Photography's Other Histories

OBJECTS/HISTORIES

Critical Perspectives on

Art, Material Culture,

and Representation

A series edited by Nicholas Thomas

Photography's Other Histories

Edited by Christopher Pinney and Nicolas Peterson

DUKE UNIVERSITY PRESS Durham and London 2003

© 2003 Duke University Press

All rights reserved

Designed by C. H. Westmoreland

Typeset in ITC Golden Cockerel by

Tseng Information Systems, Inc.

Library of Congress Cataloging-in-

Publication Data appear on

the last printed page of

this book.

Contents

Acknowledgments

This volume has its origins in a cooperative venture between the newly established Australian Research Council's Special Research Centre, the Centre for Cross-Cultural Research at the Australian National University, and the Queensland Museum. On 8 and 9 November 1997 a conference was held at the museum, convened by Michael Aird (Queensland Museum), Nicholas Thomas (director of the Centre for Cross-Cultural Research), and Nicolas Peterson (School of Archaeology and Anthropology, Australian National University) under the title *Looking through Photographs: Indigenous Histories, Presences, and Representations.* Among the wide range of papers presented were a number from practicing Aboriginal photographers, some of which have since been published elsewhere. This volume includes a selection of papers presented at the conference, along with two new papers, and reprints of three seminal essays that relate to the theme of the volume.

We are indebted to a wide range of people for assistance in preparing this volume. The conference would not have been possible without the generous funding and support of the Centre for Cross-Cultural Research and its director. The Queensland Museum generously hosted it. For organizing the conference we would particularly like to thank Jenny Newell, who did a marvellous job of overseeing its smooth operation and then followed this with the preliminary work on the preparation of this volume. Ian Bryson, Tsari Anderson, and Sally Ward also ably assisted in the production of this volume.

We would also like to thank the editor of *African Arts* and Marilyn Houlberg for permission to reprint Stephen Sprague's essay, which appeared in

African Arts 12 (1) (1978); Deborah Poole and the editor of *Representations* for permission to reprint an abridged version of her essay, which appeared in *Representations* 38 (spring 1992); and Hulleah J. Tsinhnahjinnie and the editor of *Native Nations: Journeys in American Photography* (1998; edited by Jane Alison; London: Barbican Art Gallery) for permission to reprint her essay.

Acknowledgments

Christopher Pinney

Introduction

"HOW THE OTHER HALF..."

During the ten years between 1877 and 1887, through which Jacob Riis was delivering his impassioned lectures concerning New York's "invisible" poor, photography—which he so famously championed—reached a new evidentiary crescendo. *How the Other Half Lives: Studies among the Tenements of New York* (1890), Riis's explosive conjunction of words and images, has rightly taken a central place among works on the history of photography, for it was a fulcrum of photography's collision with politics and life and an exemplary case of the image's ability to reconfigure its referent. Riis opened his work with the observation that "one half of the world does not know how the other half lives" (1997 [1890], 5), and he used photography as a shamanic trace exported from one demiworld to the other. The collection of essays in this volume was precipitated by the realization that photography itself is now in need of a similar revelation of its own other half, its own disavowed other history.

This volume seeks to change the focus of the critical debate about photographic practice. By abandoning the notion that photographic history is best seen as the explosion of a Western technology whose practice has been molded by singular individuals, *Photography's Other Histories* presents a radically different account of a globally disseminated and locally appropriated medium. In its details of the significance of colonial photographic practice in the formation of metropolitan self-identity, the book also presents case studies of contemporary photographic self-fashioning. Further, it addresses the importance of photographic records in the his-

torical and autobiographical formations that people construct for themselves, as well as the relationship between photography and other media.
Through various substantive studies, photography's mimetic doubling becomes a prism through which to consider questions of cultural and self-
identity, historical consciousness, and the nature of photographic affirmation and revelation.

Just as one might extend the history of photography far back beyond 1839
so as to incorporate entire traditions of indexical experimentation and on-
tology, so we might also extend the history of photography laterally outward to domains outside the purview of conventional narratives. Within
Buddhism, for example, there is a complex blurring with ancient ontological expectations, which places photography in a very different—and
much longer—chronology than that normally ascribed to it by historians
of photography: "The icons of the Buddha are sometimes compared to the
'original' shadow that he is said to have left in a cave at Nagarahara" (Faure
1998, 804). In central Indian popular use, "photography" is a practice that
also incorporates other media such as painting and chromolithography,
and indexicality is a property shared by these different media: photos are
not clearly marked as "modern" because their "functions are duplicated by
so many other forms of palpably ancient representation" (Pinney 1997a, 112).

This volume, which has as its genesis an international conference held
at the Museum of Queensland in Brisbane in late 1997, is notable for its
cultural and historical reach. The saliency of photography to postcolonial
debates is marked herein by the contributions of two indigenous Australians and of a practicing Seminole/Muskogee/Diné artist. The Australians,
Driessens and Aird, powerfully consider the significance of photographic
traditions in indigenous communities and the relationship between personal memories and that which is encoded in the archive. Much recent
writing that seeks to historically contextualize photography's emergence
during a period of colonial expansion has drawn on crucial insights from
Edward Said and Michel Foucault and has tended to construct photographic imagery and practice as immovably within a "truth" that simplisti-
cally reflects a set of cultural and political dispositions held by the makers
of those images. Perhaps the starkest of these contributions is that offered
by the Algerian poet Malek Alloula in *The Colonial Harem* (1987). By consciously eschewing the study of the actual political and historical consumption of images (Barthes's claim that "the reading of public photographs is always at bottom, a private reading" appears as an epigraph in

Alloula's book), Alloula spins an eloquent but untested hypothesis concerning the role of photography as "the fertiliser of the colonial vision [producing] stereotypes in the manner of great seabirds producing guano" (4). The veil that Algerian women presented to this colonial vision was received as an affront by photographers ("the whiteness of the veil becomes the symbolic equivalent of blindness; a leukoma, a white speck on the eye of the photographer and his viewpoint" [7]), and a vengeance of visibility and nudity was wreaked on this inviolability that so deeply "haunt[ed] the photographer-voyeur" (13).

Such debates tend to invoke formal readings of images that are then made to do the work of a preexisting political hypothesis. In Carlo Ginzburg's words these are "physiognomic" readings, in which the analyst "reads into them what he has already learned by other means, or what he believes he knows, and wants to 'demonstrate.'" Underpinning this approach, Ginzburg continues, is "the conviction that works of art, in a broad sense, furnish a mine of first hand information that can explicate, without intermediaries, the mentality and emotive life of a distant age" (1989, 35). Ginzburg raises a profound methodological issue of pressing relevance to all those working with imagery and artifacts, and although this is ultimately an unresolvable problem, the manner in which many arguments about the "political effects" of images overlay them with conclusions arrived at by "other means" is especially striking and troubling.

That the formal qualities of images themselves may be in large part irrelevant is suggested by their historical trajectories and the radical revaluations that they undergo. If an image that appears to do a particular kind of work in one episteme is able to perform radically different work in another, it appears inappropriate to propose inflexible links between formal qualities and effect. Instead, we need a more nuanced reading of the affinities between particular discursive formations and the image worlds that parallel them, as well as sophisticated analyses of their transformational potentialities.

What are the consequences, for instance, of the documented fact that "collectors of North African, Near and Middle Eastern descent dominate the market for Orientalist art" (Benjamin 1997, 32)? Those paintings, which Said (1978) and Nochlin (1983) have argued projected an image of largely negative alterity, are now eagerly consumed by those whose reality these images so distorted. Roger Benjamin's researches with those who market these paintings indicate that a nostalgic invocation of "indigenous identities through images of the pre-colonial past" is involved, together with "a new sense of positive empowerment expressed through the acquisition and thus redefinition of western cultural documents" (1997, 34–35).

The point here is not to attempt to invalidate Said's hypothesis—which remains of fundamental importance to all cross-cultural work—but rather to raise a set of new questions for further investigation. A greater sense of the fragility and instability of the relationship between images and their contexts might allow the exploration of why certain images prove capable of recoding while others are more resistant, and many others are completely intractable. Thus Benjamin notes that only certain types of Orientalist paintings are popular with Maghrebian and Arab customers: especially favored are nontopographically specific painted scenes, and there is little enthusiasm for photographic images and those of female nudes (1997, 34, 37).

Personal Archives

Jo-Anne Driessens's and Michael Aird's contributions to this volume recast the problem of the colonial archive. By addressing its existence not in terms of ontological generality but rather as located in a specific postcolonial moment, Driessens and Aird reveal the archive's contents as something like the cargo of a ship tossed on the waves of a heavy sea, subject to movements that produce a rearrangement and recoding. This reconfigured archive, influenced by new demands of personal recuperation, assumes a radically new role. In both Driessens's and Aird's cases the recoding of images arose from their discovery and recognition of images of family members, stored like a vein of gold in the archive. Recuperation takes the form of a homecoming: the naming of the formerly anonymous, the individuation and recognition of persons whose work in the archive had usually been to "typify"—that is, to exemplify some category. Recuperation here is a kind of particularization, the enclosing in a new space of domesticity and affection of images formerly lost in the public wilderness of the archive.

Aird wonderfully captures the creativity of the engagement of Aboriginal peoples with the archive as a "*look[ing] past* the stereotypical way in which their relatives and ancestors have been portrayed" (my emphasis). "Looking past" suggests a complexity of perspectival positions or a multiplicity of layers that endow photographs with an enormously greater complexity than that which they are usually credited. The photograph ceases to be a univocal, flat, and uncontestable indexical trace of what was, and becomes instead a complexly textured artifact (concealing many different depths) inviting the viewer to assume many possible different standpoints—both spatial and temporal—in respect to it. But for Aird only certain types of images permit this "looking past," just as only certain forms of Orientalist images appeal in the current market: he describes how an image of Andrew Ball ultimately proved wholly resistant to attempts to displace it from the space of enumeration and humiliation.

Hulleah J. Tsinhnahjinnie finds a latency in many images of Native Americans that parallels the ability to "look past." Thus in E. P. Niblack's portrait of Johnny Kit Elswa (see fig. 8 in her essay) she feels a recursive texture, at the point now of resurfacing. The portrait pictures the Haida Gwaii man with the Bear clan inscribed on his chest and the dog fish on his arms. "Tattoos," Tsinhnahjinnie notes, "went under the skin to survive, encoded beneath the skin, programmed to resurface when the time is right.... This is also how I perceive the art of aboriginal tattoo, latent images." Tsinhnahjinnie proposes a view of photography very different from Barthes's stress on the flat image's preservation of anterior temporal states. For Tsinhnahjinnie, the photograph is more like a message in a bottle, or like a seed: an object transmitted to the future, ready at any moment to burst forth.

I have noted that Michael Aird drew firm limits on the potentiality of "looking past." Tsinhnahjinnie, however, performs a more difficult recoding, which appeals to a more overtly political space of action. It is an energetic recoding, a recuperation of an image of terrible degradation that less-strenuous analysts might have abandoned forever to the practices of genocide that made possible the accumulation of large parts of the archive. George Trager's photograph of Big Foot lying dead in the snow at Wounded Knee records an ultimate subjection, but it provokes in Tsinhnahjinnie a dream. In this dream she floats, seeing Big Foot as he is in the photograph. A small girl then traverses the snow, looking into the faces of the dead: "she walked over to Big Foot, looking into his face. She shakes his shoulders, takes his frozen hand into her small, warm hand, and helps him to his feet. He then brushes the snow off of his clothes. She waits patiently with her hand extended, he then takes her hand and they walk out of the photograph. This is the dream I recall when I look upon this image of supposed hopelessness."

How are we to understand this volatility of the image? Peirce's conceptualization of the photograph as indexical has recently been much invoked ("I define an Index as a sign determined by its Dynamic object by virtue of being in a real relation to it" [1958, 391]). This relationship of physical contiguity between image and referent certainly played a central role in the truth claims of the colonial archive: photography was seen to surpass and eradicate the subjectivity and unreliability of earlier technologies of representation. Indexicality was thus mobilized as a guarantee of fixity. Photography, so Valéry observed, came to underwrite experience and history: "The mere notion of photography ... suggests the simple question: *could such and such a fact, as it is narrated, have been photographed?*" (cited in Trachtenberg 1989, xiii–xiv; see also my essay in this volume).

But the index need not only imply fixity and stability: it can as easily be used to undermine this very notion. Photography's exemplification of Peirce's index might be recast in terms of an inevitable randomness within the image. What in Peirce's terms are purely iconic images (e.g., paintings, drawings) are capable of excluding randomness because they reflect only the imagination and skill of their creators, and when those qualities are present in excess they are capable of driving out the incidental. Photographic technology, however, is founded on a paradox: the very capture of light on film implies an ineradicable surfeit. If we think of the painter's imagination and brush as a filter capable of complete exclusion, then the lens of the camera can never be closed because something extraneous will always enter into it. No matter how precautionary and punctilious the photographer is in arranging everything that is placed before the camera, the inability of the lens to discriminate will ensure a substrate or margin of excess, a subversive code present in every photographic image that makes it open and available to other readings and uses. Thus we might understand photography's indexicality to be the guarantee not of closure and fixity, but rather of multiple surfaces and of the possibility of "looking past." It is precisely photography's inability to discriminate, its inability to exclude, that makes it so textured and so fertile. Encoded "beneath photography's skin" (Tsinhnahjinnie) this excess lies waiting to resurface.

This volatility can also be seen to reflect the "misrecognition" that lies at the heart of photography. Once again, Carlo Ginzburg provides a vital route to understanding this notion. He has described what may appear to be a paradox of the completeness of those Inquisitorial records that deal with behaviors to which the makers of those records would have been especially hostile. Ginzburg agrees with other commentators that

Christopher Pinney

most Inquisitorial records are extremely suspect and reveal that the interogees' answers merely echo the questions posed by their interrogators (1989, 160). However, the Friulian trials of the *benandanti* (Inquisitorial investigations of suspected witches) stand out: Ginzburg notes that their "ethnographic value" is "astonishing": "Not only words, but gestures, sudden reactions like blushing, even silences, were recorded with punctilious accuracy by the notaries of the Holy Office" (160). Ginzburg uses these Friulian documents to argue against the suggestion that (following Jakobsen) all reported speech is "appropriated and remoulded," suggesting instead that "a conflicting cultural reality" can "leak out" from these encounters. This "leaking" was much more likely where the quoter of that reported speech—in this case Inquisitors—misrecognize what is uttered to them. As Ginzburg says, the historians' "task is much easier when the inquisitors did not understand" (162–63). He suggests that where there is "recognition" cultural filters came into play that mediated and modulated evidence to suit the agendas of the Inquisitors: where there was recognition, templates and other preexisting schemata were mobilized that appropriated the new experience to old expectations. Misrecognition thus emerges as productive: "We can take advantage ... of those invaluable cases in which *the lack of communication* on a cultural level between judges and defendants permitted, rather paradoxically, the emergence of a real dialogue—in the Bakhtinian sense of an unresolved clash of conflicting voices" (164; my emphasis).

The value of the Friulian transcripts reflects the absence of "cultural filters" that permitted the Inquisitors to mediate the evidence in terms of well-worn formulas. A "misrecognition" of *benandanti* knowledge precluded the Inquisitors from excluding anything: they didn't "know" what to exclude and as a result ended up recording everything.

This is a useful metaphor for photography: however hard the photographer tries to *exclude*, the camera lens always *includes*. The photographer can never fully control the resulting photograph, and it is that lack of control and the resulting *excess* that permits recoding, "resurfacing," and "looking past."

This dimension of "photography's other history" reflects the specific nature of photography as a technology: prephotographic technologies do not exhibit this inescapably random element. Photographs are necessarily contrived and reflect the culture that produces them, but no photograph is so successful that it filters out the random entirely. This is another ground on which we might wish to complicate Foucauldian and Saidian approaches that presuppose an absolute fit between the image and the ideological forces that appear to motivate the image, as well as those approaches that treat photographs merely as art-historical texts betraying only a grander sweeping aesthetic intentionality.

Visual Economies

A set of essays grouped together under the title "Visual Economies" forms the second section of this volume. The title is taken from Deborah Poole's exploration, in her book on Andean photography, of the inequalities that characterize representational domains. Eschewing the term "visual culture" for its supposition of consensus and homogeneity, Poole advocates a stress on unequal flows and exchanges: hence "economy" rather than "culture." She states that economy "suggests that this organization has as much to do with social relationships, inequality, and power as with shared meanings and community" (1997, 8). Clearly this is necessary as a corrective to the potentially utopian conclusions suggested by a stress on photography's volatility and infinite recodability. We must not lose sight of the extraordinary circumstances of inequality (encompassing the range from cultural, political, and economic hierarchy to systematic genocide) that gave rise to the vast majority of the images inhabiting the colonial archive. Poole has another intent: to stress the globality of image flows that exceeded the locality that the term "culture" might imply: "It is relatively easy to imagine the people of Paris and Peru, for example, participating in the same 'economy.' To imagine or speak of them as part of a shared 'culture' is considerably more difficult. I use the word 'economy' . . . with the intention of capturing this sense of how visual images move across national and cultural boundaries" (8).

Roslyn Poignant inserts photographic representations of abducted indigenous Australians in the context of a history of earlier depictions and questions the "difference" that most writings on photography attribute to its technology. Susan Sontag (1979) famously expounded the metaphorical affinity between photographic practice and "capture." Here, Poignant explores photography as an accompaniment to the literal abduction of a group of Queenslanders who were paraded as the living incarnation of a set of Western fantasies of savagery through nineteenth-century America and Europe. A fragment of an important forthcoming work, Poignant's essay is concerned with the persistence—across diverse technologies—

Christopher Pinney

of discriminatory representation. Tracing enduring tropes of "savagery" from 1600 onward, Poignant observes the intimate entwining of discourses of conceptual and visual fixity exemplified in the terms "stereotype" and "cliché"—both originally used to describe repetitive printing processes.

Poignant also develops a strategy to destabilize this apparent fixity, which resonates with the "excess" of photography discussed above. She detects a disturbance in photographic images akin to Barthes's notion of the "punctum," characterized by what Berger and Mohr (1982, 96) describe as a "quotation" from experience. However, across the centuries a continuity emerges that links the woodblock, through photography, to the digitized injustices perpetrated by global media.

James Faris traces the ways in which Navajo have been photographically depicted, and like Poignant he detects enduring structural features that regulate the manner in which certain people are represented to the archive. What may appear faulty or objectionable are not "flaws in an uneducated, unevolved, unenlightened West [rather] they are the necessary conditions of existence of the Navajo to the West." Faris's model of knowledge production is much less optimistic than Ginzburg's, seeing in the "optical unconscious" of Navajo photographic representation a limited set of ossified permutations rather than a fecund field of volatile possibilities: "There are but a finite series of means by which the West has viewed Navajo." A particularly interesting feature of Faris's analysis is his attempt to specify the limits of the representational paradigm through a contrast between published and unpublished images (a theme pursued in more detail in Faris 1997). This is one of the ways through which one can identify "effectivity" under specific discursive regimes: the choice to publish or not publish reveals contemporary understandings about which photographs do a particular kind of work (effect) and which do another kind of work. Through this sort of comparison we can transcend the inevitable limitations of the sort of formal analysis (e.g., by Alloula) discussed earlier.

Morris Low's significant contribution to this volume can help destabilize the sense of a unitary "colonial archive" through the documentation of a different colonialism—that of the Japanese in Manchuria. The reattribution of agency to those formerly denied it also entails the acknowledgment that imperialism, racism, and genocide were not the exclusive preserve of Europe and America but also have been enthusiastically performed by many other nations and cultural traditions. Low's essay can be seen as an actualization of Nicholas Thomas's (1994) invitation to explode the singular fiction of "colonialism" into diverse local practices that need to be investigated through their singularity (attending to its "dispersed and con-flicted character" [3]), rather than through an appeal to an archetypal mon-strous practice. However, Low reveals—in this singularity—a doubling or a mimicry of longer-standing models of colonialism (e.g., European nar-rative forms, colonial sartorial conventions, and stresses on "manliness"). Other studies of local colonialisms are urgently needed to explore the questions raised by Low's work.

In a subtle and sophisticated essay Christopher Wright suggests that the New Guinea photographs of F. R. Barton (which might at first appear to be exemplary instances of a voyeuristic colonial gaze) are trapped in a wider cultural history—an economy of desire that is cross-cut by Hula constructs of personhood. Barton's dubious images appear on first viewing to be utterly reducible to a set of expectations created by "ready-made in-terpretive frame[s]" and to be exemplary of the carceral and pornographic network of colonial photography. But Wright argues that this notion sim-plifies and overscripts the image with our own preoccupations: Barton's photographs are entangled in many different scopic regimes, not just that of colonial surveillance. Echoing Tsinhnahjinnie, Wright suggests that Bar-ton's images might be thought of as a form of tattoo, impregnated with diverse latent cultural codings. Wright raises the problem inherent in Fou-cauldian and Saidian approaches, namely the assumption that, in Homi Bhabha's words, "colonial power is possessed entirely by the coloniser" (cited in Young 1990, 142). The analysis presented here stresses Hula agency and the photographic image as a record of a space of complex negotia-tion—and of a "leaking out" rather than simple dominance.

Various contributors to this volume address the impact of different photographic technologies on what might be termed the "photographic event"; that is, the dialogic period during which the subject and the pho-tographer come together. These meetings encompass a diverse realm that includes lengthy negotiations under conditions of elaborate technological preparation and a fleeting invisible surveillance in which the photographer may be invisible to the subject of the image. Different essays examine the theatrical idioms of studio portraiture, the spaces of complex voyeuris-tic desire that early technologies encouraged, and the wall of silence and mutual mistrust that can also characterize certain photographic events.

Nicolas Peterson's essay sets "colonial" photographic practice centrally within the fluid political reality of Australia. He records the increasing re-cuperation of images from the archive by Aboriginal individuals and com-munities. This recuperation takes the form of a recovery from the public domain into more enclosed arenas in which they are controlled by the images' subjects and their descendants. Contrasting the free photographic access that the 1891 Elder Expedition had to Australia's native people with a 1997 legal dispute over the right to photograph on Gumaitj clan land in the Northern Territory, Peterson reveals a profound transformation in the ethical and political space within which photography operates. In contrast with Faris's stress on the relative immutability of the matrix through which Navajo are represented by the "West," Peterson demonstrates contestation and change. Photography as a technology of capture and appropriation (in the terms popularized by Sontag) is no longer free to explore the full extent of its metaphorical violence. Since the mid-1970s it has come to operate in a field of dialogue and refusal, subject to the injunctions and restraints of Aboriginal communities and national law. Peterson also observes that Aboriginal people are increasingly using the camera themselves. The use of video by remote Aboriginal communities has been famously described by Eric Michaels (1994), but regrettably no work has yet emerged that provides any substantive insight into the use of still photography in these localities.

Self-Fashioning and Vernacular Modernism

The third section of this volume, "Self-Fashioning and Vernacular Modernism" raises the issue of what questions about other practices need to be examined in order to understand photographic practice. Moving from an autonomous history of photography with its own necessary determinants, a much more culturally fluid set of possibilities opens up that reveals popular practice often to be in advance of "art" practice in its visions of the world. Attention is also given to popular practice as a *creator* of culture rather than simply (as in Bourdieu's noted study [1990]) its reproducer. Case studies from Peru (Poole), India (Pinney), Kenya (Behrend), and Nigeria (Sprague) illustrate the heterodox practices that flourish outside the metropole. These photographic practices appear to be at an ultimate remove from the disciplinary framework through which photography first impacted on these locales, and they constitute a distinctive postcolonial popular aesthetic.

In the relative absence of anthropological work on photography, historians and cultural theorists of the medium have managed to avoid asking fundamental questions concerning the social and personal space that photography comes to occupy. Through the ethnographic exploration of key issues relating to the ways in which certain forms of representation presuppose the existence of certain forms of subject (photographic historians presuppose the existence of a Cartesian or post-Cartesian subject) and particular models of time/history consciousness, photography's "other history" offers the possibility of a "provincialization" of European knowledge and experience (Chakrabarty 2000). "Vernacular modernism" might be conceptualized as a provincializing strategy, for it relocates the historical agency and centrality of Western representational practice in a new space: that of nonmetropolitan photographic practitioners whose refusal of a certain form of signification owes more to an ethical/political distaste of totalizing schemata and an imprisoning referentiality than a reading of Clement Greenberg.

Photography has been able to perform a very specific sort of work over the last 150 years in a Euro-American context because it operated in a cultural context crucially configured by the control of what Heidegger (1977) calls the "world as picture" controlled by human subjects. A specific cultural history produced a postmedieval Cartesian world as something susceptible to human agency, available to a detached gaze, and amenable to mathematical regulation: Heidegger states that "man brings into play his unlimited power for the calculating, planning, and moulding of all things" (135). It was this world within which Euro-American photography largely operated.

Photography, however, lives in many other cultural worlds as well. These worlds differ in complex ways from the Euro-American world, and yet most writing on globalized photography has assumed that theories of Euro-American experience can be exported to these other contexts (see Weiner [1997] for the most sustained elaboration of this critique). There has been almost no useful theory to address the often radically different nexus of world, human subject, and representational practice whose contours photographic practice throws sharply into relief.

In much writing on photography (as also on the consumption of a much broader range of technologies) a unitary subject is assumed rather than demonstrated, and this subject is then overlain with artifact-mobilized identities. The presence and nature of specific subjects/persons and the ways in which they can act, as well as the possibilities they have for representation and identity, need first to be investigated and established rather than simply taken as given. Heidegger's argument that the process of repre-

Christopher Pinney

senting and presenting the "world as picture," as a domain susceptible to human action, is fundamental to the constitution of the modern subject is a crucial starting point for theorizing the complex fields within which photography as (self-)representation might function.

Poole's essay on early photography in Peru explores the pathways through which photography was put to the very different task of delineating an indigenous modernist aesthetic. Figueroa Aznar borrowed heavily from European romanticism both in his life and his art, but he should not be dismissed, Poole argues, as a colonial mimic: rather he "created an approach to both photography and modernity that intentionally departed from the dominant model of European modernism." Expressive of the *indigenismo* movement, Figueroa's images stressed a theatricality rather than any attempt to capture the world "as it really is." Stressing intuition and sentiment, Figueroa, like other Cusco New Indianists, attempted to counter "the positivist inventory of their history and geography" through the production of a transformed and reworked Andean world "carefully framed and skilfully tinted."

A similar, though broader, argument is developed in my essay on the "surfacism" that characterizes much postcolonial photography. Eschewing colonial strategies of depth and indexicality, a widely dispersed "vernacular modernism" has emerged that stresses the texture of the surface of the image and the possibilities it presents for cultural reinvention. In central Indian popular practice, photography is prized not for its ability to produce indexical traces, but rather as a creative transformational space that permits its subjects to "come out better." The nature of this Indian practice resonates closely with popular West African and other postcolonial practices that also deploy what Arjun Appadurai (1997) has termed the "subaltern backdrop" and mobilize fluid identities within a ludic idiom.

Heike Behrend's essay makes a parallel distinction between early colonial practices in Kenya of "hunting with the camera" and the local appropriation of globalized glamour by the Likoni ferry photographers in modern Mombasa. Thus, as in all of the studies in this section of the volume, photography becomes a space for the inversion and critique of authorized Western models of travel, landscape, and selfhood. In Stephen Sprague's wonderful seminal essay (originally published in 1978) a similar concern with what Olu Oguibe has called the "substance of the image" emerges. Although traditional Yoruba aesthetics endure within the field of photographic portraiture (for instance, with respect to bodily postures) what is so striking about the images Sprague discusses is their "materiality"—their rupture of the smooth surface of the image that conventional dominant Western documentary practices so prize.

Cutting across all three sections of the book and across the regional diversity is a set of common concerns. These concerns include the role of photography in heightening and determining historical and biographical consciousness and the mutability of interpretational frameworks and potentialities that photographs offer. The photographs that emerge in these studies are, as Wright suggests, "supple"—that is, subject to multiple determinations in different times and places.

Although the work in this volume is concerned with the diversity and alterity within photographic practice, it also attempts to define the specificity, or the field of determinations, of photography as a technology. This endeavor includes both the processual character of picture making and its historical and cultural variation. Under the influence of theorists such as Sontag and John Tagg, much writing on photography has—in its concern with the ideological effects of picture *taking*—lost sight of the dialogic space that frequently emerges during the process of picture *making*. The concern with the political consequences of photography has effectively erased any engagement with its actual practice.

Collectively, the essays in this volume suggest that photography is a cultural practice with no fixed outcome. The technologically determinist tradition within writing on photography recently has been redeemed by predictions about the transformative effect of photographic digitization which, it is claimed, will dissolve cherished cultural certainties. *Photography's Other Histories* refutes such technological histories by revealing long traditions of photographic manipulation and concluding that it is cultural practice that is the true motor of photography.

Christopher Pinney

Personal

Archives

. . . .

1

Jo-Anne Driessens

Relating to Photographs

My name is Jo-Anne Driessens, I was born in Ipswich (Brisbane) in 1970. I was adopted at two weeks from Warilda nursing home in Newmarket (Brisbane). The name Driessens comes from my adopted Dutch/Australian family, who already had three fair children (fig. 1); outsiders noticed I had a different heritage from the other Driessens when looking through our family albums (figs. 2, 3, and 4).

My relationship with photographs began as a personal journey, which I would like to share. My interest in photography began at the age of sixteen. My adoptive family always encouraged me in my search for my birth family. While working for the Department of the Environment and Heritage I met Vicky Turner, who was studying anthropology at the time. She introduced me to Michael Aird who worked as a curator of Aboriginal photographs at the Queensland Museum. I did voluntary work for Michael at the museum on the ethnohistorical photographic collection and as a result became more interested in my Aboriginal background. While working on the photographs I couldn't help wondering if any of the people in them were my ancestors.

When I started work on the Betty McKenzie Collection from Barambah settlement in the 1930s (the settlement is now called Cherbourg) it became my priority interest. I was starting to track down my blood relatives and I knew that there was a strong possibility that my blood family came from Cherbourg.

As I was working with the McKenzie Collection trying to document the photographs, I began to understand through the photos who were the well-known community members at the time. One photo in particular of

1. My adoptive family.
Collection of the
author.

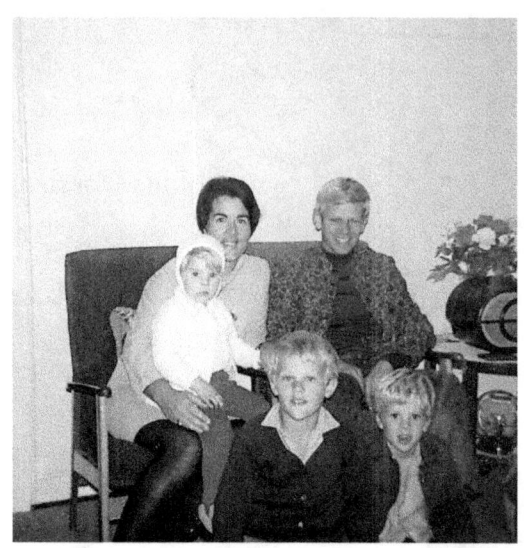

2. Me, at two
weeks old, the
day I was brought
home by the
Driessens family.
Collection of the
author.

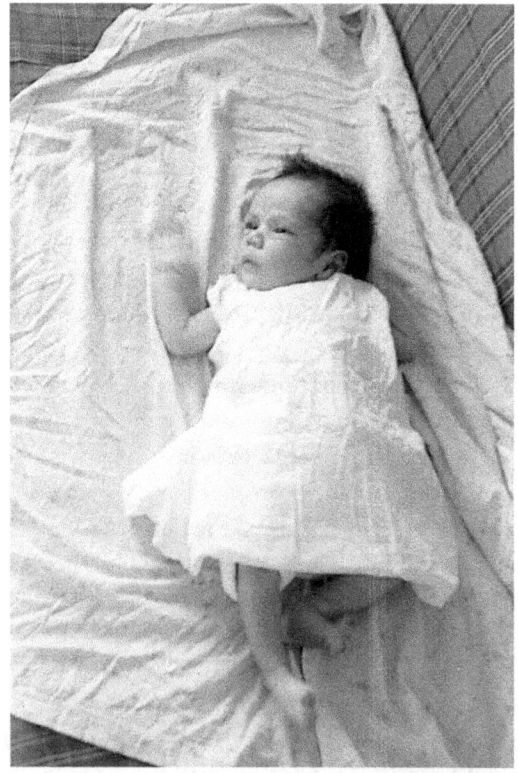

3. Sitting on a barrel with my brother and sister at home in the front garden. Collection of the author.

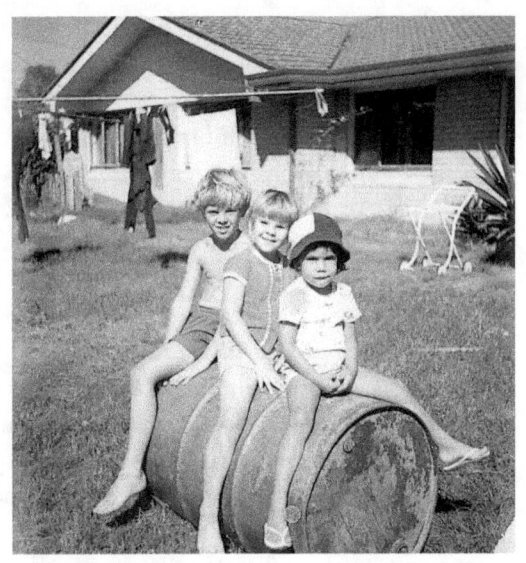

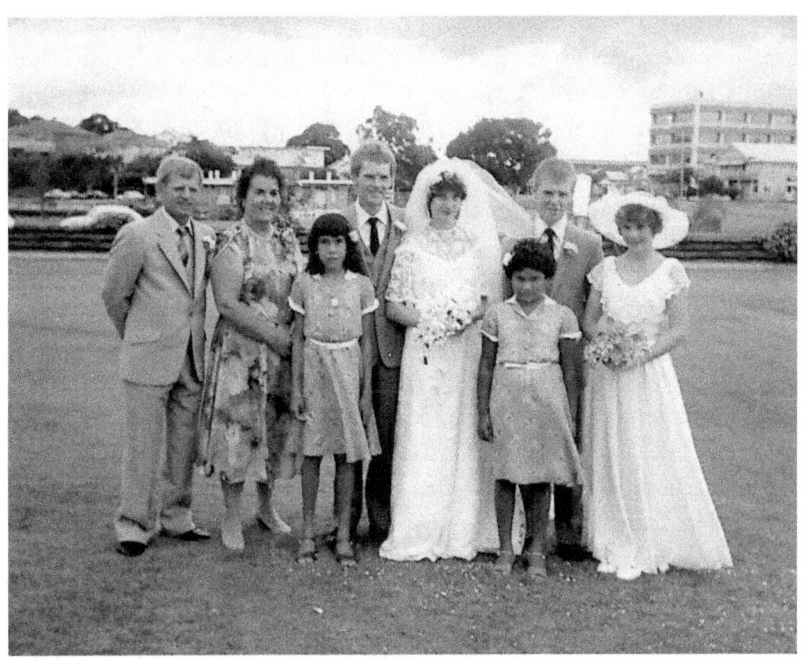

4. At my brother's wedding in January 1981. Collection of the author.

Nancy Chambers at the soup kitchen (fig. 5) I seemed to have warmed to, and it was also quite a popular one for photographic orders by the public. I had no idea then that my relationship with this photograph would be the beginning of a turning point in my life.

It wasn't until my involvement with the preparation of the book *I Know a Few Words* (Aird 1996), compiled by Michael, that I came to know my family connection to the photo of Nancy Chambers in the soup kitchen. The book evolved from a conversation between Hazel Mace and her niece, Bertha Korbe, and was planned to show how Aboriginal people in the southeast region of Queensland lost their language. It was while mixing and working with the community that I discovered that Hazel was my grandmother (nana) and that Bertha was my auntie.

I began asking them about the photographs in the McKenzie Collection and listening to their memories of that time in their life. One day my grandmother told me that she, along with her mother, was in some of the photographs in the collection. When she showed me the picture of her mother it was the picture of Nancy Chambers! If only photos could talk!

So I now have this new relationship with any photos that I view of Nancy Chambers, who I can confidently say is my great-grandmother. As I continued my journey of discovery, my next milestone was taking on a photographic cadetship with the State Library of Queensland, which at the time of this writing is now in its fourth and final year. Last year, as part of my continuing photographic journey, I completed my photographic portfolio by taking photographs at Cherbourg. People there have given me excellent feedback on my pictures.

My job, along with study, is to print and copy historical photographs of Queensland, which has included printing up the Tindale Collection photographs of Aboriginal people. Among them I found a picture of my great-grandfather (fig. 6). However, because Tindale's photographs are mainly taken to show physical types, they are very controlled and impersonal. But after a visit by my nana to the state library's Indigenous Unit in the John Oxley Library where she looked through many photographs from both Cherbourg and Yarrabah, she was fortunate to find another photograph of her father, Charlie Chambers Senior (fig. 7). It turns out he appears in a few photographs because he was a keen euphonium player, which was exciting for me as I had only seen him through the eyes of Tindale, and for me the Tindale Collection photo leaves feelings of sadness. Even so, Tindale's photographs of the old people are still a fountain of valuable information for anyone who is in a similar situation as myself.

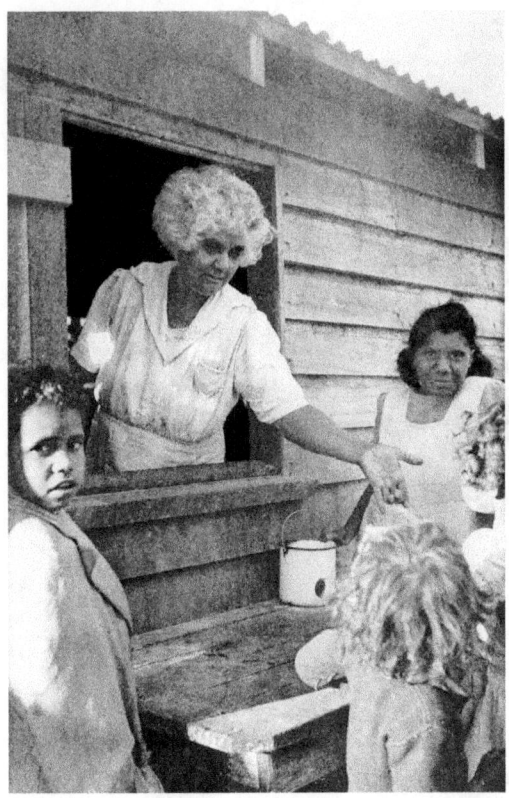

5. Nancy Chambers working in the soup kitchen. Courtesy of the Queensland Museum (EH.358).

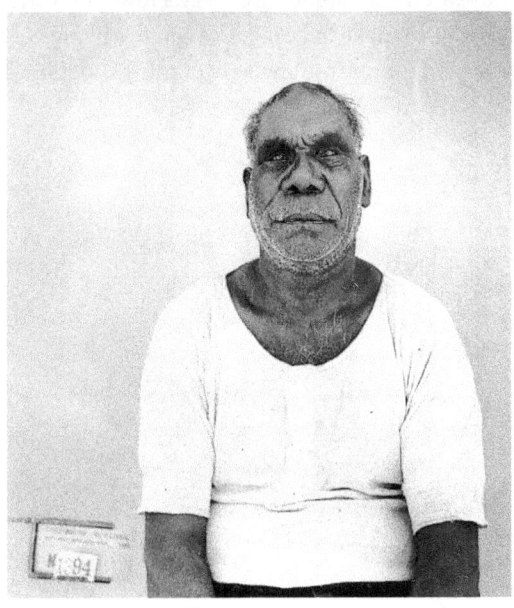

6. My great-grandfather, Charlie Chambers. Photo by Norman Tindale. Courtesy of the John Oxley Library (neg. 1394).

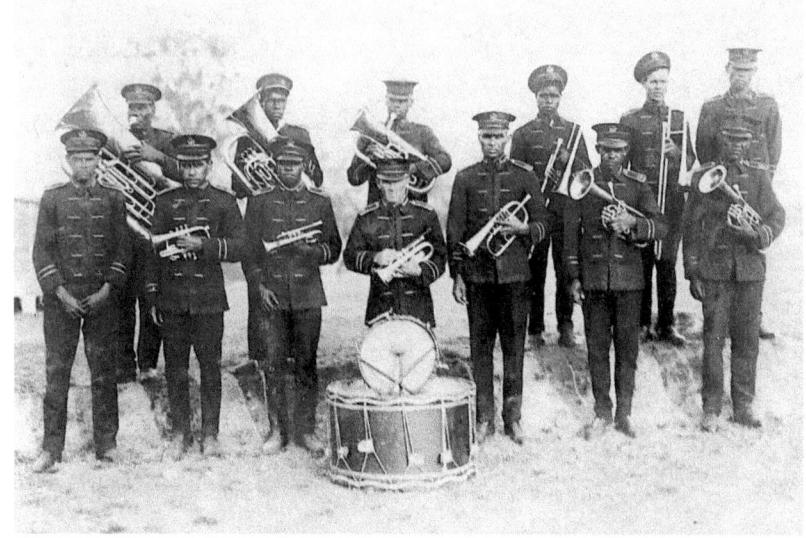

7. Charlie Chambers (back row, third from right). This photo, titled "Native Concert Party," is from the front page of the Gympie Show Souvenir Program in 1927. Courtesy of the Queensland Museum (EH.344).

Although I have mixed feelings about the photo of my great-grandfather in the Tindale Collection, it plays a very important role in my life and in my almost-completed journey of photographic discovery. However, I still expect that I have new discoveries to make in going through the many collections of photographs I have yet to look at in my new family's shoeboxes and albums.

Jo-Anne Driessens

Michael Aird

Growing Up with Aborigines

There has been a long tradition of Europeans photographing Aboriginal people, mainly as subjects of scientific enquiry. This was going on
as late as the 1930s when some scientists were still documenting what they
thought was the last of a dying race, or at least a dying way of life, and other
professional photographers were still attempting to capitalize on images
of the exotic. These colonial photographs are well known and have been
widely circulated (see, e.g., fig. 1). Perhaps, surprisingly, these photographs
are often valued by Aboriginal people despite the criticism they have been
subjected to. By contrast, however, there are other, private, barely known
bodies of photography from the 1930s that portray a different image.

The 1930s was a period when an increasing number of Aboriginal people
started to become involved with photography by choice. In the first few
decades of this century very few Aboriginal people were well-off enough
to be able to afford to visit studios as paying customers. Yet by the 1930s a
growing number began to own cameras for the first time and could afford
to have photographs developed. These kinds of photographs, often held
in Aboriginal family collections, are poorly known, as are private family
collections taken by non-Aboriginal people living in Aboriginal communities. This essay will examine these various photographic records from
the 1930s, in particular those relating to the Aboriginal people of southeast
Queensland.

Photographs taken by professional photographers or government officials have proved to be extremely valuable to Aboriginal people as historical documents, even though they are often heavily influenced by the
artistic or political inclinations of the photographer and by misguided and

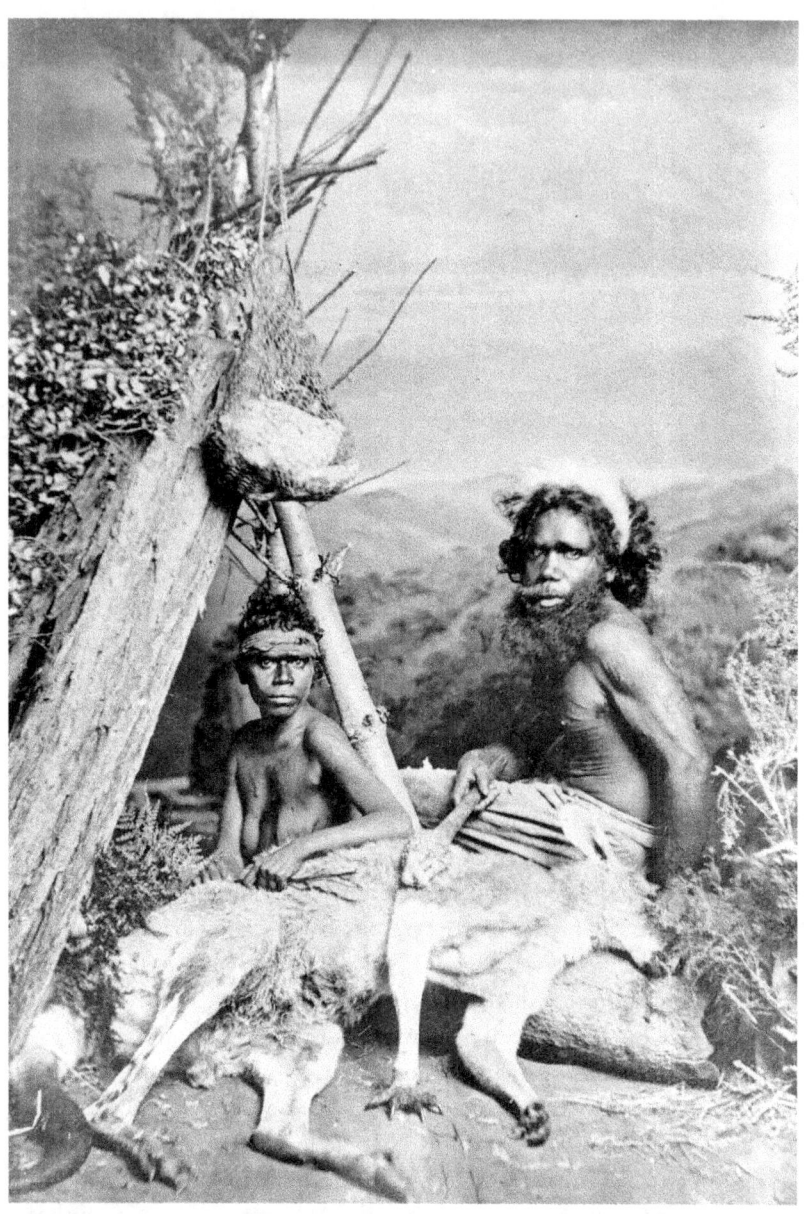

1. Man and woman, with dead kangaroo, inside a photo studio. Grafton c.1873. Photograph by J. W. Lindt. Courtesy of the Queensland Museum (EH.15).

racist beliefs resulting in the portrayal of Aboriginal people as savages, beggars, or as the last of a dying race.

I have, however, often seen Aboriginal people look past the stereotypical way in which their relatives and ancestors have been portrayed, because they are just happy to be able to see photographs of people who play a part in their family's history. I have watched as a woman viewed photographs taken in the 1890s of her grandmother posing bare-breasted in a photographic studio. This image was in contrast to the way the woman remembered her grandmother, a woman who was always fully clothed. Yet she seemed undisturbed by the uncharacteristic way in which the photographer portrayed her grandmother and was simply grateful for the opportunity to view a photograph of her taken so long ago. After working with photographic collections for over fifteen years, I myself have been able to experience, as well as share with numerous Aboriginal people, the joy and excitement of finding images of ancestors and relatives.

In 1991 I organized an exhibition called *Portraits of Our Elders*, which covered the time in the nineteenth century when Aboriginal people had little control over the way in which they were portrayed by photographers, through to the time when some of them had full control over how they were seen. These latter photographs showed a side of Aboriginal life in the 1920s that was ignored in publicly circulated photographs which almost exclusively depicted people in situations of poverty. The images were taken inside photo studios and show well-dressed and confident Aboriginal people who sent their children to schools to be educated in order to improve their credibility or acceptability within the European society. They were photographed wearing expensive clothes, and they paid for copies of the photographs for display in their homes and to give away to relatives.

There are numerous examples of how Aboriginal people attempted to become part of European society, such as finding employment in various industries, sending their children to schools, becoming Christians, and settling in urban areas. These can all be interpreted as tactics of survival, and photography was used to document this process. Survival to Aboriginal people around the turn of the century, particularly in southeast Queensland, was not just to go out into the bush and hunt kangaroos but to survive among what was happening at that time in their land. They were determined to stay in their traditional country, and every aspect of their lives became part of a strategy to survive: they had to conform. These people were in one sense being Aboriginal, but in another sense they were attempting to be "European" to survive. The later images in the exhibition represent how some Aboriginal people of southeast Queensland had gained control over many aspects of their lives, but unfortunately it was not the case for most Aboriginal people at that time.

The photographs featured in *Portraits of Our Elders* demonstrate the contrast of Aboriginal people being portrayed as "exotic" or as the "noble savage" to very confident Aboriginal people in poses of their own choosing. In particular, the photograph of Katie, Lilly, and Clara Williams gave me the idea for the exhibition (fig. 2). I was struck by this photograph; the beauty of the women and the confidence they demonstrated inspired me to put together a series of studio portraits of Aboriginal people.

One of the aims of *Portraits of Our Elders* was to look at the ownership of photographs and how they are related to by Aboriginal people today. An example is the way in which the Queensland Museum holds the photograph of Rosie Campbell, bare-breasted, (initially) unidentified with no indication of her name or where she was from (fig. 3). If you go to Stradbroke Island, to the homes where several of her grandchildren live today, there are many photographs of her. Not only is she fully clothed in the photographs held by her relatives, but the families have much information and many personal memories of Rosie as a person. Among the numerous photographs the family has of Rosie from the same era in which she posed bare-breasted is one of her fully clothed in the same studio setting.

Held within the collections of my relatives are photographs of my great-great-grandparents, William Williams and Emily Jackey. Thanks to people within my family investigating the collections of public institutions we can now take our photographic history back one more generation. For me, the photographs that I am so grateful to have are of my grandfather's grandmother's father. To have photographs of my great-great-great-grandfather is quite a privilege. This takes my family history back to the beginning of Aboriginal relations with the first European people coming to the area.

While making the final selection of photographs to be included in *Portraits of Our Elders* I considered including photographs taken in the 1930s of an old man named Andrew Ball who lived at Cherbourg, an Aboriginal settlement in southeast Queensland (fig. 4). Even though I had initially decided that the exhibition should only include photographs from the 1860s to the 1920s, it was the image of Andrew Ball that made me consider including an extra decade to bring the exhibition up to the 1930s. I wanted to use this photograph because it served to demonstrate how photography has been used as a scientific tool.

The photographs of Andrew Ball are clear, sharp studio portraits of an

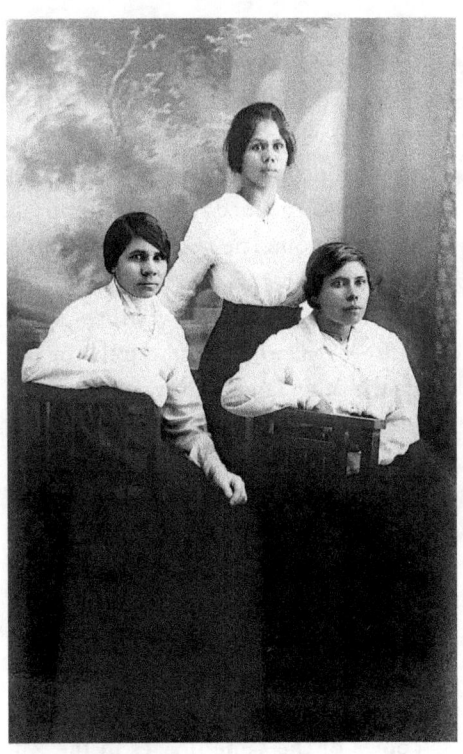

2. Katie, Lilly, and Clara Williams. Beaudesert, c. 1925. Courtesy of the Doris Yuke Collection.

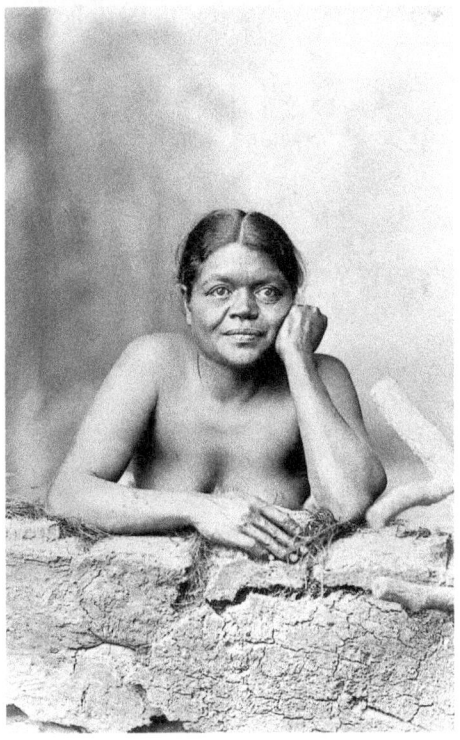

3. Rosie Campbell from Myora Mission, Stradbroke Island, 1890s. Photo by Poul Poulson. Courtesy of the Queensland Museum (EH.12).

old man sitting on a chair in a makeshift studio. In one photograph he is looking at the camera and in the other he is positioned sideways in order to assist the viewer to theorize about the shape of his skull (fig. 5). This must have been humiliating for the old man. But why does Andrew Ball look so much like a victim when other Aboriginal people who had also been put through similar humiliating situations still maintained an outward appearance of strength and control over the situation? The couple posing with the dead kangaroo featured in the J. W. Lindt photograph (fig. 1) appears to have maintained a degree of strength and control in the way they posed. The fact that the photographs of Andrew Ball were taken purely for scientific purposes sets them apart from the other studio portraits; they look obviously modern compared to those taken only a decade earlier.

Scientific interest in Australian Aboriginal people has existed for many years, but it was the 1930s that witnessed an intensification of this type of research. The information that was attached to the photographs of Andrew Ball demonstrates to what level the scientific investigation was taken. Possibly it was the degree of probing and study of physical traits that caused Andrew Ball to appear to have such a sad and defeated look in his eyes. We can only guess as to how much he objected to this type of treatment.

These photographs were unidentified in the collection of the Queensland Museum, but I came across copies of the same images in the Anthropology Museum at the University of Queensland with the following information attached:

Andrew Ball (front of head)
(a) Photo shows the almost vertical sides of his skull;
(b) Had been a black tracker;
(c) Splendid horseman;
(e) Maroochy tribe;
(f) Five and a half feet tall and under nine stone;
(g) Graceful, nimble walker;
(h) Very dark brown skin, rather oily;
(i) Whites of eyes were brownish yellow;
(j) Very correct manners when at the table;
(k) Quite famous as a boomerang thrower;
(l) Small, nicely formed hands;
(m) High-pitched tenor voice;
Andrew Ball, it is said, died at Cherbourg Mission during 1944.

Eventually I decided that I could not place the photographs of Andrew Ball alongside the earlier photographs. Ball's images did not belong, they

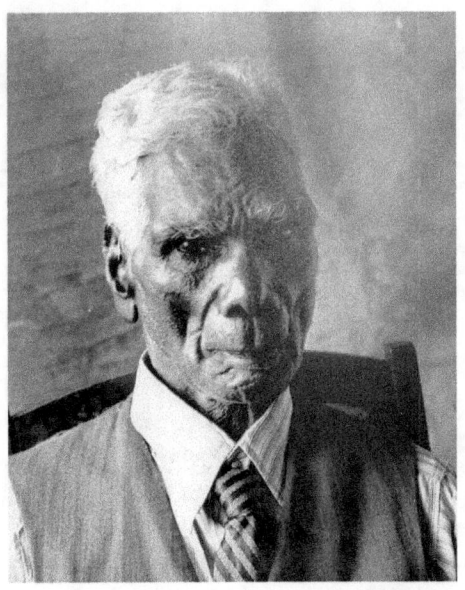

4. Andrew Ball from
Bli Bli, 1930s. Stan Colliver
Collection. Courtesy of the
Queensland Museum
(EH.921).

5. Andrew Ball from Bli Bli
(profile), 1930s. Stan Colliver
Collection. Courtesy of the
Queensland Museum
(EH.922).

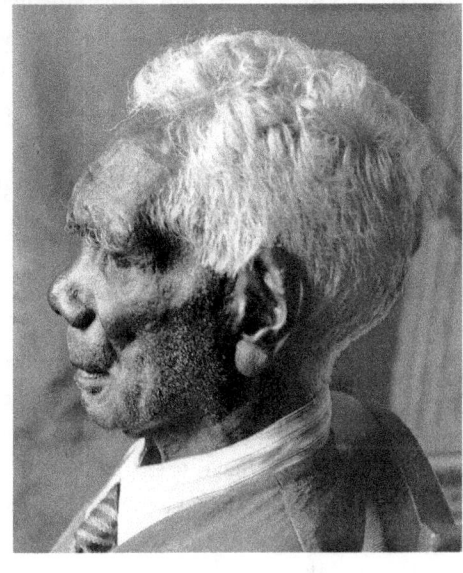

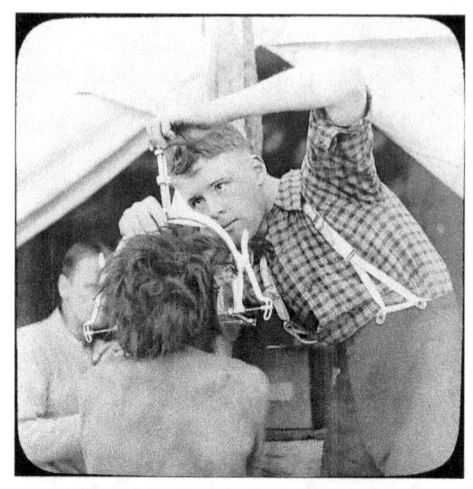

6. Tindale Expedition to Central Australia, 1930s. Herbert Wilkinson Collection. Courtesy of the Queensland Museum (EH.2204).

told of another much better known aspect of Aboriginal history, the story of Aboriginal people in the 1930s being treated as scientific objects and forced to endure this humiliation while living on government settlements. Photographs of Tindale's expedition to central Australia in the 1930s suggest what Andrew Ball had gone through. The accurate measuring of peoples' physical features with elaborate tools or by taking plaster casts of faces can be considered a step far beyond documentary photography (fig. 6). This was in stark contrast to the story *Portraits of Our Elders* was telling about Aboriginal people walking into photographic studios in the 1920s as paying customers with a degree of control over their lives and relatively free of government officials.

Not all photographers have set out with racist motivations to document Aboriginal people. Numerous photographic collections have been made by European people who have had close associations with Aboriginal people, such as clergy, police, health workers, schoolteachers, and government officials who have spent time with Aboriginal communities. Over the past few years there have been a growing number of photographic collections being donated to museums and libraries by these people or by their families. These collections are proving very popular among Aboriginal people, who are now coming into museums and other institutions searching for photographs of their relatives. These photographs are important historical documents not just because they document Aboriginal people and their daily lives but, more importantly, because they document relationships between Aboriginal and non-Aboriginal people.

Michael Aird

In 1924 Enid Elizabeth Semple, aged eight years, arrived at Barambah Aboriginal settlement (or Cherbourg, as it is now known) as the daughter of government officials. Her father, William Porteous Semple, had been appointed superintendent, and her mother took the position of matron of the settlement (fig. 7). Enid Semple, now in her eighties and known to most as Betty McKenzie, remembers back to what she calls a wonderful childhood growing up with Aborigines.

Betty McKenzie put together an important set of photographs (see, e.g., figs. 8–10). Many of the photos were taken by Betty or members of her family; others were taken by visitors to the settlement such as press or government officials who would often send photographs of their visit to Betty's family. Betty's collection is important not only for the photos, but also for her memories of the people in the photographs. It is the information she attaches to these photographs that makes them an important historical record.

Betty lived through a very important political time for Aboriginal people. However, she does not make an issue of the politics she was surrounded by, but instead chooses to focus on the happy memories of her childhood. Betty represents the caring and well-meaning attitudes of that time, attitudes that deserve to be documented: "I did not think it was a bit strange to have Aboriginal children as playmates. But the other white officials' children didn't play with Aboriginal children like I did. The little girls would come down to play with me, or say 'what are we going to do today?' At mid day they went home to the dormitory for lunch and I went into our dining room for a very different lunch. They probably had damper and jam, they had good meals but very plain, while I might have had fillet steak or whatever" (interview with author, 1997).

In 1972 Betty McKenzie gave a presidential address to the Queensland Naturalists Club titled "Growing Up with Aborigines." The title of her address may seem indicative of attitudes from a past era, but what is important about her address, as well as her photograph collection, is that they document the diversity of attitudes and relationships between Aboriginal people and government officials in the 1920s and 1930s: "It is a memory of childhood, and children don't take in the really important things, the sadder things, it's a happy memory. It isn't a considered memory of how the settlement was run, it isn't official, it isn't official at all. It is not what I know now" (interview with author, 1997). Betty did not set out purely to document Aboriginal culture, she simply wanted to document aspects of her family, friends, and the place where she lived. Many of her memories have

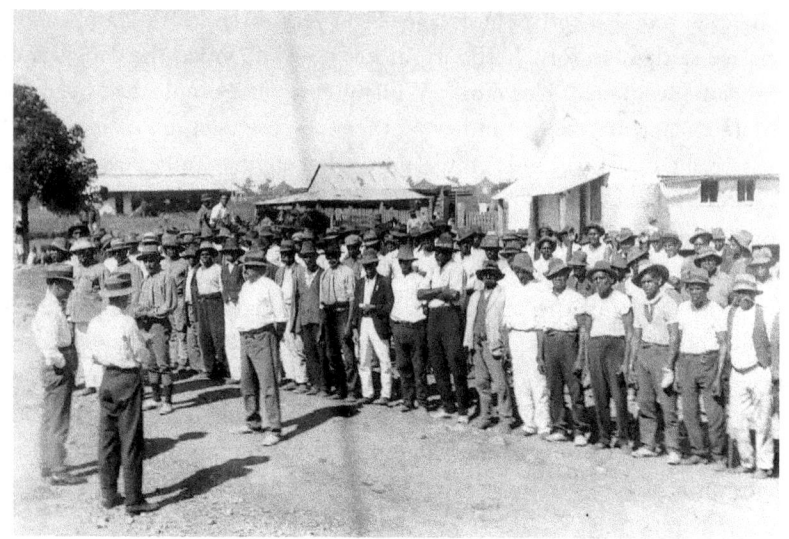

7. Roll Call at the start of a working day on the settlement, Cherbourg, 1924. Betty McKenzie Collection. Courtesy of the Queensland Museum (EH.456).

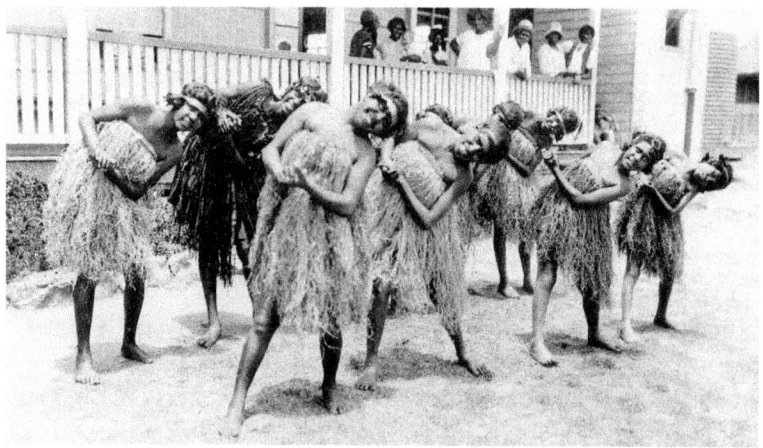

8. Entertaining visitors at Cherbourg, 1930. Betty McKenzie Collection. Courtesy of the Queensland Museum (EH.407).

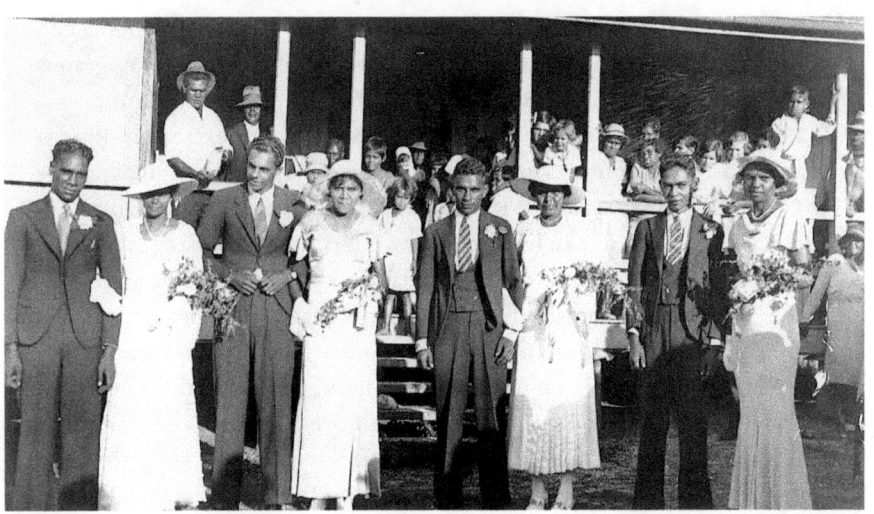

9. Wedding parties in front of the settlement's recreation hall, Cherbourg, 1937. Betty McKenzie Collection. Courtesy of the Queensland Museum (EH.434).

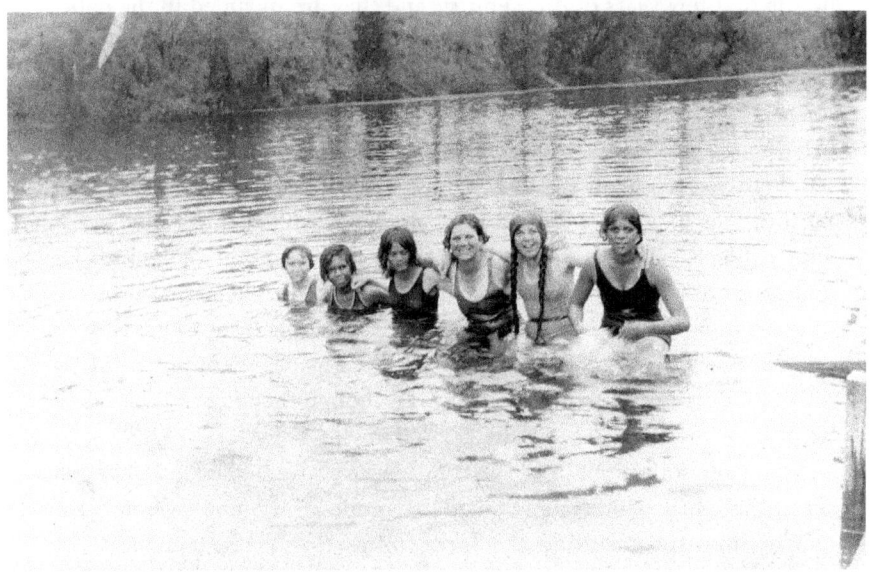

10. Tibby Williams, Naomi Chambers, Alma Willoughby, Marie Loder, Betty Semple, and Kitty Williams swimming in Barambah Creek, Cherbourg, c. 1928–29. Betty McKenzie Collection. Courtesy of the Queensland Museum (EH.897).

been recorded in the form of short stories, drawings, several published articles, and, most important, in a group of several hundred photographs that have been placed in the collection of the Queensland Museum.

Photographic collections like Betty McKenzie's are extremely important historical documents, particularly because so few Aboriginal people at Cherbourg in the 1920s and 1930s would have owned cameras. As a result, their families today do not have the photo collections that many other Australian families have. This is not to say that no Aboriginal at Cherbourg had cameras in the past: some did and their families still hold the photographs from the early part of the century. The Aboriginal people at Cherbourg were slightly better-off compared to those living on the north Queensland reserves, and some Cherbourg residents enjoyed a degree of wealth that would have enabled them to purchase a camera or occasionally to visit a photographic studio. In contrast, the people on the remote north Queensland reserves during the 1920s and 1930s would have had very little chance of being able to afford a camera, let alone have photographs developed.

The histories of Aboriginal people living on reserves are in contrast to the histories of those who did not. Photographs of Doris Yuke were taken in the first few years of this century, and they are included in the collection of her mother, Emma Somerset. Here is an example of a person who was under the control of government officials as a young woman and later managed to be exempted from the provisions of the Aboriginal Protection Act. Over a period of several decades Emma and, later, her daughter Doris managed to put together a collection of photographs dating back to the 1890s (figs. 11–15). This collection is very important to me because Doris Yuke is my mother's auntie, and as a child I knew her quite well. Her photographs represent an aspect of my family history as well as aspects of numerous other families' histories. Similarly, people from Cherbourg can look at Betty McKenzie's photographs and consider them representative of an aspect of their family history, even though they may not be related to or have any close ties to Betty or her family.

There are both similarities and differences between the Doris Yuke and Betty McKenzie photo collections. Betty's collection contains photographs of Cherbourg people painted up for corroborees in the 1920s and 1930s, but such images are not found in Doris Yuke's collection. Doris Yuke documented the daily life of Aboriginal people from the Beaudesert, Southport, and Brisbane regions who lived very different lives from the people living on reserves. Betty's photographs document the regimented work ethic experienced by the people of Cherbourg: Aboriginal people were taught the

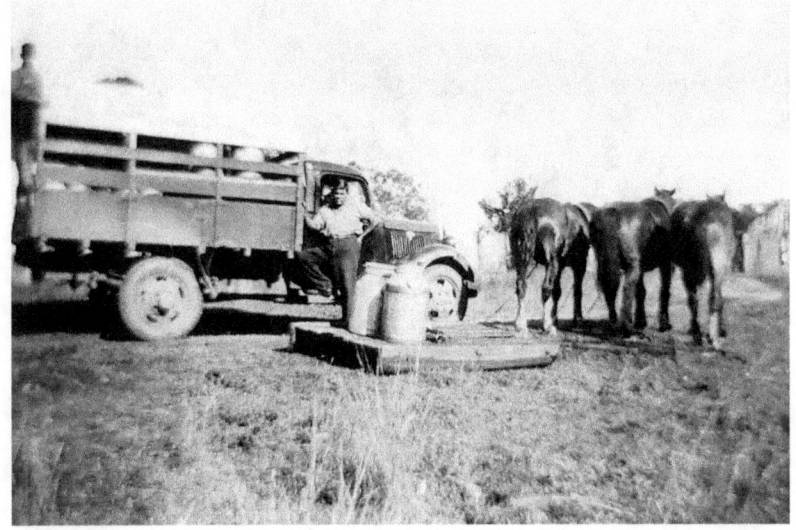

11. Tom Yuke with the truck he owned and operated by himself and used to transport milk to Beaudesert, c.1915. Courtesy of the Doris Yuke Collection.

12. Allan and Val Williams, Beaudesert, c.1915. (Allan is on the wooden horse made by their father, Ted Williams.) Courtesy of the Doris Yuke Collection.

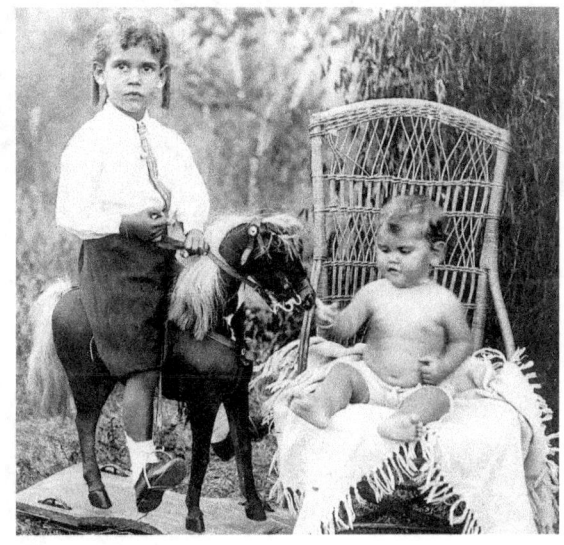

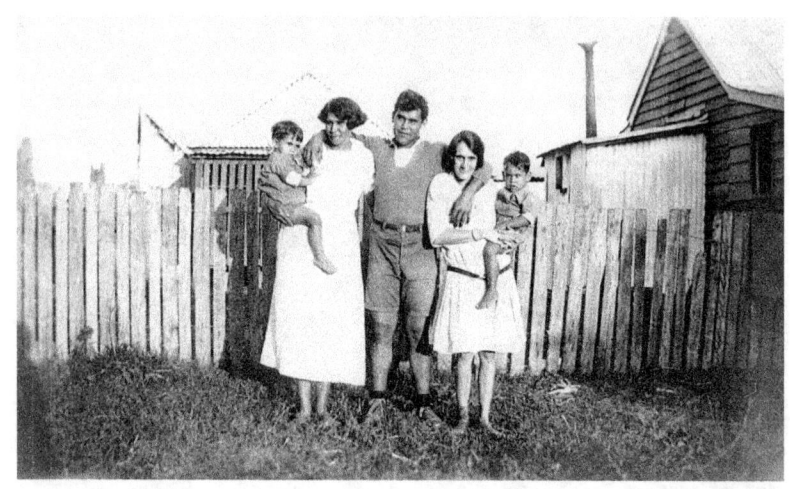

13. Allan Williams (center); Emma Williams holding her grandson, Charles
Yuke; and Doris Yuke holding her son, Douglas, Beaudesert, 1929. Courtesy
of the Doris Yuke Collection.

14. Bobby, Douglas,
and Charles Yuke
with their cousin
Joyce Yuke (on stairs)
at Tabooba near
Beaudesert, 1931.
Courtesy of the Doris
Yuke Collection.

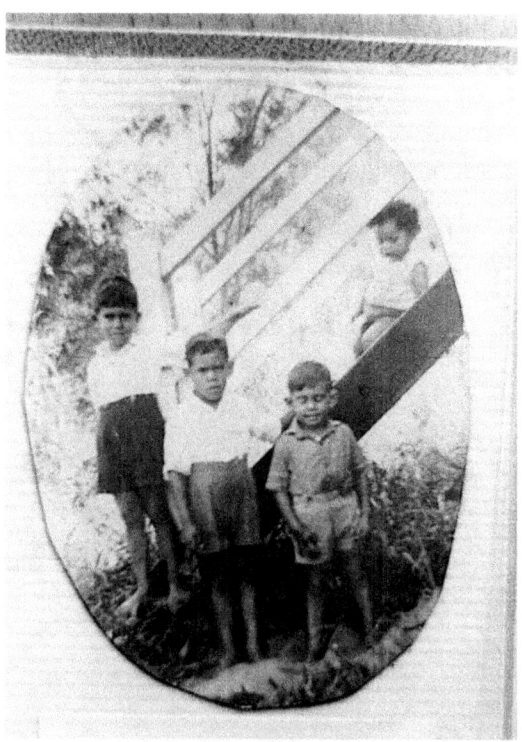

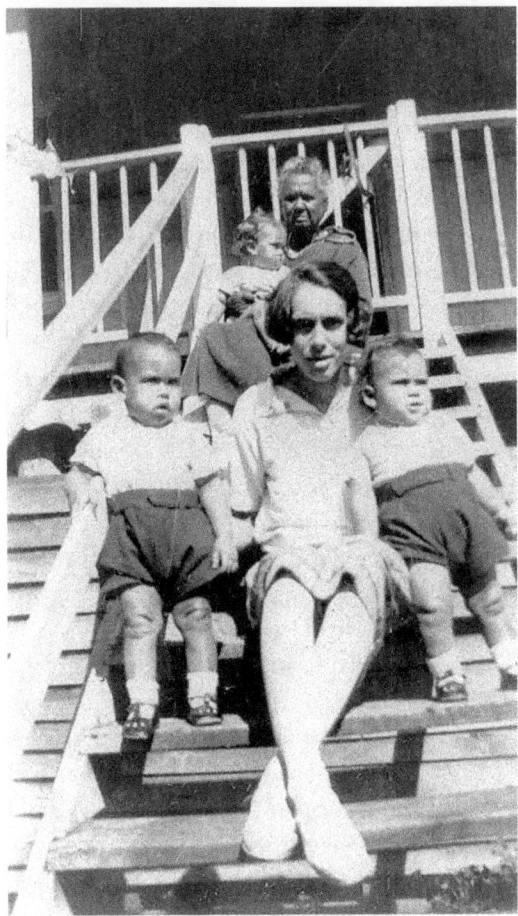

15. Jenny Graham
holding her
granddaughter, Beryl
Yuke, and Doris Yuke
with her sons, Douglas
and Bobby, at Tabooba
near Beaudesert, 1928.
Courtesy of the Doris
Yuke Collection.

benefits of industry and European society. In contrast, in Doris Yuke's collection are photographs of self-employed Aboriginal people who were in many ways part of the European economic system and owned cars and houses—something you do not see in the Cherbourg photographs.

In 1988 I copied a collection of photographs belonging to Patsy Clevens of Cherbourg, a collection begun by her mother. A few years later I returned to see that the same album had had a few photographs damaged by children, so I thought that at least I had copy negatives of this collection. I went back a few years later to find that Patsy's house had been destroyed by fire, and that she had lost her entire photographic collection. However, I was able to reproduce the entire photo album thanks to the negatives that I had made years earlier. Each time Patsy looked at a photo in this new album she would say, "Oh, I never thought I would see this photo again."

It was important for me to hear what Patsy had to say about Betty's photographs. She remembered Betty's father, William Porteous Semple, and stories about him as well as other people in the photographs. Patsy saw the photo of the Salvation Army minister Mr. Morrison, and said, "That's the guy that used to carry me around on his shoulders when I was a little girl. He used to call me Patsy but my mother called me Patty." She could go right back to the time when she was a young girl and remember a specific part of her family history, thanks to a photograph held in Betty McKenzie's collection. Patsy, who was born in 1929, is a few years younger than Betty, and she remembers Betty as being a lovely lady. This statement reflects the respect that many people from Cherbourg have for Betty, as well as the respect that Betty has for them. Maybe the younger people of Cherbourg do not look back favorably on this period of government control, nor feel that the government officials administered the settlement very favorably, but some of the older people of Betty's generation look back at the past with much fondness.

Betty often talks of the industry and the productivity of Cherbourg: the sawmill, the dairy, the crops, the piggery, and other examples of the economics of the settlement. Patsy Clevens also talked about the past with similar memories: "We used to have everything in those days, we even had our own sawmill, we used to cut our own timber to build our houses and [have] our own carpenters.... We used to have a lot of beautiful cattle here, we used to grow lovely vegetables too. In those days everybody worked. Never seen a person walking the mission, only women folk and kids were home. But now things have changed" (interview with author, 1997). These are the words of Patsy Clevens who has lived at Cherbourg all her life, and in that time she has witnessed many changes. So much has happened since the 1920s. While looking at the photographs from Betty McKenzie's collection, Patsy Clevens was reminded of what life was like there when she was young. Betty McKenzie's collection of photographs is a historical document that is important not only to Patsy and her family but also to numerous Aboriginal families.

Several years ago I showed the photographs of Andrew Ball to Patsy Clevens. At this time I had just found out that he had lived at Cherbourg, but I did not know if he had any family, nor had I met anyone who identified as being related to him. Patsy recognized Andrew as a relative of her late husband, Alic Landers. She said, "That is Alic's name, his real name is not Alic, it is Andrew, after his grandfather, Andrew Ball." Numerous times I have witnessed the complex relationships that people have with photographs. Aboriginal people are grateful for the opportunity to find images of their relatives, regardless of who took the photographs or where these photographs are held today. This essay demonstrates the relationships that Aboriginal people have with photographs that may have been taken by non-Aboriginal people, such as scientists or government officials, and it also acknowledges the role Aboriginal people have played in documenting their own histories.

Hulleah J. Tsinhnahjinnie

When Is a Photograph Worth
a Thousand Words?

Stories are always told from all corners of the world: stories of creation, stories of the ethereal, stories of survival; grandmothers, grandfathers telling stories that were told to them by their grandmothers and grandfathers; aunties relating stories about brothers and sisters. We are all familiar with the warmth of stories cradling, surrounding, supporting new generations.

I remember several of the stories related to me by my mother; as she spoke I would visualize the scenes in my young mind—just like a television, just like a photograph.

Our family photographs from the past are very few, my mother's family (Seminole and Muskogee) had a collection of family photographs that perished in a house fire during the 1940s. I would occasionally overhear my mother and Aunt Marie lamenting over the loss. Although I know them from the beautifully woven stories, I have never viewed their likeness in a photograph. My mother's father passed on before I was born. I have never seen an image of my grandfather. But in my mind—my imagined photographs—the men are strong and handsome, the women strong and breathtaking, with lustrous warm dark skin, lightening-sharp witty eyes, and smiles that could carry one for days. A photographic album full of beautiful brown people, a photographic album of visual affirmation.

My father's family (Diné) never had very many photographs, there was no furious fire to melt the negatives, there was a philosophy which was very protective. To outsiders I suppose the attitude would be interpreted as superstitious or even shy. Whatever the outsider preferred to believe, whatever the sophisticated evaluation arrived at, the outsider would leave the reservation satisfied that stereotypes had been affirmed. They never interpreted the "backward attitude" of the subject or shyness as a statement about their presence. The superstition or shyness was neither explained nor elaborated on to strangers, because the "photographer" would not have understood the nuances of privacy that the Diné perceived.

My Seminole, Muskogee, and Diné relatives may not have shared the same views about photography, but as American history would have it they did endure the same government policies created to destroy the very fabric of Native culture. All three Nations experienced forced removal from ancestral homelands.

My Seminole and Muskogee relatives were forced to walk from Florida to Oklahoma, a forced march that began in the late 1830s and is known as the Trail of Tears. My Diné relatives also have a name for their forced removal: "The Long Walk" (1867). The forced marches were in violation of every basic human right imaginable.

The focus of my relatives was the reality of survival, keeping one's family alive. Time to contemplate Western philosophy or the invention of photography was, shall we say, limited. Because of the preoccupation with survival, Native people became the subject rather than the observer. The subject of judgmental images as viewed by the foreigner—images worth a thousand words. As long as the words were in English.

When I first began reading ethnographic images I would become extremely depressed, but then recognition dawned. I was viewing the images as an observer, not as the observed. My analytical eye matured, and I became suspicious of the awkward, self-appointed "expert" narrative. From delegation photographers, expedition photographers, and ethnographic researchers, I was very cognizant of methodologies that were of the "objective" foreign eye. But even so flawed, these nineteenth-century images were very significant in filling the empty pages of my family album.

It was a beautiful day when the scales fell from my eyes and I first encountered photographic sovereignty. A beautiful day when I decided that I would take responsibility to reinterpret images of Native peoples. My mind was ready, primed with stories of resistance and resilience, stories of survival. My views of these images are aboriginally based—an indigenous perspective—not a scientific godly order but philosophically Native.

The understanding of indigenous continuance must be the understanding of indigenous religion. From healers to message receivers, enduring the past and the continuous assault by Christianity, Native religion and philosophy hid to survive and resurface at appropriate moments.

As I look into the eyes of Ayyuini (Swimmer) (fig. 1), I recall a conversation I had on a hot, humid Oklahoma afternoon in August when I was photographing Wilma Mankiller, activist and former principal chief of the Oklahoma Aniyunwiya (Cherokees). We were outside under the gracious shade of mature black-jack trees, shades of green. Cooling the sweat from my face, I raised my head pausing from the viewfinder to ask Wilma who Swimmer was. With locusts singing in the background to the rhythm of the heat, Wilma tilted her head to one side and looked at me thoughtfully and said, "He was the source of some of the strongest Cherokee medicine. He was extremely powerful. . . . How do you know of Swimmer?" Adjusting my lens I replied, "I saw his photograph in a book of nineteenth-century images of Native people, and the caption read, 'Ayyuini [Swimmer], Cherokee'—no other information, just a sliver of a caption." Wilma told me about Ayyuini and his understudies, and how no one since has equaled his presence and power. The arrival of this information was appropriate, not only in location but of the oral tradition reaffirming the feeling that I had when I looked into Ayyuini's eyes.

When I gaze upon the image of the Hinano'ei (Arapaho) followers of the Ghost Dance religion (fig. 2) and the image of the Yebichai (fig. 3), I am filled with emotion. Although Mooney and Curtis thought they were imaging a vanishing race, I see the contrary, I see perseverance.

In these photos I immediately recognize the power of survival, and my heart is filled with emotion. There is the synthesising of my existence, the very reason why this indigenous woman, typing on a laptop computer at the end of the twentieth century, exists. The persistence of that same religion lives within me, ensuring Native survival and thus refusing to surrender the soul. Native land may be taken by force or by invented written declarations, and natural resources sucked up by an infantile America, but no matter how many words are written on a piece of paper declaring ownership of land, no matter the towns and metropolitans possessing foreign names, America will always be Native land.

Native people, photographed dramatically in appropriate savage attire, vanishing before one's eyes. Native people photographed in suits of assimilation tailored to the correct perspective of a progressive new world. Such schizophrenia lamented the disappearing of the "Indian" and yet celebrated images of "Indians" accepting progress. That which could not

Hulleah J. Tsinhnahjinnie

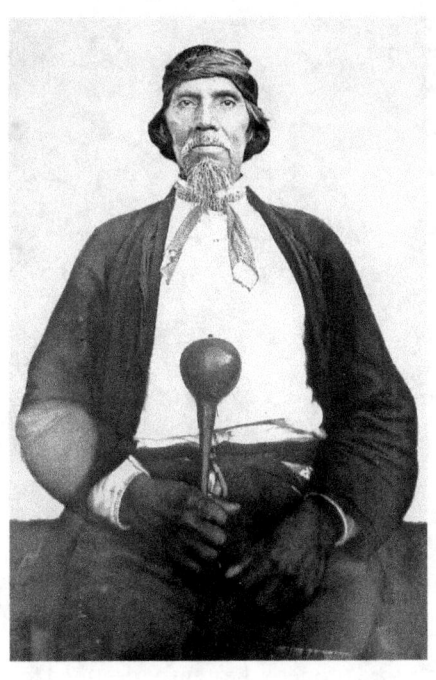

1. Ayyuini Swimmer, a Cherokee. Photo by James Mooney. Courtesy of the National Anthropological Archives, Smithsonian Institution (neg. 1008).

2. Hinano'ei [Arapaho] of the Ghost Dance religion. Photo by James Mooney. Courtesy of the National Anthropological Archives, Smithsonian Institution (neg. 55298).

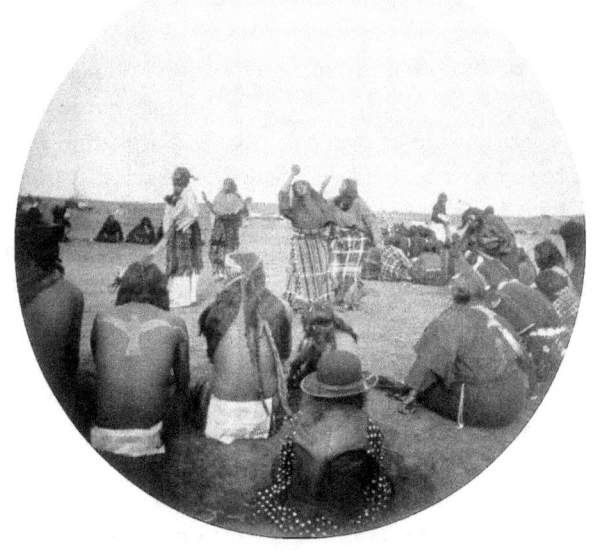

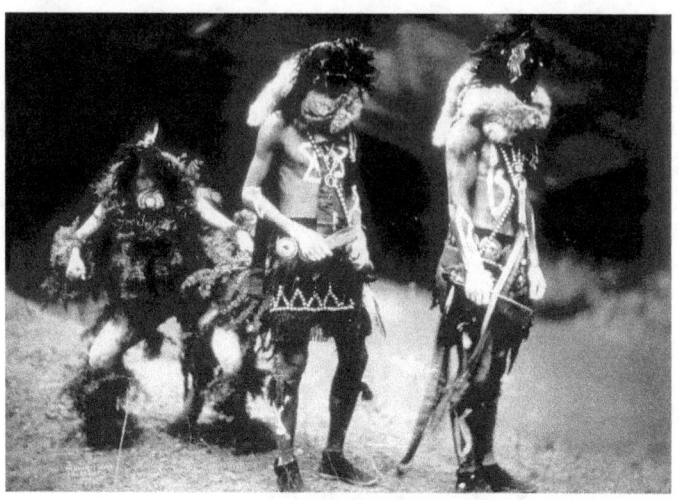

3. *Navajo War Gods.* Photo by Edward S. Curtis, 1904. Courtesy of
The Wellcome Library, London (neg. v0038486c00).

be scrubbed with soap and water, dressed properly, beaten, or destined for
extinction was and is the persistence of the indigenous soul, the persistence to exist, the strength of endurance to be faithful to Native intelli-
gence, Native religion. As I look at these photographs of religion, I think
of the ceremonies that take place today on the reservation, in the cities. I
think of those chosen to carry responsibility and of those who step forward
to take responsibility: the singers who carry the songs, those who know
the relationship of plants to people, Native-rights lawyers, activists, philosophers, writers, artists, single mothers, aunts, grandparents, individuals
who have accepted the responsibility of continuance. There is no doubt
in my mind that the people imaged in these photographs are aware of the
integral link they have to today's existence of Native religion. I am also reminded that times have not changed much and that the assault continues
in ways that aren't as recognizable as in the past but with tactics that are
just as deadly. The over-romanticizing and simplification of Native existence have been and continue to be two of the greatest assaults on Native
existence.

   I am quite aware that this is not a new story, it is a story that has been
studied and repeated. Unknown to many, the methodology of the U.S.-
planned genocide of Native people was studied and emulated.

   This story began on a June evening late in 1990 in Haudensonee land,

Hulleah J. Tsinhnahjinnie

where I was in residency at the Center for Conceptual Photography in Buffalo, New York. Earlier Jolene Rickard had invited me to visit her reservation, and that day I was given the grand tour. In the evening I rested at her parents' house while Jolene was out on errands. Jolene's father and I were sitting in webbed lawn chairs sipping ice tea, the scent of citronella candles wafting in the air. Mr. Rickard was sharing Tuscarora history. He asked if I knew of "Old Man Clinton"; I replied "No." The crickets seemed to soften their voices as Mr. Rickard began telling me about Clinton Rickard: the stories were incredible, one was particularly haunting.

In the early 1930s, a German investigation team arrived at the Tuscarora Nation and sought out Clinton Rickard. They were searching for information about the genocidal practices of the United States, past and present, and Clinton Rickard was an authority on Native American history and law. The investigation team asked questions and took notes, they returned a second day full of questions and notebooks. As I listened to this story my soul shivered, Jolene's father was giving me a gift, a story. The Tuscarora Nation was not the only Nation visited by investigation teams. Later, I related this story to a friend involved with the Jewish museum in San Francisco, who then told the people at the museum. Most were skeptical, but one said that she had heard of such a visitation on the Shoshone reservation. This story has yet to evolve as "hard evidence" to the doubters, for me this story need not be in print form for it to be true, the oral transference of information that summer evening in Haundensonee Territory will always be more *real* than words in a book.

When oral history coincides with photographic evidence the impact can be disturbing. The photographic evidence of U.S. genocidal practices is not extensive (if there is no evidence of genocide then there was no genocide). But the few photographs available are poignant: The images of the massacre at Wounded Knee, the bodies of Sioux people stacked on a wagon for a mass burial, and the photograph of Big Foot, frozen in death (fig. 4).

I had a vivid dream of this photograph. In my dream I was an observer floating—I saw Big Foot as he is in the photograph, and my heart ached. I was about to mourn uncontrollably when into the scene walked a small child, about six years old. She walked about the carnage, looking into the faces of those lying dead in the snow. She was searching for someone. Her small moccasin footprints imprinted the snow as she walked over to Big Foot, looking into his face. She shakes his shoulders, takes his frozen hand into her small, warm hand, and helps him to his feet. He then brushes the snow off of his clothes. She waits patiently with her hand extended, he then takes her hand and they walk out of the photograph. This is the dream I recall when I look upon this image of supposed hopelessness.

The complexity of the subject being photographed never seems to be included in the thousand words. It seems the thousand words get reduced to a generic title void of the subject's voice, especially in the case of the indigenous subject. What better photograph to illustrate this than the photograph taken in 1879 by John K. Hillers (fig. 5). It's an innocent enough photograph. A documentation of the Zuni mission school run by Taylor Ealy (standing right). Miss Jennie Hammaker (standing left) was their teacher, twenty-seven students, one baby, five Zuni men, one Zuni woman, and two (unfocused) observers on the roof. No one is named except for the white people, nothing new. A very dry photograph.

Except for the Zuni woman standing behind the children, standing behind the children in a very maternal, protective way. The woman is We'wha, a respected member of the community, involved in the ceremonies, an excellent artist and cultural ambassador for her people. We'wha traveled to Washington in 1886 to meet national leaders and the president. We'wha influenced whites and Native people alike, an incredible life. This beautiful woman was a man.

We'wha was born into this world a male, lived her life as a woman, and then departed this world as a man (1896). This photograph is a perfect example of those complexities that cannot be reduced to a three-sentence caption.

In today's politically correct language We'wha would be referred to as gay, but even that is not correct, "gay" is a foreign, alienating word. The anthropologist would label We'wha berdache whereas contemporary Native gay and lesbians prefer the self-described title of two-spirited society.

The history of the two-spirited society is very limited due to assimilation, Christianity, and the need to survive. As written by Will Roscoe in *The Zuni Man Woman:*

> The abandonment of the dress accrued throughout Native North America. Persons learned of an Isleta berdache in the 1930s who had adopted men's clothes and another at San Felipe who wore men's clothing at his job in Albuquerque and women's clothing while in his pueblo. Among the Diné [Navajo], most berdaches stopped cross-dressing in the early 20th century, and several observers have cited the impact of white ridicule. . . . In some cases, cross-dressing and gender mixing were actively suppressed by Indian agents (or their suppression was contemplated, as in the case of Pueblo agents in the 1890s). . . . Of course berdaches were not alone in abandoning

Hulleah J. Tsinhnahjinnie

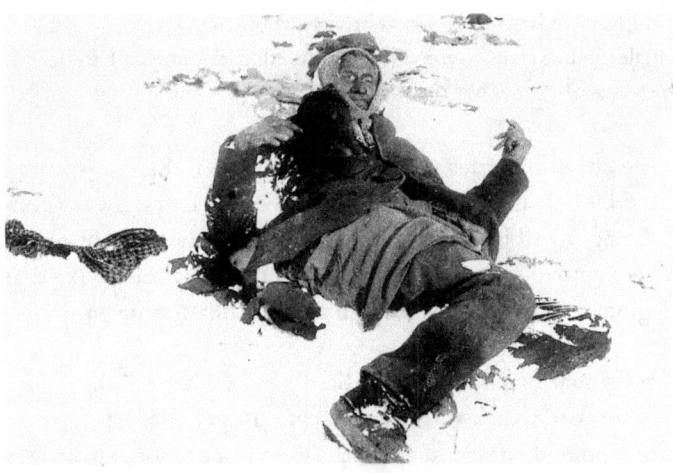

4. Big Foot lying dead in the snow at Wounded Knee, South
Dakota, January 1891. Photo by George Trager. Courtesy of the
National Anthropological Archives, Smithsonian Institution
(neg. 55018).

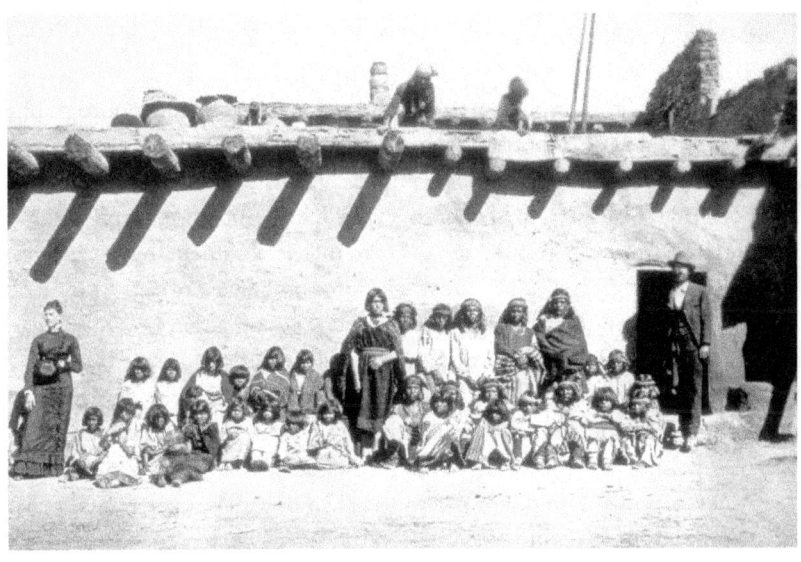

5. Children in front of their school at Zuni Pueblo with their teacher, Jennie
Hammaker, and the school administrator, Taylor Ealy, 1879. Photo by John
Hillers. Courtesy of the National Anthropological Archives, Smithsonian
Institution (neg. 2251-D-2).

traditional clothing. Indians who wore Native clothing in the white world —
male or female or berdache were often ridiculed. Eventually, all Indians
made compromises in how they dressed, at least in the white setting.

Similar to the survival tactics of indigenous religion, the two-spirited
society survived by becoming invisible. Being invisible by no means con-
notes defeat. Being invisible signifies the condition of the current political atmosphere. The two-spirited society faced a dilemma much like that
of Native religion: conform to the specifics of assimilation or go under-
ground.

Similar to missionaries knocking on the doors of Native homes, presenting the proper road to heaven, so approaches the gay and lesbian community spouting polemic political agendas defining a proper existence, a
missionary approach that does not include indigenous philosophy, much
less historical or cultural perspective. One must even be aware of the complexities of the self-described title "two-spirited society" a definition, a
contemporary definition in English, when there exists proper titles in several aboriginal languages: surviving titles that are neither alienating nor
judgmental; words describing one's position in community; words before
contact with Christians or anthropologists. In the Zuni language, We'wha
was Ihamana.

When is a photograph worth a thousand words? When photographs
were occupied with "a thousand words" of text the "official" language often
would fall short and many times completely miss the point.

Aboriginal beauty. Curtis photographed a beautiful Acoma Pueblo
woman (fig. 6) staring into the lens. It is an intense moment, not exactly an
endearing stare. Curtis was the voyeur photographer aware of the physical.
What of her mind? Her thoughts of yesterday, today, and tomorrow? I can
relate to the energy that she emits. It reminds me of the summers when my
father, a painter, would travel to Monument Valley or Canyon de Chelly to
paint the landscape and sell the paintings to the tourists who were watching him paint. My brother, sister, and I would play nearby, climbing the
red rocks, playing in the sand. The tourists would call us over and take our
picture, sometimes giving us a quarter, the look I perfected was the look
that the Acoma woman is giving Curtis: "Take your photograph and. . . ." I
like this image: perhaps I am projecting, but isn't this what it's all about?

The nineteenth-century photographer who, I believe, truly imaged
Native women with love and a humanizing eye is Jennie Ross Cobb (Ani-

Hulleah J. Tsinhnahjinnie

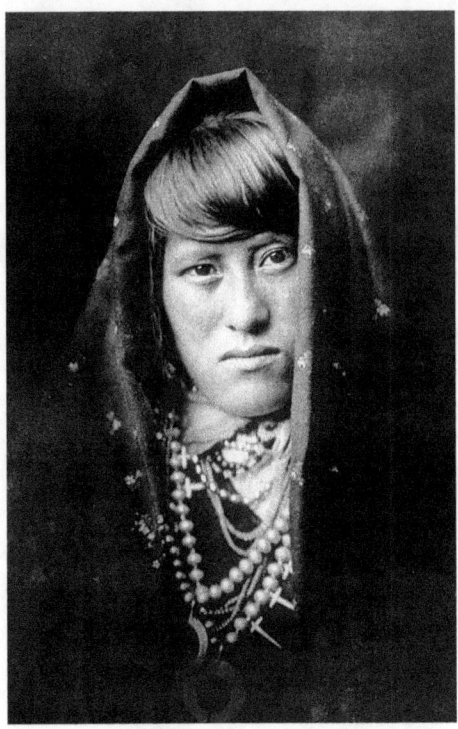

6. *An Acoma Woman.* Photo by Edward S. Curtis, in his *North American Indians*, vol. 10 (Cambridge: Cambridge University Press, 1907). Courtesy Guildhall Library, Corporation of London.

yunwiya). Photographs of Native women at the Aniyunwiya (Cherokee) women's seminary (fig. 7), images of Native women living in the contemporary, relaxed poses, smiling to a friend. Photographs by a Native woman photographing Native women at the end of the nineteenth century: images Curtis, Vroman, Hillers, and the many others could not even begin to emulate, when the eye of the beholder possesses love for the beheld.

Images of the early non-Native photographers documenting Native people will always be interesting, but of more interest to me is the aboriginal perspective, the aboriginal photographer. The "discovery" of early Native photographers is exciting, there are more—I can sense them. They also know when to surface.

Several aspects of Native beauty are resurfacing: the photograph of Johnny Kit Elswa (Haida Gwaii) by Ensign E. P. Niblack, with the Bear clan inscribed on his chest and the dog fish permanently on his arms (fig. 8). Aboriginal tattoo—the brazen illustration of identity. Tattoos went under the skin to survive, encoded beneath the skin, programmed to resurface

When Is a Photograph Worth a Thousand Words? 49

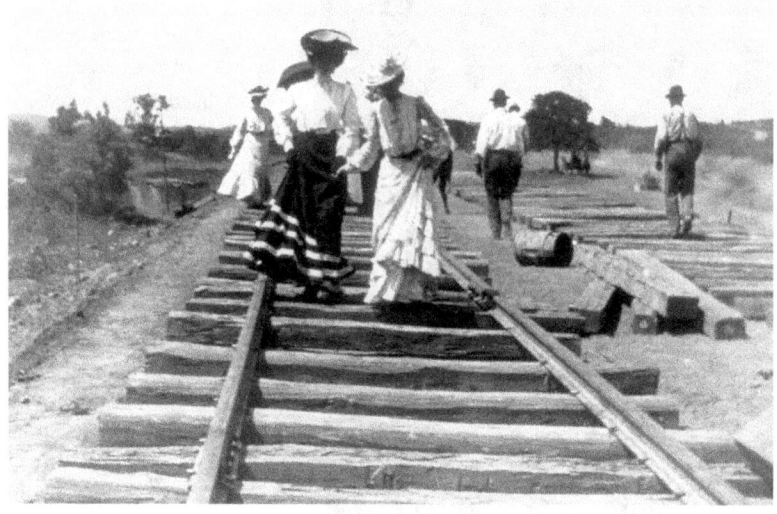

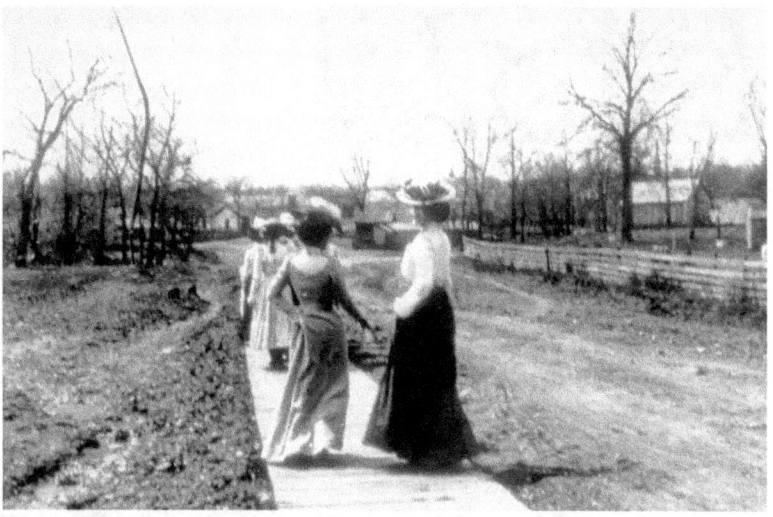

7. *(Top)* "When the train came to Tahlegnoh 1902. Ozark and Cherokee
Central Railroad, Fayetteville to Okmulgee."
(Below) "Students strolling along a broadwalk that led from the Cherokee
Seminary for Women into Tahlegnoh," c.1900–1901.
Photos by Jennie Ross Cobb. The Jennie Ross Cobb Collection. Oklahoma
Historical Society.

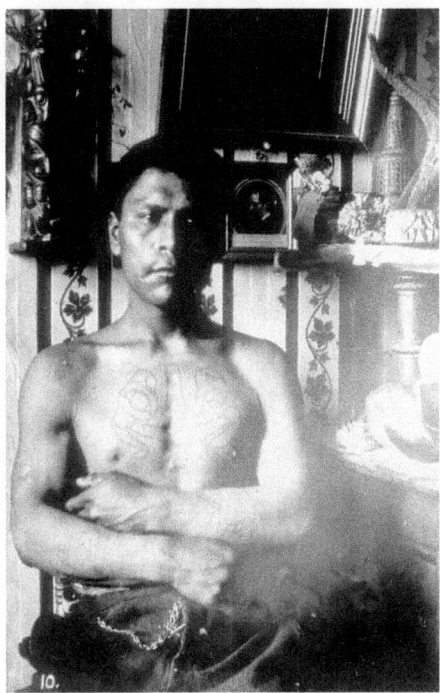

8. Johnny Kit Elswa (Haida
Gwaii). Photo by E. P. Niblack,
1886. Courtesy of the National
Anthropological Archives,
Smithsonian Institution
(neg. 4117).

when the time is right: this is also how I perceive the art of aboriginal tattoo,
latent images.

I have been considering tattoos for years. The Muskogee, my mother's
people, adorned themselves with tattoos to signify status of power both
spiritually and socially. From Atearoa to Florida there was a submergence
of *moko*, of tattoo. Today there is a healthy resurfacing.

I am in the process of researching and receiving information. Research as
in the "Western" academic sense, scrutinizing, investigating, collating assembled notes from museums, ethnological reports, etching, observances
from those who were sincerely curious and yet simultaneously whose pre-
conceived assumptions prepared the climate for the submergence of tattoo.

I receive information via the aboriginal internal world—information by
dreams, ethereal coincidences, and the very important oral tradition of the
aboriginal people around the world. The reemergence of aboriginal traditions, the wave of rebirth, people surviving, harvest dances being danced
and songs returning in dreams . . . information resurfacing.

When Is a Photograph Worth a Thousand Words?   51

When I begin to tell my stories to my many nieces and nephews, I will first create photographic albums in their young minds, . . . where the men are strong and handsome, the women strong and breathtaking, with lustrous warm dark skin, lightening-sharp witty eyes, and smiles that could carry one for days. A photographic album full of beautiful brown people, a photographic album of visual affirmation.

Hulleah J. Tsinhnahjinnie

Visual

Economies

. . . .

2

Roslyn Poignant

The Making of Professional "Savages"

FROM P. T. BARNUM (1883) TO THE

SUNDAY TIMES (1998)

The Narrative

In October 1993, news flashed round the world that the mummified body of a North Queensland Aborigine, called Tambo, had been found in the basement of a recently closed funeral home in Cleveland, Ohio. This macabre event brought to public attention the little-known story of the removal abroad of Tambo and his companions, nine Aborigines from the Palm Islands and nearby Hinchinbrook Island, all of whom were probably picked up in Townsville by the showman R. A. Cunningham, who was acting as recruiter for the American circus impresario P. T. Barnum. During the circus season of 1883, the Aborigines were featured in Barnum's "Ethnological Congress of Strange and Savage Tribes," together with the Zulu, Nubians, Toda, and Sioux performers who had been similarly dispossessed on other colonial frontiers. After the season, through the winter of 1883–1884, Cunningham and the Aborigines toured the dime museums of the northern United States until, in Cleveland, Tambo was the first to die—only a year after leaving Sydney. Unknown to his companions, he was subjected to the ultimate indignity: his embalmed body was put on show in Drew's Dime Museum. (It remained on display there and elsewhere in Cleveland well into the twentieth century.)

It was part of Cunningham's pattern to move the group on whenever there was an incident, and sometime between leaving Cleveland and arriving in London a few weeks later another young man died. For several years, Cunningham continued to tour the seven survivors through the showplaces of Europe, their numbers steadily reduced by death. On their travels, in addition to their show appearances, they were examined, measured, and photographed by anthropologists. Early in my investigations of the Aborigine show group I wondered if it would be possible to recover their story. Reasoning that the group may have been regarded as British subjects, I searched the register of "British Deaths Abroad." There, at a likely date, I found the single entry "Jimmy." It was a long shot, but I paid my £5 and sent away for the certificate. With it came confirmation: Jimmy had died in Darmstadt, Germany, on 31 May 1885, and his occupation was given as "Australian Savage" in the Cunningham Company. It was never again to be as easy to recover what Americans call "vital records." The manner in which the unwilling travelers were represented in both scientific and popular accounts (the sources on which this outline draws) served to obscure their individual identities, so that deconstructing the linked graphic, photographic, and textual representations associated with their performance and display has been crucial to the recovery of their particular histories, however fragmentary.[1] In any event, my main concern here is with the visual.

Aboriginal lives were made captive, not only in the sense of loss of agency but also within late-nineteenth-century discourses that linked the colonial frontiers to the metropolitan centers of North America and Europe. Together with other indigenous performers, they became enmeshed in Western systems of popular entertainment and education involving display and performance, which marked the emergence of the modern world as spectacle. I call the arena where this engagement took place the "show-space." This term is more than a collective name for the actual places of exhibition. Rather, it is a cultural space that, among other things, serves as a zone of displacement for the indigenous performers and a place of spectacle for the onlookers—that is, a chronotopic space (Bakhtin 1981, 84, 250–53) in which historically specific relations of power between colonizers and colonized are made visible. Within this space the personal stories of these people intersected with another narrative concerning the links between popular culture and anthropology. The language lists, bodily measurements, and photographs of the physical anthropological accounts of Cunningham's group were part of a classificatory project that postulated a hierarchy of races in which Australian Aborigines and other hunter-gatherers were rated low in the scale. Such dubious social-evolutionary notions provided the ideological underpinning for their dispossession. At the same time, they provided the rationale for the treatment of indigenous performers as expendable.[2]

Although recovering narrative has been central to my research, a parallel concern (and a main concern in this article) is to investigate the representational processes—what Homi Bhabha (1983) calls "the processes of subjectification"—that "made" Tambo and his companions into professional savages. My investigation is complicated by the public exposure the story has received since Tambo's repatriation and his burial on Palm Island in February 1994, 110 years after his death. The historical photographs in particular have been deployed in the several different but interrelated narratives of the descendants of other Palm Islanders, and of non-Aboriginal commentators and public alike.[3] Although some of these new narratives are part of the process of cultural renewal taking place in the community since the "return" of Tambo, much of the reporting about these events comes close to reanimating the sensational and derogatory language of nineteenth-century circus literature. Thus the shifting ground of the present fosters both the emergence of new narratives of identity and the persistence of old stereotypes—albeit in new digitized clothing. Re-presentation is a relentless process. I propose here to interrogate both old and new representational forms, concluding with a particular example from an article about present-day Palm Island in the *Sunday Times* supplement, London (1998), in which one of the historical photographs—a portrait of Jimmy—was digitally manipulated to represent not Jimmy himself, but the ghost of Tambo.

Let me begin with two representations, one photographic and the other graphic, of Tambo and his companions. The photograph of the group in their cowhide show costumes, taken before Tambo and another young man died, is the only one known showing all nine group members (see fig. 1). Although the photo was almost certainly taken in the United States,[4] Cunningham registered its copyright in London on 28 April 1884, giving the photographer's address as the same as his own temporary address. The implied London location is an impossibility, given that by April 1884 two of the men were already dead; that a copy of the photo has survived in the British copyright files can be attributed to Cunningham's deviousness. Although the Aboriginal names of each group member were recorded both by Cunningham (in his pamphlet) and several European anthropologists, all except one—the second young man to die—have come to be known by their given English names. In an essay elsewhere (Poignant 1997) I have shown that by relating this photograph to other named photographs

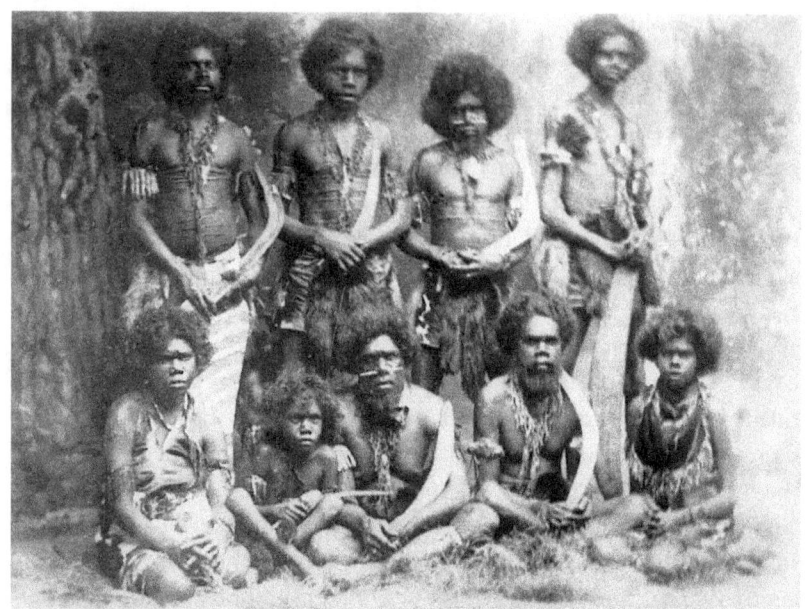

1. Only known photograph of all nine of the first group of North Queensland Aborigines removed by R. A. Cunningham in 1883. The identity of the
photographer is uncertain; although it is attributed on the copyright form to a
William Davis of 416 Strand in London, this cannot be correct because the
photo was taken before the group reached England. Courtesy of
the Public Record Office, U.K.

and to anthropologists' descriptions of the seven who had survived to
reach Europe, it has been possible to identify the nine not only by name
but also by the language groups to which each belonged. Here, however, I
shall simply introduce them.[5]

Jenny; her son, Little Toby; and her husband, Toby, are seated left; Tambo
and his wife, Sussy, are seated together, right; and behind them, Jimmy
stands a little apart. These are the six Manbarra from the Palm Islands. From
left to right, the three Biyaygirri men from Hinchinbrook Island—Bob,
a man whose name may be Wangong, and Billy—stand together, distinguished by their horizontal scarifications. It was not until this photograph
enabled me to identify Wangong(?) by his body marks as Biyaygirri that
I realized it movingly reflects Aboriginal relationships—not an arrangement imposed by the photographer. Although many of the later photographs made of the seven who survived to reach Europe were taken with

Roslyn Poignant

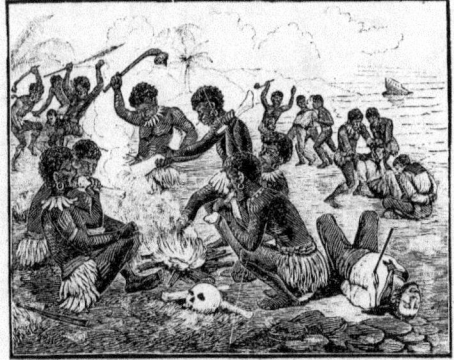

HISTORY OF

R, A. CUNNINGHAM'S
AUSTRALIAN
ABORIGINES.

TATTOOED
CANNIBAL
BLACK TRACKERS
AND
BOOMERANG THROWERS,
Consisting of Two Tribes, Male and Female,
COPYRIGHT.

2. Front cover
of *A History of R.A.
Cunningham's Australian
Aborigines*, copyright
registered in London on
10 April 1884. Courtesy
of the Public Record
Office, U.K.

anthropological intent, this photo of the whole group was taken for commercial reasons—the sale of photographs being part of the exploitation of indigenous performers, together with the sale of pamphlets, circus route books, and artifacts. While the photographs, both commercial and anthropological, have in their archival existence over the past hundred years frequently become separated from their contexts of production and circulation, the graphic representations, when they have survived, usually are accompanied by captions or other contextualizing letterpress.

For example, the cover illustration of the 1884 English edition of the pamphlet *History of R. A. Cunningham's Australian Aborigines* is not derived from the photograph (see fig. 2),[6] although by the 1880s the use of photographs for reference was well established. It pictures not Aborigines but "savages" of late-nineteenth-century Western imagination. Although in this instance depicted as vaguely Fijian-looking "savages"—whatever their supposed racial origins—were said to be characterized by "ferocity" and "treachery," their bodies were self-mutilated, and they lacked language and

The Making of Professional "Savages"   59

3. Billy, photographed in the studio of Tuttle & Co., February 1883. McCaddon was Barnum's business manager during this period. McCaddon Collection of the Barnum and Bailey Circus. Manuscripts Division. Department of Rare Books and Special Collections. Princeton University Library.

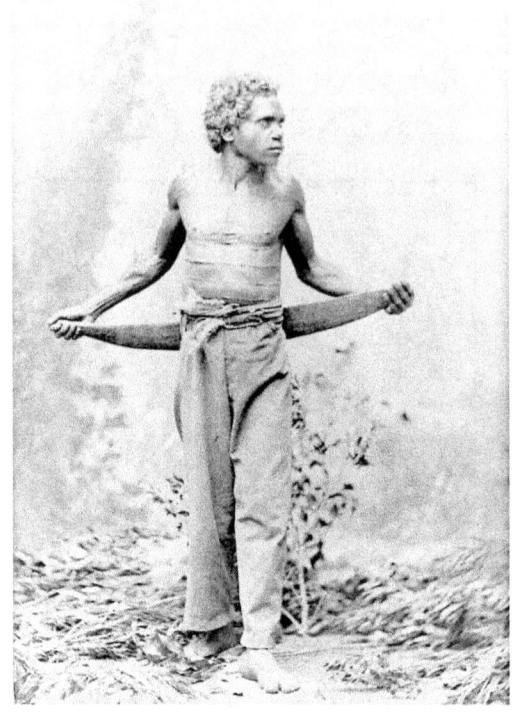

ate people. These traits are signaled in the illustration by the depiction of a cannibal feast on the seashore—a graphic representation that is generically related to a number of other images, both contemporary with it and earlier.[7]

I propose in this essay to trace briefly the iconographic elements and technological advances that in the course of the nineteenth century facilitated a negative construction of "savagery." By contrasting photographic and graphic representations of the same subject I am not proposing the apparent actuality of the photograph as a foil for the obviously fictive graphic representation. In the photograph the men's nosebones, their bare, scarified torsos, and their weaponry were meant, along with their bushy hair, to signal "wildness"—even if (at least to our eyes) these signs are undermined by the passive pose of the subjects. On the other hand, an earlier photograph of Billy taken in the Australian studio of Tuttle and Co., posing with his weapon held horizontally behind him and his hair neatly cut, is the picture of an amenable and employable "native" (fig. 3). This was almost certainly the impression Cunningham was aiming at when he dis-

Roslyn Poignant

patched the print to Barnum.[8] Looked at another way it could also suggest a more active participation by Billy, who might have been eager to play a new social role defined by European clothes and goods. The stereotypical elements in a photo's construction do not preclude its value evidentially or ethnographically. Considered together, the various photographs of Tambo and his companions both advance the narrative and expose the processes of subjectification. I suggest it is the interrogation of them—in conjunction with texts—that helps to destabilize the "fixity" and disrupt the stereotypical imaging of the group in either form, photographic or graphic, by returning something of their individuality to them.[9]

In my larger project, "Captive Lives," on which this paper draws, I am concerned with what W. J. T. Mitchell calls "the whole field of representations and representational activity" (1994b, 6) relating to the exhibition of Tambo and his companions. I am concerned with performance and display and with textual and pictorial representations—both graphic and photographic—that enable the excavation of their story: the popular ephemera of advertising and presentation, such as broadsides, posters, and illustrated papers, as well as anthropological reports. I am concerned with the interlayering of these various forms of representation and with the interpenetration of the factual and fictional in images, scientific and official reports, registers and contracts, and frontiersmen's tales and romantic novels. At the same time, I place some emphasis on the visual, because I regard visual documents—and oral when available—as important in the "making" of social and cultural histories contrary to received histories. Indeed, the image-rich nature of the representational field of the late nineteenth century sparks its own form of excavation and accommodates a flow between deconstructive processes that unlock meaning and constructive processes of reformulation. Although for the period under discussion it is difficult to recover, even partially, aspects of past performances and displays—let alone the totalities—the representational activities most accessible to us take visual and written forms. These forms are the representational fragments from which it is possible to construct a new narrative, or even new knowledge.[10]

In the mid-1930s the historian Walter Benjamin, in the course of his own excavations of nineteenth-century life, kept "a kind of album" for his never-to-be-finished "Arcades" project, *Passengen-Werk*, in which he assembled image material (pictorial and textual), including many photographs, that "were the concrete 'small particular moments' in which 'the total historical event' was to be discovered" (Buck-Morss 1991, 71).[11] Benjamin referred to these "concrete" and particular representations as dialectical images, and he proposed that montage was the process by which interpretation-*cum*-representation took place. By "montage" he meant more than simple juxtaposition without commentary. As I see it, the uncovering or interpretation emerges from the process of montage by the interrogation of the dialectical relationship between image and image, text and image, or by probing the dialectical field within a particular image. In the case of the "Captive Lives" project there is a virtual "realm" of imagery that forms part of my assemblage of textual and visual documentation of the Aboriginal travelers' lives, and of the nineteenth-century sociocultural constructions, both popular and anthropological, into which they were drawn. What Mitchell calls "the multidimensional and heterogeneous terrain" of this field of representations—"a patchwork quilt assembled over time out of fragments" (1994b, 419)—has sparked a methodology of both research and interpretation that, in turn, has flowed into the process of presentation—re-presentation—of the narrative.

The Frontier

To relate what I mean to this particular history, there was no place for stories of these Aboriginal travelers in the anecdotal histories generated on the North Queensland frontier. When the full thrust of the invasion, both overland and from the sea, began in the early 1860s, the eldest in the group, Toby, would have been about twenty, and the youngest, Sussy (the wife of Tambo), would have only just been born. The probable pattern of their lives during these years has to be pieced together from documentary sources. For instance, Billy, Bob, Wangong (?), and their wives and children, would have been among the handful of Biyaygirri who survived punitive drives across Hinchinbrook Island and the nearby mainland in the 1870s.[12] By the 1880s Townsville had become the principal center of the region— linked by rail to the mining hinterland it had telegraph links and flourishing newspapers. It had even been visited by a circus. The steamer on which Cunningham traveled from Darwin to Townsville had forty Malaysians aboard who had been recruited to work in the pearl and bêche-de-mer industries. The frontier was already a very hybrid society in which the remnants of the different Aboriginal communities were being forced into the towns.

The frontier was also a very public one. Although reports of "the sick-

Roslyn Poignant

ening and brutal war of races" provoked widespread debate in southern cities,[13] in the settler accounts "the blacks" were written out of history. In *Advance Australia!* (the title says it all) Harold Finch-Hatton (who left the colony at the same time as Tambo and his companions) wrote, "whether the blacks deserve any mercy at the hands of the pioneering squatters is an open question, but that they get none is certain. They are a doomed race, and before many years they will be completely wiped out of the land" (1885, 148). However, one writer, A. J. Vogan, chose fiction "to throw light on Australia's shadow side," and there was a limited public for his novel, *The Black Police* (1890), among the supporters of the Aborigines Protection Society. The book's engraved frontispiece showed squatters attacking an Aboriginal camp, but most of Vogan's on-the-spot sketches, such as that of the Georgetown killing field, remained unpublished for over a century.[14] By contrast, the dominant frontier narrative found succinct but powerful expression in the montaged picture story *Sketches of Life in North Queensland* (fig. 4). Published in the *Illustrated London News* in 1884, it reached a far-larger public, probably a million.[15] Claiming its authenticity from the photographs on which it drew, in its "concrete particulars" it encapsulates the triumphalist view of events. Furthermore, it conveys the dynamics of land taking in the way a single image could not: first the sheep and then the cattle, contiguous with the Aborigines' displacement and degradation. Its message was the generation of wealth through the development of primary industry in north Queensland, and there is no place in this narrative of the dominant society for personal stories such as that of Tambo and his companions. Their removal raised only a ripple of concern in Sydney when Billy and Jimmy tried to escape and were recaptured. Indeed, until they reached Europe and were interviewed by anthropologists, only three seem to have been mentioned by name in newspaper reports: Billy and Jimmy in Sydney and Tambo in America.

In the 1880s, Tambo and his companions became entrapped in an already powerfully constructed stereotype of "savagery." Earlier stories from North Queensland's shifting frontiers had played a part in its formation; these stories had fed into an imperialist narrative that spoke of civilization's triumph over savagery on a number of frontiers, including Australia and the Pacific, Africa, and the Americas. A most frequently retold story was that of the shipwrecked Eliza Fraser. For instance, Henry Stuart Russell, in his *The Genesis of Queensland* (1888), retells at some length Fraser's story and that of the wreck of the *Stirling Castle*, even though it had taken place fifty years earlier. Moreover, he dwells with some relish on the theme of cannibalism.

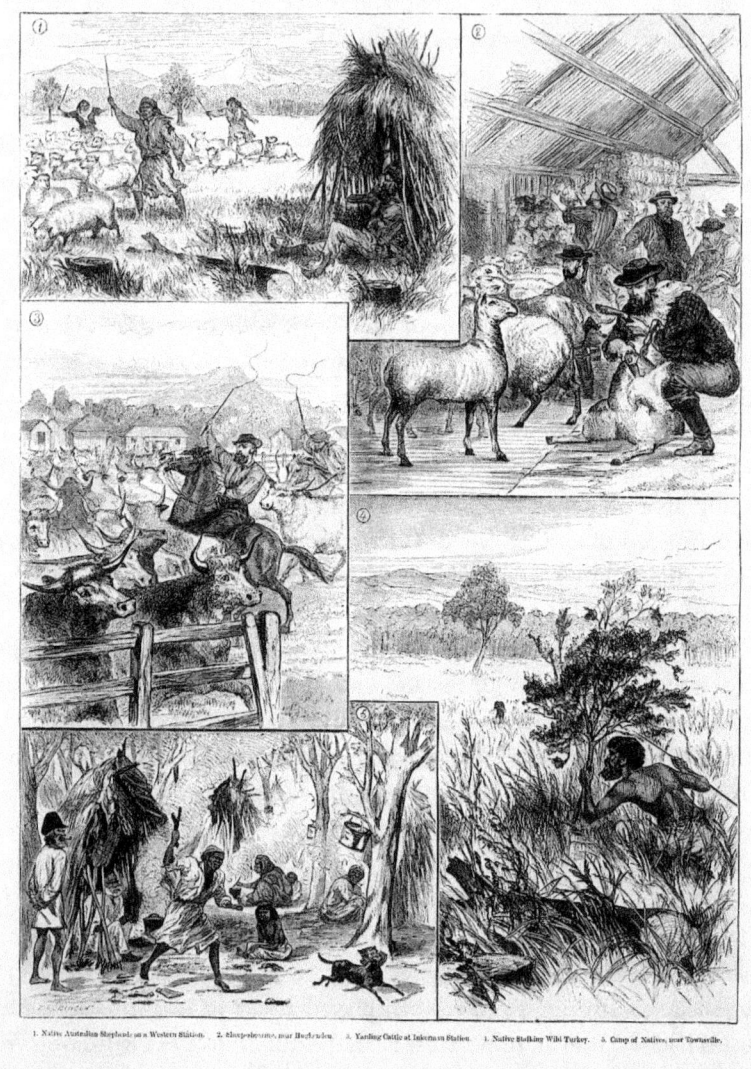

4. "Sketches of Life in Queensland," *Illustrated London News,* 19 January 1884.

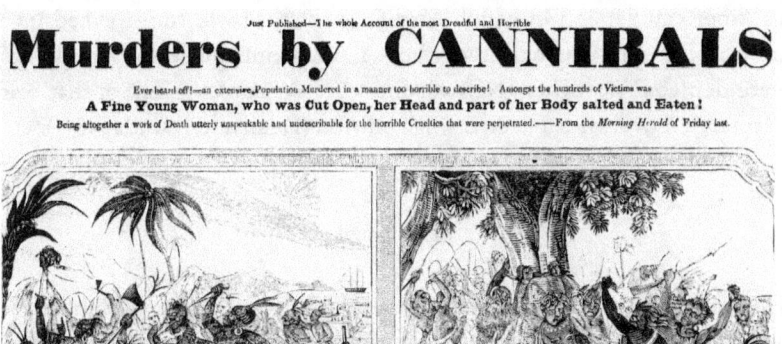

5. "Murder by Cannibals," a broadside c.1840. Rex Nan Kivell Collection.
Courtesy of the National Library of Australia.

Exploration of the many transformations of Eliza's story has proved a
fruitful field for scholarly investigation (see, e.g., Schaffer 1993; Healy 1997;
McNiven, Russell, and Schaffer 1998). In Russell's version, my attention was
caught by his opening description of an encounter with a sandwich-board
man in Hyde Park, who was advertising the exhibition of a woman said
to be Mrs. Fraser. According to Russell, this happened about the time of
Mrs. Fraser's return to England in mid-1837. Was Russell writing from rec-
ollection or was he only deploying an imaginative narrative device? Either
way, his description reveals his familiarity with the broadsides and posters
telling the "horrible" stories in circulation in London at the time. One of
these, *Murder by Cannibals* (fig. 5), about a different shipwreck, is identical
(except for its border) to the broadside for the *Ballad of the Stirling Castle*,
published by Catnach in 1837 (Schaffer 1993, 47).[16] Multiple uses of the same
woodblock to illustrate a different story on the same theme was commonplace (O'Connell 1999; Meggs 1998, 81), but even when a new block was
made, the same pictorial elements tended to recur—the ship in the bay and
the massacre on the shore, usually showing a foreground figure of a mor-
tally wounded (sometimes decapitated) European man. See, for example,

The Making of Professional "Savages"

an American version in which Mrs. Fraser's story was transformed into an American captivity narrative where, in the frontispiece, the Aborigines were depicted as vaguely Native American—a characterization that was also carried over into a later English edition (Dean and Munday 1837).[17]

Encounter

The conventions of visual narrative employed in these representations have deep roots in earlier representations of encounters between Europeans and the inhabitants of exotic lands. Jan van der Straet's engraving *America* (c.1600) provides an early example of the encounter genre: a ship in the bay with landing craft drawn up on an exotic shore. The meeting is between allegorized figures of "the navigator," carrying his instruments of science, and a feminized "America," surrounded by animals and plants of the New World. In the background, farther along the shore, a cannibal feast is depicted in a supposedly more informational style. These stylistic tensions direct attention to what Peter Hulme refers to as the "colonial anxiety . . . between European, native and land" (Hulme 1986, 1; fig. 1).[18]

By the late eighteenth century the recurring visual elements associated with "encounter" had been turned to different ideological usages. At the time of the anti-slavery movement, an engraved book "by one Chambon" dated 1764 (which Hugh Honour describes as the first full account of the operation of the slave trade) deploys them in a more naturalistic style. Lamenting relatives stand on the shore as a small craft transports slaves to a waiting vessel in the bay. The same pictorial elements are also marshalled for a specific didactic purpose in George Moreland's painting *African Hospitality* (1790), which depicts a compassionate encounter between Africans and shipwrecked Europeans. Widely disseminated as an engraving (by J. R. Smith), it was meant to complement Moreland's earlier *Execrable Human Traffick*. Both paintings were inspired by an antislavery poem (Honour 1989; figs. 15, 20, 52–53, 66–72).

By the nineteenth century the dominant expression of the encounter genre carried more negative connotations (although positive representations of it were produced, particularly as paintings and drawings).[19] The popular printed imagery produced for tales of missionaries, traders, and settlers, who followed the Western voyagers into southern seas and encountered the resistance of indigenous peoples, mobilized the same visual language (the ship in the bay, the melee of savages on the shore, the mas-

Roslyn Poignant

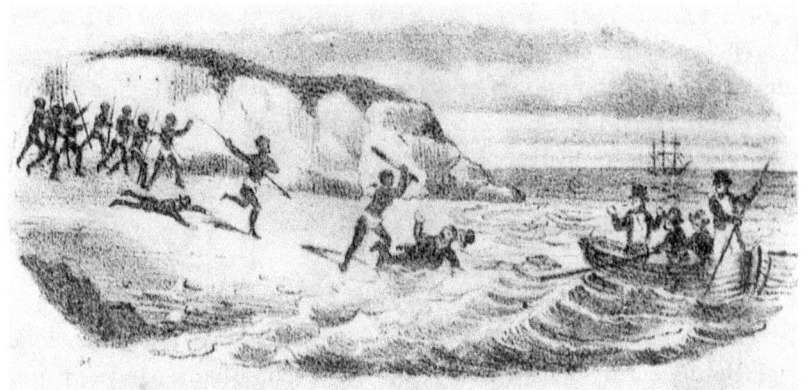

6. Sheet music cover, "The Missionary's Requiem," published c. 1843 to commemorate the murder of Rev. John Williams on the beach at Eromanga (Vanuatu). Rex Nan Kivell Collection. Courtesy of the National Library of Australia.

sacre, the cannibal feast) evoking the terror of shipwreck and being cast-away, cut adrift from the civilized world and physically overwhelmed, if not physically obliterated. The process is demonstrated well by a sequence of representations, contemporary with the Mrs. Fraser illustrations, which are part of the production of a Baxter oil print commemorating the mur-der of the Rev. John Williams of the London Missionary Society on the beach at Eromanga (Vanuatu) in 1839. As Bernard Smith first noted in the 1960s, the instructions written on the preliminary watercolor to darken the skin tones of "the natives," and to make the dying Williams "more heav-enly," have been carried out to a brutalizing degree in the final oil print (Smith 1960, 245; plates 155, 156).[20] Both the Baxter print and the cover of *The Missionary's Requiem* (fig. 6) would have had wide circulation. On the sheet music, however, the same pictorial elements—ship in the bay, the running natives, and the massacre—have been reduced to a simple sign de-noting "savagery." Displays of indigenous performers before metropolitan audiences appear to have fostered the same derogatory attitudes.[21] By mid-century Charles Dickens expressed the prevailing sentiment of the age when, on seeing an exhibition of "the Pygmy Earthmen" at the Westmin-ster Aquarium, he wrote, "I call him savage, and I call a savage something highly desirable to be civilised off the face of the earth" (1853, 337).

Although the Baxter print of the Rev. Williams purported to repre-sent an actual event, its execution was shaped by prevailing ideas about the correspondences between appearances and inner character (Lavater 1775–78, 19–20) that could be systematized according to type through techniques of physiognomic observation. These widely held notions about the visible embodiment of race (and class) found an application in art (Cowling 1989). For instance, Gottfried Schadow's *National-Physiognomieen* (1835), prepared as an artist's guide from "outlines of portraits of savage tribes," influenced representational conventions. His methods bridged the work of earlier scientists (such as Camper and Blumenbach) who codified and classified human beings according to physical features (particularly facial) and underlying skeletal structures, and that of the artists of the eighteenth-century scientific voyages, whose published engravings (not original drawings) provided some of the models for his line drawings of national/racial types. Although these techniques of draftsmanship contributed to nineteenth-century realism in art, they also supplied a legible code for works of satire and caricature and for the popular representations of the indigenous Other. These outcomes were compounded by the application of increasingly mechanical means of reproduction, and they require a closer examination of the part played by changing print technologies in consolidating the negative aspects of visual representations of savagery.

In thinking about these developments it is important to recognize that the emergence in Europe of the reproduction of images—pictures and diagrams—by the woodblock narrowly anticipated Gutenberg's printing press. The woodblock was soon to be followed by other reproductive graphic techniques such as copper engraving and etching, and later in the nineteenth century by lithography and photography (Ivens 1953, 1; Meggs 1998, 58–69; Jay 1993, 66–69; O'Connell 1999, 210). The urge to re-create the "real" implicit in the development of these representational processes was constantly countered by the creative inventiveness of craftspersons and artists on the one hand, and by the reductionism that flows from constant repetition of form on the other. It was also shaped by prevailing ideologies, for human sense perception is itself culturally bound (Benjamin 1968, 222).

The steady ascendance of visual media over the past two centuries is undisputed. Here I want to focus only on those aspects of these developments that may help to illuminate the relationship between fixity of form and fixity of ideas, which is reflected in the dual meaning of the words "stereotype" and "cliché" (both initially terms for repetitive printing processes).[22] The printed image added an intimate, easily handled and disseminated visual dimension to what until then were largely oral systems of communication—although the dynamics of visual storytelling were already established in visual communicative processes such as stained glass, the illuminated manuscript, and a variety of popular arts such as painted furniture and votive paintings, as well as in more ephemeral graphic forms. The replication implicit in printing and in the various stages of production (such as a separation of functions between draftsman and the block makers) encouraged the recycling that made for the visual cliché. The process was quickened with the quantitative shift that came with the industrialization of printing from the beginning of the nineteenth century, particularly the development of the stereotype, as a method of replication. In the simplest terms, metal stereotype plates were made by first taking an impression of the original setup of type or woodblock in a mold of papier-mâché or similar material, which was then used to cast the stereotype in metal.[23] Although by mid-century this system would be replaced by the electrotype process, through it the word became endowed with its cultural meaning of fixity early in the century.

The next acceleration of output came with the mechanization of paper making, the introduction of steam-powered presses, and in 1827 the invention of the multiple cylinder presses, which took curved-metal stereotype plates. This enabled the low-cost, high-speed production and circulation of all print media: broadsides, handbills, posters, billboard advertisements, newspapers, and the first serial pictorial publications, such as the English *Penny Magazine* (begun in 1832). Initially sponsored by the Society for the Diffusion of Useful Knowledge, the *Penny Magazine* was one of the first pictorials to reach an estimated public of half a million (see P. Anderson 1991; Jackson 1885; Fox 1988; and Meggs 1998).

These developments in print technology and media in the course of the century flowed from, and at the same time were implicated in, the formation of the industrialized, urbanized, and largely literate societies emerging in Europe and America. The pictorial press has been regarded as the cultural production that best characterized the age (Ohmann 1996, 36). It developed in response to the increased purchasing power and leisure time of the new urban classes (both those of middle rank and the so-called respectable sections of the working class), with their insatiable appetite for news, commodities, and self-improvement.[24] Much emphasis has been placed on the democratizing force of the process. But the social values expressed were those of the dominant white, male-oriented middle classes. As the century advanced, the various national mass-circulation newspapers and the illustrated journals mirrored for their consumers the modern world of spectacle in which they were themselves immersed. It was a world not only of home events but also of foreign ventures, most notably colonial wars, which were presented in terms of civilization's triumph over savagery. The positive self-imaging of what Benedict Anderson calls "imagined communities" of nations involved an opposite. These were several, but the indigenous inhabitants of the colonies is the Other relevant to this narrative.

At the Circus

In America, the expansion of communications—both transportation and informational systems—underpinned most other developments. Take, for example, the circus: in the 1830s, while still in its infancy, the circus pioneered the use of illustrated newspaper ads (almost as soon as it was technologically possible) and its posters dominated the scene (Kelly 1969, 184). From the 1870s, P. T. Barnum led the way in developing the traveling circus as an industrialized form of mass entertainment. His stated target audience was the middle classes and their respectable working-class allies (Adams 1997, 90). He and his partner, William Coup, made use of the expanding railway network to penetrate the largest and most profitable centers on the East Coast and in the Midwest of North America. Dismountable carriages made the show highly mobile, and duplicate sets of canvas reduced the time lost between showplaces. The success of such an operation depended on capturing the attention of whole communities: a cast of many hundreds seen by tens of thousands, very often in the course of a single day. In the 1880s Barnum's circus used up to three advance publicity carriages, which were movable workshops as well as transporters. Illustrated newspaper advertisements, a promotional publication called the *Advance Courier*, posters, and billboards summoned the crowds from the surrounding districts, often from up to forty miles away, and excursion trains brought them in (Flint 1977, 1983; Parkinson n.d.).[25] Before the movies, the circus was probably the most influential instrument of mass culture in shaping public attitudes,[26] through an extraordinary range of linked representational activities.

Barnum's involvement with the display of living people for commercial gain began in the mid-1830s when he toured the slave Joice Heth, who was alleged to have been 161 years old and to have nursed George Washington (Reiss 2001). From 1850, Barnum continued to display "living curiosities"

Roslyn Poignant

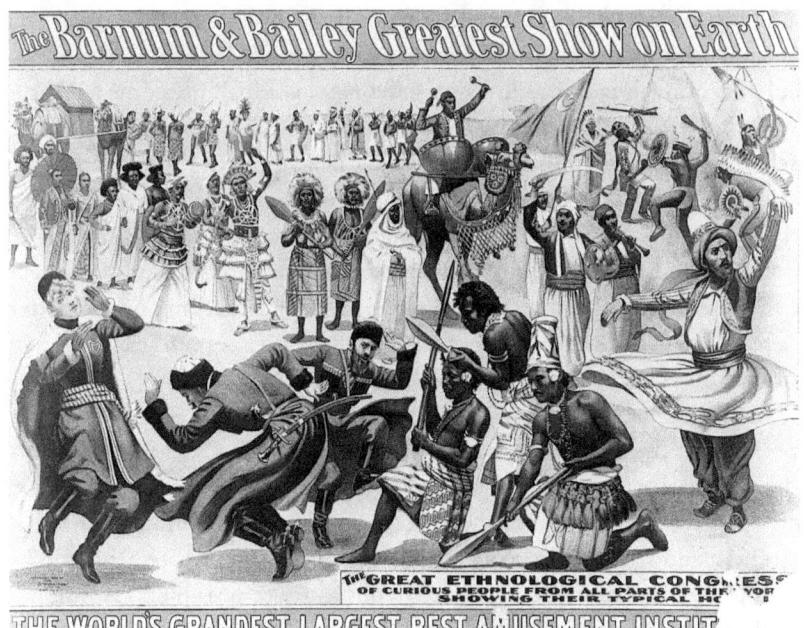

7. Poster produced for Barnum's "Ethnological Congress," c.1883. Courtesy of Prints and Photographs Division, Library of Congress.

in his American Museum. After the museum burned down, Barnum concentrated his resources on the development of the circus. In his advertisement in *Harper's Weekly*,[27] Barnum—emerging from the flames engulfing his museum—offered a new spectacle: "The World in Contribution" ... "A Great Travelling World's Fair."[28] Included in "the menagerie" were three Fijians, but when General Ra Biau, the smallest of them, died in York, Pennsylvania, in 1872, Barnum's attempts to introduce "savage curiosities" to the circus faltered. Regardless, he continued to advertise them in the *Advance Courier* for the following season. The Fijians thus became the prototype "cannibal savages," providing a model for the illustration of Tambo and his companions on the cover of Cunningham's pamphlet and elsewhere in advertisements.[29]

In 1881 P. T. Barnum and J. Bailey merged their circuses with a third partner, James Hutchinson, to form a three-ringed circus billed as the "Greatest Show on Earth," and Barnum determined that the main feature would be the "Ethnological Congress of Strange and Savage Tribes" (fig. 7). His recruitment of what he referred to as "type specimens" of humankind was a highly organized affair, and R. A. Cunningham was only one of several agents so engaged. Hundreds of letters were sent abroad to American consuls. Barnum already had links with the new national museums in Washington and New York, and he solicited a testimonial from Spencer Baird, secretary of the recently established Smithsonian Institution, because, he said, "the authorities are *reluctant* about letting their people leave the country unless they are first satisfied that the party taking them is responsible."[30] Baird replied that he could only furnish information in reply to direct enquiries about Barnum. Nevertheless, he hoped that "my official letter herewith will answer all the purposes. You, of course, can use your own discretion as to the mode of employing it."[31]

According to his letter on 9 August 1882, addressed to agents, Barnum expected that the indigenous people recruited "would also possess extraordinary peculiarities . . . such as singular disfigurements of the person, dexterity in the use of weapons, dancing, singing, juggling, unusual feats of strength and agility etc." "With this object in view," he wrote, "I should be glad to receive from you . . . photographs as far as possible."[32] A number of these photographs, sent by agents, have survived in the archive of Barnum's business manager of the period, Joseph McCaddon (see fig. 3). The lithographic poster (fig. 7) featured the "Grand Parade," which always took place on the morning the circus arrived in a town.[33] Although not included in the poster, according to press reports Tambo and his companions led the parade with Jumbo the elephant on 7 May in Baltimore, and when they danced the Zulu hissed at them.[34]

Each of the indigenous groups on display with Tambo and his companions were featured in the twelve-page *Advance Courier*,[35] where the captive Aborigines are depicted as captors (fig. 8). Again the pictorial elements are the same as forty years earlier: the ship in the bay, the massacre on the shore, and the cannibal feast. The explicitly racist language of the letterpress leaks over into the newspaper reports of the performances, and it is very difficult to gain any idea of how Tambo and his companions were perceived by the public, except through the screen of circus publications.

On another page of the *Courier*, the "ferocious Zulu" and the "extraordinary Todars" (*sic*) are paired. By comparison with the stereotypical power of the circus advertisements, their photographs also appear to show what they are like, yet there is much more unity than difference between the photographs of the different groups. Consider the similarity between the Zulu group in figure 9 and the Aborigines shown earlier in figure 1. The

Roslyn Poignant

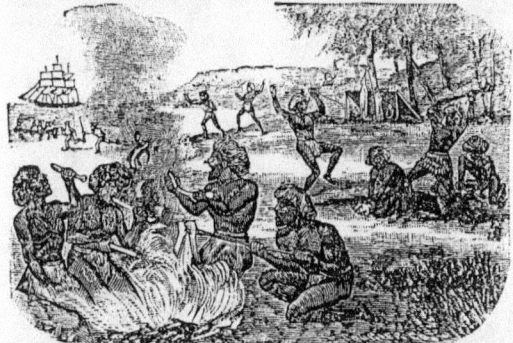

8. "Australian Cannibals," *Advance Courier*, 1883, p. 4; copy overstamped 28 August, Jackson. Courtesy of the Bridgeport Public Library.

similar pose, costuming, and captioning emphasizes their roles as professional showpeople. Again, the photographs provide a starting point for the recovery of personal histories of each of these groups, as they do with the Aborigines. The stereotypical nature of the representation is underlined further when one finds that, even in the same circus season, the same pictorial elements are used to represent the fake "wild men of Borneo" (fig. 10), which was performed by two small-statured white men who traveled the circus and dime museum circuits for about thirty years.[36]

Although Barnum frequently supplied stock cuts for newspaper ads, the block makers for the *Cincinnati Enquirer* (fig. 11) appear to have drawn on photographic sources. Even so, some of the same pictorial motifs persist, particularly the decapitated foreground figure. In Cleveland, Ohio, where Tambo died, the local *Penny Press* used the same image as on the cover of

The Making of Professional "Savages"

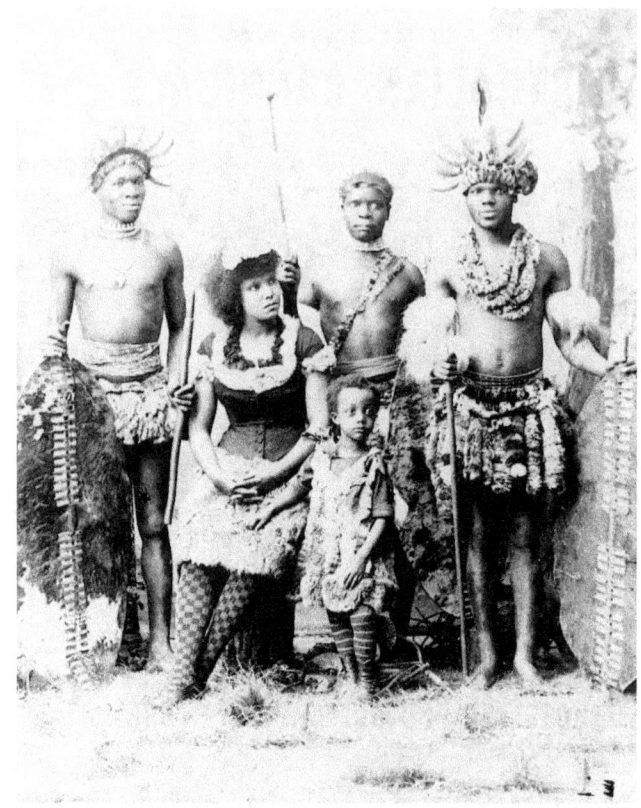

9. Zulu Warriors. Photographed by Charles Eisenman. The
photographs of all the indigenous groups who performed
with the Australian Aboriginal group are together in the same
collection. McCaddon Collection of the Barnum and Bailey
Circus. Manuscript Division. Department of Rare Books and
Special Collections. Princeton University Library.

Cunningham's pamphlet (see fig. 2).[37] The ephemeral nature of these news-
print sources and circus literature, particularly the products of Barnum's
publicity machine, has made it easy to overlook the cumulative power of
these textual and graphic representations to fix the savage stereotype. The
reach was even across oceans and borders: the transnational nature of Cunningham's operation is emphasized both by the production of editions of
his pamphlet in several European languages and by the printing in Germany of an English-language poster.[38]

Roslyn Poignant

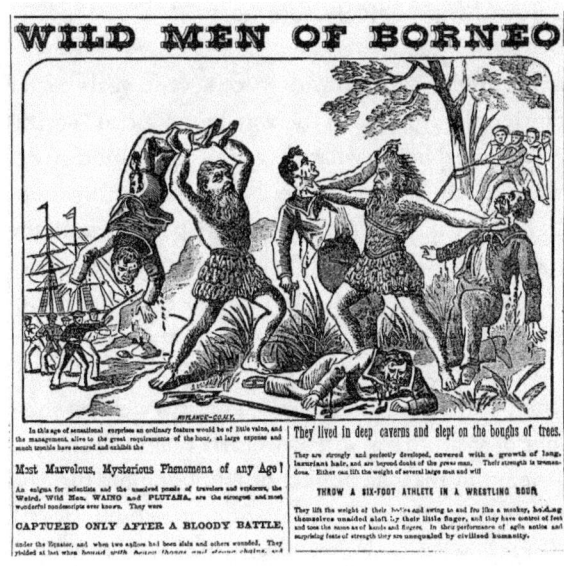

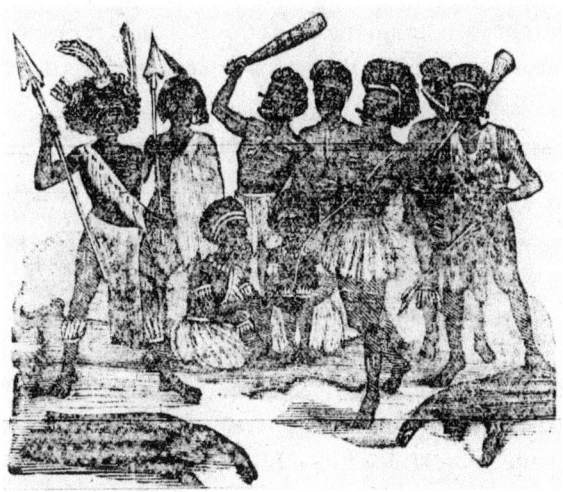

(Top image) 10. "Wild Men of Borneo," Roylance & Co.,
New York. (Above) 11. "The Australian Bushmen," *Cincinnati
Enquirer,* 13 January 1884; advertisement for the group's
performance at the Dime Museum. Courtesy of
Newspapers Division. Library of Congress.

In Europe, Cunningham toured the group widely for several years, as far as Moscow and Constantinople. And along the way he obtained "certificates as to their [the Aborigines] being what they are represented" from eminent "Professors" throughout Europe.[39] These troupes of indigenous performers, what the Germans called *Völkerschauen*, were popular with the public but, compared with America, it is difficult to assess the size of the audiences to which they were exposed. From 1877 in Paris, the Jardin d'Acclimatation in the Bois de Boulogne added what were called ethnographic displays to its attractions,[40] with the approval of the Parisian anthropologists. In 1883, when four different indigenous groups were on show at the Jardin, the number of visitors was cited at nearly one million. William Schneider makes the point that the public for ethnographic displays was of the same magnitude as for the mass-circulation press (1982, 125–51). In 1885, however, the displays were temporarily suspended, so that Billy, Jenny, and Little Toby were shown at the Folies-Bergère. Although this shift of venue reflected a shift in attitude among the anthropological fraternity as to the scientific value of such displays, their popularity as entertainment continued throughout the European showplaces.

Nevertheless, photographs taken of the seven Aborigines who survived to reach Europe are embedded in the linked histories of anthropology and photography. High on the scientists' agenda for the examination of the members of these touring companies of indigenous peoples was the systematized measurement of bodily features and physical performance that provided the comparative data for the anthropologists' classificatory project. By the 1880s, however, the effectiveness of the camera as an anthropometric recording device was in doubt because of the difficulties of achieving the uniformity of process required. Therefore, the photographs of Billy and his companions by Prince Roland Bonaparte (in Paris) and Carl Günther (in Berlin) are more appropriately described as being of an anthropological genre. From our perspective today both the photographs and the anthropologists' descriptions—read against the grain—are invaluable documents of identification and enlightenment about them as people.

I have written elsewhere (Poignant 1997) on this theme, particularly about the power of a photograph of Billy, Jenny, and Little Toby to compel the interrogative reading that launched my research project into their containment within the show-space (fig. 12). Although taken by the anthro-

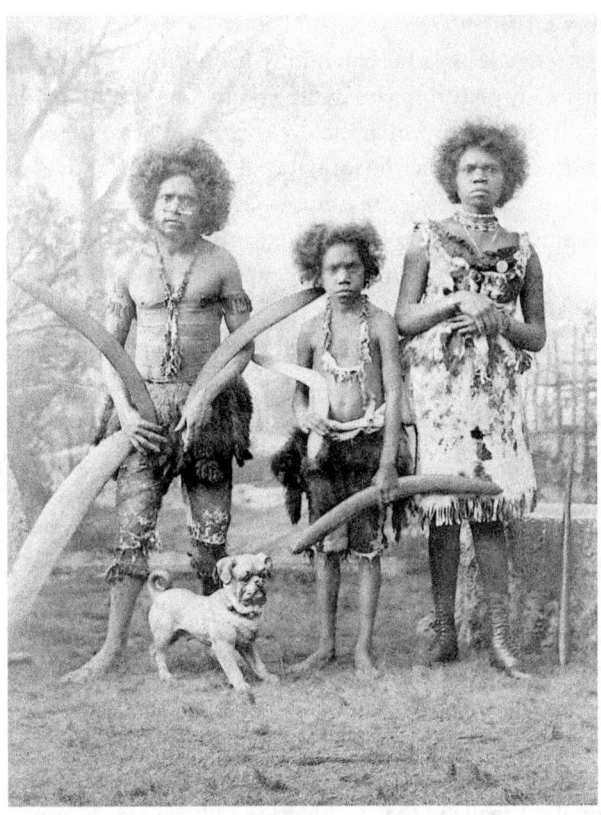

12. Billy, Jenny, and her son, Little Toby, photographed by
Prince Roland Bonaparte in Paris, November 1885.
Courtesy of Royal Anthropological Institute.

pological photographer, Prince Roland Bonaparte, the photo is more like
the commercial portraits of the group, the sale of which played a part in
the economy of their exploitation.[41] I read it as a "quotation" from experience (Berger and Mohr 1982, 96), a record of a moment of confrontation
that serves to disrupt both the scientific and the commercial scenarios.
The location of the photograph is not entirely clear, but there are elements
in its construction—the performance costumes, the digging stick leaning
against the "wall," the partly out-of-focus European pastoral backdrop, and
the dog in the foreground—that suggest a performance space (such as the
stage of the Folies-Bergère) rather than a photographic studio. Their body
language—Billy's tilt of the head, Little Toby's apparent dejection, Jenny's
folded hands and tensely raised shoulder—together with their confron-

The Making of Professional "Savages"   77

tational looks convey an air of resistance. Add to this the knowledge—from written sources—that Jenny's husband, Toby, has just died (Topinard 1885). Further, in an already disturbing image, the point (the "punctum," in Barthes terminology [1984, 27]) to which the eye is drawn, with a horrible fascination, is the stuffed pug dog in the foreground. The visual "shock" of it activates what Barthes describes as the obtuse—as opposed to the obvious meaning—a surplus of meaning that "belongs to the family of pun, buffoonery, useless expenditure. Indifferent to moral or aesthetic categories . . . it is on the side of carnival" (1977, 55). This cruel visual pun, with its Janus-faced message of callous indifference and terror, must have had an initiator. Could it have been Cunningham or Bonaparte who placed the stage prop in the frame? Emblematic of death and embalmment, the stuffed dog offers an absurd and cruel commentary on the three survivors' existential extremity.[42]

My attempt here to read, cross-culturally, fleeting expressions of emotions and subtle nuances, as they have been arrested by the mechanics of the camera, is obviously a subjective exercise.[43] But I have had many opportunities to observe the effect of this photograph on others. It is Billy's head in this image that, more than any other, has been excised and used to illustrate various newspaper reports about Tambo's "return," maybe because of his appearance read as wildness and/or his anguished expression. At first I thought that this use arose because I had not yet located a photo of Tambo, but gradually I realized that an identified likeness of him was not the most important requirement for representing him, either within the community or by others. Indeed, on Palm Island at the time of Tambo's funeral in February 1994 a mythical image was created: a graphic representation of an Aboriginal head merged with an outline of the island (again, I write more about its significance in Poignant 1997). On the other hand, the public circulation of the story has confirmed that the potential also remains for the persistence and transformation of old stereotypes.

This Spectred Isle

On 1 February 1998, the *Sunday Times* supplement (London) published a report about the Aboriginal community of Palm Island, described on the cover as "Devil's Island." It highlighted the number of youthful suicides there, claiming there had been forty since 1994 (although the probable figure of fourteen is horrific enough). Because of the appalling living con-

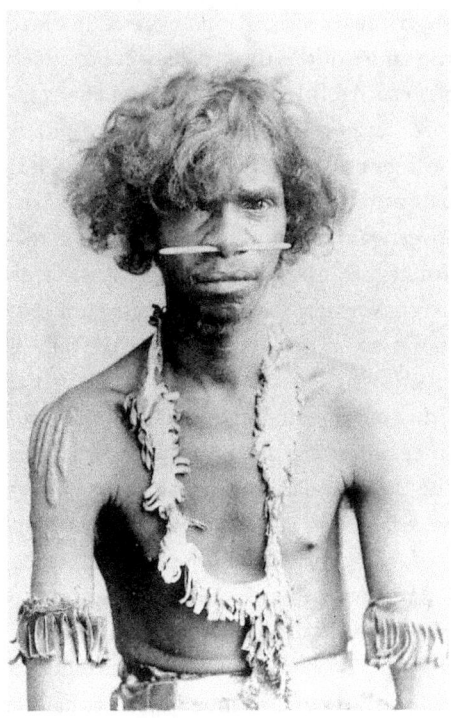

13. Jimmy, photographed by Carl Günther in Berlin, July 1884. Copy from the collection of Prince Roland Bonaparte. Courtesy of the Bibliothèque Nationale and Société de Géographie.

ditions and the downright robbery of the older generation of Palm Islanders of wages never paid over many years (Kidd 1997), those who knew the state of affairs were diffident about voicing objections to an article that at least raised these issues, no matter how negative the tone. For some readers, however, the nonsensical account of Captain Cook at Palm Island in June 1770 (facts easily checked in any newspaper library) would be enough to call into question the rest of the article, especially when accompanied as it was by a recognizably improbable description of Cunningham's troop of musket-men seizing and carrying off the group of Aborigines and sailing directly to America. As usual, evil is more banal: Cunningham used public transport. My quarrel, however, is not so much with this relentless sensationalizing as it is with the spurious attempts at "authenticating" the reporters' story by image manipulation.

The authors chose to frame their story, "This Spectred Isle," within a retelling of Tambo's removal and the return of his "ghost," presenting the local youths as believing themselves to be helpless victims of supernatural forces. To illustrate this largely fictional account, the picture editor obligingly provided a red image of the ghost by digitally manipulating a photo of

Jimmy, not Tambo (fig. 13).[44] Although images of both men were available to them postage-stamp-sized from the same source, the broadsheet produced for the "Captive Lives" exhibition, presumably Jimmy was selected because his nose bone made him look more "savage." So poor Jimmy was digitally demonized and superimposed on a photo of a group of Palm Islanders outside the local store.[45] The visualization of the "spectre" produces a frisson of difference. Whatever the investigatory claims of the article, the manipulated image suggests that, unlike "us," these people are still savages. This notion was given wider currency when the *Sunday Times* subheading — "It's the most violent place in the world" — was repeated by the *Guiness Book of Records* (1998), causing further distress to the Palm Islanders. In the words of Geoff Batchen, "digital imaging remains an overtly fictional process" (1997, 211), and fantasy continues to play a crucial part in the processes of subjectification that underwrite power relations (Bhabha 1983, 30–35). Photographic manipulation, however, has always featured as a visual narrative device, and the issues, as before, are to do with aesthetics, ethics, moral rights, and power relations. My purpose here is to draw attention to the continuities; in this instance how the digitized transformation of the late-nineteenth-century photo of Jimmy has facilitated the persistence of an old stereotype of savagery, in the service of continued discriminatory practices.

Notes

With such a long-term project my debts are so many and so great that the conciseness of my acknowledgments list should not be taken as a measure of the considerable gratitude I feel to many individuals and institutions. I wish to thank Walter Palm Island and family and the Palm Island community for the warm support that enabled me to balance my overseas research with local experience. My U.S. research in 1993 was partly aided by a grant from the British Academy, supplemented by the Royal Anthropological Institute and the Tambo Repatriation Committee. Thanks are also due to the Australian Institute for Aboriginal and Torres Strait Islander Studies, particularly Dr. Stephen Wild and Dr. Geoffrey Gray; the National Library of Australia, particularly Michael Richards and Irene Turpie; and Professor Nicholas Thomas and the Centre for Cross-Cultural Research at the Australian National University. I also wish to thank the librarians and archivists of the Australian National Library, both pictorial and exhibition divisions; the Bibliothèque Nationale and Société de Géographie; the Musee de l'Homme;

Roslyn Poignant

the Bridgeport Public Library; the British Library; the Chicago Historical Society; the Hertzberg Collection at the San Antonio Public Library, particularly Jill Blake; the Library of Congress; the Library of the Department of Ethnography, British Museum; the Milner Library Special Collections at Illinois State University, particularly Steve Gossard; the National Anthropological Archives in the National Museum of Natural History of the Smithsonian Institution, Washington, D.C., particularly Paula Richardson Fleming and James Harwood; the Smithsonian Institution Archives, particularly William Cox and Libby Glenn; the John Oxley Library of the State Library of Queensland; the Princeton University Library; the Public Record Office, London; and the St. Bride Print Library, London. Thank you to Dr. Kate Darian-Smith, Elizabeth Edwards, Nicholaas Heijm, Peter Mesenhöller, Dr. Christopher Pinney, Dr. Paul Turnbull, Dr. Kay Schaffer, Christine Winter, and Christopher Wright for their support. Finally, I valued the comments of colleagues at the CCCR conference *Looking through Photographs* in Brisbane in November 1997, where a short version of this paper was delivered, and I wish to say thank you for the opportunity to give a longer version in Adelaide in December 1998 at the conference convened by Associate Professor Kay Schaffer for the Cultural Studies Association of Australia.

1 Cunningham returned to the same district in 1892 and removed a second group of eight Aborigines. Their story will not be dealt with here. Although R. Virchow's examination of the three members of the second group to reach Germany established that no members were the same as any in the first group, the two groups continue to be confused; see, for example, Corby 1993.

2 Pseudoscientific language pervaded show publicity. For instance Krao, the hairy girl from Laos, was billed as "The Missing Link: A Living Proof of Darwin's Theory of the Descent of Man" (broadside in Bodleian Library, Oxford).

3 Oral accounts have proliferated. Also, something of both nineteenth-century and present-day stories has been told in a touring exhibition, "Captive Lives: Looking for Tambo and His Companions," which I curated (in close consultation with the Palm Island community) for the National Library of Australia.

4 Although unlikely, because of the show clothes, the photo could also have been taken in Australia or New Zealand, on route to America.

5 The most important and detailed account was that of two Belgian anthropologists, E. Houzé and V. Jacques (1884), and it is largely from this account that information can be gleaned about the first group as individuals, as well as about their culture and languages (Dixon 1983).

6 Cunningham also registered copyright on his pamphlet in London. There must have been an American edition on which it was based, because the inside text describes the group of nine, while the back cover refers only to the

seven survivors to reach England. Copies of German and Swedish editions have also survived.

7 It was of no account that some of the group proved to be good linguists. According to several reports, Cunningham said they were not cannibals.

8 Billy's photograph has survived in the collection of Joseph T. McCaddon in the Princeton University Library. The photo invites a more detailed analysis than is possible here. In an Australian photo-historical context such a studio photograph of an Aborigine would be regarded as a typical image of displacement.

9 Homi Bhabha explores the dependence of the colonial discourse on the concept of "fixity" "as a sign of cultural/historical/racial difference," and he sees the stereotype as "its major discursive strategy" (1983, 18).

10 Taussig sees such representational fragments as "inscription[s] on the edge of official history" (1986, 209).

11 Here I am using "image" generically to embrace graphics and photographs. For the discussion on Walter Benjamin's idea of montage and the dialectical image, and Adorno's critique of it as no more than juxtaposition, see Buck-Morss 1991 (66–77). See also the discussion in Taussig 1986 (166, 199–203). Following Buck-Morss, I take a broader view of the interpretative process Benjamin proposed.

12 According to Houzé and Jacques (1884), Billy and Bob left wives and children behind. Local records claim that only some seven Biyaygirri survived the massacres. For a report of the oral account, see Jones 1961 (171).

13 The outstanding example is a series of articles and letters reprinted from the newspaper the *Queenslander* as a pamphlet titled *The Way We Civilise* (1880).

14 Watercolor sketch dated 25 October 1888, in an album of sketches by Arthur J. Vogan, John Oxley Library, State Library of Queensland.

15 Also published in Stirling 1884. Circulation figures are unreliable until the end of the century (Reed 1997); the relationship of readership to circulation is estimated as 1 to 5 (Anderson 1991, 3).

16 Sandwich-board advertising apparently had its heyday from the 1820s to the 1840s in both Europe and America. Catnach achieved printruns of half a million for popular subjects such as murders and trials. Broadsides printed by woodblocks were gradually superseded from the 1840s on by the increased distribution of lithographic posters, newspapers, and the pictorial press.

17 Frontispiece to Dean and Munday 1837. The caption reads: "Mrs Frazer [*sic*] & part of the Crew of the Stirling Castle who had Escaped from the Wreck in the Long Boat being seiz'd and Stripped by the Savages."

18 Bernard Smith refers to such compositional mixes as "exotic conflations" (1992, 80).

19 On the A. C. Gregory expedition, the ethnographic artist Thomas Baines in 1857 made an oil painting of an encounter with Aborigines near the mouth

of Victoria River, N.T. This work amounts to a group portrait—the attention to the individual is not emulated in popular imagery (Rex Nan Kivell Collection, National Library of Australia).

20 The two Baxter originals are in the Rex Nan Kivell Collection, National Library of Australia. In the eyes of the public, authority would have also accrued to the image because of its iconographic kinship with the representations of the death of Captain Cook at the hands of "savage" Hawaiians.

21 The exhibition of humans from the margins of the known world has a long history, but I have picked up this story from the early nineteenth century, when such shows became progressively more organized and institutionalized.

22 In doing so, I am also side-stepping a discussion of, in the words of Gilman, "the cognitive procedures, through which we structure the world, and which underlie the representations of the world which make all of us produce stereotypes" (1991, 10–15).

23 Although the process was not invented by Firmin Didot, around 1794 he named it "stereotype."

24 In the final decades of the century, American pictorials were transformed by advertising revenue and print technology: the photo-mechanical age had begun (Reed 1997, 76).

25 Route books were published that set out the detailed itinerary of the circus.

26 Up to this point I have been speaking of popular culture, meaning "popular in the main sense of widely disseminated" (see Ohmann 1996, 11–30, for useful discussion on the emergence of mass culture toward the end of the nineteenth century).

27 The *Harper's* ad is dated 29 March 1873, but the image was probably in circulation as a poster and advertisement from 1872.

28 The circulation of *Harper's Weekly* in 1872 was 150,000 (Ohmann 1996, 26).

29 After the initial report in the *York Daily* on 15 May 1872, the death of "Barnum's cannibal" and his later exhumation and fate, reported in the *York Dispatch* in April 1897, became an off-repeated story (see the *York Gazette and Public Advertiser*, November and December 1993). Barnum also replaced another deceased member of the group with a black American woman from Virginia.

30 Barnum to Baird, 25 October 1882, Smithsonian Institution Archives, permanent Administrative Files.

31 Baird to Barnum, 31 October 1882, Bridgeport Public Library.

32 Barnum's letter to agents, 9 August 1882, Smithsonian Institution Archives, permanent Administrative Files.

33 Until the 1880s most posters were printed by letterpress using engravings and wood and metal types, but from that decade they began to be superseded by large, colorful lithographic posters (Kelly 1969, 186).

34 Also noted in *My Diary, or Route Book of P. T. Barnum's Greatest Show on Earth and*

the Great London Circus, for the Season of 1883, proprietors: Barnum, Bailey, and Hutchinson. Although no longer with the circus, the Australians continued to be listed as late as 1885.

35 The same *Advance Courier* was reissued in 1884. Initially, such recycling made tracking the group difficult. The *Advance Courier* was printed in bulk and over-printed as necessary with show place and date.

36 Cutting from the *Advance Courier*, Consolidated Shows, Madison Square Garden, c.1884.

37 The source could have been Barnum's organization, although the poster houses also kept great stores of stock cuts (Kelly 1969, 186).

38 Copy in Historisches Museum, Frankfurt am Main, Germany. Thanks to Peter Mesenhöller for directing my attention to this source.

39 Copies of both the testimonials and the letter are in the Galton papers (R. A. Cunningham) 227/6, University College, London. Thanks are due to Dr. Paul Turnbull for sharing this find with me.

40 Established in 1859, in effect the botanical and zoological gardens.

41 At this point, although Cunningham must have needed new photographs of his much-reduced group, it is unlikely that the anthropological photographer, Bonaparte, made them available. To date, prints of these photographs have been found only in institutional collections. I have located another of the three, taken after 1885, by commercial photographers Negretti and Zambra, Crystal Palace, London.

42 Adorno refers to such dialectical images as "puzzle pictures," which shock by their enigmatic form and thereby set thinking in motion (as discussed in Taussig 1986, 368).

43 The reading of body language and facial expressions is something all humans do as a part of living and surviving. Apparently there are areas of the brain that are specialized for reading the complexities and subtleties of facial expressions (Zeki 1999, 179). This cognitive process is to be distinguished from the nineteenth-century practices of physiognomy and phrenology that played such an important part in racial stereotyping.

44 I had hoped to reproduce the *Sunday Times* montage but permission was not granted.

45 I know the photograph was copied from this source, because I was asked for but declined to supply prints. I also know the *Sunday Times* did not get a print from the collection where it is housed, although they credited that institution (correspondence between the author and the *Sunday Times;* and the author and the French Geographical Society).

Roslyn Poignant

James Faris

Navajo and Photography

As exemplar of the photographic practices on Native Americans, outlined here are what might be called "photographic registers in the
imaging of Navajo" (see table 1). This information cannot, of course, be
claimed to cover all imaging practices on all Native Americans, but what
is noted here is quite likely typical in essential features of much of the
experience of many indigenous people to Western photographers. These
registers are not argued as stemming from any single locus, and there is no
agency or extradiscursive site of privilege for such an outline. This is not
a map that is exhaustive. In addition, some of the unique experiences of
Navajo are noted.

Navajo people of the U.S. Southwest (mostly in the states of New Mexico
and Arizona, and some in Utah) are today the largest pre-Columbian group
north of Mexico. They number some quarter of a million people, who
live principally in an area (a reservation established by military force and
treaty) of some twenty-four thousand square miles. This area is largely
high desert and mountains, and it was left to Navajo because European
Americans at the time considered it largely useless. Navajo resistance to
European American expansion resulted in punitive measures, and in the
mid-nineteenth century several thousand Navajo (probably about half the
total population of the time) were forcibly rounded up and marched some
seven hundred miles to an incarceration site in an attempt to settle them.
This project failed (not because it was judged wrong or immoral but because it proved to be financially nonviable) and those remaining alive were
allowed (or forced) to return to Navajoland some four years later (1868).
This incarceration and the westward push of expanding capitalism also co-

Table 1. Registers in the photography of Navajo.

Surveillance	1. Documentary (official, unofficial, advocacy)
	2. Anthropological (asset in communicating anthropology's view, archive, racial, museum)
	3. Casual (early tourist, traveler, worker in area, gaze)
Humanist	1. Sentimental (vanishing race, lost culture, family of man)
	2. Victims (dead, dying, nonfunctional or misfunctional)
Commercial	1. Aestheticist (color/silver/weaving/herding/turquoise, fashion, body parts)
	2. Landscape (extension of trees, desert, red rocks)
	3. Studio (personal, postcard)
Alternatives	1. Late modernism (modernist photographic gestures mocked, different voice privileged)
	2. Navajo photographers (silences, effacement, defacements)
	3. Unintended, unpublished (resistances)

incided with and was accompanied by the earliest photography of Navajo —significantly, as captives.

Prior to the arrival of Europeans, Navajo were gatherers and hunters who rapidly adopted horses and livestock on the introduction of these animals to the New World. On forced settlement, many Navajo adopted farming and ranching practices, particularly of sheep. Today, of course, there are Navajo in every walk of life—proportionally an excess of physicists, artists, and academics, but underrepresented in medicine, law, and photography—but a slight majority still makes much of their living by sheepherding and ranching.

Anthropology and Western science claim that Navajo are very late comers from the far north to their present homeland; indeed, arriving just in time to greet the first Europeans coming north from Mexico in the sixteenth century. Navajo, of course, have another view of their history (labeled "myth" by Westerners, including anthropologists). Despite this major contradiction, a favorite photographic trope is to image Navajo as autochthonous in their dramatic landscape. Nevertheless, photography, normally opaque to any time except the fraction of a second necessary for exposure, is enlisted evidentially (anthropologically) against a Navajo his-

James Faris

tory and their indigenous claims. In a curious perversity, Western "reality" is imaged, not Navajo.

Photographic Registers in the Imaging of Navajo

Rhetorical and subjective working classifications may be established for the major categories of Western photographs of Navajo to the present. They constitute a catalog of the lenses through which Navajo are viewed, and the Western values attached to images of this American people. These classes guide photographers and are in turn guided by and bear on established discourses of conquest and racism.

I am not talking here about intention or motivation—which are not relevant in any case. These categories, these registers, then, are not based on consciousness or announced desire, for all photographs are subjects of ambition and desire. Thus, on the one hand, consciousness and themes of assimilation, adaptation, and pastiche, and, on the other, preservation, nostalgia, and pastoralism, are not classes of this catalog and are present in almost every photograph. It could hardly be otherwise.

This classification is informed by a political interrogation or objection to the West's imaging of Navajo. Judgments are political and subjective. The valence, which I argue adheres to these photographs, are not flaws in an uneducated, unevolved, unenlightened West. They are the necessary conditions of existence of Navajo to the West, exemplars and important features of its relationship with Navajo. They are the imaging devices for the maintenance of a specific and shaped difference—they can be thought of as an "optical unconsciousness" (Benjamin 1968). They saturate practically all ways Navajo can currently appear to the West. This scheme is another Western template—another ordering, normalizing catalog, and one more project by outsiders on images of local people made by outsiders. And as such, it cannot claim to be informed with Navajo consciousness. It is not intended to be. And, readers may notice, serious alternatives, whether by local people or outsiders, are placed somewhat separately and outside this scheme. Ever more of these are now beginning to appear, and this scheme will become increasingly historical. Nevertheless, it still applies, as of this writing, to most Western photographic projects on Navajo.

Of course these classes merge, blend, and mix. But they do establish something of the limits and boundaries of the way Navajo have appeared or can appear to the West. Obviously this suggests that there are but a finite series of means by which the West has viewed Navajo. And as noted, these photographs are guided by a series of other discourses (as are all photographs). These are often discourses premised on the hierarchies of civilized/savage, sedentary/nomadic, modern/traditional, anthropological knowledge/local ideology, and West/Other. Yet occasionally there is a truly grand photograph within this registry (see fig. 7). I prefer to think of these somewhat as "simply luck," as has cultural critic Lucy Lippard (1992). And this classification, as noted in discussing conscious intent, also ignores sets, collections, and series as particular ordering entities. The U.S. government, for example, obviously maintains pictorial archives to justify and promote its own projects, agendas, and views of Navajo. And there are the many aesthetic—that is, beautiful, charming, cute—art photographs that are so vital to the region's huge contemporary tourist industry.

Quite obviously other photographs are possible. And they exist. They are the photo-machine snapshots, some of the studio portraits from towns bordering the Navajoland, and other Navajo-generated photographs. And Navajo input is also evident in the hosts of resistances that appear in archival collections but never surface in publications, and in explicitly political photographs by contemporary Navajo photographers (see below, and fig. 9).

None of this is new and certainly in part could probably ground almost any Western photographic production for almost any minority people. But this presentation is based on a rather exhaustive examination of the archival and published illustrations of one Native American people from the inauguration of photographic imaging to the present (Faris 1996).

Other Views of Existing Photographs, and Alternatives

The deliberate destruction of the existing photographs and filmic materials of Navajo subjects is an alternative that has been requested, although presumably it is not really ever under serious consideration. Photographs and films of sacred materials, of the dead and dying, are argued to have been very dangerous to those involved, and there have been requests that such images be returned to Navajoland to be destroyed. Such queries have never, however, amounted to a formal request by the higher Navajo authorities who might have sufficient status or power to make such a demand, so archivists need not worry. It is an expression of local people who remember the history of the photographic and filmic events and know the consequences.

Readers will have heard these stories because they are legion. Yet there is such an evidential or aesthetic or historical or some other value attached to these images by the West, that their return to and/or destruction by the photographic subjects is considered idiocy or some type of Luddite ir-rationality—or not, ultimately, in the best interests of the people making the request. After all, it is usually argued that archives and museums have a responsibility to the wider society and only Western history is impor-tant. It is the view here, however, that such requests ought to be treated carefully and seriously. Navajo frequently consider untoward photographs (those that they did not agree to have made, or over whose distribution they have had no control) to constitute a danger to them by their very existence, whether or not publicly available or published, and numerous lawsuits have been filed based on such objections. They have not, how-ever, been successful, as the torts governing photographic access in the United States are not premised on any sorts of non-Western cultural sen-sitivities but on issues of privacy. Indeed, it has been adjudicated that per-sons of "reasonable sensitivity" cannot object to having their photographic image made in public places (see Moreland 1991). That the notion of "rea-sonable sensitivity" is exclusively bound to European-American cultural discourses, is not, of course, acknowledged. Navajo culture, in such legal tests, has been judged not "reasonably sensible."

Of course there are other alternatives, such as many under consider-ation in this volume; for example, the rereading of photographs by new viewers, the admission of readings previously disallowed, and particularly, the new readings and new uses by local people. And there is particularly innovative work by local photographers. There have also been a few anti-exhibitions and reexhibitions. This, however, is usually such a threat to existing museums of Native Americans (whose very important gift shops —heavily stocked with photographic volumes—furnish an ever-increasing amount of their overall budgets), tourist directors, and the local art trade, that despite occasional conversations, such exhibitions are seldom forth-coming. These antiexhibitions are regarded as holding history hostage to the present or as promoting dissent and as unwelcome introductions of things best forgotten. The West has never been generous to exposures of its more unsavory history or threats to its own statements of the his-tory of others. Hopefully, in time there may emerge a sufficient corpus of

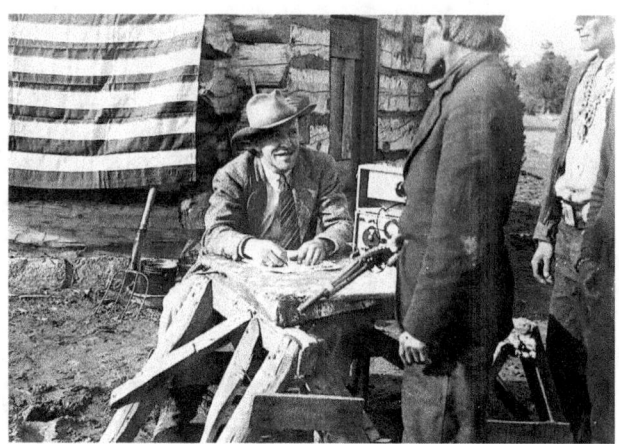

1. Navajo Indians register for selective service, 1941. This old Navajo Indian came around with an Aston (1849) pistol, ready to tackle Hitler's armies. Photographer unknown (probably Milton Snow). Courtesy of the National Archives, Washington, D.C. (NA/BIA/RG75N/box 22, Navajo 229-1333. Navajo 352). The man is posing with his pistol, while other activities take place outside the frame of this widely published propaganda photograph.

photographs by Navajo photographers, or others, to fill the future archives so that a truly postcolonial study might be undertaken. Thus far, however, such work is scarce, and the current project must necessarily examine a thoroughly colonial archive.

In such examination it is important to see which photographs have been culled for publication and which have not. For example, in attempting to recruit Navajo to World War II, the federal government spent much time and attention stressing Native patriotism (this was before, in some areas, Navajo—indigenous Americans—had the right to vote). But a careful look at the total archival corpus reveals that the government did not simply set up recruiting sites to have Navajo rush to them in an outburst of patriotism; rather, they had to rely on Navajo ceremonial gatherings to attempt to recruit them to the war effort. We were never told this when the photographs were published, and one has the impression—intended by propagandists—that Navajo flocked to recruitment stations (figs. 1 and 2).

The same discrepancy emerges when comparing other published photographs with the unpublished sources. Readers are now all familiar with Ed-

James Faris

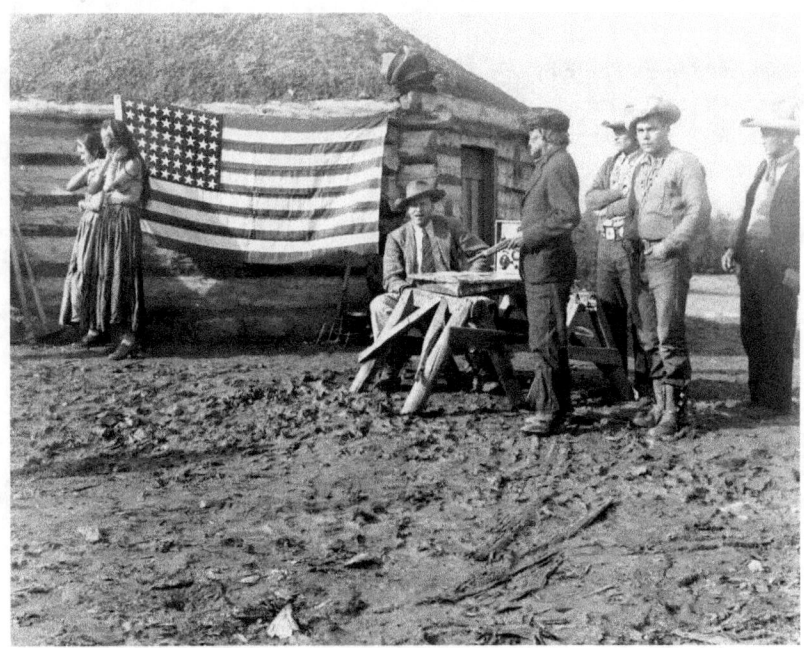

2. John McPhee (seated) registering Navajos for selective service. Photo by Milton Snow, 26 February 1941. Courtesy of the Milton Snow Collection, Navajo Nation Museum, Window Rock, Ariz. (NH 1-22). This photograph is interesting for several reasons. The registrar has some sort of electronic device or transmitter on the table (probably with a recorded message in Navajo). To the left are two girls, bare to the waist, clearly in the middle of a Navajo healing practice, perhaps an Enemyway. Government agents frequently used Navajo traditional events for their own purposes, as it was difficult to contact large numbers of scattered Navajo otherwise. Here Selective Service registration is taking place at a Navajo healing event.

ward S. Curtis's (1907) famous and now-ubiquitous photographs of Native Americans. Among some of the most famous of these photos are the masked Navajo God Impersonators. Research into an early trading family's unpublished photographic archive revealed that Curtis's masked Navajo were often phony—they were actually photographs of a European-American trader's son in Navajo gear! (figs. 3 and 4). Of course, the more familiarity with the biographies of photographers, and the more familiarity with a people's history, the better for this essentially forensic endeavor. Curtis's turn-of-the-century project was motivated by a nostalgic concern for the "vanishing race." Indeed, one of Curtis's Navajo photographs be-

Navajo and Photography

3. *Zahadolzha-Navaho.* Photo by
Edward S. Curtis (probably
summer 1904), in *North
American Indians,* vol. 10
(Cambridge: Cambridge
University Press, 1907), facing
p. 108. Courtesy of the Libraby
of Congress (LOC LC-USZ62-
39425). Fringe Mouth is an
important God Impersonator,
especially during the last two
days of the Nightway, a Navajo
healing practice. Charlie Day, a
European American trader's
son, is the impersonator here
(note the skirt, bag, and belt,
and see also figure 4).

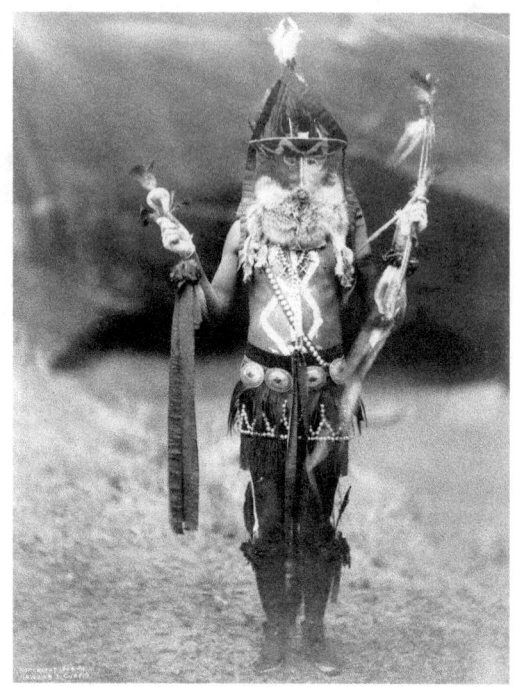

4. Charlie Day, costumed
as a God Impersonator, but
without the mask. Photog-
rapher unknown (possibly
Sam Day II); date unknown
(probably c.1903–4). Indenti-
fication by and photograph
courtesy of Sam Day III.
(Enlarged and cropped by
Gretchen Garner, University
of Connecticut.) Note the
skirt, medicine bag over the
shoulder, and concha belt,
seen in figure 3.

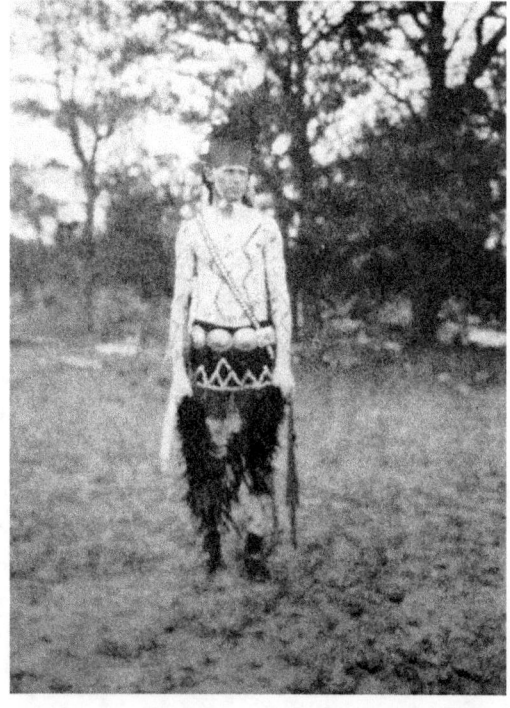

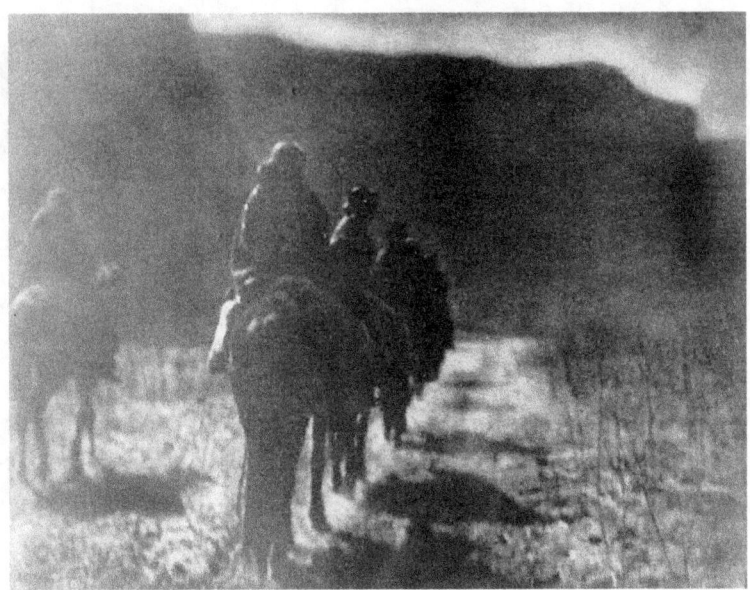

5. *The Vanishing Race.* Photo by Edward S. Curtis, 1904, in *North American Indians*, supplemental portfolio to vol. 1 (Cambridge: Cambridge University Press, 1907), plate 1. This obviously posed photograph has been very widely reproduced—the photograph is the specific archetype of this important discourse on Native Americans.

came the prime source of this archetype (fig. 5). And certainly only a decade or so earlier than Curtis's first work there was a public outcry to eliminate Native Americans as a threat to European-American westward expansion. Now a people successfully conquered, the photographs for public consumption of Native Americans were to be sentimental and nostalgic (mighty warriors as victims) but also shells of their former selves—no longer a threat to European-American expansion and evidence of the success of European-American expansion, of Manifest Destiny. This meant that Native Americans could not appear happy, prosperous, flourishing— or even simply persisting or surviving—they had to appear "vanishing." It should be clear that these sorts of photographs are an early pastoral version of advocacy or victim photography, such as represented today by people like S. Salgado or S. Meiselas—the aestheticizing of misery.

None of this work was simply accidental: Curtis was funded by J. P. Morgan, published by Harvard University, and acclaimed in Washington among Bureau of Indian Affairs bureaucrats (at this time, the bureau was

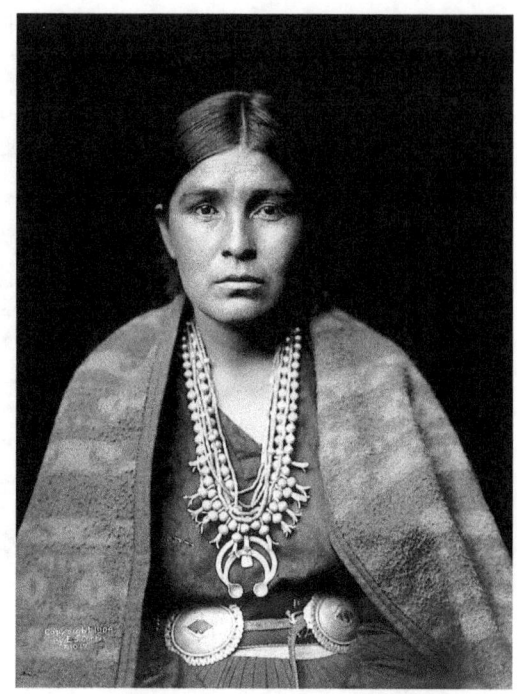

6. *Navaho Woman.* Photo by Edward S. Curtis, n.d. (probably summer 1903). Courtesy of the Library of Congress (LOC LC-lot 12311). This dour, posed photograph of a woman (posed elsewhere in Curtis 1907 [vol. 1, facing p. 76] as *The Blanket Maker*) provides a view of Navajo common for the time (and subsequently): bejeweled, straight-faced, sad, stoic, certainly inscrutable, and perhaps "vanishing." The jewelry was the property of Curtis.

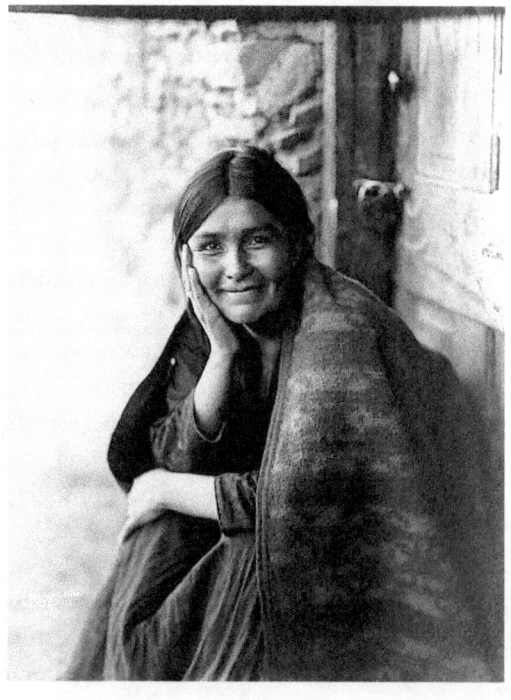

7. *A Navaho Smile.* Photo by Edward S. Curtis, n.d. (probably summer 1903). Courtesy of the Library of Congress (LOC LC-USZ62-46943). This lovely image of the same woman seen in figure 6 could not show greater contrast. Indeed, her entire face changes, and years disappear. If this smile reflects Curtis's relationship with his models, then he got on very well. Here there is no jewelry, no dark backdrop, no contrived pose. This grand photograph was never published.

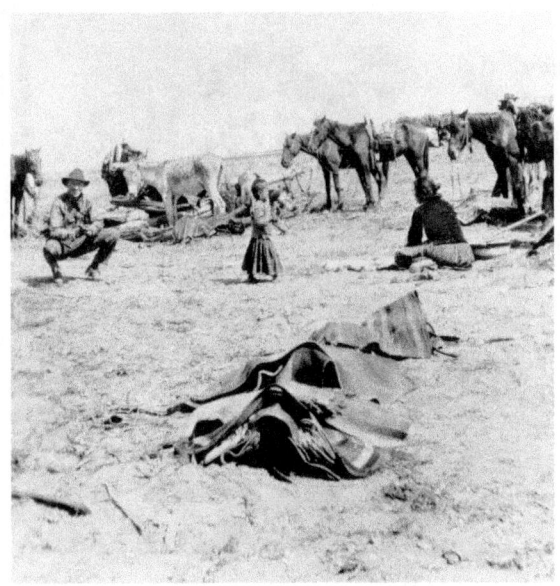

8. Camp scene taken by "Tin Horn," 6 July 1914.
Courtesy of the Arizona State Museum, University
of Arizona (PIX278-x-8). Tin Horn, the first recorded
Navajo photographer on which I have data, made this
photo on the occasion of an Enemyway at Kayenta,
Arizona. His ostensible subject, the European
American (and undoubtedly owner of the camera)
has been moved left of center so that Tin Horn might
include a Navajo child, a woman (probably the child's
mother), horses, donkeys, and tack.

still under the War Department). Curtis, however, left many unpublished
images, and some of happy, smiling, nonvanishing individuals. To illustrate
just one contrast, consider the Navajo woman who appears at least a couple
of times, once as *The Blanket Maker*, in another as *Navajo Woman* (fig. 6), in
Curtis's massive published twenty-volume collection. There is little question she looks somber. However, buried in the unpublished Curtis materials in the Library of Congress is another photo of the same woman, this
time in a lovely intimate portrait minus the vanishing trope, the jewelry,
and the dour expression (fig. 7). This grand photograph was not published
because it did not conform to the required project. One might argue that
it is because Curtis was honest enough that we are today fortunate to have

Navajo and Photography   95

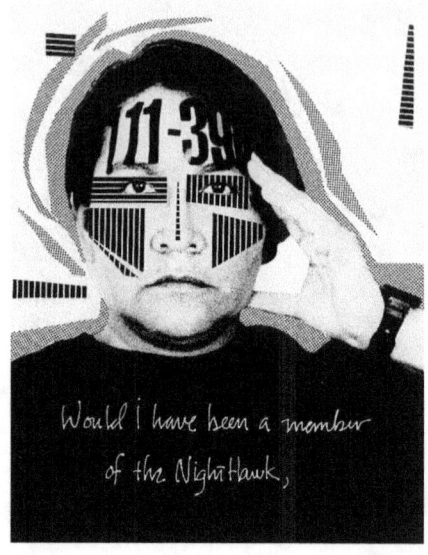

9. *Census Makes a Native Artist,*
from the *Creative Native* series,
1991, by Hulleah J. Tsinhnahjinnie
(who is also the model).
Courtesy of (and photo by)
Hulleah J. Tsinhnahjinnie.

it; or perhaps with his extensive exposure during this massive project, he could simply not resist the persistent warmth of ordinary Navajo.

Nothing here is very profound, nor does it take much effort to reflect any of this, certainly not to note resistances (and with regard to photographs of Navajo, the archives are filled with them) seen in actual photographs of threatening individuals, of dropped eyes, of turned backs, of raised hats and blankets to avoid photographers. These images are never published—they are, indeed, considered "bad" photographs. But they also reveal something of the way local people *could* resist, short of violence, which, as they knew only too well, brought down the full fury and devastation of the U.S. authorities.

Of course, this is apart from newer uses of existing photographs, other photographic possibilities. Local people themselves are probably best equipped to discuss this. Consider a few photographs taken by Navajo. The first is the earliest documented Navajo-composed and imaged photograph, by a man known only to us as "Tin Horn." Notice how the Navajo child, and various items, have been foregrounded in the photograph, whose ostensible purpose was to image the grinning white man who obviously brought along the camera (fig. 8). The second example is a triptych by the exciting contemporary Navajo artist and photographer, Hulleah J.

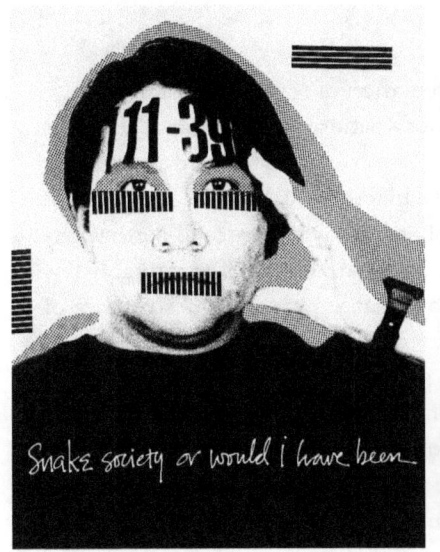
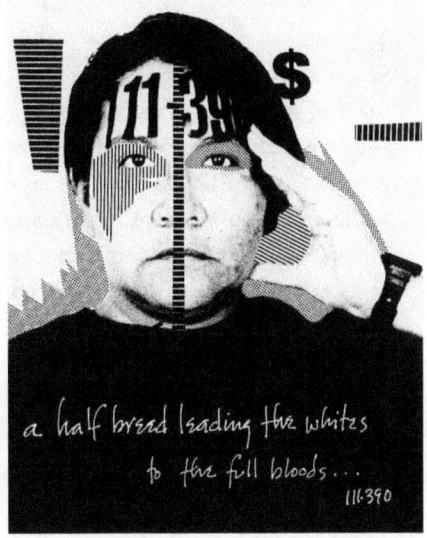

Snake society or would i have been

a half breed leading the whites to the full bloods...

111·390

Tsinhnahjinnie, who is also the model (fig. 9). Originally from a series, these three photographs form a 40´ × 30´ collage. They were stimulated by the "good intentions" of Public Law 101–644, signed into law in 1990, which required Native artists to prove their Native heritage. Because Tsinhnahjin-nie's mother is Seminole/Creek, her "exact identity" in "full-blood" terms (Navajo father; Seminole/Creek mother) is questioned by the West, and in the image she is defined by her Bureau of Indian Affairs census num-ber, tattooed across her forehead. The caption, with her eyes and mouth shaded in succeeding views, and finally divided (halved) by the American eagle and dollar symbol, states: "Would i have been a member of the Night Hawk, Snake society or would i have been a half breed leading the whites to the full bloods. . . ." This text raises the problematic issue of the West's set-ting identities (especially in terms of "blood" quotas); defining who is and who is not a native artist; and imposing exterior identification criteria on Native Americans, as if it were a "gift" to local people to protect them from non-Native American creations posing as Native American. Tsinhnahjin-nie (1993) likens such government "gifts" to the blankets given to Native Americans in the last century—items sometimes deliberately laced with smallpox.

Conclusions

Susan Stewart has argued that "the liberation of representation into a domain of signification always opens onto a pattern or structure of absences —that which is the task of the representation to bring forward as a 'making present'" (1991, 6). This essay has argued that the visual and discursive space available in most Native American photography to date (and particularly for photography of Navajo) has been very narrow and of remarkably few registers. It has been characterized by what Stewart calls "a structure of absences." The available tropes appeared early and have been maintained rather consistently. While each subsequent photographer of Native Americans attempts to distance herself or himself from all previous work (possibly as a sales strategy, as well as to avoid the not uncommon charges of photographic exploitation applied to earlier practitioners), the photography, except for various technical innovations, is remarkably the same. There is simply limited space allotted in the West's representation of the Rest. This may be beginning to change with new readings (viewings) of the corpus, but significantly it is challenged most obviously in the small corpus of Navajo photographers at work.

The two Navajo photographers illustrated here are interesting in this regard. Is there space in the chart of representations for them? I think there is, but in alternative and interesting ways largely unavailable in the published corpus of Western photographers. They rest, at least in the readings (viewings) I have given them, as alternatives to the registers outlined in table 1. Tin Horn turns an intended documentary and recording photograph into an engaging snapshot, rather like a warm family photo. But it is clearly of the wrong family. This was very likely done in violation of the white man's (and undoubtedly camera owner's) instruction. This photograph gives voice to the unvoiced. It photographs the European American, as probably instructed, but he is moved to the side, the owner of capital marginalized and rendered less significant.

Hulleah J. Tsinhnahjinnie deliberately steps outside the available registers. Her overtly political expressions combine effacement and resistance, and privilege not only a Native voice but also a Native model—herself. Tsinhnahjinnie used her own position—indeed, herself, but also her Native identity—to mock not only a government policy but the very notion of imposed identities. She used her "ambivalence" in imposed identity terms to pose an irony—rising to ridicule. She denied Western discourse, and any possibility that a Westerner could have even made this photograph.

James Faris

Thus, in the case of two selected Navajo photographers—one almost accidental, the other subtle and professional—we can see space that they liberated for themselves, space unavailable in the registers argued heretofore to govern Western photographic projects of Native Americans. I am less sanguine about the possibilities of liberating existing images of Native Americans by Westerners or of reclaiming them to progressive ends. Perhaps they remain, however grand and aesthetically pleasing, rather like alchemy or other great enterprises of the past. And unless one tries to argue that medieval alchemy really did evolve and was necessary to contemporary chemistry, opening the absences or exceeding the space made available by classic Native American photography must probably rest on nonparadigmatic Native American photographers.

Morris Low

The Japanese Colonial Eye

SCIENCE, EXPLORATION, AND

EMPIRE

This essay explores the role of photography in the Japanese colonization of Manchukuo (also known as Manchoukuo or Manchuria) from
the images in the reports of the First Scientific Expedition to Manchukuo in 1933, in which photography is prominent. The Japanese used colo-
nial/neocolonial science as part of the process of colonization to demonstrate the need to bring modernity to the region. The term "colonial
science" refers to the overt use of scientific research for territorial expansion and domination, and also to the use of a colony or territory as a
source of scientific and often commercially useful material and data by
the home country. The expedition was formed in May with the full team
arriving in Manchukuo in July and leaving in October. At the time Japanese photography was expanding into journalism and scientific studies,
and the information given in the expedition reports is designed to provide
evidence for how far the Japanese had come compared to the less-civilized
people whom they colonized. Photography helped authorize the colonization by authenticating the conditions in Manchukuo, thereby providing
an important tool for taking stock of Japan's informal empire. By making
Manchukuo visible it became appropriable (Friedberg 1993, 15), but barely
had photography played its part in the appropriation before it was being
questioned by the Japanese themselves.

Colonial Science in Manchuria

Manchuria was the subject of colonial science well before the Japanese arrived. In 1896 the Russian botanist Vladmir Komarov and two other naturalists used their time there not only to make botanical collections but to explore the regions where the lines for the new Manchurian railway were to be marked out (Bretschneider 1898; Noda 1971). By the end of the Russo-Japanese War in 1905, the Japanese had won dominance over southern Manchuria, and the rail lines from Mukden to the port of Dairen (Dalian; formerly known as Dalny) had been built by the Russians along the line surveyed by the naturalists.

The South Manchuria Railway Company (SMR) was established by Japan in 1906, with half of the original capital of the company being provided by the Japanese government. The SMR dominated the Manchurian economy with its control over railways, coal mines, and industrial plants. The railways provided Japan with the means by which to exploit Manchuria's natural resources, as well as the territory beyond its borders. The next few decades saw a period of intense railroad rivalry between China, Russia, and Japan, in which economic and territorial rights were at stake (Wei 1980).

The first president of the SMR was Gotō Shinpei, who had been chief civil administrator in Taiwan during the period 1898 to 1906. Gotō advocated a scientific approach to colonialism that stressed the need for research for colonial development and that included the use of railways as a force for "progress" (Young 1966). In Gotō's eyes, colonial policy must restructure the social and physical environment in order for certain social changes and evolution to occur. Gotō invited Japanese scholars to examine and compile information on Chinese legal history and customs in order for Gotō and his administrators to implement certain reforms (Myers 1973, 435).

The Japanese colonial administrations showed a concern for the history and cultural traditions of the territories. Research and publications on cultural heritage and historic preservation resulted in a positive contribution to their subject peoples by Japanese colonial rule. This work included multivolume histories, biographical dictionaries, and huge compendiums of the fauna and flora of various places (Peattie 1983, 211). Colonial universities and colleges were established in Seoul, Taipei, Lushun, and Manchuria during the 1920s, but the majority of students were Japanese. Scientific research that was conducted in the colonies tended to be limited to studies that were deemed "necessary for local development," and pure research was confined to the imperial universities in mainland Japan.

In the years leading up to the 1930s, Japan used the plague as one of a number of reasons for increasing its influence in Manchuria. There are a large number of scientific papers published in English by research staff of Japanese institutions in Manchuria and China that indicate how epidemics provide opportunities for scientific research and promote the notion that the Japanese presence was a necessary and desirable one (Nathan 1967). If disease was to be controlled not only in the laboratory but throughout Manchuria and China, the Japanese would have to be present in the area and impose certain disciplines on the population.

The proximate excuse to do this did not, however, come from science but from political manipulation. Lieutenant Colonel Ishiwara Kanji, who had been assigned to the Kwantung army in late 1928, developed a solution to the problem in Manchuria by suggesting that it be made into a new state. In 1931 Ishiwara and staff officers of the Kwantung army organized a small explosion to occur on 18 September near a SMR line just outside Mukden. The Kwantung army used this event as an excuse to attack the army of Chang Hsueh-liang (Zhang Xueliang) and occupy Mukden. Japanese spokesmen declared to the public that Japanese occupation was necessary because of the inability of China to maintain peace and order in the region. By late November Japanese forces began to enter territory to the far north of Mukden, and one month later the occupation of Manchuria had met with success. By January 1932 the Kwantung army and SMR had cooperated in drawing up development plans for the new state, and in March Manchukuo was born (Barnhart 1987, 31–33).

The Japanese news media enthusiastically promoted the war, with newspapers vying with each other to track the progress of the Kwantung army. It can thus be said that the conflict with China was accompanied by "war fever" (Young 1998, 58), and the news war in Japan in turn encouraged technological innovation in newspaper production and the diffusion of radio. Young argues that "to a large extent, Manchurian empire building took place in the realm of the imagination" (17), and the mass media played an important role.

The new name of Manchukuo was a means of imposing a new identity on the Manchurian space, and it was a means by which the Japanese established their domain. As in China, the Japanese imposed their own place names and architecture (Duus, Myers, and Peattie 1989). They also created a break with traditional time and declared a new history. Although Manchuria was never formally a colony, the Japanese gained virtual control by the establishment of Manchukuo.

The most prominent Japanese organization supporting scientific research in Manchuria was undoubtedly the SMR, Japan's engine of progress
in the region (Myers 1989). In recent years there has been a spate of books,
mainly reminiscences, that have been published in Japan on the SMR (Itō
1988). The company established a number of research institutions—two
such were the Central Laboratory and the Geological Institute, both in
Dairen. These institutions employed scientists who were given the task
of finding exploitable resources and developing manufacturing processes
that would lead to the creation of new industries (Kinney 1928; Sugita 1990).
The laboratories authenticated knowledge and lent legitimacy to colonial
policy. Such activities or "public services" were, it seems, funded from the
earnings of the SMR railway operations and the mines it operated, and the
activities were considered as being part of the industrial and cultural development of Manchuria.

Institutions such as the Manchukuo Institute of Scientific Research and
the Manchurian museums produced English-language research reports
that served to disseminate throughout the world the achievements of Japanese colonial science in Manchuria. The museums reminded readers of
the reductive nature of the scientific enterprise, housing within their walls
and journal pages the gems of knowledge that they had collected. They
provided the public face of "objective," "nonpolitical" science, and thus
Manchuria would provide knowledge for the rest of the world, and a space
in the Asian continent for the Japanese.

Although the scientific journals published by the institutions appear to
be highly technical, they show many characteristics of colonial science
that are of interest to the historian. Endō Ryūji's paper on fossils published
in 1937 by SMR's Manchurian Science Museum does refer briefly to changes
in the region's peace and order. Endō outlines how bandits and antiforeign
feeling in the Hsaio-shih area in 1928 prevented much fieldwork, whereas
in the 1930s (with occupation by the Japanese) he was able to reexamine
some of the localities (Endō and Resser 1937).

Many of the papers published suggest an emphasis on studies that could
be of commercial benefit. The papers show how the mapping of Manchuria depended on economic as well as strategic factors. But perhaps
more important, the text of the very many papers produced established, by
their sheer volume and continued publication, a type of authority derived
from scientific discourse, from "knowing" Manchuria, which legitimated
the Japanese presence there and enabled them to survey the landscape.

What is also clear from the papers is the existence of research networks

1. Viscount Toki Akira, vice-parliamentary secretary of the War Office of Japan. From *Report of the First Scientific Expedition to Manchoukuo; Epilogue, General Index, and Obituary* (Tokyo, 1940).

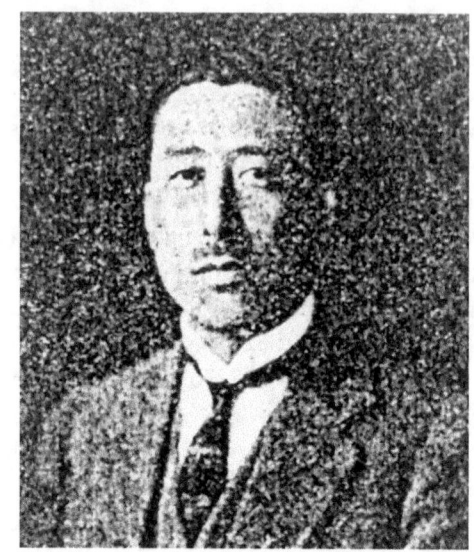

2. Professor Tokunaga Shigeyasu, Waseda University. From *Report of the First Scientific Expedition to Manchoukuo; Epilogue, General Index, and Obituary* (Tokyo, 1940).

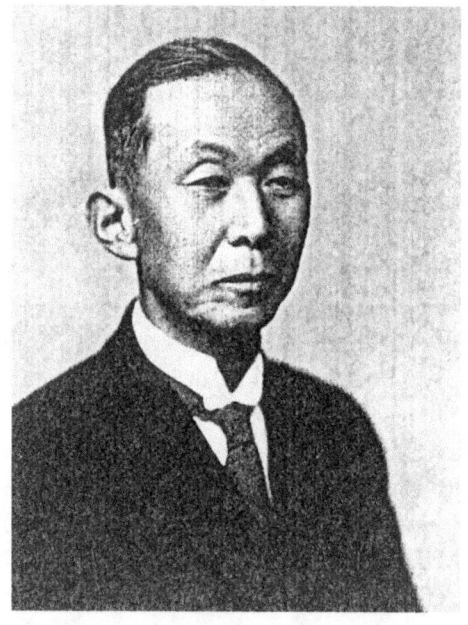

between Manchurian institutions and universities back in Japan. These links facilitated data collection and provided channels for the flow of specimens to the home country and thus for the making of local knowledge global. There were, for example, amateur scientists who, while normally preoccupied by commercial work for Japanese companies in Manchuria, would come across interesting fossils about which they would report to scholars in universities in Japan. For them, the center and the periphery was Manchuria. Publications also show a flow of information to scholars back in Japan, as well as the flow of research funding emanating from the center and moving to the periphery. In the process, Manchuria and its occupants were reduced to fossil-like specimens that could be counted, described, classified, and rendered harmless.

Thus science was a technology of control. It provided a vocabulary with which to transform the subjugated peoples into what would become, in 1938, the Greater East Asia Co-prosperity Sphere, a new order in Asia that would initially bring together China, Manchukuo, and Japan. As Hardt and Negri argue, "the triple imperative of the Empire is incorporate, differentiate, manage" (2000, 198). Territorial expansion involved an inclusive moment when all within its boundaries would be welcome, but "science" would be used to help differentiate and military control brought in to help manage and hierarchize differences.

The First Scientific Expedition

As Stefan Tanaka has pointed out, early Japanese research on Manchuria tended not to involve any fieldwork or data collection in the region of study. Rather, scholars focused on collecting important documents (Tanaka 1993, 242). The First Scientific Expedition was a belated attempt to remedy this situation (*Report* 1934–40). Instigated by the dapper Viscount Toki Akira, vice-parliamentary secretary of the War Office of Japan (fig. 1), the expedition was led by the distinguished scholar Tokunaga Shigeyasu, professor at Waseda University (fig. 2).

Science structured the way that members of the expedition saw Manchukuo and reported on it. Twenty-five impressive volumes of scientific papers were produced from the expedition. Members of the expedition met with sufficient hardships during the trip to be awarded the Asahi Cultural Prize of 1937. The newspaper *Asahi shinbun* had been one of the sponsors of the expedition, along with the Japanese Foreign Office, the South

Manchuria Railway Company, the Foundation for the Promotion of Scientific and Industrial Research of Japan, and others. Tokunaga also acknowledges the assistance of officers of the Kwantung army during the expedition. *Asahi shinbun*'s media coverage, reported in a timely fashion by using planes, ensured a successful reception for the expedition on its return.

The expedition was more symbolic than useful. The report, published between 1934 and 1940, consisted of a description of the journey and many volumes of scientific papers. These were divided into six parts (a general report, followed by sections on geology, geography, botany, zoology, and anthropology). The text was written in both English and Japanese to assure both local and international audiences of Japan's good intentions in Manchukuo. It was important to be seen as willing to freely share scientific results with the rest of the world.

The photographs discussed in this essay are a selection from the sixty-nine images in the general report by Tokunaga. The hundreds of other photographs contained in the report serve as illustrations to scientific papers and hence are very specific in content. They include topographical images of diggings and of the geography of the province of Jehol; examples of excavated fossilized specimens; and many photographs of butterflies, freshwater fish, and local birds. The final section on anthropology is devoted to an examination of the ancient artifacts that were excavated in the region. The sheer bulk of images and text was done in part as an effort to promote and reinforce the scientific value of the expedition. As Tokunaga wrote in the final volume published in 1940, 149 new species and 64 new subspecies were found (*Report* 1940, 4). Of these, 68 were animals and 124 were plants, and 21 were identified as being extinct animals and plants.

But in addition to its contribution to science, the voluminous report (around 4,000 pages and 820 plates) formed a picture of a sparsely populated geographic region ready for the taking, one that could be used to further Japan's expansion and absorb some of its excess population. Its position on the periphery suited its perceived role as part of Japan's protective buffer zone (Tanaka 1993, 247).

The expedition mapped out the new space of the Japanese empire, as it progressed through the puppet state of Manchukuo in 1933. The portable space carved out by the expedition, and by the camera, was marked by the Japanese flag, a symbol that allegedly struck fear into the hearts of the "natives." It was not only the flag, however, that symbolized the Japanese presence. Dressed in traveling garb not unlike that of British explorers, and accompanied by around thirty troops, the expedition members evoked associations with European explorers in nineteenth-century Africa. Because Japan came late to colonialism, it was able to draw on the old and new technologies of observation and documentation. The expedition appropriated some of the forms and narratives of exploration created by Europeans, along with notions of manliness.

The expedition trekked through the desolate terrain of Jehol province, which was added to Manchukuo in 1933. Tokunaga saw Jehol as "virgin land remaining untouched with [sic] scientific work." He declared that the expedition was evidence of the closer relationship between Japan and Manchukuo, and that it was conducted in the lofty hope of "developing Asian civilization" (1934, 45). Jehol was metaphorically portrayed as feminine and ready for the taking. In the process, its occupation would contribute to a greater pan-Asian identity.

We can also tell much from the silences and absences in the report. Prior to setting out for three months in Jehol, expedition leader Tokunaga and his assistant N. Naora spent twenty days visiting Ku-hsiang-tung on the outskirts of Harbin, where they conducted paleontological and anthropological work. This event helps us to understand the discrepancy between the June starting date of the expedition and the July arrival of the rest of the members of the expedition. This imprecision in the actual beginning date of the expedition is a telling one because it avoids the need for photographs of the twenty-five white-Russian laborers who were employed to assist them (Tokunaga 1934, 48). The reversal of power in Manchuria that this implied may have overly complicated the simple narratives and racial hierarchies that the photographs were seeking to establish. Although the population of Manchuria was estimated to be 90 percent Han Chinese in 1931 (Mitter 2000, 23; Jones 1949, 5–6), Harbin was an "un-Chinese" city; that is, its many Russian residents and its hybrid mix of architectural styles, thanks to the earlier development of a Russian rail line in Manchuria, gave it a distinctly European feel (Fogel 1996, 271). The large number of Russians competing with the Chinese for work as laborers upset expectations regarding racial hierarchies (Jones 1949, 76). In many ways, the elegant city of Harbin did not conform to stereotypes that may have been hoped for by the media.

The involvement of the major newspaper *Asahi shinbun* did ensure wide coverage in Japan of the expedition. Its central role in the expedition of providing timely reports helped determine the expedition's perceived success. The press was important in promoting the idea of the explorer as hero, regardless of the actual results of expeditions. Japan was no different from England and the United States in this respect (Riffenburgh 1994): the reports generated from their experiences in the "frontier" were also derivative of explorers' accounts. *Asahi* had launched a photo-illustrated magazine, *Asahi gurafu*, ten years prior to the expedition, in the tumultuous year of 1923 when the great Kantō earthquake destroyed much of Tokyo. The company also launched *Asahi kamera* in 1926 for the All Japan Association of Photographic Societies, which served to bring together various amateur photography groups (Kaneko 1996, 40, 43). It was thus against the backdrop of an image-hungry media feeding a mass-consumer society that the expedition occurred. Visual representations served to help integrate Japanese society and usher in modernity in a way hitherto unknown (Clark 2000, 27).

How could the expedition's activities be justified? Scientific knowledge, or the data collection that passes for it, has very specific settings such as laboratories or takes certain forms such as expeditions. Whether exploration is used as a pretext for territorial expansion or not, certain types of equipment and clothing are deemed necessary for the gathering of facts previously unknown to the Japanese and perhaps to Westerners, but certainly known to the people resident there. How is it that the scientific world could call the local knowledge of "natives" new "discoveries" uncovered by the scientific expedition? It has been argued that "many of the characteristic signs of a good [scientific] witness were thought to exist as a consequence of the actual physiology of the human body" (Johns 1993), and dressing for the part helped. Not surprisingly, the creators of the knowledge were always men, and their bona fides could be confirmed by their actions and status. In Japan, this meant affiliation with an imperial university and connections with an influential professor.

Copies of the early volumes of the report, dated October 1934, were received by the Linnean Society of London on 10 December 1934. They tended to confirm British attitudes at the time that "Manchuria was destined by the accident of history to become the cockpit of international ambitions. Nominally Chinese soil, and yet outside China proper, its strategic and industrial importance caused world statesmen to realise the complications which might arise from the presence of a predominant foreign Power attempting to occupy and exploit it" (Etherton and Tiltman 1934, 5); and that "developments financed and carried out by the Japanese in Manchuria have transformed the country from an empty, backward land into an area destined to play an increasingly important part, under whatever regime, in the industrial economy of the Far East" (5–6).

Morris Low

Seeing the Sights of Manchukuo

The militaristic tone of the expedition, escorted as it was by some thirty soldiers, along with its much-trumpeted successful conclusion, were further proof of Japan's ability to match European colonial powers and to exert its superiority over the people of other Asian countries. For the Japanese, military success was evidence of Japan's modernity (Mackie 2000, 192). In the report of the expedition, we see the commanding gaze over the landscape in the form of photographic panoramas. Since the late nineteenth century, panoramic oil paintings of military conquests were popular attractions in places such as Asakusa. Photographs also instilled a similar sense of nationalistic euphoria. They delivered a visual experience of the new territories under Japanese control (Iizawa 1995).

The extended photographs in the expedition report are joined together like a panorama, allowing spatial mobility and giving the viewer some sense of the body moving over the terrain. They illustrate how in the 1920s and 1930s the Japanese were introduced to new ways of looking at things, thanks to the "real" photographs provided by science. Whether it be the body under the gaze of the camera for medical purposes, photographs of the heavens for scientific purposes, shots of biological specimens under microscopes, or aerial photographs of the land, the Japanese during this time were being introduced to ways of viewing things that differed dramatically from the ways of the past (Iizawa 1989, 12). In the name of science, the expedition observed the local people, using their various types of equipment to record the event. Observation of cultural difference facilitated defining the Japanese national character. Protected by troops and with progress checked via plane, the expedition was not unlike tourism.

Mark Elliott has recently explained that, even for Chinese, up until the early part of the twentieth century Manchuria was an isolated geographic region, a space that had an identity that was distinct from the rest of China. Ironically, not until after 1931, with the creation of "Manchukuo" as part of Japan's informal empire, was it really transformed into a "place." It was, ironically, in the 1930s and early 1940s under the Japanese that Manchuria enjoyed a more independent identity. Its strategic importance was the subject of a large literature (Elliott 2000, 639).

A manifestation of the expansion of the Japanese empire was the growth of international tourism, and a considerable literature also grew up around it. In the fourth edition of *Peking, North China, South Manchuria and Korea*, published by Thomas Cook and Son in 1920, the South Manchuria Railway Company urged travelers and tourists journeying between Tokyo and Peking to "travel via the South Manchuria Railway, which runs from Fusan to Mukden and passes through magnificent scenery and furnishes the last link in the newest highway round the world" (Cook 1920). Thomas Cook and Son further reassured travelers that they would "find something different, something new—yet ancient, an [sic] unique change from the 'modern civilisation series' of Europe and the Far West. . . . Fortunately, beyond a mere fringe of the coast-line of this great 'grandsire of empires,' . . . today the Chinese people are as simple and primitive in their habits and customs as they have been for ages past" (i).

Prompted, no doubt, by such urgings, the 1930s saw a boom in Japanese tourism. The expansion of Japan's sphere of influence, along with its renewed confidence, created new opportunities for consumers. The First Scientific Expedition to Manchukuo can be likened to an upmarket outback safari, combining a chance to see the natives, pick up some souvenirs, and taste a sense of danger without getting killed. Commentaries at the time describe Manchukuo more like a theme park than an informal colony. The expedition's report helped construct Manchukuo as a tourist attraction by providing the documentation (MacCannell 1976, 41). Like all good theme parks, there was the threat of danger. The expedition encountered anti-Japanese guerrillas whom they invariably described as "bandits." It has been estimated that in mid-1932 there were some 300,000 to 400,000 such people in Manchukuo opposing the Japanese army, but by the time of the expedition their numbers had been greatly reduced (Wilson 1995, 263).

The photographs in the expedition's general report are numbered and bear captions. They are assembled in a clear sequence, rather filmic in nature, and tell the narrative of the expedition, in the process miniaturizing the landscape and shaping it for consumption by the reader/potential settler (Stewart 1993, 146). As Tokunaga, the expedition leader, relates, "prior to proceeding to the research we solemnly performed the inauguration ceremony at Hsinking on August 2, 1933, and on October 12 all of the party returned to Hsinking just for a time making the expected investigation and research. As to the entire course in details [sic] I have explained with illustrations in Section I of the present report" (1940, 3). Given the circular nature of the expedition's route, photographs in serial order were seen as a useful way to convey to readers the sense of progress made by the expedition.

The snapshots of the countryside, towns, and even toilets are strangely devoid of people (fig. 3), and these images are in line with other propaganda

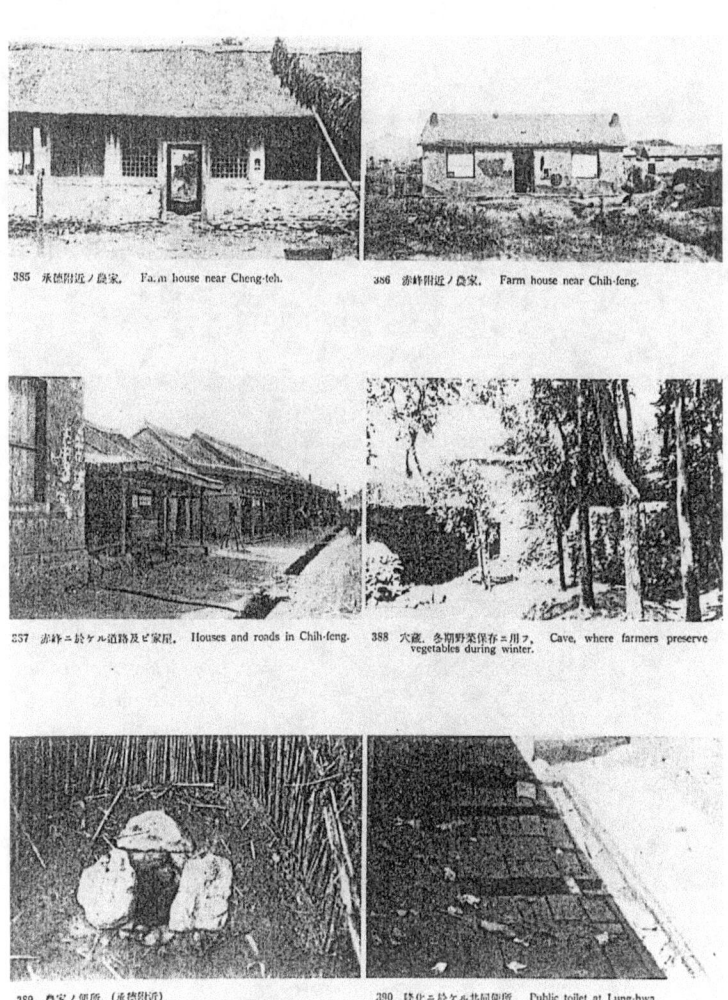

385 承徳附近ノ農家. Fa. m house near Cheng-teh.   386 赤峰附近ノ農家. Farm house near Chih-feng.

387 赤峰ニ於ケル道路及ビ家屋. Houses and roads in Chih-feng.   388 穴蔵. 冬期野菜保存ニ用フ. Cave, where farmers preserve vegetables during winter.

389 農家ノ便所. (承徳附近) Toilet of a farmer's house. (near Cheng-teh.)   390 隆化ニ於ケル共同便所. Public toilet at Lung-hwa.

3. Page showing images of empty residences. From *Report of the First Scientific Expedition to Manchoukuo* (Tokyo, 1934).

that often implied that no one lived in the region—that it was *terra nullius*. Uninspiring photographs of a dilapidated, solitary "farm house near Chih-feng" (figs. 3 and 4) highlight this idea. The Manchukuo framed by the camera lens was one that the Japanese had imagined. It is only when we are to be shown people who are grotesque and different, with swollen necks (fig. 5), do the locals in the southern districts of Jehol warrant a picture. These pictures are rather taxonomic in nature yet the people photo-

The Japanese Colonial Eye   111

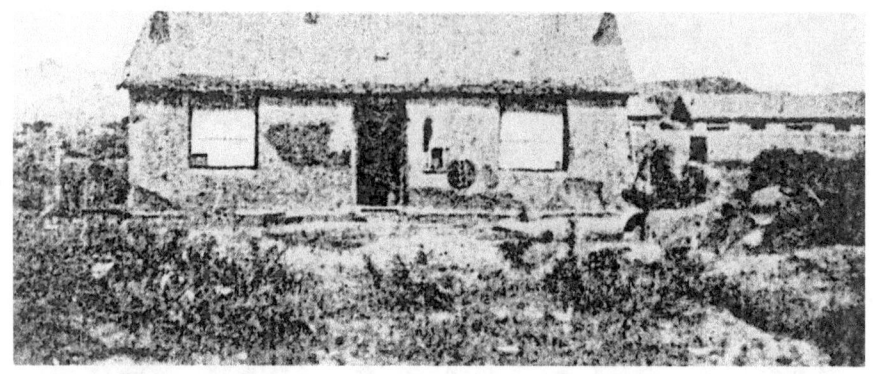

4. "Farm house near Chih-feng." From *Report of the First Scientific Expedition to Manchoukuo* (Tokyo, 1934).

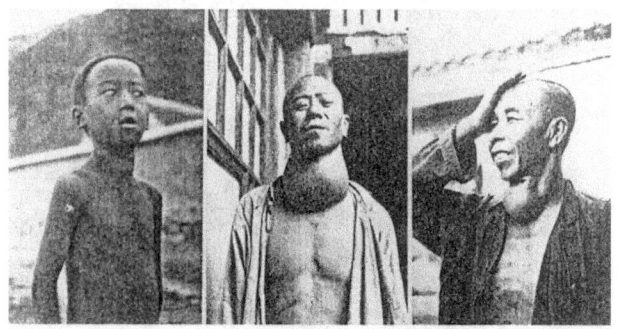

5. Page showing images of local people in Jehol province suffering from endemic goiter. From *Report of the First Scientific Expedition to Manchoukuo* (Tokyo, 1934).

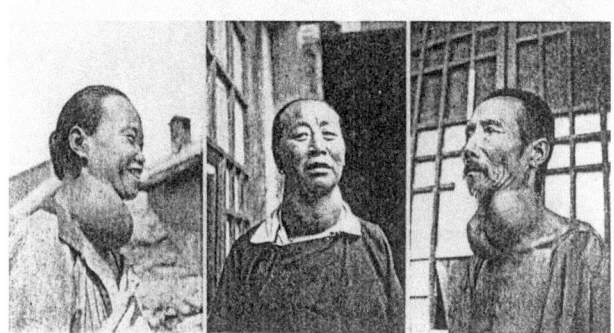

甲状腺腫患者.
In the southern districts of Jehol, more than half of the townfolk suffer from Endemic Goiter, so throughout Jehol tens of thousand people must be the victims of the disease. The cause of the disease has not yet been discovered.

graphed seem to be somewhat bemused, as if indulging the Japanese and thus resisting dehumanization.

Masculinity and Self-Cultivation

The expedition's journey served a variety of purposes. It can be seen as a way of nurturing budding colonialists and heroicizing Japanese imperialism. At the ceremony on 2 August 1933 for the commencement of the expedition at Hsin-king, the new capital of Manchukuo, members of the expedition swore that they would "exalt the spirit of loyalty and patriotism, and . . . act impartially for the honour of the corporation [the expedition], formed by friendship and co-operation" (Tokunaga 1934, 55). This was done in the presence of the emperor of Manchukuo. The harsh conditions that the men subsequently experienced made them more conscious of their bodies: "Situated in the southern extremity of Manchoukuo, Hsing-lun-hsien district is so steep a land as to allow no auto to pass, and in consequence rarely has any scientist's body of Japan ever explored the land" (61). At the end of the expedition we are reminded of its greater significance for the Japanese. On 12 October, a dispersion ceremony was held at Hsin-king Shrine, where the expedition began. The photograph of the ceremony (fig. 6) shows members of the expedition bowing in the direction of the Imperial Palace of Japan (64).

From the images of the expedition we can gain a sense of the changes in masculine identity as Japan underwent modernity. We see traces of the interplay between Japanese notions of masculinity and Western modes of masculine identity. The photographs show how the Japanese removed their laboratory coats and suits and donned tropical and military uniforms, reshaping their physical selves and their masculinity in the process (figs. 7 and 8). Members of the expedition literally had to dress the part. Photographs show them as selfless pioneers, but not entirely comfortable with the role or the clothing. They adopted the garb of British colonials in order not to surprise the natives, who no doubt were meant somehow to be used to domination. In the eyes of the local inhabitants, these uniforms would have empowered and masculinized the Japanese men, but those very same uniforms served to discipline and regulate the wearers as well.

This Western-inspired masculine identity served to create a sense of difference from the Manchurians—one of the cultural strategies of Japanese colonialism. The report's urbane images of Viscount Toki and Professor

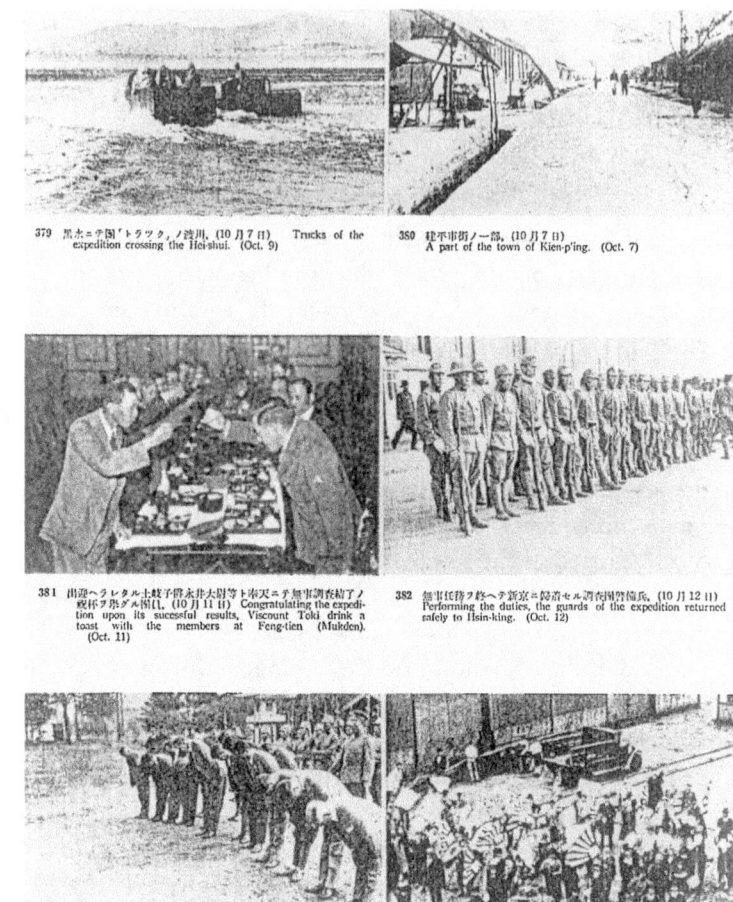

379 黒水ニテ囯「トラツク」ノ渡川。(10月7日)   Trucks of the
    expedition crossing the Hei-shui. (Oct. 9)

380 建平市街ノ一部。(10月7日)
    A part of the town of Kien-p'ing. (Oct. 7)

381 出迎ヘラレタル土岐子爵永井大尉等ト帝天ニテ無事調査結了ノ
    祝杯ヲ挙グル図[1]。(10月11日) Congratulating the expedi-
    tion upon its successful results, Viscount Toki drink a
    toast with the members at Feng-tien (Mukden).
    (Oct. 11)

382 無事任務ヲ終ヘテ新京ニ帰着セル調査国警備兵。(10月12日)
    Performing the duties, the guards of the expedition returned
    safely to Hsin-king. (Oct. 12)

383 新京神社殿前ニ於ケル解開式。(10月12日)
    Dispersion ceremony before the Hsin-king Shrine. (Oct. 12)

384 神戸ニテ調査団ヲ歓迎ノ光景。(10月21日) Enthusiastic wel-
    come extended towards the expedition at Kobe. (Oct. 21)

6. Page showing images of the return of the expedition. From *Report of the First Scientific Expedition to Manchoukuo* (Tokyo, 1934).

Tokunaga (figs. 1 and 2) highlight this, as does the obituary for the professor in the final volume. Tokunaga contracted pneumonia and died of heart failure on 8 February 1940, just as the final report was being checked by proofreaders. This was a somehow fitting end to the drama of the expedition. As Nakai Takenoshin wrote in Tokunaga's obituary:

The difficulties of a work of this kind—the first in the history of our country—can hardly be appreciated in the initial stages, but we have come to

Morris Low

realise that our late leader alone could have brought it to a successful conclusion under the prevailing conditions of national emergency. To his example of undaunted courage and untiring energy we owe not only the success of the exploration itself, traversing regions infested by bandits, braving epidemics, rigours of climate and shortage of supplies, but also the completion of the study of materials collected and the many other steps leading to the final publication of results after some eight years of arduous and often disheartening toil, severely handicapped owing to the national emergency by depletion of staff and scarcity of appliances. (*Report* 1940, 6)

Tokunaga thus was a martyr for science and the nation.

Joshua Fogel has written of the research trips of third-year students of the Shanghai-based Tō-A Dōbun Shoin (East Asian Common Culture Academy), which was established by the adventurer Arao Kiyoshi and would eventually become a university. The institution stressed practical training on contemporary aspects of China, including the language. The annual summer vacation trips were an extension of this approach to education, and served to reproduce an ideology of manhood based on exploration. The trips first began in 1907 and continued until 1942. Small groups of students traveled throughout China and neighboring areas, producing, like the Manchukuo expedition, mammoth reports (450 to over 1,000 pages) on various aspects of Chinese life (Fogel 1996, 134, 283–84). These documents helped Japan stake its claim in Manchukuo. And, in forming part of the "colonial library" (Mudimbe 1994, 17) of Japanese imperialism, the texts reveal the various discourses at work.

In 1933, the same year as the expedition, eighty-six of the ninety students who participated in the annual research trip went to Manchukuo. Divided into twenty-six groups, they scattered throughout the countryside. Like the members of the expedition, they describe a lack of order among the people residing there, but perhaps because of their youth and training they tended to be more sympathetic to the plight of the Chinese they saw, and they questioned the Japanese sense of racial superiority (Fogel 1996, 185–87). The students' involvement with Chinese society and culture was deeper than that of the scientific expedition, which used Western methods of data collection to justify the distance they placed between themselves and their objects of study.

Endō Ryūji provides another example of a Japanese researcher conducting fieldwork. As mentioned earlier, in terms of encounters with local people, he refers briefly to changes in the peace and order when he outlines how bandits and antiforeign feeling in the Hsaio-shih area in 1928 proved

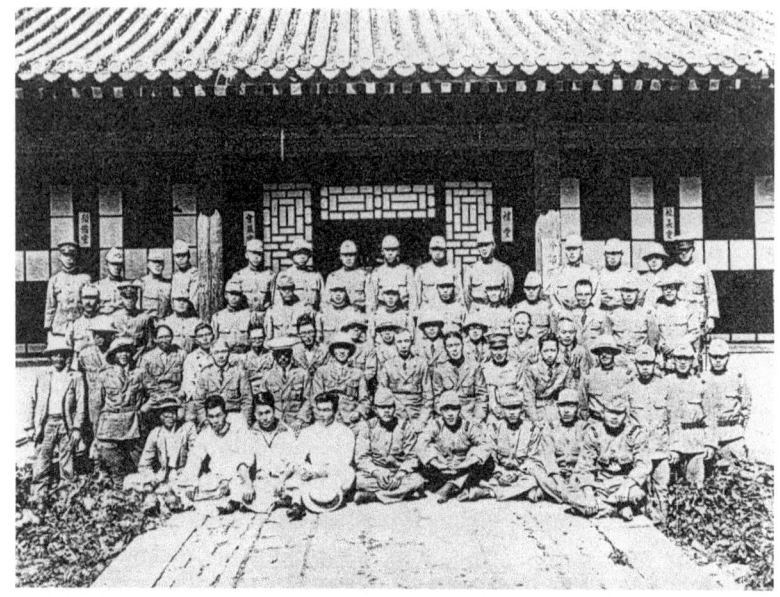

7. Group photo of expedition team. From *Report of the First Scientific Expedition to Manchoukuo* (Tokyo, 1934).

8. Profile of a team member. From *Report of the First Scientific Expedition to Manchoukuo* (Tokyo, 1934).

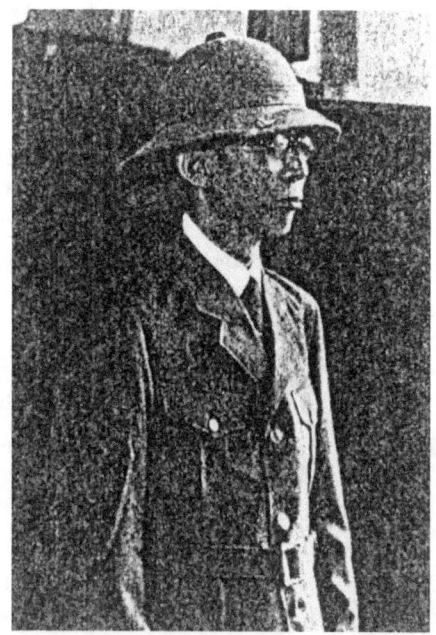

to be an obstacle to fieldwork, whereas in the 1930s (with occupation by the Japanese) he was able to reexamine some of the localities (Endō and Resser 1937). The enthusiasm of Japanese scientists like Endō in persisting with their work in the face of real danger shows how determined they were to sort and organize China and Manchuria and thus reduce the region to manageable proportions suitable for the pages of academic journals. This desire can be partly understood by the way in which "objectivity" assumed a distance between the observer and those being observed, between colonizers and the colonized. The people of Manchuria were not so much the Other to the Japanese, but rather a people lower in the hierarchy in terms of industrial development, hygiene, rationality, and order. To show this the Japanese used Western labels to specify and categorize—in effect mapping an Asian people with a Western tool of empire.

In the years after the completion of the expedition, attitudes to the "truthfulness" of photography changed. The English-language newspaper the *Japan Times and Mail* tried in 1937 to explain this notion with a book titled *The Truth Behind the Sino-Japanese Crisis: Japan Acts to Keep Eastern Civilization Safe for the World*. What is so fascinating here is that it was only four years after the expedition that the "truthfulness" of photography is questioned. A page of three photographs, titled "How China Fools Public Abroad," shows a lonely, burnt Chinese baby sitting on railway amid wartime devastation. Below the photograph is another image depicting the same baby, an older boy, and a man posing them for the photograph. The third photograph shows the standing boy in place of the baby. As the caption reads, "These photographs show how, through clever posing, war pictures can be made to win the sympathy of people abroad by misrepresenting the truth. The picture at the top is a photograph widely circulated in the United States. In it a Chinese baby is shown as the only apparent survivor in a scene of desolation.... In the picture below, at left, which was taken at exactly the same spot as the photograph at the top, a rescue worker is shown placing the child between the tracks, apparently for photographic purposes (*Japan Times and Mail* 1937, 18).

On 7 July 1937, a clash occurred between Japanese and Chinese troops at Marco Polo Bridge near Peking. That month, the Japanese imperial army and navy prohibited the publication of photographs deemed to be detrimental to the war effort. In August, fighting broke out in Shanghai that led to a full-scale conflict, and in September imports of photographic equipment into Japan were restricted (Ono 1998).

Conclusion

As Vera Mackie (2000, 196) has argued, Japanese modernity was indeed a colonial modernity, and colonial space could at times provide an imaginary space in which the Japanese could carve out their own dreams. The scientific objectification of Manchukuo in the expedition's reports facilitated the appropriation of its history and its future. While some of the rhetoric was pan-Asian, it is clear that the expedition was done for the greater glory of the emperor of Japan and the nation he symbolized.

The expedition also served to reinforce the self-worth of the Japanese as men, scientists, and colonizers. Jehol province was virgin territory and the men could assert themselves there, safe in the knowledge that they had the scientific tools and military might to do so. The photographs referred to in this essay reinforced the difference between the more urbane members of the expedition to Manchukuo and the "backward" subjects of territories under Japanese control. The photographs reflect the eye of Japanese scientists who, whether they liked it or not, became colonizing subjects. The emptiness of Jehol reinforced the notion that it was ready for colonization, and images of the "uncivilized" people were evidence that they could benefit from Japanese medical science and better hygiene.

Through the use of Western science and the camera, the Japanese sought to impose a modernity on the Chinese and the people of Manchuria as part of their own colonialist project. We can conceive the use of photography as part of cross-cultural communication, a spectatorship that provokes thoughts and action. A certain "look" involves power relations that can subjugate or empower. But the empire could strike back, and the Japanese became all too aware that the object of their gaze could manipulate visual images as well.

Nicolas Peterson

The Changing Photographic Contract

ABORIGINES AND IMAGE ETHICS

Until the late 1960s, anthropologists and others in Australia published images of restricted Aboriginal religious activity with little thought of possible Aboriginal concerns about such publication. Although this practice is indefensible from a contemporary point of view it seemed unproblematic until that time, partly because it had been going on for over a hundred years and partly because the vast majority of images published were in academic journals or ethnographies difficult to obtain. Further, the great social, cultural, and spatial distance between the Aboriginal people of remote Australia, where the images were taken, and the regions of settled Australia, where the images circulated, meant that the images rarely found their way back to the communities or areas in which they would cause concern.

In the immediate post–World War II period what protests there were about photography were mainly from the government in the context of the assimilation policy, and largely pertained to images that perpetuated negative stereotypes such as those of urban or rural poverty or of people affected by alcohol.[1] Since the late 1960s, however, the situation has changed dramatically. Publication of images of restricted religious activity is now unthinkable, even by popular magazines.

In this essay I want to look at the emergence of a public concern with image ethics in relation to photography involving indigenous people and their culture in Australia. Image ethics go far beyond the publishing of pictures of restricted activities or objects, of course, to issues of representation and informed consent, but as far as such a history of public concern can be established, it is the conflicts around this matter in particular that have been central to the emergence of a public consciousness of the issue. Furthermore, anthropologists, being among the principal makers, publishers, and precipitators of conflict over such images, have been central to this history.

Although the ethical issues extend worldwide, it is mainly in the case of Fourth World people, such as indigenous Australians or native North Americans (e.g., see Brumbaugh 1996; Faris 1996; Powers 1996), where the anthropologists, photographers, and the public archives holding the images are within the same polity, that there is now unavoidable pressure to address these issues. The past carelessness of anthropologists and others in their treatment of images was brought about not just by colonial inequalities, pragmatics, and situational ethics but also by a more principled, even if problematic, scientific concern with the importance of open inquiry and freedom of access to information (see Powers 1996 regarding archives), all of which remain relevant today.

Because the vast majority if not all the photographic contracts entered into with Aboriginal people, until recently, would have been verbal, the amount of evidence in relation to the number of photographs taken is infinitesimal. What follows is inevitably sketchy, but it provides a preliminary outline of the history of image ethics, including the emergence of public concern about the terms of the photographic contract between Aboriginal Australians and others and the consequences for the prevalence of certain kinds of images. This history can be divided into three phases: 1840s to c.1920, c.1920 to 1971, and 1971 to the present. I shall begin with two incidents, one from 1891 and the other from 1997, that show how remarkably the situation has changed.

Two Photographic Encounters

On 3 September 1891 the Elder Scientific Exploring Expedition, having reached a position near the Barrow Range in the Great Victoria Desert in Western Australia, was suffering from a grave water shortage. Richard Helms, the naturalist on the expedition, recorded the following event in his journal entry for that day:

We came to camp at about 2 P.M., having just before caught a little native girl of about five to six years of age. She screamed terribly when she saw us approach. The poor little thing trembled in all her limbs when we got hold of her, and she handed us immediately the large lizard she had in her hand. When the caravan came up she received some water, of which she drank greedily, became pacified after that, and ate some of the sugar given to her. Later she got some jam, and at times was incited to a smile, but she submitted more passively than otherwise to our treatment of her. Everyone tried to be kind to her. (1896, 300)

David Lindsay, the leader of the expedition, records the event slightly differently:

[T]his child will be able to show us some water. We had dinner, the child sitting close by me, eating such a dinner as she never dreamed of, quite happy and apparently without fear of the strange white men. She is the first female we have had in camp and the first one the doctor has had an opportunity to photograph; she was much afraid of the camera, and I had great difficulty in keeping her quiet. (1893, 94)

The resulting photograph (fig. 1) confirms the entries: the girl's distress is patent, and she is clearly an unwilling captive of the camera's gaze.[2]

One hundred and six years later, on 20 February 1998, Mr. Yunupingu, the chairman of the Northern Land Council and senior member of the Gumaitj clan, appeared before a magistrate in Darwin in the Northern Territory of Australia to face three charges (see Reeves 1998, appendix Q):[3]

— that on the 4th April 1997 at an area on the beach side of the Gove Yacht Club he unlawfully assaulted Mr. McRostie, a professional photographer
— that he unlawfully damaged a Canon camera belonging to the photographer
— that on the same day and at the same place he unlawfully damaged property, namely a Kodak slide film, to the value of $18 belonging to the photographer.

On 4 April 1997 the photographer, Mr. McRostie, looking for a suitable backdrop for wedding photographs at the Gove Yacht Club, walked off the lease on which the club stood and went down to the beach where he took some photographs. The beach is Aboriginal land belonging to the Gumaitj clan. Walking the short distance back to the clubhouse, yet still on Gumaitj land, he was invited by an Aboriginal man from the Dalwangu clan to take photographs of his two naked children. However, the Dalwangu man should not have made this invitation because he was on Gumaitj land and it was disrespectful to Mr. Yunupingu, who was present. He should have

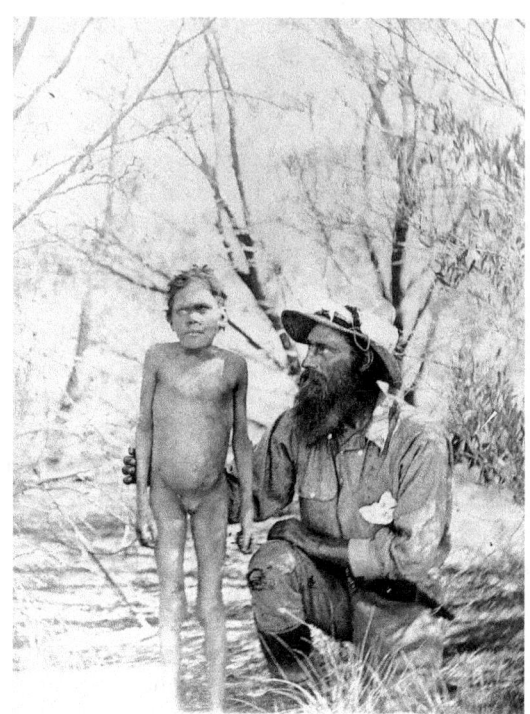

1. David Lindsay holding an Aboriginal girl before the expedition camera in 1891. Courtesy of the Royal Anthropological Institute.

directed Mr. McRostie to seek from Mr. Yunupingu, as a senior landowner, permission to photograph the children.

Mr. Yunupingu became aware that photographs were being taken of the naked children, one sitting on each of the Dalwangu man's legs. Mr. McRostie invited the other Aboriginal people present, including Mr. Yunupingu, to gather for a group photograph. Mr. Yunupingu declined and said: "Have you taken photographs of the children?" Mr. McRostie said words to the effect of, "Yes, I did." Mr. Yunupingu said, "Yes? Give them $50." Mr. McRostie said, "No." This exchange was repeated. Mr. McRostie said he had permission to take the pictures.

Mr. Yunupingu walked across to him and demanded the film. Mr. McRostie said "What for?" and Mr. Yunupingu replied to the effect that, "You have taken and captured—taken a spirit images [sic] of the children." A tussle resulted with Mr. Yunupingu gaining control of the camera and removing the film before returning the camera to Mr. McRostie.

From the evidence the magistrate was satisfied beyond reasonable doubt that (1) the thirteen clans in east Arnhem Land are subject to the operation of Yolngu law on their lands. That law is real and governs the life of

Nicolas Peterson

Aboriginal people in and on their own clan lands; (2) the senior elder of a clan has the responsibility to protect the land which his clan owns; (3) it is wrong for a stranger to come into or onto Yolngu land without permission of the senior elder; (4) it is wrong for a person to take photographs of Yolngu land for commercial purposes, without permission; and (5) if a stranger trespasses or takes photographs for a commercial purpose without permission, he is expected to expiate his wrongdoing. The magistrate dismissed the charges.[4]

The incident in the Victoria desert is a long way from that in Arnhem Land in both space and time, and it stands in marked contrast. In that incident a picture was taken of a naked child who was caught and held against her will and then made to stand before the camera, the ultimate subject of the colonial gaze. No consent to taking the photograph was sought from either the girl or any adult related to her, and the members of the expedition felt free to physically restrain her in front of the camera. Given that the camera and photograph were entirely unknown to the people of the area at that time, informed consent would have been impossible to secure. However, it is interesting that the expedition photographer took a number of other photographs of Aboriginal people, from the same area, where the people clearly cooperated with him and where the expedition narrative makes clear that they also allowed him to measure and examine them. This may have been seen as part of the reciprocity for the food and tobacco that seem to have been given to most groups encountered (Helms 1896, 296–97).

In the second incident two naked children and a man went willingly before the camera, but the image was taken without consent from the person on whose land the people stood, and the image was immediately destroyed. The full strength of Australian law came down on the side of the Aboriginal protagonist's rights to control image making according to his own customary practices. This was in a context where many Aboriginal people own their own cameras and are great takers and consumers of photographs.

The 1840s to the 1920s

It is a commonplace that ethnographic photography in the colonial period encodes power relations, and that Aboriginal people were not only subjects of but also were subjected to the camera. However until the arrival of the pocket Kodak camera in Australia in 1895, following the invention of roll film in 1888, photography in the studio was much easier than it was outdoors, and the snapshot was not yet a real possibility (see Davies and Stanbury 1985, 1; Willis 1988, 126). Any photographic encounter required a significant level of cooperation from the Aboriginal people concerned, except in special circumstances such as the Elder Expedition photograph or in cases of pictures taken of people in custody of one sort or another. Setting up was often an elaborate procedure, and exposure times in the early years of photography were relatively protracted, which resulted in the need for people to pose for the camera, even if this only meant standing still in front of it. Aboriginal people must have had a wide range of reasons for cooperating, including fear, a sense of obligation, and inducement.

Surprisingly, there is evidence of the circumstances in which some of the very first photographs of Aboriginal people were taken. Douglas Kilburn established Melbourne's first permanent photographic studio in 1847 (Willis 1988, 9; Davies and Stanbury 1985, 186), and he took a number of daguerreotypes of Aboriginal people (fig. 2). An account in the *Illustrated London News* on 26 January 1850, about photographs Kilburn must have taken before 1848, carried the following story:

> It appears that Mr Kilburn, the brother of the eminent Photographer, of Regent-street, has long resided in Australia, and felt anxious to portray the curious race of Aborigines by aid of the Daguerreotype. Mr. Kilburn had much difficulty in prevailing upon any individual to sit, from some superstitious fear that they possess, imagining that it would subject them to some misfortune.[5] He lost no opportunity in persuading them, by small bribes, when they wandered into Port Phillip, usually for the purposes of begging; but, in return, they appeared always willing to render any assistance in chopping wood, &c. At length, Mr. Kilburn succeeded, and the result is here presented to the reader. (53)

Two features, in particular, of nineteenth-century photography encode the asymmetrical and racialized power relations between photographers and their Aboriginal subjects—features that clearly facilitated the taking of photographs even though, of course, some level of cooperation was necessary. The more common feature is encoded in the line-up genre in which the occupants of a hut, or a group of huts, are lined up in front of the hut(s) in team-like fashion (fig. 3). These photographs had to have been organized, and it can be assumed that in most cases they were organized by the photographer. The other way such power relations were encoded was in women's turned-down dress tops to reveal the breasts (fig. 4). The some-

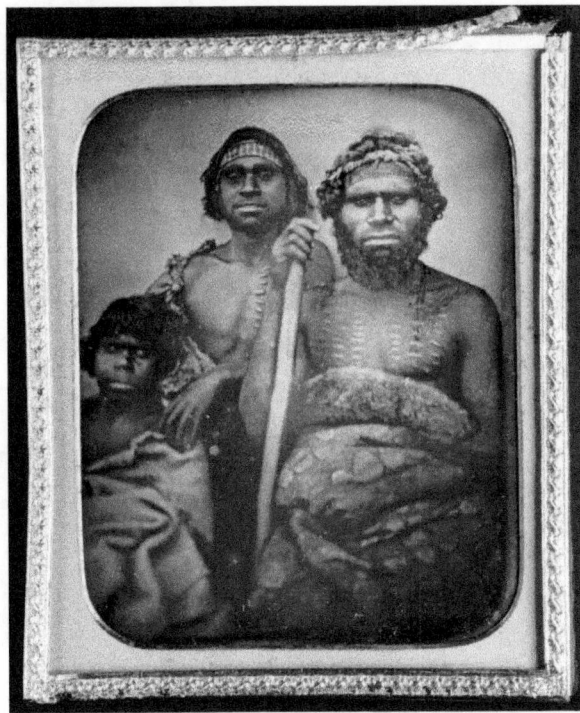

2. A group
of Victorian
Aborigines.
Photo by
Douglas T.
Kilburn c.1847.
Courtesy of the
National Gallery
of Victoria.

what puzzling feature of these photographs was that the photographers often make no attempt to hide the fact that they had asked the people to take their tops off, because the tops frequently simply hang down, carelessly, around their waist. How the women felt about removing their tops and whether they were paid to do so presumably would have varied greatly from situation to situation, but what is evident is that Aboriginal women certainly did not always accede to requests to pose in states of undress.

Frank Gillen, the post and telegraph stationmaster at Alice Springs in the 1890s was also the subprotector of Aborigines, and he had a deep interest in and knowledge of central Australian Aboriginal life. When Baldwin Spencer, professor of zoology at the University of Melbourne, visited Alice Springs in 1894 they formed a strong friendship and collaborative anthropological partnership that lasted until Gillen's death in 1912. On 20 December 1895 Gillen described in a letter to Spencer the following experience:

> Your parcel of tobacco was duly conveyed to old Poll whom it has utterly demoralised. She bids me Yabba, "Thank you long Puff-fessa, me big fellow look out longa rat and all about lizard by and bye long cold weather." I hoped

The Changing Photographic Contract

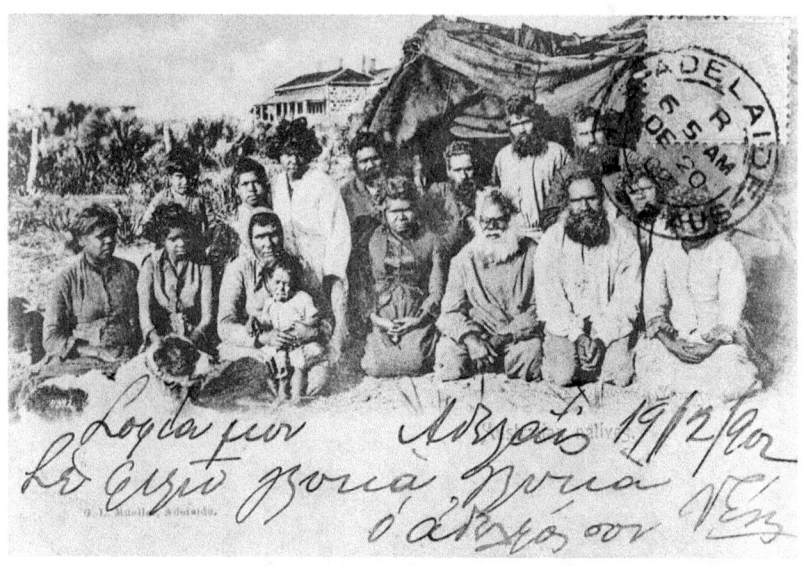

3. A typical line-up photograph, on a postcard published by G. Muller of Adelaide. It was posted on 20 December 1902 and addressed to Egypt.

4. A typical turned-down-top photograph. Courtesy of Ron Blum.

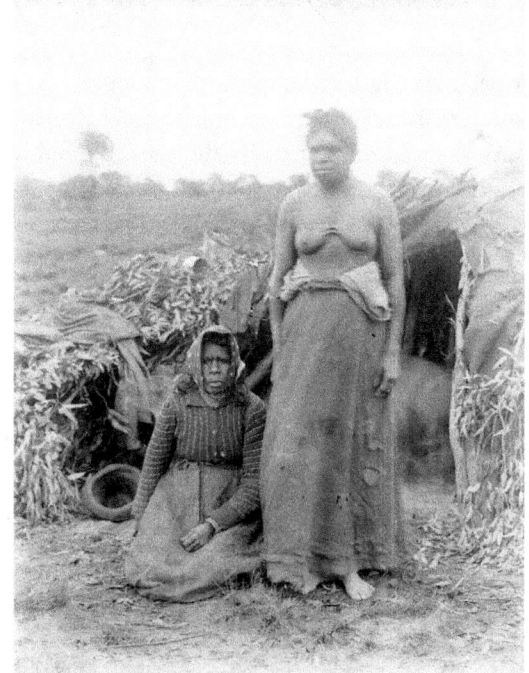

to send you a photo of her au naturel by this mail but when, after handing her your tobacco, I approached her on the subject with exceeding delicacy, she gave me a look which I shall never forget and scathingly remarked, "You all same Euro, you canta shame! You no big fellow master! You piccaninny master." The emphasis on the piccaninny was something to remember for ones lifetime. Since then she reverted to the subject to tell me that, "That one big fellow master Puff fessa no yabba like it that him no poto-grafum, poto-grafum, poto-grafum lubra [Aboriginal woman] all day. Very good long bushie lubra, no good longa station lubra" and in a final burst of indignation she wound up saying, "No good no good potografum lubra cock!" (Mulvaney, Morphy, and Petch 1997, 89–90)

In Gillen Poll was dealing with one of the most sympathetic and amenable of Europeans, and one who would quickly heed her refusal, but nonetheless the event provides evidence of the kind of complex negotiations that lie behind many photographs. Ramsay Smith also provides evidence on the same issue:

For certain anthropological purposes, especially connected with the subject of body markings, we wish to have photographs of some of the dark ladies, beauties and others, in fewer habiliments than are usually considered fashionable; but we immediately encounter difficulties. Argument, entreaty, pecuniary or narcotic inducements are all so much waste matter or ineffective energy. Then by patient inquiry we discover the reason. The women are afraid they will be laughed at by others of their tribe; and [they] . . . cannot stand ridicule. After this the way is clear. Two will always agree to come to be taken. Neither will split on the other without the other being able to say "You're another." (1924, 133–34)

Another domain where the colonial camera was persistent in its intrusion, clearly against the desires of Aboriginal people (although the evidence for reluctance is not encoded in the photographs), was in the sphere of religious activity. It is in this sphere that people with anthropological interests have been most deeply implicated. In the letter from Gillen quoted above, he reports people's reluctance to have photographs taken of the enactment of a form of sorcery: "I am sending you a parcel of photos by this mail including set of Kurdaitcha pictures also set of Illapurrinja (lubra Kurdaitcha) for description of which see notes. . . . I had great difficulty in procuring the Kurdaitcha pictures and greater still in getting the Illapurrinja. On the whole I flatter myself I have done a good deal of useful work since last mail" (Mulvaney, Morphy, and Petch 1997, 90). Interestingly Charles Kerry, photographer and owner of a major studio in Sydney that published

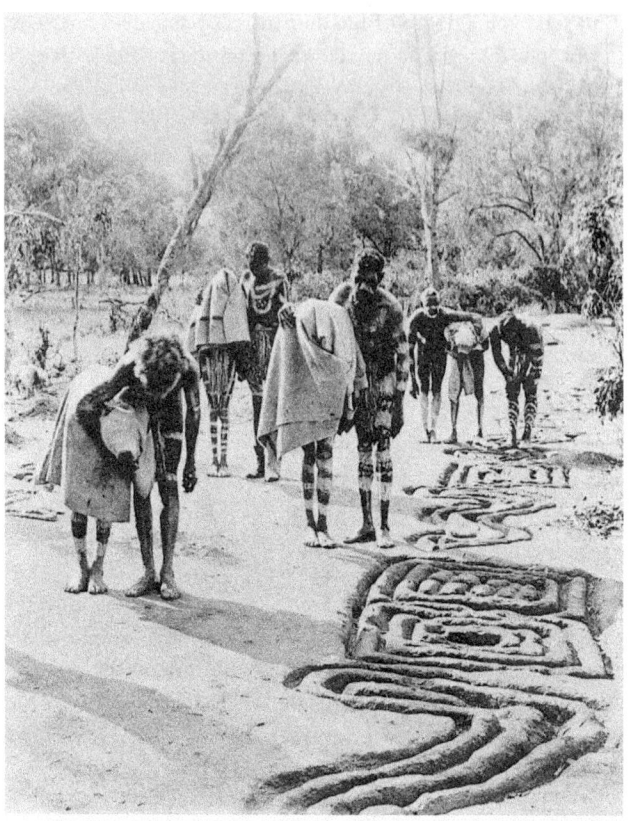

BORA CEREMONY.
Series 5—Australian Aboriginals.

Kerry (Copyright) Sydney.

5. One of the images Kerry took at the bora ceremony in
central northern New South Wales, published as a postcard
that circulated in the first decade of the twentieth century.

many postcards as well as other commercial images, was experiencing the
same difficulties photographing an initiation ceremony in north-central
New South Wales in 1898, 1,500 km to the southeast of Alice Springs (fig. 5):

> The photographs of an Aboriginal Bora Ceremony which I have forwarded
> to the Royal Society form part of a series secured by me in the Winter of
> 1898, locality Lower Macquarie River, N.S.W. I was indebted to Mr. F. Hill,
> the owner of the adjoining station "Quambone," for the privilege of being
> present on the occasion. Many of the natives were in his employ, and all
> were under heavy obligations to him for protection and kindness extend-

Nicolas Peterson

ing over many years. He was probably the only white man who could have both gained entrance to the Bora ground and introduced a friend. Enormous difficulties, however, had to be overcome to break down the prejudice against allowing a white man to see this secret ceremony, and even when successful in gaining admittance to the scene of operations we were frequently requested, sometimes ordered, to leave again. . . . Such information as I could glean from an interpreter present, also appeared to have very little bearing on the ceremony, and the final impression I gathered was that I was being wilfully misled, or else that the ceremony itself was almost meaningless. (1899, xxvii–xxviii)

The ethical position of missionary Siebert in his photographic endeavors seems even more problematic: "It was only after I had used all manner of subterfuge that I was able to get . . . [the] holy of holies of the magical dance onto my photographic plate" (see Swain 1993, 227). Whatever the reasons the photographers had for insisting on taking images of women bare breasted or of lining people up, the taking of images of ceremonial activity, particularly secret ceremonial activity, was usually justified on scientific grounds, as Gillen's letter suggests.

The grounds for the Aboriginal people's objection to the taking of these kinds of ceremonial photographs are not always entirely clear and could well be different in each case. In particular it is not clear whether the issue was the taking of a photograph in the first place or the concern about its use subsequently. There is a prima facie reason to suppose that it was the latter issue that was of major concern. This is not only because in many cases the photographers had already seen what it was that they wanted to photograph, but more fundamentally because of common attitudes about knowledge among Aboriginal people.

Knowledge, particularly knowledge related to religious matters, is not common property in Aboriginal societies but rather is highly controlled, particularly by the senior members of a clan or group. Seeing and knowing about an object or performance does not authorize a person to speak to others about it: the information is only for their own benefit and only those acknowledged as the rightful controllers of the knowledge can disseminate it to others. This has often been, I believe, a source of misunderstanding between those Aboriginal people who have allowed photographers to photograph secret objects or performances and those people taking the photographs in the past. Aboriginal people have probably believed that at least those photographers who know something about their way of life will treat the photographs as purely for private consumption.[6]

The Changing Photographic Contract

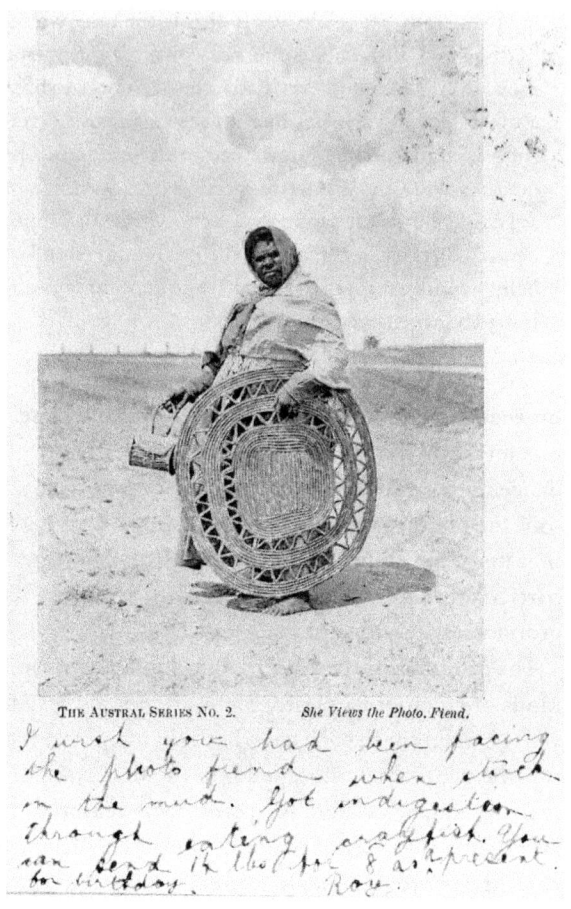

THE AUSTRAL SERIES No. 2.   *She Views the Photo. Fiend.*

I wish you had been facing the photo fiend when stuck in the mud. Got indigestion through eating crayfish. You can send Ih the[?] 8 as present for birthday.   Roy.

6. "She Views the Photo. Fiend." A postcard in the
Austral Series no. 2, posted in the first decade of the
twentieth century.

Undoubtedly Aboriginal people were under considerable pressure to be photographed, especially at the turn of the century when photographic technology had improved. An indication of this pressure is encapsulated in an early-twentieth-century postcard caption: "She Views the Photo. Fiend" (fig. 6). The postcard shows a woman holding a large mat and a basket made by her, and she stares at the camera with a quizzical, if not hostile, look.[7] The caption makes it clear that the photographer is a highly enthusiastic devotee of photography, and further suggests that he may not have sought permission to take the image (although the stationary posture

Nicolas Peterson

and the orientation of the body, so that the sun falls on the face, makes this unlikely). If the photographer did pose the subject then the implication of the caption would be that only somebody addicted to photography would bother to have taken this image. Perhaps both implications might be picked up by viewers. The image and caption elicited an interesting response from one viewer, a man writing to an unmarried woman: "I wish you had been facing the photo fiend when stuck in the mud. . . ." The comment is interesting in that it shows a certain empathy with the Aboriginal woman in the image—I wish you too had been caught in an awkward position—suggesting that the sender was responding to the look on the face.

Overall, it can be said that photographers in this period generally had easy access to Aboriginal subjects. For the most part the Aboriginal people would have been shielded from knowledge of the circulation of the images taken, especially when published in books with limited distribution. Most sacred ceremonial photographs were published in such volumes, with the major exception being the leading Sydney commercial photographer Charles Kerry's set of New South Wales *bora* photographs, which circulated widely as postcards (although whether they found their way to the Quambone population is not known).

The 1920s to 1971

The conditions of access to Aboriginal people for professional photographers began to change in the 1920s with the growth of the reserve system. Aboriginal people in settled Australia were in many places removed to reserves, and because of this relocation they became less easy to photograph, not only because the reserves were often out of the way but also because permission to visit them had to be sought from the superintendents of the reserves. More generally, with the demise of the social-evolutionary framework in academic circles there was much less interest in Aboriginal people. Further, for reasons that Pinney (1992, 81–82) discusses, photographs largely disappeared from monographs in this period.[8]

While there were plenty of people who took photographs of Aboriginal people, the majority were not commercial photographers but people engaged in anthropology, such as Donald Thomson and Charles Mountford, or those who were doing missionary work—both professions with privileged access to Aboriginal communities.[9] Although much of this photographic work circulated through academic journals and monographs, some of it was published in widely circulated magazines (for example, Thomson in the *Illustrated London News*, and both Thomson and Mountford in *National Geographic*) or in popular books.[10]

The assimilation policy acted as a further restraint on commercial photography in the immediate postwar period, as bureaucrats were often suspicious of photographers documenting conditions that were an embarrassment to the government or mission body administering the village on the government's behalf. A case in point was the Warburton Range controversy involving the poor living conditions of desert Aboriginal people in Western Australia (for example, see Grayden 1957, 22). The freelance photographers who were given access were those who by the nature of their interests were not likely to cause problems, such as people working in a "before it is too late" documentary mode, such as Axel Poignant (e.g., see A. Poignant 1957 and R. Poignant 1996).[11]

These trends affected publicly available images quite dramatically, as the range of postcards from this period demonstrates,[12] and the number of images declined substantially. Many of the photos that were available were recycled images obtained from museums or state libraries,[13] drawn caricatures of traditional life, or posed images by professional photographers showing activities such as fire lighting or spear throwing with the mainly male subjects in loincloths. The line-up photograph in front of impoverished self-improvized dwellings had virtually disappeared.

The physical and cultural gulf between settled and remote Australia still protected anthropologists and others from facing the issues related to the circulation of images (for example, Simpson 1951),[14] and they continued publishing photographs of secret ceremonial activity, largely in ethnographies and books. Such books were, for the most part, too expensive and largely irrelevant to people who could not read, and the few that did find their way north were usually in the hands of people more or less sensitive to the problems surrounding the photographs in them.[15] Very few restricted images found their way onto postcards because commercial photographers rarely had time to build up the links that would allow them to attend the restricted ceremonies.[16]

Films were the first images to reach remote Aboriginal communities and create major concern among the people there. Almost universally in remote Aboriginal communities during the 1960s and 1970s there was a Friday or Saturday evening film show attended by almost everybody. Film programs were put together by the national film lending library in Canberra and normally included a short film (often a documentary) along with

Nicolas Peterson

a popular feature film, and these programs then circulated from community to community. The two documentary films that caused the first major consternation in the early 1960s were made by David Attenborough—*Artists of Arnhem Land* and *Desert Gods*—both of which included restricted ritual sequences (see Attenborough 1963). Presumably the films were included in the programs for Aboriginal communities because the people in Canberra thought they would be of local interest.

In 1964 the Australian Institute of Aboriginal Studies, as it was then called, embarked on a major ethnographic filmmaking program of recording men's restricted rituals in the belief that the rituals were rapidly disappearing. By 1965 the Institute had its own film unit virtually dedicated to this purpose, which during the next four years produced over a dozen films of men's restricted ceremonies. By 1967 questions began to emerge about the distribution and circulation of these films, but still at this stage it was agreed with the participants in the films that as long as they were not shown in remote Australia they could be shown to anthropological audiences in the south (see Bryson 2002).[17]

The Institute's film director's views on the circulation of these films reflected the older attitudes: the Institute was an academic research body dedicated to the values of science. By restricting the distribution of these extremely interesting and important ethnographic documents the Institute was elevating the narrow ethic of tribal law above the larger values to which the Institute was, by definition, committed (see fig. 7) (Sandall 1976).[18]

However, in 1969 the Institute began to change to a much more restrictive policy on the use and distribution of ceremonial films made by its film unit, and it eventually adopted a buy-back policy in the 1970s. The audience issues raised by this filming program and the movement to restrict their distribution and circulation prefigured many of the changes that were to take place regarding still photographs.

The transition taking place at this time is clearly captured in a paper published by Catherine Ellis (1970) on the role of the ethnomusicologist in the study of desert women's ceremonies. The paper includes eight photographs relating to the ceremonies, each of which has printed on the actual image a copyright symbol and the sentence, "The taking of even one copy of this photograph is strictly forbidden." This clearly recognizes that even the obscure and specialist nature of the journal in which the paper was published, *Miscellanea Musicologica*, might no longer keep the images circulating in the academic domain. Nevertheless the advancement of knowl-

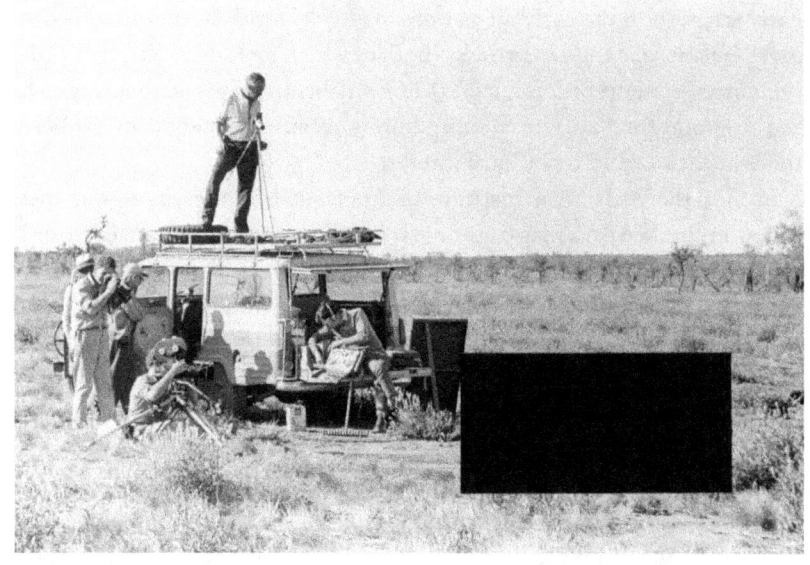

7. The scientific gaze. The film unit of the Australian Institute of Aboriginal Studies (as it was then) at work documenting a restricted men's ceremony in central Australia in 1966. Photo by Nicolas Peterson.

edge, and possibly of career, still justified their inclusion, despite the clear awareness of possible Aboriginal concerns. On the penultimate page of this long paper the following statement appears: "ATTENTION FIELD WORK-ERS: Great offence can be caused if this material is shown to tribal Aboriginal people. The author strongly requests in the interests of further research that this not be done" (207).

1971 to the Present

Although Aboriginal people achieved the full political rights of citizenship by the early 1960s in most states, this had little immediate effect on the kinds of commercial photographs in circulation. The reason for this remained the remote location of north Australia, where the so-called traditionally oriented people lived—those who had been the main subject of photographic interest from the 1920s onward. Until the election of the Whitlam Labor government in 1972, very few Aboriginal people from re-

Nicolas Peterson

mote Australia visited the southern part of the continent; indeed, relatively few even got to leave their communities to visit local regional centers because of limited access to transport, lack of money, and bureaucratic controls. However, because of the explosion of funds available in Aboriginal affairs following the election of the Labor government and the great emphasis it placed on consultation and the establishment of many new Aboriginal organizations, people from remote Australia suddenly started to travel in considerable numbers to the major urban centers and to establish networks with the Aboriginal activists there. In the climate of political activism from the late 1960s onward some of these urban people took up the issue of the circulation of restricted images.

The 1970s saw two defining events in this respect. The most crucial, because it marked an absolute watershed in anthropological use of photography, was the Yiwara affair. In 1969 an archaeologist published a very well-written, popular book, *Yiwara: Foragers of the Australian Desert* (Gould 1969), about the Aboriginal people of the Warburton area. Aimed at an audience of upper-secondary students and first-year undergraduates, it found its way into a number of school libraries. The cover showed a head-and-shoulders portrait of an Aboriginal woman from Warburton.[19] It appears that around 15 May 1971, an Aboriginal schoolgirl from the town of Laverton (the regional center for Warburton) who had been on a school trip to Perth returned home with a copy of the book, which had attracted her attention because the woman on the cover was a close relative. She had shown the book to her father who became very angry because eleven of the fifty-two photographs showed restricted ceremonial objects and activities. Moreover, it was rumored that there was a threat to the young girl's life because she had seen these images.[20]

The subsequent events and the long-term ramifications of the affair were complex, but the immediate formal result was that there was an embargo on permits for researchers who wanted to work in Western Australian communities. A change was also made to the research permit granting system so that instead of the decision being made solely by bureaucrats in the Department of Native Welfare, the Aboriginal community concerned also would be involved. This move galvanized the anthropological world, and the Australian Institute of Aboriginal Studies called a major conference, "The Aborigines and the Anthropologists: Problems of Field Access," to be held 9–10 August 1971, at which the federal minister responsible for Aboriginal matters was present, along with forty non-Aboriginal academics. Among the six resolutions passed at the conference was the following: "That this Conference recommends to the AIAS Council that it revise its 'Code to Fieldworkers,' taking into account the need for added comment and direction upon the collection and publication of material, including photographs, made available in confidence to a research worker, or of data of a secret sacred character." A second recommendation seems almost prophetic, given the Yunupingu case mentioned at the outset, although this is accidental because native title did not exist at that period, nor at the time did it ever seem likely that it would: "That while recognizing the wish of Aborigines to use the permit system to protect their privacy this Conference urges that a more satisfactory protection of Aboriginal privacy will come from the holding of titles to land by Aborigines."[21]

The slow grappling with the full ramifications of these issues is revealed in a publisher's note placed opposite the title page of a 1973 institute publication on eastern Arnhem Land, titled *Australian Aboriginal Bark Paintings and Their Mythological Interpretation* (Groger-Wurm 1973), which included many photographs of paintings and much restricted information on sites and myths:

Publisher's note
Readers are asked to cooperate with a specific condition placed on secret/ sacred material in this book by Aboriginal men and/or women. All knowledge relating to these rituals (sites) is normally confined to the men and/or women who have been inducted into them. Many Aborigines are eager to have the material recorded and published as a matter of permanent record, but it is necessary to handle it with great discretion. Because much of this material is secret/sacred it may cause great distress if it is discussed with any Aborigines before it has been established that he has the correct standing in his society and is willing to participate in discussion.

This was the Institute on the cusp of balancing its image of itself as a scientific research institute while at the same time taking seriously Aboriginal concerns about image circulation. The situation was all the more confusing because it was not a matter of simply showing images of restricted ceremonial activity or even of the key sacred objects but rather photographs of paintings juxtaposed with text about their deeper meanings.[22]

The second defining event secured a more or less complete transition to a virtual ban on all publication of images of a restricted nature.[23] In 1976 the Pitjantjatjara Council sought an interlocutory injunction against both anthropologist Charles Mountford and Rigby, the publisher of Mountford's

Nomads of the Australian Desert, which included a number of images of restricted places, objects, and activities taken in the 1930s and 1940s. It was
argued that the Aboriginal people who had allowed him to take photographs of secret objects and sites had only done so in confidence, and that
publication amounted to a breach of that confidence.

Compensation by way of monetary damages was seen to be inappropriate, and an interlocutory injunction restraining publication and distribution of the book in the Northern Territory was deemed more appropriate.
This led to the book being withdrawn from publication (see also *Pitjantjatjara Council and Peter Nganingu v. John Lowe and Lyn Bender,* in McCorquodale
1987, 275).[24]

Concomitant with these changes was the beginning of a move in the
opposite direction. As Aboriginal people became more familiar with photography and started buying the new inexpensive cameras and taking their
own photographs, the widespread aversion to seeing pictures of the dead,
especially the recently dead, started to change in some areas.[25] Warnings,
similar in form to the publisher's note above but in regard to people being
portrayed who might be dead, started to appear at the front of films and
in the more profusely illustrated books.[26] While attitudes to images of deceased people, particularly those recently deceased, are still variable, in
many areas pictures of such relatives are eagerly sought from anthropologists and others. As yet, however, Aboriginal people do not seem to be following the common practice of the Torres Strait Islanders of encapsulating
a photographic portrait in a transparent capsule on grave headstones.

Conclusion

Since the mid-1970s Aboriginal people have gained a great degree of control over the reproduction of photographic images that involve them. The
highwater mark of this control was the Australian Institute of Aboriginal
and Torres Strait Islander Studies' bicentennial volume, *After Two Hundred
Years: Photographic Essays of Aboriginal and Islander Australia today* (Taylor 1988),
in which Aboriginal communities both negotiated the terms on which the
photographers involved in the project entered their communities and participated in selecting and captioning the images in the volume. The Institute also put out a primer for the photographers involved in the project
concerning restrictions on taking photographs in Aboriginal communities
(Michaels 1994). Although it was the events outlined above that brought

the ethical issues of the photographic contract to the fore and changed the practice of anthropologists and others, it is land rights, as the Institute conference foresaw, that has given Aboriginal people real control.

A case in point is the immediate consequence of the handover to the Pitjantjatjara in October 1985 of Uluru (Ayers Rock), one of the major tourist sites in the country, thereby giving Aboriginal people a majority on the management board of this national park. Among the changes was the erection of the following notice:

PHOTOGRAPHS
Traditional owners request that you respect their customs & refrain from photographing local Aboriginal people.
Having one's photograph taken is considered culturally inappropriate as the image captured on film, believed to be part of one's spirit, is removed from that persons control forever.
Thank you for your co-operation. (photo in *Weekend Australian Magazine*, 18–19 October 1986, 3)

Ironically the photograph adjacent to the image of the notice in the *Weekend Australian* was of a Pitjantjatjara man, Tony Tjamiwa, who was interviewed for the article and apparently allowed his photograph to be taken. This inconsistency suggests that the writer of the notice had some difficulty articulating the grounds on which Aboriginal people objected to having their photograph taken. Although fear of being photographed has, as indicated above, been present since photography began in Australia, and there are a number of cases reported where it was seen as soul theft or the like, there are good grounds now for being skeptical of this reason for the objection to having a photograph taken. Apart from anything else Aboriginal people of the area have had their photographs taken for many years and, in the past, numbers of them have negotiated for payment with tourists who wanted to take their photograph. Many Aboriginal people now have cameras, and old and new photographs are much valued.

The difficulties around Uluru are that it is sold as a tourist destination in which Aboriginal culture features strongly and it is an attraction to tourists. Understandably, tourists are keen to have photographs of Aboriginal people in keeping with the overall climate of commercialization of their culture, and they tend to take photographs of Aboriginal people unasked. In part this may be due to different understandings of what is public and what is private space. Although Uluru is definitely public space from a non-

Nicolas Peterson

Aboriginal point of view, from an Aboriginal point of view it is clearly seen as an Aboriginal space in which Europeans are outsiders. As such it is not hard to imagine that Aboriginal people feel that the behavior of non-Aboriginal people should be circumspect and that permission should be asked by people wishing to take their photograph.

There are situations that facilitate photographing people with whom one does not have a personal relationship. Principal among these is being outdoors in a public place where a formal or informal performance, activity, festive occasion, or demonstration is going on. Thus if Aboriginal people are dancing or demonstrating some technique or aspect of their material culture at a tourist destination or public gathering, photographing them unasked is usually unproblematic, and even photographing those people observing the performance is usually achieved without difficulty because observation and photography are components of the situation—indeed, an audience is usually required. As Henderson (1988, 97–98) says in her discussion of access and consent in photography in public places, as a person's activity becomes less focused and more personal so it becomes more private even in a public space, and the pressure to secure consent becomes stronger. People generally do not like being singled out, especially when there is no clear reason why.

Photographing children is an exception to these constraints (fig. 8). Children are less fully cultural or social than adults, and as such are seen and treated as moral juniors. Parents and other adults can give consent to them being photographed, even against their will. Commonly, however, they are willing collaborators with the camera, and it is a great deal easier to get spontaneous images of them because, depending on age, they are usually less self-conscious about their appearance and, as Henderson says, "less likely to anticipate the 'possible horrors' of photographs as they might appear in publication" (1988, 98). Further, such images can often have a universal appeal. Noel Wallace, who with his wife, Phyl, published a photographic book on Pitjantjatjara children, has this to say:

> Photographing the Pitjantjatjara children is a pleasant task, but not without its own peculiar "occupational hazards." The more sophisticated children, who know about cameras, line up and display toothy smiles as soon as they see one appear; the less sophisticated, with the natural curiosity of children everywhere, want to see what you are doing—with the result that the scene in the viewing screen disappears, and a single, very out-of-focus eye takes its place—or you find three or four little tousled heads all vying with each

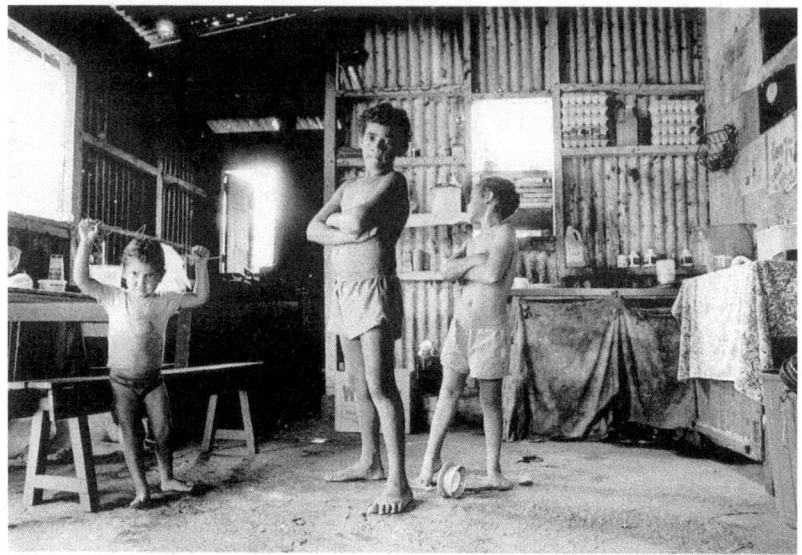

8. A good example of children being used to mediate photographic access to areas where living conditions are poor, and which the adult residents do not necessarily want to be associated with in a public way. The image also makes a political point about the conditions in which Aboriginal children are growing up. Courtesy of the Australian Institute of Aboriginal and Torres Strait Islander Studies.

other, and the photographer, to look into the top of the camera—and all the children have left the picture that you were going to take and are now behind you!

However, the universal technique applies in the Musgrave Ranges, like any other place where there are children—become part of the scenery by always being there and they become engrossed in what they are doing and no longer notice you, or the camera.

I have shown these children as they really are, some dressed, some naked; not made more photogenic or "cute" by asking them to remove their sometimes tattered clothes.

May the reader share our enjoyment of these delightful children. (1968, 6)

Aboriginal adults can relieve the pressure that they are under to be photographed by agreeing, or not objecting, to their children being photographed, thus diverting the photographer's interest.

This trend of the prevalence of images of children in photographic publications on Aboriginal people is widespread and can be seen in the

Nicolas Peterson

recent work of three freelance photographers: Jon Rhodes's publication on Kiwirrkura (1998); Heide Smith's book on the Tiwi (1990); and Penny Tweedie's book *Spirit of Arnhem Land* (1998), in which the first six images of people (including the cover) are of children. Such images are also seen in the posthumous publication of a selection of Donald Thomson's photographs, titled *Children of the Wilderness* (1983).

Such has been the opposition of adults to photography outside of performance, activity, and demonstration that for a ten-year period from the late 1980s there were almost no images of people in postcards relating to Aboriginal people.[27] Instead, images of people were replaced with pictures of paintings and artifacts. The occasional images of Aboriginal people were marked by two features: they were nearly always old, recycled photographs, often twenty or more years old; or they were pictures of people performing their culture, such as dancing, lighting fires, or throwing boomerangs. These images are marked by a complete disjuncture with contemporary living conditions or everyday circumstances. As Aboriginal people have secured title to increasing portions of the continent, currently at around 16 percent, it has become a domain in which commercial and other photographers can only operate with difficulty and persistence.

The photojournalist Penny Tweedie, in an interview for the *National Times* issue of 5–11 December 1982, reports that it took her almost three years of "waging a battle with bureaucracy" to secure permission to enter Arnhem Land for a project to produce a photographic book on life in the region. What she does not say is that the bureaucracy was an Aboriginal one, although contradictorily it is often the non-Aboriginal employees of those bureaucracies that are the fierce protectors in cases like this, and the area that she refers to as a reserve controlled by the Department of Welfare had in fact become Aboriginal land in 1977. She comments that "to say one was a photographer was almost to commit a crime. They were so suspicious. Those government organisations that work for and with the Aborigines are so protective that they saw me as just another media person who was going to rip them off" (25).

This trend is not, I think, confined to Australia. Ethnographic films, documentaries, and the media generally have in more recent times allowed their subjects to speak. As a result they are more generally accorded the rights of individuals, including the right to have some say in the capture of their image on film. Increasingly, freelance and other commercial photographers are finding it difficult to take informal pictures of adults in the documentary mode, with the consequence that images of children are proliferating in documentary photography worldwide. There is, no doubt, a certain irony in this increased awareness of image ethics among those with a documentary bent resulting, at the beginning of the twenty-first century, in the depiction of the radical Other as a child.

Notes

I thank David MacDougall, Howard Morphy, and Frances Morphy for their helpful suggestions and comments.

1 The preferred images of this period are typified by those supplied by the Commonwealth government information service or published in the New South Wales Welfare Board's magazine *Dawn/New Dawn*, which are characterized by smiling people, neatly combed hair, and the use of flash.

2 I am indebted to Leslie Devereaux, who provided me with a detailed unpublished analysis of this photograph and its background.

3 Reeves (1998) reproduces the whole of the *Decision of Mr Gilles, SM in R v. Yunupingu* in the Northern Territory's Court of Summary Jurisdiction (ref. no. 9709243). The account here is drawn from the decision.

4 The legal importance of the case was his reason for doing so: it was because he acknowledged that the recognition of native title means that Aboriginal laws and customs in relation to land may be enforced on Aboriginal land, if the people so wish.

5 This is the classically referred to fear of having their spirit stolen or the like. It suggests that even at this early stage Aboriginal people would have had some familiarity with images, presumably because they had to come into the studio to have their photograph taken, and there they were shown photographs, including the ones taken of them. Anthropologists like Baldwin Spencer, and later Donald Thomson, also developed their films in the field and presumably printed some images at the same time. Ramsay Smith is another person who has reported this kind of belief in Australia: "A mother said that if the piccaninny died and the photograph 'lived,' the child would never have any rest or peace" (1924, 133).

6 It would, of course, be fascinating to know what motivations Aboriginal people attributed to Europeans who wanted to photograph them in any particular context, but I have not found evidence about this so far.

7 The caption on a second version of the same photo indicates that the mat and basket were made by her.

8 Compare any of the classic functionalist monographs (e.g., Warner 1937; Kaberry 1939) with books by Spencer and Gillen, for instance.

9 Although Catherine de Lorenzo (1993) has written an unpublished history

of photographic images of Aboriginal people, no detailed analysis has been made of the photographic work of people like Thomson and Mountford or the output of missionaries. The history of the publication of this work is complex, especially because much of it was published long after the images were taken.

10 For example, see the *Illustrated London News*, 23 July 1938, 17 September 1938, 24 September 1938, 15 October 1938, 22 October 1938, 25 February 1939, 15 July 1939, and 12 August 1939, for heavily illustrated articles by Thomson; see *National Geographic*, January 1946, March 1948, and December 1949, for articles by Mountford and Thomson. For a listing of Thomson's other popular pictorial images of Aboriginal people, see Thomson 1972, 33–36.

11 Although many of Axel Poignant's 1952 photographs of Aboriginal people in the Liverpool River area of Arnhem Land have been used in publications by other people, it was not until his wife published a book in the 1990s about taking the photographs back to the people that a representative sample of his superb photos was brought together in one place. But see McCarthy (1957) who was the first to publish a substantial number of Poignant's Aboriginal field photographs.

12 I make this statement on the clear impression gained from examining these images for many years. I have yet to make a formal analysis.

13 For example, see the Australian Museum's republication as postcards of the Dick photographs from northern New South Wales (see McBryde 1985).

14 This book was a reporter's account of the American-Australian Scientific Expedition to Arnhem Land, which was a major anthropological expedition.

15 Often these books were treated by their European owners in a way that was similar to the treatment of restricted sacred objects by Aboriginal people themselves, which was presumably reassuring for them.

16 One exception was a set of postcards circulating in Alice Springs showing a restricted Warlpiri site and men decorated for a ceremony—the same site and ceremony that was featured in David Attenborough's film (see below). It seems that these were from Mountford's photographs.

17 The first anthropologist to be concerned with the issue of showing scientific record films of restricted ceremonial activity to wide audiences was Olive Pink. She made the arrangements for Dr. John Cleland, Dr. Fry, and Charles Mountford to film a Warlpiri increase ceremony at the Granites in 1936, on the condition that the film was not to be shown in public. Mountford promptly breached this condition, and Pink wrote to Cleland in the following terms:

> [I] also have a letter, two in fact, stating that in spite of that definite promise in writing it was later shown in both England and America and worse still [at] Adelaide University Partys [sic].

You will remember that you were then *guests* (!) at my camp to *see* a ceremony arranged for me and paid for by me (the ritual payment)

I invited your party to *see* it. Instead Dr Fry and Mr Mountford *took possession* and both photographed and filmed it. (Naturally I thought only as a record!). Scientists honour. It was a secret ceremony (to which Mountford would not have been admitted!) except for me.

They specially disliked the running about and moving photographs they told me afterwards (Sacrilege!).

Also I have your telegram still, saying your party would not trespass on my research subjects at Granites in 1936.

Yet it did so. . . .

I hope *you* will be responsible that in Mr. Mountford's paper on art (as an *Art Teacher* a particular Study of mine) he does not use *Granites data* to illustrate it. That would be a betrayal of both the natives and of me.

Those drawings and carvings (rock and others) are not art *to them*!!! They are a *secret religion*.

(Miss Olive Pink to Dr John Cleland, 14/12/1938, archives of the South Australian Museum, Adelaide.)

18   These views were first formally expressed by Sandall to the Institute in February 1969 (see Bryson 2002, 44). For a later and somewhat different argument on why early film material on secret ceremonies should be available, see Cantrill and Cantrill 1982.

19   It is a reflection of the growing awareness of photographic ethics that Gould provided the name of the woman on the cover of the book.

20   This is based on a report written for the Department of Native Welfare in Perth by an employee of the department, Malcom Griffiths, in 1971.

21   Letter from AIAS to conference participants, 24/8/1971, AIATSIS correspondence archives, ref. 71/33, AIATSIS, Canberra.

22   The issues here are complex, and there is a great deal more that could be said. For example, in Morphy and Layton 1981 see Morphy's fascinating discussion of how Aboriginal people in eastern Arnhem Land were quite aware of the problem of the public circulation of their restricted religious art (they were producing the images for sale), and how they dealt with this problem. The issue that has taken much longer to address is the circulation of image-free text that deals with restricted materials.

23   This qualification is occasioned by the sad affair of the publication of photographs of restricted men's ceremonies by T. Strehlow in 1978. Driven largely, it seems, by a desire for money, Strehlow sold a number of images to the German magazine *Stern*, which in turn sold them back to *People* magazine in Australia, a very widely circulated and popular weekly pictorial (Kimber 1992, 206). Needless to say, this event caused an enormous outcry.

24 As it happened, the withdrawn copies of the book were destroyed in a fire shortly afterward.

25 In eastern Arnhem Land people may now display, on the coffin, images taken during the deceased's youth. In general, older people and those closely associated with the deceased are not keen to see images of their dead relatives, but usually have no objection to others seeing them privately. Françoise Dussart reports that a Warlpiri woman was not comfortable having deceased people cropped from a photograph of her dancing with them, because it embarrassed her. Presumably this was because the cropped photograph would have reminded her of the context in which the deceased were present. Dussart was interested in the body-painting design the woman was wearing, and the woman agreed could be drawn, but the figure was not to have a face because it might not look like her, and it would be wrong for an unknown person to be wearing that particular design.

26 Today such warnings appear in the front of many publications, particularly those put out by Aboriginal organizations, and often serve a symbolic function as much as a practical one.

27 See note 12.

Christopher Wright

Supple Bodies

THE PAPUA NEW GUINEA PHOTOGRAPHS

OF CAPTAIN FRANCIS R. BARTON,

1899–1907

The photographic collection housed in the basement of the Royal Anthropological Institute (RAI) in London contains more than 1,500 glass
negatives taken in Papua New Guinea by Captain Francis R. Barton between 1899 and 1907. During this period Barton was government secretary,
resident magistrate, and finally administrator of the Territory. He was a
keen and prolific photographer and took hundreds of photographs around
Port Moresby and on his official tours; images through which we can trace
his encounters with diverse Papuan cultures. But he also took a considerable number of overtly staged photographs of young girls, and it is one
of these that I want to consider here. I have chosen to focus on this one
image, with all its attendant "difficulties," in order to raise a series of questions about contemporary critical approaches to such early photographs.
The presence of the photographs as material artifacts housed in the RAI archive allows me to perform this work on them, and it is their history as
artifacts that also concerns me here.

The photograph of a Hula girl called Luikama from the southeast coast
of Papua New Guinea (fig. 1) was taken by Barton in Port Moresby probably sometime between 1904 and 1907, the period during which he developed this particular style of his photographic work. The photograph

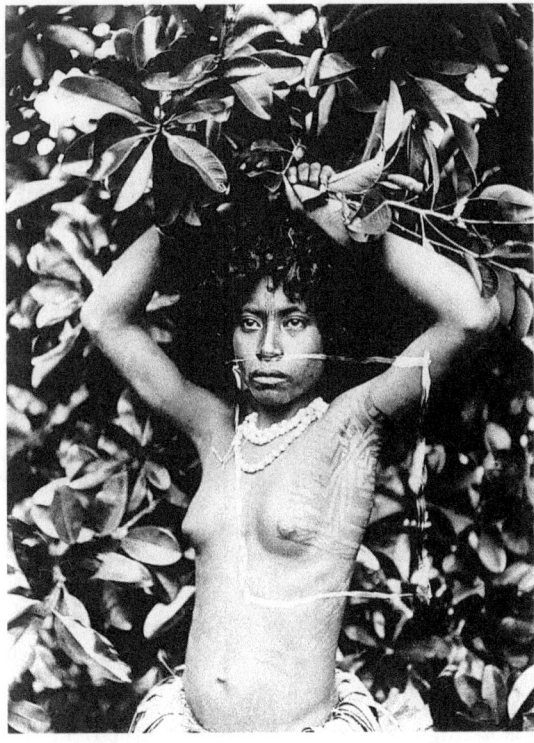

1. A Hula girl
called Luikama,
Port Moresby. Photo
by Francis R. Barton,
probably c.1904–1907.
Courtesy of the Royal
Anthropological
Institute (RAI
no. 20524).

presents a challenge, the hand-drawn box in the center of the photo confronts us directly with Barton's intention(s), and also makes us acutely aware of our own intentions in looking at the photograph. The box has a disturbing tactile quality, and the acts of voyeurism and framing that it signifies can be unsettling, at least to an audience that wants to "understand" the photograph within an anthropological framework; and questions of audience, such as the "us" I have referred to, are vitally important here. The photograph challenges us to create a narrative for it; it suggests that there is a beyond to which it can lead us. But how, and within whose history, can this photograph be inscribed and assimilated, and what is at stake in this process? Through an extended consideration of this one photograph (although bringing in several others as counterpoints) I want to trace some of its multiple histories.

The photograph's sexual content, and intent, is seemingly obvious. Luikama's pose, the decontextualization of her body, her display and circulation as an object—both within the photograph and as a photograph—are all the products of a colonial desire.[1] It is as though Barton were merely performing or reenacting a colonial gaze of which Luikama is the victim. The unequal power relation on which the photograph rests—Barton the colonial official, Luikama the "innocent native"—allows the projection of a stereotype, and the photograph becomes an example of colonial and anthropological surveillance in which Luikama is reduced to an object. In this respect it is perhaps the complicity or contamination of our own sight with Barton's that is potentially unsettling. However, I am wary of how such understandings of the photograph can, if taken on their own, fail to recognize both some of the cross-cultural complexities of the encounter and some of our own assumptions about photographs, particularly those of others.

The photograph was taken, to consider just one aspect of intention, in the name of an ethnographic science. Barton's interest was, at some nominal level at least, in Luikama's tattoos. This is why he drew a frame on the glass negative, isolating her tattooed armpit. Yet, surely this is not the subject of the photograph? Tattoos were frequently represented in late-eighteenth and early-nineteenth-century engravings as disembodied body parts, an array of buttocks, arms, legs, and faces (Thomas 1997, 68), and this fragmentation and objectifying style was continued in later photographic representations of tattoos. But here, the hand-drawn frame within a frame is ambiguous; in isolating and producing the "scientific detail" it simultaneously fetishizes Luikama's body and reveals Barton's intervention. It makes Barton's gaze all the more obvious, and in so doing paradoxically threatens the very aura of science that provided the impetus for its addition. Here ethnography is a pretext, a ruse that allowed Barton to indulge his voyeurism, the referencing of tattooing serving to veil what might otherwise make the photograph less acceptable within the context of ethnographic science. The photograph of Luikama makes apparent an overlapping series of desires involved with looking, collecting, and classifying that were central to processes of colonial appropriation.

This, then, is an initial inscription: Barton's attempt to redeem the photograph for ethnographic science, as though by drawing the box as an afterthought he could somehow transform the glass plate in some alchemical way. Inscriptions like this are performances through which photographs acquire meanings and are embedded in histories. A series of inscriptions, which function as frames or contexts, can be traced through the photograph; from ethnographic science to classical or romantic idealism, and pornography. Hundreds of photographs of naked or seminaked young girls similar to this one of Luikama (although, importantly, minus the hand-

148   *Christopher Wright*

drawn box) were offered for sale as prints in the busy *carte de visite* and cabinet card shops of nineteenth-century London. The photograph seems to move from one site of inscription to another with apparent ease, or to exist simultaneously in several spaces at the same time.

Barton considered himself an amateur anthropologist and was a friend of the prominent British anthropologist Charles G. Seligman, having met him when Seligman visited Papua New Guinea in 1904 as part of the Cooke Daniels Expedition. Barton carried out some field research for Seligman, and the two kept up a written correspondence. In 1910 Barton contributed to Seligman's *The Melanesians of British New Guinea* a chapter on the annual *hiri* trading expedition carried out by the people of Port Moresby. Barton avidly read the work of contemporary anthropologists and quoted A. C. Haddon's advice concerning the desirability of information collected "on the spot" in the introduction to his own article on tattooing (Barton 1918). At some level Barton saw himself as proceeding with a systematic anthropological survey of tattooing, and he was concerned to produce anthropologically sound observations.

Barton also drew lines on bodies as well as on glass negatives (fig. 2).[2] Tattoos presented certain technical difficulties for early photographers in the Pacific, and their lack of definition on dark skin was a problem much commented on. Barton solved this problem by painting over existing tattoos, tracing their exact shapes in his own mixture of soot and oil, to create an artificial contrast more suitable for photographing. However, Seligman (1910, 74) argued that Barton's practice presented a "coarser appearance" than the "really beautiful harmony" that originally existed between the color of the tattoo and that of the skin. Like the hand-drawn box, Barton's overpainting reveals other difficulties, such as the need for some kind of external intervention in order to make things fully visible. Yet his process of reinscription seems confusing here; Barton painstakingly painted over Luikama's tattoos to make them stand out and thus allow their full observation, but he then posed her and composed the photograph in a highly stylized manner, before finally, after the glass negative had been developed, drawing the box to isolate the "scientific detail." It is as if the "focus" of the photograph were not considered sufficient on its own.

Thus the photograph becomes a record of this performance of overpainting; a crystalization of this literally colonizing process of inscription through which Luikama's body is territorialized. However, this reading is to some extent based on a series of assumptions about photography and colonialism through which certain inscriptions are linked to form trajec-

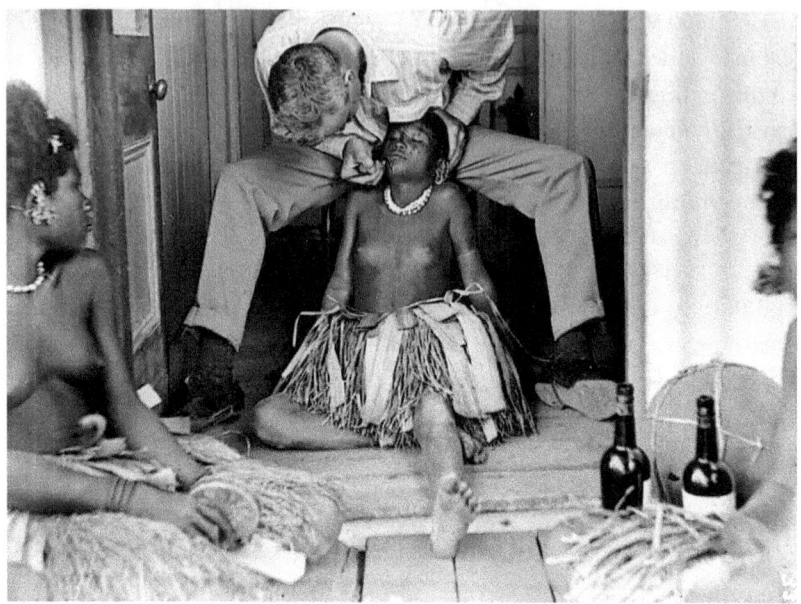

2. Barton painting over a young girl's tattoos, near Government House, Port Moresby. Photo by Guy Manning, c.1899–1907. Courtesy of the State Library of New South Wales (ON 3, box 28, no. 333).

tories: the lines of movement that connect photographs from one context to another, and the inscriptions that form the specific sites that plot trajectories. In the wake of theorists like Michel Foucault and John Tagg, among many others,[3] we have a ready-made interpretive frame for this photograph, one in which a male colonial gaze is implicated in the subjection of other, often female, bodies. Within this frame the focus has been on photography as a carceral technology, a part of the colonial apparatus of surveillance that "imprisons" others by "fixing" them—in an analogy with the chemistry of photography—as particular "types" and as objects for display. Yet there is a sense in which such frames can, if taken on their own, remain largely within a colonial perspective; the emphasis tends to be on the colonial gaze to the exclusion of other histories and perspectives. There are cross-cultural issues of revelation, display, and the construction of individuality at stake in any discussion of this photograph of Luikama, as well as issues of surveillance and the imposition of a colonial power.

One reading of Luikama's tattoos by a Victorian audience, both popular and scientific, would have been as indicators of an assumed "savagery." Tat-

Christopher Wright

toos marked physical and cultural difference, and, like other surface effects such as physical deformities, were frequently understood by some late-nineteenth-century European audiences in terms of their links to a depth, a "primitive" interior that is also revealed in the photograph. Cesar Lombroso, one of the founders of modern criminology, argued in 1911 that the desire to be tattooed was a biological feature of the criminal "type," a kind of genetic disposition that often came along with a passion for other forms of excessive ornamentation, bodily mutilation, strange clothing, and obscure slang (Lombroso, cited in Gell 1993, 12). These dispositions were also considered to be shared by "primitive humanity"—not in the sense that they were similarly regarded as criminals, but that both were considered to be lower on an evolutionary scale than "civilized" society, and thus somehow morally deficient or degraded. Yet we must also remain aware that there were other audiences, such as sailors, soldiers, or those considered part of the Victorian "underworld," to whom tattoos—although not necessarily those of someone like Luikama—indicated a sense of belonging and a positive difference, among a range of other connotations. What is important here is the formation of a group or nexus of related inscriptions—the links that connect various Victorian notions of "savage," "criminal," morally degenerate, and sexually illicit—that cluster around Luikama's tattoos and form one trajectory for the photograph.

Facial and bodily blemishes were frequently edited out of European portrait photographs of the late nineteenth century precisely because it was thought that they too readily revealed inner deficiencies of the self. Through a similar play between surface and depth, nineteenth-century audiences, and indeed contemporary ones, might see Luikama's individuality revealed in the photograph. Although these might be widely divergent notions of individuality, we still tend to make the equation between a photographic portrait and an individual as though they were in some respects equal units. We press the shutter release and capture the individual, and in achieving this act there is a sense in which photography retains some of the combination of technological precision and magic that was established at its inception (Benjamin 1985). The knowledge of Luikama's name certainly encourages a reading of the photograph as a kind of portrait, as though it represents her inner self. The photograph thus becomes a material artifact that in some sense contains, or stands for, her individuality, although here perhaps it is the masking of an individuality that is at stake. We see the stereotype *and* the individual.

For us, life is often seen as an inward depth that can be exteriorized and

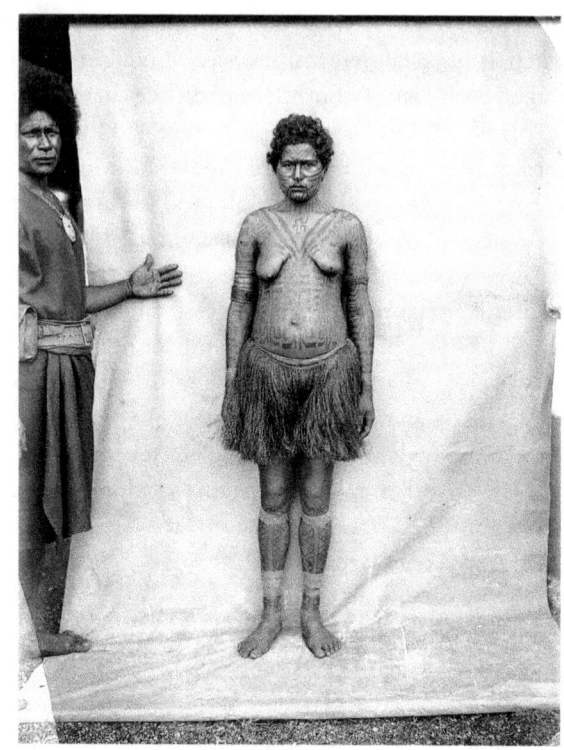

3. A woman from Maiva (west of Port Moresby) with her tattoos overpainted by Barton, with a member of the Armed Native Constabulary. Photo by Francis R. Barton, c.1899–1907. Courtesy of the Royal Anthropological Institute (RAI no. 20318).

expressed in the articulations of the body, in features that belong to an individual. Barton listed the names of some of the hundreds of young girls he photographed, whereas the names of men and women are listed far less frequently, suggesting that he was concerned with capturing their individuality. He considered himself as having a "relationship" of some kind with individual girls, so much so that he wanted to have his own photograph taken with them (Wright 1997). The photograph is a site for the intersection of two, or more, individuals, but not necessarily for their meeting. In this sense photographs resemble Melanesian artifacts, frequently discussed by anthropologists as being the products of relationships between people.

Through these processes of inscription—the literal overpainting, and the cultural and historical stereotyping that also amount to inscriptions— Luikama's body is made to bear a series of signs. Like the bodies arranged and displayed in Barton's anthropometric-style photographs (such as fig. 3), Luikama's body is decontextualized, cut off from one set of social relations,

Christopher Wright

and circulated in a colonial space that makes a territory out of the body. The foliage replaces the white-sheet backdrop of the anthropometric examination and serves to "naturalize" the body at the very moment when it is actually divorced from other contexts. Through the photograph and its space the body is mapped and Luikama is inscribed as "primitive," sexually different, and available as a spectacle. The photograph's space constructs a perspective of examination; Luikama's body, lacking any social context or "background," becomes the sole focus of our attention. In the emphasis placed on "type" Luikama's individuality is denied, and she is made to represent the whole cultural group. Yet there remain unresolved tensions between Barton's relationship with Luikama and his treatment of her as a "type," between her representation within a more aesthetic frame and an objectifying scientific one. In drawing the box it is as though Barton has attempted to transform an aesthetic vision into a scientific one, but in so doing has drawn attention to the processes of inscription involved in both. I want next to consider some Hula processes of inscription.

For the Hula people of Hood Bay east of Port Moresby, and for neighboring south coast Papua New Guinea cultures, Luikama's tattoos signaled a different set of meanings, which included marking her as female, as Hula, and, by the apparent absence of marks on her stomach and upper chest, as currently unmarried. According to Barton's account (1918, 25) the designs on her armpit, called *kadidiha*, were formed as part of the sixth stage of tattooing carried out on young girls. The *kadidiha* marked the end of a first set of tattoos; the second set was begun with the approach of puberty, and culminated in those called *kopa*, inscribed between the navel and the chest just before marriage. There is another photograph of Luikama by Barton that shows that the inside of her upper thighs, *kio gunina*, have been tattooed, which would suggest that she had already begun this second stage. As well as a series of patterns that were required for all young girls, the arrangement of certain tattoo designs also indicated specific clan affiliations and links with female relations.

Barton was interested in discovering the etymological roots of Hula words for various tattoo patterns, but he was not concerned with tracing their links to existing social institutions and relationships, or their functional efficacy as "a linking element in the sequence of social intention, action, and result" (Gell 1993, 3). He treated tattoos solely as signs, and he focused on certain aspects of their representational content with no concern for their practical effects or with the forces that they both draw on

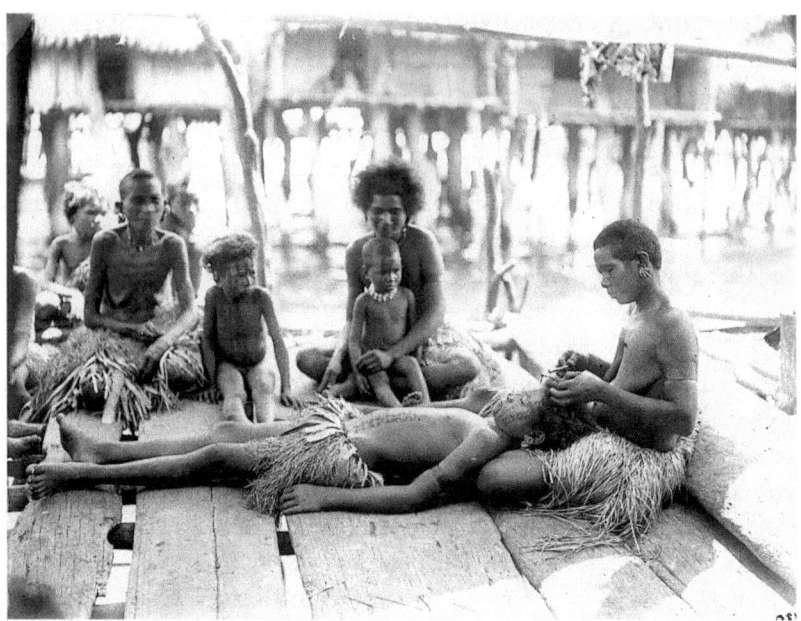

4. A young girl being tattooed in Gaile (Kaile) village (east of Port Moresby). Photo by Francis R. Barton c.1899–1907. Courtesy of the Royal Anthropological Institute (RAI no. 20286).

and create. Yet in approaching tattooing as a form of ornamentation Barton inevitably brought into play a whole series of other inscriptions, including those of the "primitive" and morally illicit.

Writing of tattooing in Polynesia and eastern Melanesia, Alfred Gell has argued that "tattooing institutions . . . helped produce a certain mind-set, a certain frame of social classification, a certain notion of person, self-hood, and empowerment, which was an enabling factor in the reproduction of [the] specific types of social and political regimes" (1993, 3). As well as being directly linked to the processes of reproduction through their connection to life-cycle events such as puberty and marriage, tattoos reproduce a particular type of person. In addition to indicating clan affiliations and relations with living maternal kin, Hula tattoos also signal relations to ancestral spirits, both human and animal. The skin is the site for the demonstration of these relations.

In many south coast Papua New Guinea cultures the tattooing of young girls was a performance carried out in public view, usually by a maternal aunt (fig. 4), although this does not discount the possibility of particu-

Christopher Wright

lar or required audiences, or of potentially different ideas of what consti-
tutes "public view" in Papua New Guinean cultures. There are, for example,
Barton photographs similar to figure 4 that show an audience composed
largely of men. However, Barton's comment that men's knowledge of tattoos and the names of specific patterns was "very imperfect," as well as
the far less frequent tattooing of men,[4] suggest that it was largely a female
form. Comparing the space of this indigenous inscription with that of Barton's site of overpainting (fig. 2) raises fundamental questions of display
and consent.

Tattoos are involved in processes of revelation: they are made to be seen
but also to be hidden. In light of this, the important question is seen by
whom and hidden from whom? Guise, writing in 1899, discusses an important annual Hula celebration in Hood Bay called the *kapa* (1899, 215).[5] During the stage of this festival known as *kuiriga*, young girls who have been
recently tattooed around the lower abdomen are displayed to the gaze of
onlookers by lining up on a ceremonial wooden *dubu* platform. At a given
signal, the young initiates take off their "petticoats" and throw them behind themselves. Guise states that "the girls quite enjoy their position, and
do not show any shame" (216). Guise also notes that the tattooing of the
lower abdomen was considered a necessary factor in sexual attraction, and
he surmises that tattoos are linked to sexuality and reproduction in at least
two ways: first, they are required as an initiation that differentiates a mar-
riageable woman from an unmarriageable girl; and, second, they possess an
erotic charge of their own in the eyes of young men. In terms of the audience for the *kuiriga*, Guise says: "Very few, if any, men seem to care to look
on at the 'ceremony', old women, widows, and married women who have
daughters, constituting the majority of the bystanders: and it is amusing
to hear them pass experienced remarks on the tattooing, and referring to
the days when they joined in the kuiriga. The Government has suppressed
this part, insomuch that no girl is allowed to doff her petticoat" (216).

Tattoos are a permanent mark of the initiates' change of status and their
ability to endure pain. They also represent the inscription of a Hula sexuality, and they may well have indicated a more generalized Hula notion
of becoming properly human. Their importance in these respects is perhaps why early missionaries were so keen to eradicate the practice. Guise's
quote also reveals the colonial government's attitudes to the display of
young bodies. Did the referencing of tattooing and an aura of anthropology allow Barton to circumvent government prescriptions about the
visibility of young girls' bodies?

Supple Bodies

There is a sense in which tattoos are completed in relation to an audience (fig. 5), by being looked at, or by being "seen" to be hidden by a skirt, displayed but not necessarily revealed. Tattoos are processual, not just marking a point in time but forming a part of ongoing, lived relationships. Melanesian initiation is often about the creation of particular types of adults rather than just marking a transition to adulthood, and it is a process that continues throughout a person's lifetime rather than a single event. What is important here is that Hula tattoos were designed for certain audiences and contexts of display.

The photographs that Barton took were themselves caught up in varying contexts of display. Barton took lantern slide copies of many of his photographs with him when he traveled on tours of inspection within Papua New Guinea, and he gave slide shows to large village audiences. Sadly, he did not record local responses to his photographs in any detail, although others have reported the interest with which they were viewed (Lett 1949, 74). There is one photograph of Barton himself in the Royal Anthropological Institute's collection: he is seated in a large wicker chair on the grounds of Government House in Port Moresby, showing an album of his photographs to two young Motu children (Wright 1997). Both of these examples of Barton's activities indicate that he was actively involved in displaying his photographs to Papuan audiences, and the lantern slide shows suggest some kind of shared space of display for the photographs.

On his return to Britain in 1907, however, Barton showed his photographs to a very different audience. He gave at least two lectures at the Royal Anthropological Institute that he illustrated with his own photographs. The area isolated by Barton's secondary framing in the photograph of Luikama was made into a lantern slide, and it was used by him in a lecture on tattooing given at the institute. Furthermore, it was also reproduced in the scientific article on the same subject that he wrote for the Institute's journal, where it is captioned "4.—*Kadidiha* (No.30)" (1918, plate 8). There it is the fragmentation of the body, the isolated detail, that magically transforms the photograph of Luikama into "ethnographic science." This, then, is another of the photograph's trajectories, a movement that links the events of one afternoon in Port Moresby (fig. 6) with the royal institutions and gentlemen's clubs of London, with a group of men sitting in a darkened room watching images projected on a wall. Two connected performances of the photograph: one of its production, the other of its consumption.

A small article in *Popular Science Monthly* in 1899 referred to some of the

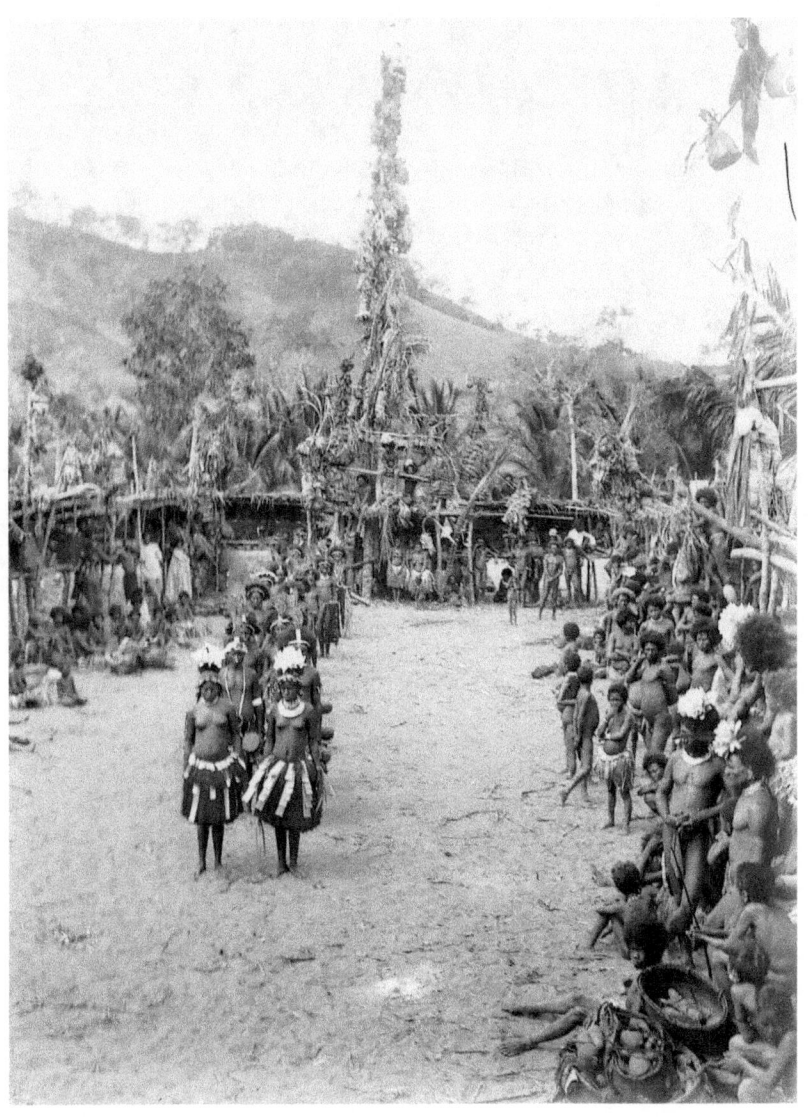

5. Young girls dancing at a feast in Konebada Village, Port Moresby. Photo by
Francis R. Barton, c.1899–1907. Courtesy of the Royal Anthropological Institute
(RAI no. 20637).

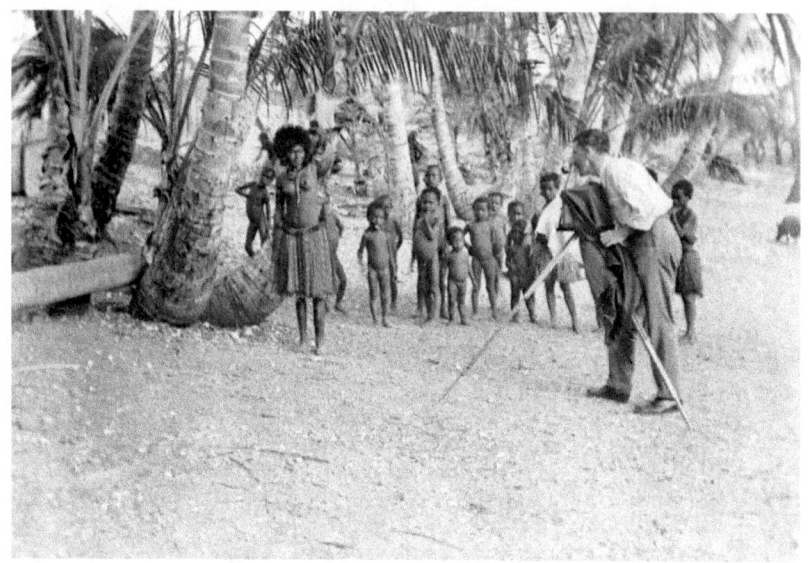

6. Arthur Jewell photographing a young woman in Hanuabada village, Port Moresby. Photo by Guy Manning, c.1899–1907. Courtesy of the State Library of New South Wales (ON 3, box 26, no. 324). Barton himself took scores of photographs of young girls in similar poses.

problems encountered in the production of photographs of Papuan children:

> Many savages dislike to have their pictures taken, some being restrained by motives of superstition; but in New Guinea Professor Semon found being photographed a great joke for all the boys and girls. He had much trouble in isolating a single individual, so as not to get thirty or forty persons into his picture instead of the one he wished to immortalize. "Wishing," he says, "to portray one young girl of uncommonly good looks, I separated her from the rest, gave her a favourable position, and adjusted the lens, surrounded all the while by a crowd of people behind and beside me, the children cheering, the women most ardently attentive, the men benevolently smiling. Evidently my subject was proud of the distinction she enjoyed and the attention vouchsafed her. Quite suddenly, however, this simple savage, untaught as she was and innocent of the laws of reticence and prudishness, became convulsed with shame, covered her eyes with her hands, and valiantly resisted every attempt to make her stand forward as before. At the same time I noticed that the hue of her features changed, the brown of her face became darker and deeper than before, a phenomenon easily explained by the fact of

Christopher Wright

the blood rising into her head. Had she been a brown girl we would have said that she blushed. At all events the physiological process was the same as that which forces us to blush." At another time, when the author had got two little girls into position to be photographed, their mothers came up and forbade his taking them that day, but promised to present them on the morrow. On the next day "both the little angels were solemnly brought to meet us nearly smothered in ornaments, their hair decorated with feathers and combs, their ears with tortoise-shell pieces, their little throats surrounded by plates of mother-of-pearl and chains of dingo teeth, legs and arms hung with rings and shells, teeth, and all sorts of network.... Here, again, one may see that mothers are made of the same stuff all over the world, Papuan mammas being equal to any of our peasant women or fine ladies in the point of vanity as far as concerns their children."[6]

Throughout the latter half of the nineteenth century, photography in Europe developed alongside a new conception of childhood, and the "places" of child and photography were similarly commodified and fetishized. A utopian image of an innocent childhood was linked to a desire to photograph youth before it "slipped away," but conversely the sexuality of childhood was also frequently alluded to. The reading of images of childhood as innocent is partially based on an awareness of the adult sexuality that is missing or latent; a kind of see-sawing occurs between innocence and knowledge. Perception of one value inevitably involves some kind of acknowledgment or recognition of the other.

One notorious Victorian example of photographs that involve this kind of ambiguity are those of young girls taken by the author Lewis Carroll (Charles Dodgson). Some of the girls in these photos were naked, or as Carroll tellingly referred to them, in their "primitive dress" (Carroll, cited in Mavor 1995, 11). Like Barton, Carroll listed the names of the girls in his photos, although he also included their dates of birth as though to authenticate their "girlishness." Further, he was obsessed with the height of the young girls he photographed, and he meticulously recorded the figures in bound volumes and marked off the height of individual girls on the doorframe of his house. Carroll considered height to be the prime indicator of childhood; those under a certain height were children, those above it were not (Smith 1998, 105–8).

Although some of Carroll's photographs were more overtly concerned with sexuality—for example, the orientalist pose of Evelyn Hatch reclining nude—others, such as the 1859 image of Alice Liddell in *The Beggar Maid*, are far more ambiguous in terms of their sexuality. In this photo Alice poses leaning against a moss-covered wall in artfully torn rags that hang off her shoulder, and she stares directly back at the camera. The perspective of Carroll's photograph of Alice is similar to Barton's photograph of Lui-kama; the central focus on the child's body is reinforced by the lack of dis-tracting context. Recent discussion (Mavor 1995) of Carroll's nude photo-graphs has cast his images of clothed young girls in a different light for contemporary audiences, but Tennyson, Britain's poet laureate, declared at the time that the photograph of Alice was the most beautiful he had seen (Higonnet 1998, 125). In his photographic masquerade of Alice as a beggar maid, Carroll inscribes her as a class Other and references the "primitive-ness" of her imaginary status, but her difference is seen to be staged and therefore less threatening. The play between the recognition of her "sav-age" mask with its conflation of the "primitive" and sexually illicit, and the "innocence" that lies behind it, contributes to the ambiguous or latent sexuality of the image.

Recent discussion of Julia Margaret Cameron, a photographer contem-porary with Carroll, has taken an almost opposite trajectory to his. Largely reviled at the time for their "sentimentality," Cameron's deliberately soft-focus photographs of naked children, sometimes as cupids complete with paper wings, have recently been reclaimed as evidence of a feminine aes-thetic and maternal eroticism that provides an alternative to patriarchal sexuality and history (Mavor 1995, 43–69). The latent sexual content that is considered suspicious in photographs of young girls taken by men is seen in a positive light in similar photographs taken by women (Higonnet 1998, 125). The gender of the person taking the photograph becomes of vital importance here; would we be less suspicious if the photograph of Lui-kama had been taken by a woman? Would a woman have taken this kind of photograph? In looking at Barton's photograph of Luikama we need to take into account the contexts provided by this kind of nineteenth-century imagery of children — of which Barton would doubtless have been aware — but we also need to consider our own contemporary contexts for assessing this kind of imagery. A reading of Carroll's, and Barton's, photo-graphs as sexually ambiguous is influenced by the current unease and sus-picion surrounding the activities of almost any adult male photographing young girls.

Barton was an avid photographer, and a major influence on his work may well have been the popular style of pictorialist photography that was emerging at the turn of the century. Photographers such as Alice Bough-ton, Clarence White, and Frank Holland Day were producing works that created a strong association between children's bodies and a sense of "primordial innocence" (Higonnet 1998, 129–30). Clarence White in particular frequently photographed naked children in pastoral idyllic settings, often including actual classical statuary. He also treated the negative and printed the photograph to achieve a soft focus that distanced its subject matter. The link between young bodies and "natural innocence" became a central theme of pictorialist photography in the early years of the twentieth century. It was the referencing of "antiquity" that allowed photographic images of naked young bodies to be idealized as classicism, whereas nakedness was considered "indelicate" and far less acceptable in those images that located themselves more firmly in the present.

Through the Victorian cult of the child, photography and childhood were laminated together, both focusing on a similar concern with presence and absence. There is a slippage between the spaces of photograph, child, and the "primitive," as though they share common trajectories and strategies of representation. By reflecting the nostalgia Victorians associated with childhood, the photograph reminded them that what was definitely there was now no longer there. Both photography and childhood were shaped by disappearance and a play on temporality. Barton took numerous photographs of children's games during his time in Papua New Guinea, and he later wrote an article on the subject for the *Journal of the Royal Anthropological Institute* (Barton 1908). He considered the cultures he encountered to be, like children, on the verge of disappearing.

Images of innocent young children in photographs and genre paintings were extremely popular with Victorian audiences. John Everett Millais's famous 1879 painting *Cherry Ripe,* which showed a young girl in a white dress and bustle-bonnet, and which later became the Pears Soap advertisement, sold 600,000 copies within a few days when it was reproduced as a color centerfold in *Graphic* magazine (Higonnet 1998, 51). These kinds of mass-media images of childhood innocence contributed to a more general concern with protecting that innocence, and photography was seen as a perfect technology for preserving or "immortalizing" it, and as such was bound up with the various processes of defining the limits of childhood.

As well as being the subject of popular imagery, the bodies of young girls were entangled in a great deal of academic debate and legislation in Victorian society in the latter half of the nineteenth century. Various pieces of legislation, such as the Contagious Diseases Acts, the Offences against the Person Act, and the Criminal Law Amendment Act or the Stead Act (named after William Stead's 1885 exposé in the *Pall Mall Gazette* of child prostitution and "white slavery" in London, which raised the age of consent for girls from thirteen to sixteen), all concern attempts to determine and fix the parameters of (mostly female) childhood and thus simultaneously control adult sexuality (Gorham, cited in Mavor 1995, 19). Factions within the Social Purity Movement of the 1870s lobbied for raising the age of consent to twenty-one, a significant jump from the existing age of twelve, which dated back to thirteenth-century legislation and continued to be endorsed by the 1861 Offences against the Person Act. Although in 1875 the Social Purity Movement successfully had the age of consent raised to thirteen, and it was subsequently raised to sixteen, the category of adolescence itself did not come into use until the turn of the century.

These debates all demonstrate adult fears about childhood and about relations between children and adults; debates that revolve around consent as a key factor. Consent was of great concern to photographers like Carroll, and because the children he photographed were considered incapable of giving their consent he sought it instead from their parents. He wrote lengthy letters to the parents of the young girls he photographed explaining exactly what he wanted to "borrow" their children for, in an attempt to legitimate his own relationships with children and differentiate them from those illegitimate ones that were the subject of contemporary Victorian fears about child abuse (Smith 1998, 100). Consent is also an important issue in Barton's photograph of Luikama. The perceived lack of it, its impossibility given the circumstances of the photograph's production, adds to a reading of the photograph as the imposition of colonial surveillance and sexual fantasy. Yet the issue of consent in relation to this photograph has to confront the possibilities of other conceptualizations of sexuality and agency. Under what conditions can we imagine that Luikama could give her consent?

Given these frames of reference, the sexual content of Barton's photograph of Luikama is rendered more problematic and uncertain than the projection of any simple colonial stereotype of "primitive sexuality." Perhaps for Barton the sexuality of the girls he photographed was not perceived as the active sexuality of adult women. A sexuality that, to certain sections of Victorian society, was threateningly "animal," in need of socialization, and supposedly only redeemed and controlled through marriage and Christian morality. In this light he could have seen Luikama as both woman and not-woman, sexually knowing and yet innocent; her sexuality was latent, both present and absent.

In tracing some of the trajectories in which the photograph is entangled I

Christopher Wright

have tried to show that there are multiple histories of sexuality, childhood, and tattooing that could productively be taken into account in considering the photograph of Luikama. These would include the approaches of Victorian audiences, Hula or Papua New Guinean audiences, and contemporary audiences, and therefore need to be considered cross-culturally. For example, the discussion of photography and tattooing and their focus on the child body as the bearer of signs suggests both similarities and differences between Victorian and Hula attitudes. It is possible to draw some parallels between the status of Victorian children and that of Hula initiates. There is a similar concern with transition and the ambiguous status, in terms of both sexuality and individuality, of those who are not yet fully adult. They share a concern with the body and its images as the site of transformation. But equally a contrast could be made between the Victorian aesthetic ideal of the undecorated body—exemplified by Greek sculpture—as literally embodying the height of civilization; and Hula ideas of body decoration as precisely that which defines human qualities. How Victorian and Edwardian notions of "natural innocence," particularly in relation to photographs of children, might contrast or overlap with Hula notions of nature and culture is another history of the photograph that could be traced across cultural borders.

Rather than focusing solely on a colonial gaze and the construction of various stereotypes, it is necessary to track how these interact with indigenous constructions. The photograph of Luikama is entangled in the histories of different scopic strategies, not just that of colonial surveillance and its object.

The androgynous status of children in some Melanesian cultures is a feature frequently commented on by anthropologists. In order to assume a place in the reproductive order the androgynous child must be actively placed in a single-sex category, and the body is frequently the site of this construction. Marilyn Strathern has discussed how Melanesian initiation ceremonies, rather than making a self-contained individual, often serve to make individuals incomplete: "What is produced is a sexually activated person, a potential reproducer, an incomplete person whose identity must be completed in relation with another" (1988, 27). In many Melanesian cultures a person's identity is the product of a complex set of social relations, the links she or he has with other individuals rather than the possession of an individual.

In contrast to Victorian culture, the body in Hula culture is not seen as the expression of an inner individuality, the sign of a person belonging to her or himself. So, tattoos, rather than the surface expression of an interior individuality are, for the Hula, evidence of an exterior individuality that is constructed through relations with others. For the Hula it is not the individual that is tattooed, but rather a specific kind of individual that is partially created through the external relations that are realized in both making and displaying the tattoos. Tattoos are the evidence, the manifestations of these external relations (Strathern 1997, 99).

Before tattoos make sense to any audience or reader, they give pain to the living body, they hurt. The Hula eye that looks at tattoos does not just read them, it also winces, it senses the pain. The Hula body is malleable, a ground for inscription. Barton treated tattoos as the inscription of an evolutionary narrative, he wanted to discover a vocabulary of tattooing by tracing the designs of tattoos back to their roots in Melanesian and Southeast Asian words for various animals (1918). For Barton the role of Hula tattoos is to signify, to efface themselves before a meaning that is located elsewhere, in a complex table of orthographic similarities or in an assumed "primitiveness" or "innocence." For the Hula tattoos involve beauty and sociality, they are forces as much as signs.

Lutkehaus and Roscoe (1995, 21) discuss the links between beauty and power in Melanesia, and the way that physical attractiveness, such as that achieved through tattooing, implies the power and the ability to seduce both humans and valuable objects. Yet, of course, it is within the context of Hula culture that Luikama's display of her body has that power and efficacy. Her depiction in a photograph that takes no account of that context in its strategy of representation—that is also taken away from local audiences and displayed to others, reproduced, circulated, and finally placed in an archive—discounts or neutralizes that power.

Barton's performance in taking the photographs, and what subsequently happens to them, ignores the social relations through which Hula sexuality and individuality are manifested and sustained; Barton substitutes a different set of relations and other audiences. His photographs could be seen as an attempt to impose one type of inscription over another; to replace one context of revelation with another.

In this light the photograph that we started with is not, then, a portrait of Luikama—or rather it can only be seen as such within certain trajectories and in relation to particular audiences. To read the photograph as a representation that stands for an individual is to ignore the ways in which individuality is constructed in Hula culture. Any assumptions about the presence of an individuality in the photograph need to be put in a cross-

Christopher Wright

cultural perspective: for many Melanesian cultures' self-objectification is not a desirable outcome of any representation but a positive danger. Melanesians do not want to be seen individually, because for them individuality lies in relationships. In an extremely thought-provoking consideration of one of her own photographs of a Hagen dancer from the highlands of Papua New Guinea, Strathern discusses how the dancers' decorations show a capacity to draw in relationships, but are "not a portrait if we mean that inner individuality must show in the features, for individuality lies not so much in the appearance as in the act of assembling" (1997, 99). To say that they are a representation implies a medium, and although we might see the features of the body as a medium through which a portrait represents the individuality of a person, this is not necessarily the case in Melanesia. Similarly, Hula tattoos do not "represent" relations with others but are only there because of them, they are the result of activated relations: as Strathern says, "we witness an outcome: the result or effect of mobilizing relations" (99).

Barton's photograph is like an attempt to tattoo Luikama, to inscribe and fix her as permanently as the pigments used to mark her skin. Both photographs and Hula tattoos have similar effects to the "initiation objects" of the Rauto of New Britain described by Thomas Maschio, which "can be said to memorialize the identities of past owners, when the initiates have them placed on their persons their own identities participate in, and are augmented by, ancestral identities" (1995, 156). Photographs, like tattoos, bring into being other selves, including spirit selves.[7] There are cross-cultural ideas of "containment" at stake here, and in some senses we treat photographs in a way similar to Hula attitudes toward tattoos: as evidence or containers of relations. Photographs are material "artifacts" that demonstrate relations with others, the living and the dead, helping to fashion particular types of individuals through these relationships.

It is perhaps finally *our* myth of photography's ability to steal souls, our belief in its ability to capture individuality, that is the starting point for a reading of Barton's photograph of Luikama as only concerned with the imposition of a colonial gaze over an individual. This trajectory tends to pose the problem in terms of a binary opposition between type and individual, or object and subject, automatically privileging the latter over the former. We assume the presence of an individuality in the photograph that then contributes to a reading of it as the inscription of a stereotype that masks that individual. But the ways in which the Hula construct individuality in the relationships between individual and group disrupts this redemptive strategy. Luikama's individuality evades the photograph, it is located elsewhere, and we are left with the question of what a photographic representation of Hula individuality would look like. How can we, or should we, see the individual and not the group? A consideration of Barton's photograph in these terms is one route toward a cross-cultural understanding of processes of representation, an understanding that would enable future representations of cultural Others to both take account of and convey indigenous aesthetics.[8]

I want neither to redeem Barton's photograph nor to reduce Luikama to simply the object of a colonial gaze, a project that actually avoids some of the more disturbing aspects of us looking at the photographs now. We can gesture to another point in time in which the objectification and voyeurism took place, rather than confront the possibilities of our own. Even if Barton's photograph of Luikama did not capture her individuality in the sense that I have discussed here, it still had, and potentially has, many adverse effects that do need to be considered. Photographs involve acts as well as representations. What I want to suggest here are other creative and productive ways of looking at these kinds of photographs. Although understanding them as evidence of the misuse of colonial power is an important aspect of any consideration of them, the individuality that frequently gets assumed in these histories needs to be approached more critically. In many discussions of photographs like Barton's the emphasis has been too heavily weighted toward one side of the equation, on the colonial gaze itself rather than on the entanglement of that gaze with indigenous notions. Such a focus can retain a colonial perspective and ignores some of the borrowings and appropriations that have occurred in both directions as a result of encounters between cultures. The pierced, scarred, and tattooed European and American bodies displayed in recent publications like *Modern Primitives* (Vale and Juno 1991) show the continuing impact of perceived "tribal" attitudes on our own body culture.

Photographs trace multiple trajectories: for all their superficial fixity and their inclusion in structures like the archive that seek to contain them, they are processual and constantly in motion. What brings meanings to photographs are performances of them, specific readings and enactments. The photograph crystalizes these performances, providing a site where meanings both appear and disappear. What is important is not so much what the image contains, a meaning that resides within it, but what is brought to it, how it is used, and how it is connected to various trajectories.

Potentially productive future uses of collections like Barton's include repatriation[9] and the kind of visual work exemplified by the Australian photographer Leah King-Smith. The history of photography as a technology of colonial surveillance has been discussed to the point of exhaustion, and along with the tracking of Barton's photographs across cultural borders these uses represent creative new directions for the history of his work as both artifacts and representations. They would also take the photographs out of the realm of academic debate and actively connect them to other histories and trajectories.

The supple bodies of my title are not those referred to by Barton in his letters or articles (1908, 259) or those imagined and represented in his photographs, but rather those of the living malleable bodies of Hula culture, a suppleness that enables their beauty and efficacy. They are also the "bodies" of photographs and their spaces, bodies that, like those that are tattooed, reveal our construction through relations with others.

Postscript

In producing a contact print of Barton's photograph of Luikama for this volume, the photographic studio involved decided to "clean" Barton's hand-drawn box from the glass negative. Before they did so they made one contact print with the box still in place, making this print the only surviving record of Barton's actions.

Notes

The research on which this article is based was funded by the Leverhulme Trust as part of a project to catalog sections of the Photographic Collection of the Royal Anthropological Institute. I am very grateful for their support.

I owe a particularly great debt to Max Quanchi, Queensland University of Technology, for drawing my attention to the photograph of Barton overpainting tattoos (fig. 2) and for generously sharing with me his own research on early photography in Papua New Guinea. Thank you Max.

I want to thank Christopher Pinney and Roslyn Poignant for their valuable advice, and Nicholas Thomas for his helpful suggestions. I would also like to thank Nicolas Peterson for inviting me to the 1997 conference *Looking through Photographs*, and the Centre for Cross-Cultural Research at the Australian National University for covering the cost of my flight. Many thanks are due to Jenny Newell of the Centre for her hard work during the conference, and I also would like to thank all the other participants and the audience at the conference. Finally, but most important, I owe a great deal to Joanna Wright for her companionship and support.

I would like to thank the following individuals and institutions, all of whom have helped me with my research for this article: Elizabeth Edwards, Pitt Rivers Museum, Oxford; Harry Persaud, British Museum, London; C. G. Sheehan and Lynn Perkins, John Oxley Library, State Library of Queensland; Michael Quinnell and Jennifer Vaisey, Queensland Museum; Alan Davies and Martin Beckett, State Library of New South Wales; Valerie Helson, National Library of Australia; Joe Naguwean, Michael Somare Library, University of Papua New Guinea; Tukul Kaiku, National Archives and Public Records Services, Papua New Guinea; Wilma Marakan, National Library Service, Papua New Guinea; Carole Edwards, Foreign and Commonwealth Office, London; Diane Langmore and John Ritchie, Australian Dictionary of Biography, Australian National University; Judith Bailey, University of Queensland Library; and Barbara Berce, Australian Archives.

The Barton photographs in this article are reproduced courtesy of the Photographic Collection of the Royal Anthropological Institute. I owe both the institute and its staff a great debt. I am also very grateful to the State Library of New South Wales for permission to reproduce figures 2 and 6.

1 The photographic process resembles a kind of miniaturization, and this aspect could be productively explored in light of the role such processes play in Lewis Carroll's writing and also his photography, which I refer to later.

2 I am very grateful to Max Quanchi for drawing my attention to this image.

3 There is a line of critical writing about the colonial photography of the nineteenth century that has its origin in the work of John Tagg (1988), who took as a starting point Michel Foucault's (1979) discussions of the role of vision in the development of the modern prison.

4 Men usually only received small facial tattoos in the event that they had committed homicide.

5 Guise's article "On the Tribes Inhabiting the Mouth of the Wanigela River, New Guinea" was read by Mr. T. V. Holmes at a meeting of the Royal Anthropological Institute on 8 November 1898, and was accompanied by a series of lantern slides made from Guise's photographs. The article was subsequently published in 1899.

6 I am very grateful to Roslyn Poignant for pointing out this article to me.

7 Another productive avenue of research would be to trace the connections of Victorian ideas concerning psychic photography (the belief in photography's ability to capture images of spirits and other emanations, often in the form of direct manifestations, onto the photographic plate rather than representations in the accepted sense) with Hula attitudes toward tattoos as the manifestations of ancestral spirits.

Christopher Wright

8   The discussion by Nicholas Thomas (1997) of contemporary photographs of Samoan tattooing is particularly interesting in this respect.

9   Although I have initiated several projects involving the repatriation of photographs from the Royal Anthropological Institute's collection, I have not yet carried out any work of this kind in Papua New Guinea.

Self-Fashioning

and Vernacular Modernism

. . . .

3

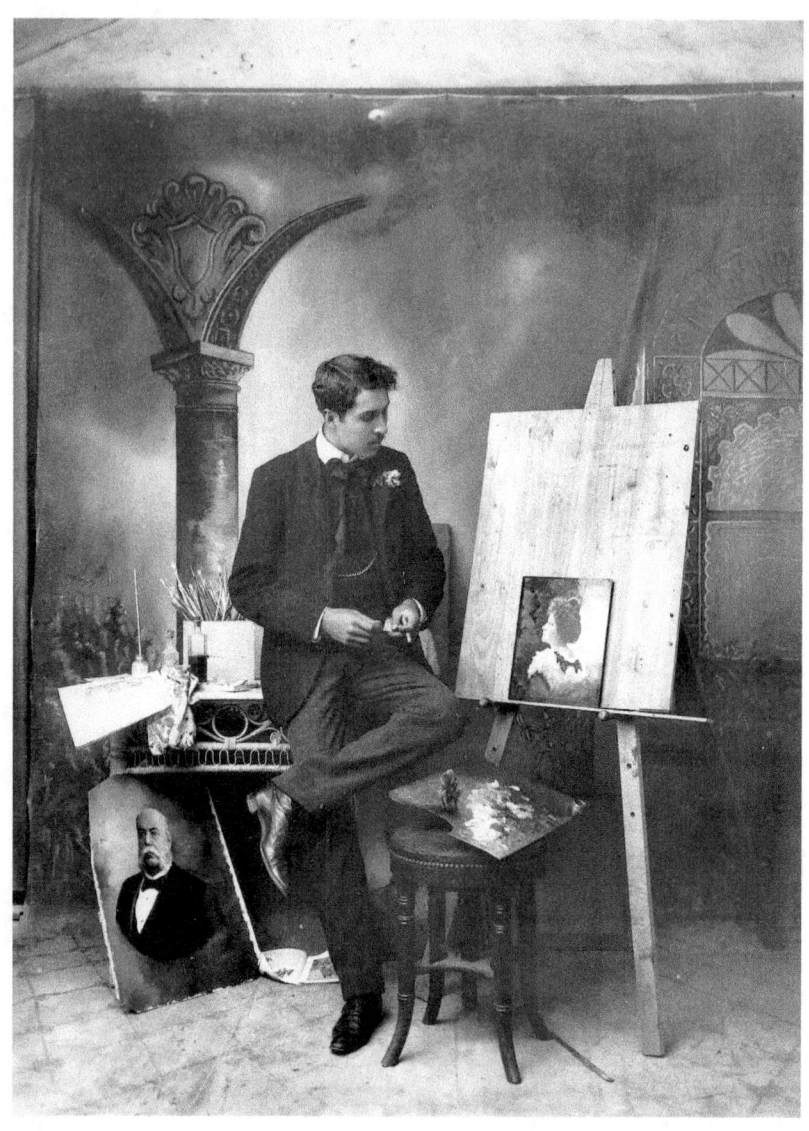

1. Figueroa Aznar, self-portrait with easel. Courtesy of Figueroa Aznar Archive, Cusco, Peru. Photo by Juan Manuel Figueroa Aznar, used by permission of Luís Figueroa.

Deborah Poole

Figueroa Aznar

and the Cusco *Indigenistas*

PHOTOGRAPHY AND MODERNISM IN EARLY-

TWENTIETH-CENTURY PERU

Sometime in the early 1900s, the Peruvian artist Juan Manuel Figueroa Aznar arranged his easel, paints, stool, palette, two open photo magazines, and two portrait canvases in front of a studio backdrop. On the backdrop, which he also used for occasional work as a commercial photographer, he had painted on one side a Spanish colonial archway and, on the other, one half of a traditional Andean religious altar. Having arranged his utensils and easel in front of this scene, Figueroa then set up his camera, prepared the plate, composed the image, and arranged for another person to release the shutter. He straightened his suit, adjusted the flower on his lapel, and posed, cigarette in hand and one leg crossed casually over the other, to contemplate his work of art (fig. 1).

But where, exactly, do we situate the object of this carefully framed and contemplative gaze? Is it the not-yet-finished painting? The thematic space uniting artist, easel, and paints? Or the still-broader frame of an anticipated image that has just been composed on a chemically coated, and industrially produced, plate of glass? How, in short, are we to understand the relationship of this turn-of-the century Peruvian dandy, photographer, and painter to the representational technologies he so skillfully wields?

A glance at the embedded pictorial frames of this particular self-portrait suggests that Figueroa was himself suggesting such questions about the relationship between photography, painting, and art. The stretched and painted canvas is framed by an easel. The easel is in turn framed by a stretched and painted backdrop. This entire scene is then framed by the awkwardly visible and slightly rumpled upper edge of the canvas backdrop. This interior frame—which could easily have been edited from the plate —dismantles the illusion a backdrop is intended to convey. Juxtaposed next to the even sharper line left by the negative edge itself, the void left visible by this painted backdrop's edge reveals the photographer's awareness of the technological and artistic artifices enabling his own romanticized and introspective gaze into the world of easel, palette, and disguise.

In what follows I suggest that Figueroa did indeed have a very particular interest in understanding and, to a certain extent, dismantling the artifices of both photography and art. Like the dandified self-image he assumed, his approaches to these problems borrowed heavily from the literature and art of European romanticism. Yet, contrary to the concept of an amusing colonial mimicry that our own first viewing of this provincial Peruvian dandy might evoke, his reappropriations and reworkings of these borrowed European elements were neither innocent nor misconstrued. Rather, Figueroa created an approach to both photography and modernity that intentionally departed from the dominant mold of European modernism. In the following discussion of his life, I am particularly interested in exploring the ways in which this tangentially modernist style was shaped by Peruvian understandings of photography and art, and by a provincial intellectual and regionalist movement known as *indigenismo*.[1]

Photography and Art in Peru

Juan Manuel Figueroa Aznar was born in 1878 in the small town of Caras in the Andean highlands of the Peruvian department of Ancash. Soon after Juan Manuel's birth the family set up residence in Lima, and it was in this turbulent and war-torn city of the 1880s that the young Juan Manuel spent his youth and completed his primary and high school education at the Colegio N.S. de Guadalupe.[2] He then went on to study at the Academia Concha, a privately endowed municipal fine arts institution in Lima. Following his studies at the Academia, Figueroa worked his way through Ecuador, Colombia, and Panama as a portrait painter. While in Colombia, Figueroa may well have learned of such developments in art photography as aca-

Deborah Poole

demicism and naturalism, both of which were practiced quite early in Colombia by Antioqueño photographers such as Melitón Rodriguez (see Serrano 1983; Arango 1988).

The Peru to which Juan Manuel returned sometime in 1899 or 1900, however, was strikingly different in many respects from both Colombia and the western European countries where art photographies first emerged. The vast majority of the country's population consisted of Quechua- and Aymara-speaking peasants employed in small-scale community agriculture or as peons on semifeudal agrarian estates. The small elite of rural landlords who owned these estates lived in provincial cities that, with few exceptions, were isolated from the modernizing currents of industrial capitalist development.[3] Lima, the capital of this predominantly rural country, was home to a small but prosperous oligarchy whose wealth was based on sugar and cotton plantations built from the accumulated profits of the prewar guano (bird manure) and nitrate trade. Production in both the guano fields and the plantations they engendered was based on indentured contract labor from China and on sharecropping by coastal and highland peasantries. Little or none of the income from these properties was invested in industrial development. As a consequence, Lima lacked the bourgeois and emerging middle classes who served as both the European and Colombian audiences for pictorialist and amateur photographies.[4]

In these different social and class settings, "art photography" had emerged to fulfill a historically specific set of representational tasks. These tasks were related to the split between an aesthetic discourse based on notions of artistic creativity, manual production, and the author; and the forms of scientific epistemology, mechanized technology, and commodity production informing bourgeois industrial society (see Benjamin 1968; Sekula 1983, 1984). Pictorialist photographies resolved this problem by transforming the scientific (or industrial) qualities of photography into "art" through the photographer-artist's personal (i.e., manual) intervention into the mechanical technology of focus, tone, framing, angle, and texture. The photographic print was in this respect no longer a mass-reproducible commodity but a unique "work of art."

In early-twentieth-century Lima, by comparison, the ruling class was still firmly entrenched in its traditional modes of domination and had not yet been confronted by the challenge of industrial forms of commodity production or mass-marketed art (kitsch). In this society of patronage and family, success as an artist depended on access both to family resources and to the prestigious allure that artistic training in Europe, particularly Paris, acquired for those artists with the means to study abroad (see Eléspuru 1968; Lauer 1976). More specifically, with respect to Figueroa's personal situation, success as a visual artist meant success as a painter, and painters had not yet been forced to confront the artistic marketplace whose traumas had paved the way for both pictorial modernism and art photography in Europe.

The failure of aestheticized and pictorialist photographies to take hold in Lima must, then, be understood with respect to the specific class and social structures that defined contemporary Peruvian reality. This fact has two important consequences for how we read Figueroa's photographs. First, it suggests that Figueroa's photographic work was never considered, or perhaps intended, to be "art." Second, it suggests that Figueroa's early decision to turn to photography was not so much an artistic choice as a practical solution to the dilemma created by his relatively marginal social position in the closed and highly stratified society of oligarchic Lima. For an artist with neither upper-class family ties nor European training, apprenticeship in a successful photography studio was one of the few available routes through which to pursue a viable career in portraiture, the genre of artistic representation in which Figueroa had so far specialized.

By 1900, the business of photographic portraiture was a thriving—even somewhat saturated—industry in Lima, with little room for either artistic experimentation or the bohemian aesthetic that Figueroa had cultivated in his travels abroad. Some forty to fifty studios competed to serve a market made up of the relatively stable population of Lima's oligarchy and merchant class (see McElroy 1985). These fashionable studios, which were ranked in accordance with the prestige and class position of their respective clienteles, defined a dominant portrait style based on the rigid poses and stylized theatricality of the nineteenth-century *carte de visite*.[5]

Given the formulaic nature of their composition and content, the "artistic" qualities of such photographs were ascribed to the varying qualities of their surface effects. In the early years of Peruvian photography, when the prestigious French studios of Courret, Garreaud, and Manoury dominated Lima's portrait trade, this aesthetic quality was explained in terms of the technical and lighting effects produced within the print itself by the (European-trained) photographer.[6] As photography became more widespread and national, however, the Peruvian photographers—who often could not count on European pedigrees to authorize an artistic status for their machine-made images—began to look toward other means of differentiating the aesthetic value of their commercial products. The favored

Deborah Poole

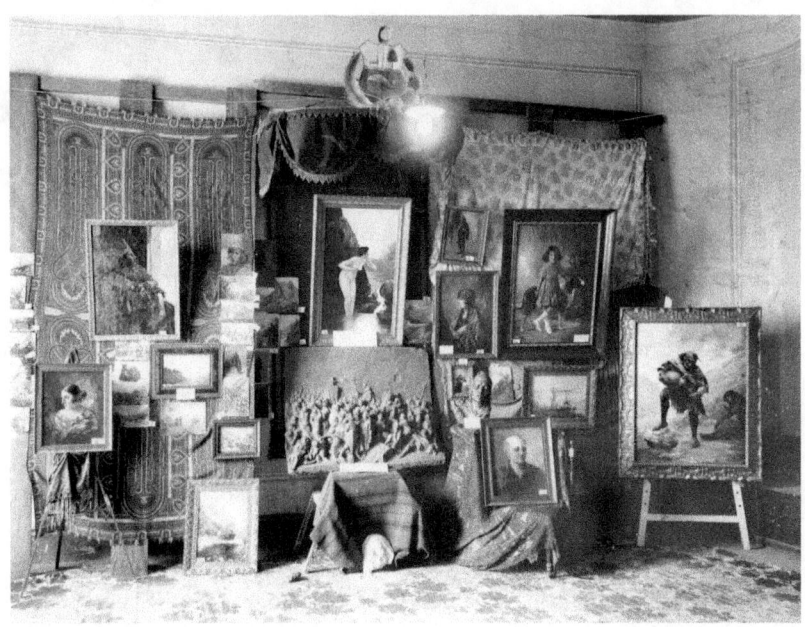

2. Figueroa Aznar's atelier with paintings and work table with *foto-óleos*. Courtesy of Figueroa Aznar Archive, Cusco, Peru. Photo by Juan Manuel Figueroa Aznar, used by permission of Luís Figueroa.

solution was to transform totally the machine-produced image into a hand-produced "work of art." This was accomplished through retouching techniques by which faces and figures were altered in the negative and color added to the final print.

Of these retouching techniques, the most radical was that known as *fotografía iluminada* (illuminated photography) or *foto-óleo* (oil photo) (fig. 2). In *foto-óleo*, oil-based paint was used to idealize the subject's features, add color, and even create backdrops and special effects not present in the original negative. Because of its painterly qualities, the *foto-óleo* provided both the aura of an original work of art *and* the allure of modernity ascribed to photography as an industrial and, above all, imported technology. More important, from the point of view of the upper and merchant classes who at first monopolized the market, *foto-óleos* retained this allure while simultaneously denying the democratic nature of photography as a mechanically reproducible portrait technology that threatened to become increasingly accessible to Lima's working and servant classes. Precisely because of its contradictory combination of exclusivity and availability, *foto-*

óleo rapidly became one of the most popular art forms in Lima. During the first decades of the twentieth century, well-attended exhibitions of *fotografía iluminada* were regularly held in the major photography studios and reviewed in the national press.

The popularity of the *foto-óleo* speaks for the extent to which Lima's photographic culture differed from the contemporary Colombian and European art photographies with which Figueroa may also have been familiar. Whereas the pictorialists sought to render photography an art by intervening *as artists* in the chemical and mechanical process of photographic production, the Peruvians sought to separate completely the photographer's labor from that of the artist. Even this conservative compromise was resisted by Lima's foremost critic, Teofilo Castillo, who, as late as 1919, attacked *foto-óleos* for their "immoral" effects on Lima's popular classes. Castillo claimed that insofar as *foto-óleos* displayed "a value more industrial than artistic," the public should be protected from their "unculturedness and tackiness" (*incultura i cursilería*).[7] Castillo's virulent defense of traditional aesthetic values in the name of the public good echoes Charles Baudelaire's much earlier charge in 1859 Paris that photography would spread "the dislike of history and painting amongst the masses" ([1859] 1980, 83).[8] The seeming anachronism of the Peruvian critic's attacks on photography sixty years later—when photography was already an accepted artistic form in Europe and North America—reflects not so much the late arrival of photographic technology and ideas to Lima as the ways in which analogous class structures informed the two critics' perceptions of photography.[9] For Baudelaire writing in 1850s France, photography was a threat to painting precisely because it confused the functions of bourgeois industry and the elite art *salon*. For Castillo, the *foto-óleo* as "industrial" or bourgeois kitsch had similar resonances for the cultural values of an oligarchical society faced with the prospects of President Augusto Leguía's modernizing state.[10]

Neither the technology of photographic portraiture nor the technique of *foto-óleo* could, however, be forever defended from the demands of Lima's lower classes. As increasing numbers of studios began to offer a commercial version of the prestigious *foto-óleo*, other critics intervened to ensure that the "artistic" *foto-óleo* remain a perquisite of the few fashionable studios who used photographers either trained in, or visiting from, Paris, London, and Rome. These in turn depended on the artistic aura assigned to their work to retain both their monopoly on prestige and their loyal, wealthy clientele. The photographs and *foto-óleos* produced by nationally trained photographers, or by the more poorly equipped photo studios that serviced Lima's working class and merchant sectors, were reciprocally relegated by the critics to a status of technology or "craft."

Although it is not known in which studio Figueroa worked, in 1901 he exhibited two *foto-óleos* — one of a woman playing the piano, the other of "a young woman half covered with vaporous tulles" — in a department store on Mercaderes Street, where Lima's most fashionable photography studios were located. A review of the exhibit notes that Figueroa's work "reveals the effort to go beyond the routine," but it adds that his figures were rigid and lacked the polish of Lima's more accomplished and European-trained studio portraitists.[11] Clearly entry into Lima's exclusive social and artistic circles would not be easy for a newcomer such as Figueroa who lacked the crucial sine qua non of a European education.

Provincial Intellectuals and the Bohemian Aesthetic

Like all born artists, Juan Manuel Figueroa led an elegant
and refined bohemian life. — Julio G. Gutiérrez[12]

In 1902, Juan Manuel Figueroa moved to Arequipa, the urban and commercial center for southern Peru's booming wool export trade. At the time of Figueroa's arrival, Arequipeña society was dominated by a small but prosperous oligarchy whose wealth was based on the commercial export trade. Unlike the Lima oligarchy, they depended very little on the guano trade, and therefore lost little in the War of the Pacific. Unlike other provincial elites in Peru, they had relatively reduced agrarian holdings and bought their wool instead from the large haciendas of Puno and Cusco. The city was also home to a relatively large number of foreigners, in particular British agents of the wool export houses and a small Spanish and Arab merchant class (Flores-Galindo and Burga 1978). As a result, Arequipa's photographic and artistic establishment, though smaller, was both more cosmopolitan and more receptive to new talent than that of Lima.

In this setting, Figueroa found work in the new, yet already nationally recognized, photographic studio of Maximiliano T. Vargas. In Vargas's studio Figueroa painted backdrops, posters, and *foto-óleos* for what was to be Arequipa's most luxurious photographic studio. It is probable that Figueroa learned many of his techniques of studio lighting from Vargas, who was also the instructor for Martín Chambi, another photographer whom Figueroa would meet in Cusco. Vargas's influence on both Figueroa and Chambi can be traced to his skills in photographic portraiture, and, perhaps more importantly, to his early interest in taking studio portraits of Indian subjects.

Although these influences show up clearly in Figueroa's later work, his early work did not immediately develop Vargas's insights into either the Indian or photographic composition. Instead, Figueroa remained during these years immersed within the world of the *foto-óleo* and therefore within the all-encompassing dichotomy of photography versus art. In 1903 an exhibit of Figueroa's *foto-óleos* and landscape and portrait canvases was mounted at the Vargas studio and at a nearby jewelry store. It was the *fotografías iluminadas*, however, that the critic for Arequipa's *La Bolsa* newspaper singled out as most expressive of Figueroa's artistic potential. The young artist, he wrote, "distinguishes himself above all for his good taste in the selection of details which give life to his portraits." Figueroa's *iluminaciones* could compare favorably, he continues, with the paintings of Carlos Baca Flor, Daniel Hernández, and Alberto Lynch—three Paris-based Peruvian artists—were it not for the "small defects [that] originate . . . in large part from his lack of schooling."[13] Other reviews of his Arequipa work likewise focus on the *foto-óleos* as a means through which the undesirable realism of photography might be sentimentalized and improved. For his growing Arequipeño public, Figueroa was an artist "of the modern school [who] loved reality, albeit embellished and invigorated by art and sentiment."[14]

In 1904 Figueroa moved to Cusco, a smaller city located 11,000 feet above, and several weeks' traveling distance from, Lima. The Cusco of Figueroa's time was home to some 19,000 Quechua-speaking Indians, a scattering of *mestizo* and Arab traders, an even smaller group of white landowners, and a half dozen or so Italian and Spanish families engaged in the wool and alcohol trade, as well as in a nascent textile industry (Herrara 1981,107–8; Valcárcel 1981). The contrast between the luxuriant lifestyles of these landowning and emergent bourgeois sectors and the impoverished Indian peasants on whose labor and wool the regional economy depended was structured in ways similar to the class and cultural oppositions found in other contemporary Latin American cities.

Figueroa's early work in Cusco would seem to suggest that, at least initially, his sympathies lay with the more prosperous pole of Cusco's cultural life. Indeed, the warm reception Cusco provided to the aspiring young photographer and artist must have been a welcome contrast to Lima and Arequipa, where he had been refused full recognition as an artist. Figueroa's first Cusco exhibit in October 1905 was of *fotografía iluminada*, the ambivalent form of art/photography with which Figueroa had hoped to appease the taste of Lima's demanding ruling elite. The work was exhibited in the studio of Vidal González, a Cusqueño studio photographer with whom Figueroa had worked since his arrival in Cusco.[15] In his review of the exhibit, the anonymous art critic for Cusco's *La Unión* newspaper presaged Figueroa's future as one in which the artist would have to overturn all of his metropolitan ambitions. Although Figueroa's work reflected, he said, a "nobility of the soul," it was restricted in both scope and spirit by the too "powerful influence of Lima."[16]

During the next several years, Figueroa established himself as a prominent figure in Cusco's small but vital intellectual circles.[17] His success reflected his ability to resolve the distance between his earlier, more metropolitan notions of art and the locally grounded identity called for by his first Cusqueño critic. An article by José Angel Escalante, a leading Cusco intellectual, describes a visit in August 1907 to Figueroa's atelier on the hacienda Marabamba outside of Cusco.[18] The familiarity with which Escalante recounts Figueroa's hunting activities, artistic progress, and newly grown beard reveals Figueroa's status as a well-known figure in Cusco cultural circles. The paintings completed at Marabamba formed the core of a lavishly reviewed benefit exhibition held in late 1907 at the University of Cusco.[19] Among the 126 paintings that Figueroa purportedly exhibited, none were of the Indian, Inca, or Andean themes that would later characterize his work.[20]

In Cusco, it was the individual per se, and not his or her social and academic formation, that was idealized as the source of artistic and general intellectual ability. Sentiment was valued over skill, passion over science, color over form, and instinct over tradition. In later *indigenista* philosophy, the source of this natural talent would be defined as the Andean landscape itself. At this early period, however, it was expressed primarily through certain consciously contrived bohemian identities associated with the artistic personality. On this front as well, Figueroa's natural status as an outsider to Cusco placed him in a position of artistic advantage. For Cusqueños, Figueroa—four years after moving to Cusco—was still "our guest, the well known Limeño painter . . . through whose veins runs Andalucian blood and in whose spirit Moorish atavisms endure."[21] An impediment to his artistic acceptance in Lima, this outsider status buttressed a studied bohemian identity that was to be Figueroa's trademark in Cusco society (fig. 3).

The bohemian identity attributed to Figueroa in 1900s Cusco borrowed

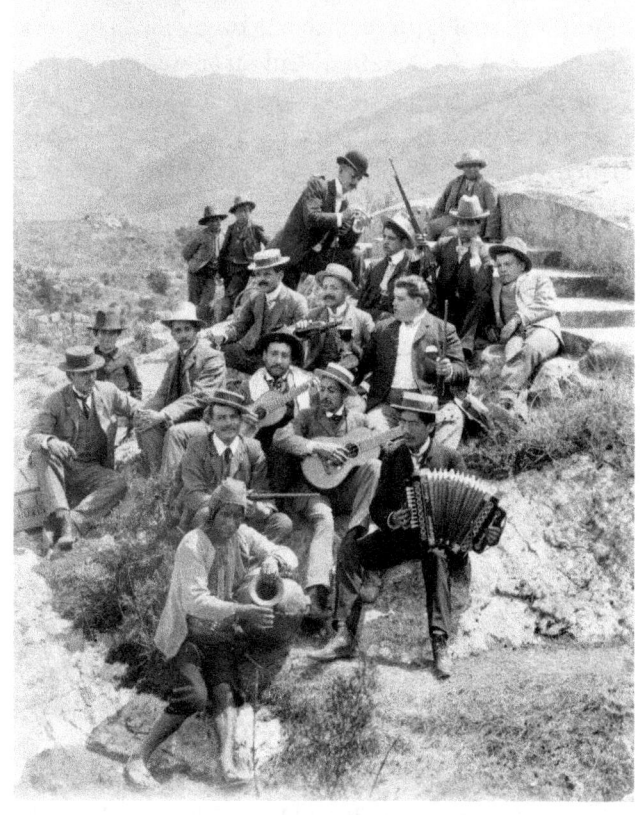

3. *Bohemios* in Saqsahuaman (Cusco). Courtesy of Figueroa
Aznar Archive, Cusco, Peru. Photo by Juan Manuel Figueroa
Aznar, used by permission of Luís Figueroa.

its terms of reference from the earlier nineteenth-century tradition of
bohemianism that had originated in the rapidly expanding metropolitan
settings of Paris and other European cities. In these cities, and under the
pressures of marketplace competition and the mass production of both
culture and art, young intellectuals and artists made the conscious endeavor to renounce the materialist values of bourgeois industrial society.
Modeling themselves on such modes of otherness as gypsies or *saltim-
banques*, the bohemians of Paris set the precedent for an emerging modernism based on the cult of individuality, fashion, and "art for art's sake"
(Grana 1964; Grana and Grana 1990; Brown 1985).

Deborah Poole

The first, and in many ways most striking, difference between this classic European bohemian setting and rural, seigneurial Cusco is the nearly total absence of the defining structural feature of European romanticism: the literary and artistic marketplace (Williams 1983). Unlike his nineteenth-century European counterpart, the early-twentieth-century Cusco artist was not confronted by the challenge of a large new middle-class reading and art-consuming public.[22] While there was some limited local market for journalism, prior to the university reform of 1909 there was very little public at all for literary journalism and even less for the visual arts. In fact, the first public purchase of works exhibited in Cusco's Centro Nacional de Arte e Historia's annual show was not until 1922.[23] As a result, the image of marginalized artistic genius used to describe Figueroa and other Cusco artists was inspired not, as in Europe, by aversion for bourgeois art consumers but rather by the Cusqueños's rejection of the cultural dominance of Lima. Figueroa was seen by his Cusco contemporaries as a "bohemian" because he was not from Cusco. He was seen as a bohemian "genius" because of the natural affinity for nature and beauty that had drawn him to the Cusco landscape, and because of his personal and aesthetic rejection of Lima society and urban life. In this way an identity and discourse that, in Europe, had been structured by urban artists' emerging aesthetic and social enmity toward the bourgeois consuming classes was instead tailored in Cusco to fit the quite different needs of a provincial discourse of regionalist demands.

Although its terms were derived from a vocabulary of European romanticism, in Cusco the image and meaning of the "bohemian" social rebel were thus reshaped to fit local political ends. The artist as spokesman for Cusco's own cultural project stood opposed to a place—Lima—and not, as in Europe, to a class—the bourgeoisie. This slight twist in the Cusco bohemian tradition meant in turn that it would be nature, in the guise of geography or place, that the first Cusco bohemians would privilege in their definition of the sentiment or emotion that inspires artistic genius, and not the gypsies or other social outsiders on which the European bohemian ideal was molded. In Cusco, these ideas about nature, individualism, and the bohemian rebel were perhaps best articulated in the popular ideal of the *walaychu*. In Quechua, *walaychu* refers to a man who replaces social or family ties with a restless, wandering existence, yet who, unlike the European bohemian, is neither entirely carefree nor uprooted. Rather, the *walaychu* replaces his family and community tradition with a deeply sentimental attachment to the land. This emotional attachment to a province, region, or landscape is then credited as the source of the *walaychu's* heightened artistic and musical sensibilities. The Cusqueño intellectuals saw themselves as building on this spatially grounded concept of aesthetic sensibility to form a community based on shared artistic sentiment. Because of its Andean roots, this community was seen to exclude both Lima and the forms of European mimicry that the Cusqueño intellectuals believed had undermined Lima's "spiritual" authenticity.

Figueroa cultivated this bohemian identity in a short but locally remarkable theatrical career in which he chose romantic roles, such as that of Luciano in Joaquin Dicenta's play *Luciano o el amor de un artista.*[24] Offstage, as well, he supplemented his artistic persona with a carefully cultivated image as a "restless spirit, wanderer, and adventurer" who continued—despite his upper-class in-laws—to work in the mining ventures that had also been his father's trade.[25] In shaping this public persona of "artist and man of action," Figueroa fused the more down-to-earth profession of miner with the lofty vocation of portrait painter to create a public persona based on the ideal of the artist existing on the fringe of society.[26]

Indigenismo (1910–1930)

The end of Figueroa's public bohemian career came with his marriage in July 1908 to Ubaldina Yabar Almanza. By this time, Figueroa was already a well-known figure about town. In his wedding announcement he is described as "the likeable artist, the inimitable colorist, the popular bohemian."[27] Exploiting the romantic possibilities of his public persona, he courted Ubaldina by first painting an image of the Virgin with Ubaldina's face, and then donating it to the church of San Francisco where, as Juan Manuel well knew, a cousin of Ubaldina was the priest. It was, perhaps, only through such a gesture that Figueroa could have met Ubaldina— whom he had before then only admired from afar—because the Yabars were one of Cusco's most distinguished families. Ubaldina's uncle, for example, was bishop of Cusco, and the Yabar family owned several large haciendas in the province of Paucartambo. The bulk of Figueroa's surviving photographic plates are portraits of her family, taken in the intimate space of their Cusco family home, or on one of the Paucartambo haciendas. Figueroa's favorite space for creating these family portraits was the formal salon where Bishop Yabar received his guests. Known as the "blue salon" for its richly colored carpet, the remarkable layered imagery of its walls testify to the monumental centrality of visual imagery in the social and religious life of Cusco (fig. 4). Although the extent to which such traditional use of images affected Figueroa's photographic work is unknown, several surviving plates show evidence that Figueroa did experiment with recreating the iconographic space of Cusco-school colonial religious paintings (fig. 5).

Other family portraits from this same period reveal the uncomfortable contradictions of an affluent artistic life in racially divided Cusco. In one photograph, for example, we confront a branch of the Yabar family outside a hacienda in Urbamba (fig. 6). Nestled in luxuriant grasses, this family displays all the finery of a Cusco Sunday outing. Emerging from the darkness of the eucalyptus grove behind them, a peasant who is barely perceptible—and certainly far from the consciousness of the group that poses for the camera—peers curiously at the photographer and his subjects. Was he a houseboy, a servant, or simply a peasant who happened by? Did he come with the family from Cusco; and in what capacity did Figueroa know him? Did the photographer place him in the background? Or, more likely, was he excluded from the photograph only to reappear insistently within the frame, as occurs in so many other Cusco photographs from these times?

At first an anecdotal, almost accidental, presence in his photographic work, this shadowy presence of Cusco's Indian peasants moves into an increasingly central place in Figueroa's identity, sentiment, and art. While his experiences on the Yabar family's haciendas afforded Figueroa an opportunity to observe the Indians on whom Cusco's economy depended, it was the intellectual and political discourse of *indigenismo* that would determine the ways in which Figueroa would paint and photograph the Indian.

Indigenismo was a pan-Latin American intellectual movement whose stated goals were to defend the Indian masses and to construct regionalist and nationalist political cultures on the basis of what *mestizo*, and largely urban, intellectuals understood to be autochthonous or indigenous cultural forms. Within this broader vanguard movement, Cusqueño *indigenismo* occupied a privileged position because of Cusco's history as capital of the Inca Empire. This history made Cusco a particularly contested site in the battle to wrest a Peruvian national history away from the endless scrutiny and historicizing gaze of the European and North American scientists, archaeologists, and historians whose expeditionary itineraries and reports consistently mapped Peruvian history onto that of a fallen Inca Empire. In reclaiming Inca history and geography as their own, the Cusqueño *indigenistas* introduced the previously forbidden figure of the *contemporary* Andean Indian into the Peruvian literary and artistic imagination,

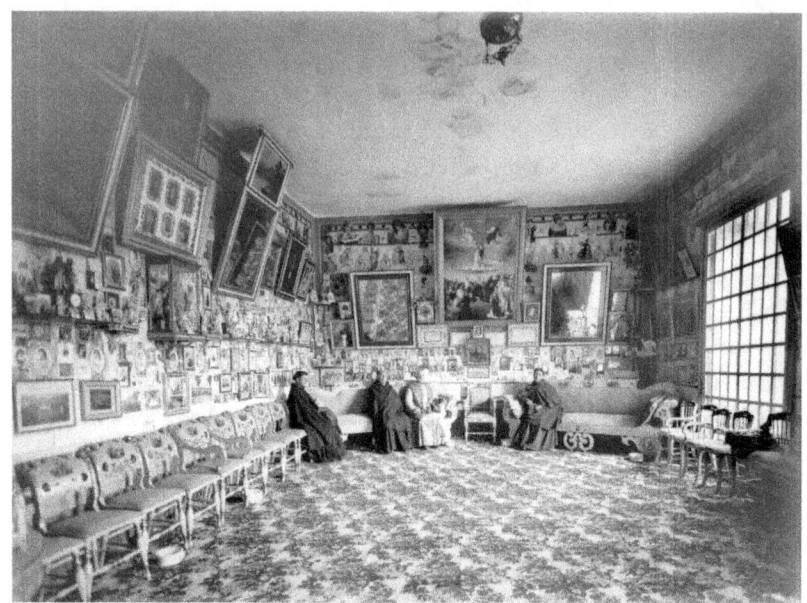

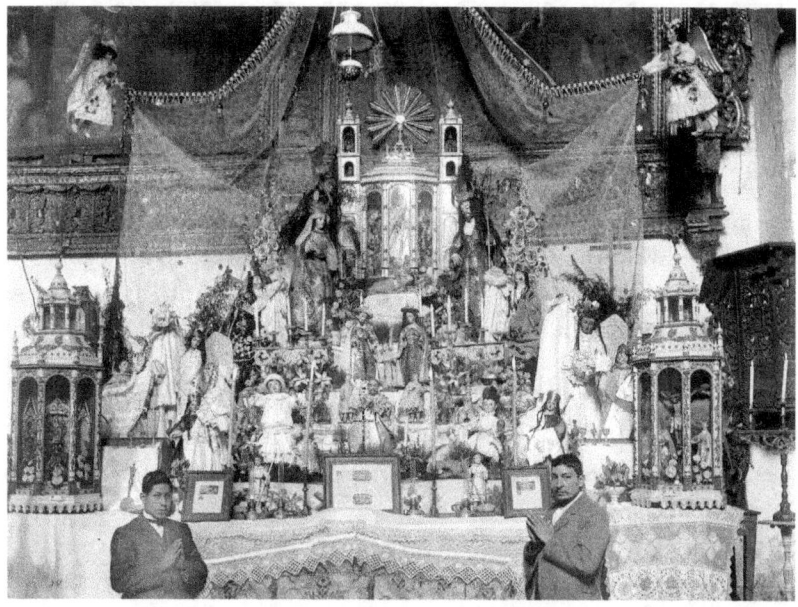

4. *(Top photo) Salon azul* of Monsenor Yabar, bishop of Cusco. *(Above)* 5. Altar in Cusco. Both courtesy of Figueroa Aznar Archive, Cusco, Peru. Photos by Juan Manuel Figueroa Aznar, used by permission of Luís Figueroa.

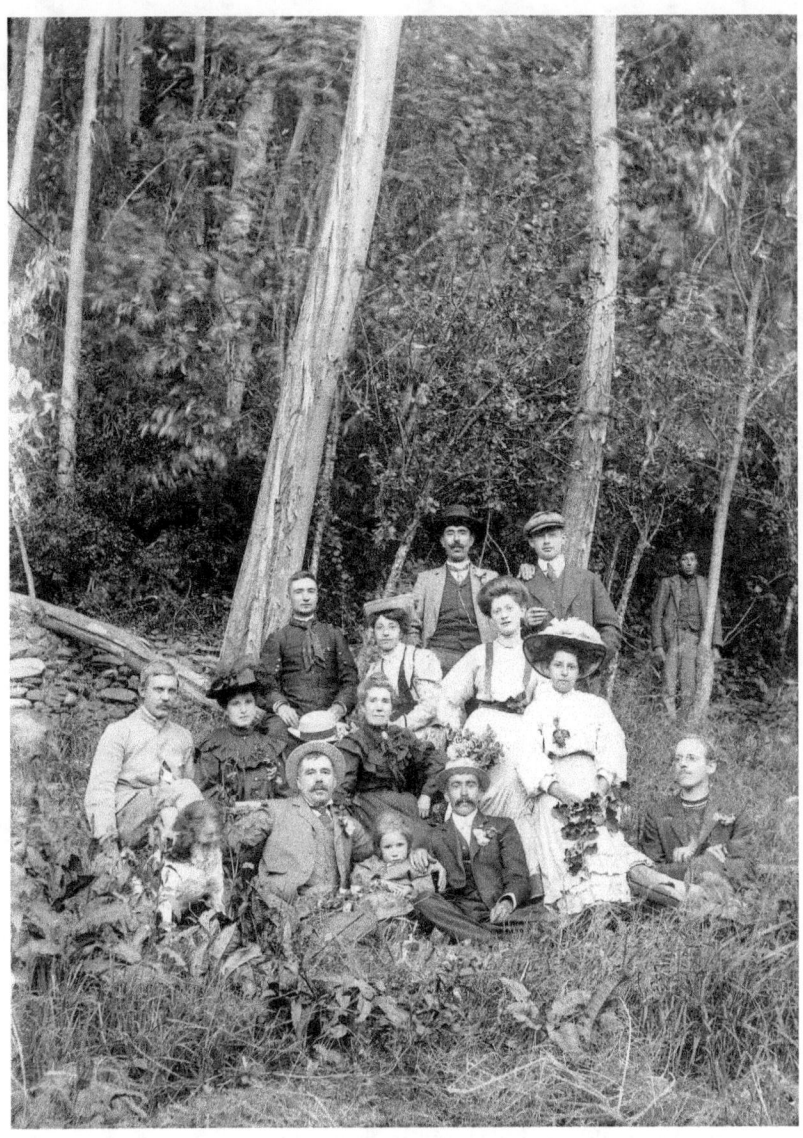

6. Yabar family in Paucartambo. Courtesy of Figueroa Aznar Archive, Cusco, Peru. Photo by Juan Manuel Figueroa Aznar, used by permission of Luís Figueroa.

as well as into Peruvian nationalist discourse, jurisprudence, and domestic policy.[28]

Although the roots of Cusco's *indigenista* movement can be traced to colonial and nineteenth-century literature about Indians and the Incas, what has been called the golden age of Cusco *indigenismo* is more usefully situated in the period from 1910 to 1930.[29] During this period, *indigenista* writing about the Andean countryside, the Inca past, and Indian culture coalesced with, and responded to, political demands for greater regional autonomy and decentralization. These demands in turn responded to the economic modernization projects and shifting class alliances of President Augusto Leguía's "Patria Nueva." Within this context, the most important factor motivating the Cusqueño intellectuals' interest in the Indian was a series of violent peasant uprisings in the mid-1920s. These uprisings in Cusco's high pastoral provinces, together with the processes of economic modernization occurring in the department's agrarian valley provinces, threatened the cultural and social hegemony of Cusco's agrarian-based seigneurial class.[30] It was in this context that intellectuals from Cusco's upper and middle classes began their campaign to validate an authentic Indian identity for *all* Cusqueños.

Two major works produced during this period were to determine the future course of Cusqueño thinking about the "Indian problem." These were Luís Valcárcel's *Tempestad en los Andes*, published in 1927, and José Uriel García's *El nuevo indio*, published in 1930 as a rebuttal to Valcárcel's nationally acclaimed *Tempestad*. Whereas Valcárcel saw post-Conquest colonial history as a process of racial and cultural degeneration and advocated a return to the values and purity of pre-Conquest Inca society, García saw colonial history as a process of cultural and racial improvement. The true Indian, he argued, was not pure (or "Incaic") but rather the mixed, or *mestizo*, product of Cusco's colonial past. In conformance with this historical vision, García's *indigenista* mission was to create a "New Indian." He rejected Valcárcel's vision of Andean culture as an inherited constant (or received tradition) that could be resurrected according to the historical or archaeological methodologies of empirical description and scientific induction. Instead, García's emergent Andean culture was to be a product of directed *mestizaje* (cultural mixture). The New Indian intellectuals who would guide this mission were to be forged by melding the spiritual or *telluric* power of the Andean landscape with the intellectual prowess of a *mestizo* avant-garde.

Deborah Poole

Far from being a carbon copy (or much less, imperialist imposition) of European modernism, *indigenismo* was a deliberately iconoclastic pastiche of philosophical, aesthetic, and discursive borrowings. The result is a "modernism" that mimics the European only partially and thus appears, from the point of view of European modernism, to have contradictory structures and purposes.

The most visible contradiction that emerges from this process is that which exists between the Cusqueños's enthusiastic subscription to the *ideal* of an avant-garde and their simultaneous rejection of the formalist and internationalist languages of abstraction and modernity through which the modernist avant-garde constituted itself in European literature, painting, photography, and music. For García's New Indians, modernity, and in particular the rhythm or velocity of modern life, were perceived as threats to the very landscape from which Andean peoples drew their spiritual and emotional strength. For them, "*indigenismo* [was] a return to the land ... an instinctive battle against the new concepts of the Twentieth Century."[31] Similarly, for New Indianist artists such as Figueroa, abstraction, formalism, and modernity remained taboo.[32] As a result, in the eyes of a European, North American, or Limeño observer, most of the Cusqueño *indigenista* paintings appear to be strikingly naive, overly stylized, romantic compositions; they appear, in short, to be "bad art."

The Cusqueños's rejection of modernist pictorial idioms, however, cannot be quite so summarily dismissed. They were both exposed to and knowledgeable of modernist pictorial styles. Most were trained in European art. Cubist and other abstract formalist styles of painting were exhibited in Cusco and summarily attacked by the Cusco critics.[33] Rather the Cusqueños's collective decision *not* to imitate this style was consciously made according to two political criteria. On the one hand, it was precisely the formalism and academicism of European painting that had become most closely identified with the hegemonic culture of Lima. On the other hand, the political and social legitimacy of New Indianist discourse remained necessarily situated in a local history and environment. This political and historical grounding in regionalist, anticoastal politics made the Cusqueños justifiably wary of the European formalist aesthetics that celebrated a *dis*connectedness from such historical constants as representation and tradition.

Figueroa's approach to painting and photography was molded both by his personal experiences in Cusco and Paucartambo, and by the ways in which the *indigenista* discourses of Valcárcel and García shaped an understanding of art, ethnicity, and the intellectual avant-garde that was in many ways specific to Cusco. The two decades of *indigenista* ferment in Cusco between 1910 and 1930 correspond to the period when Figueroa was most active in photography and, although he left no written records, when *indigenista* concerns clearly informed his studio photos of idealized Indian "types" (fig. 7), stylized theatrical groups (fig. 8), and bohemian self-portraits (fig. 9). In these and other such carefully composed scenes, Figueroa uses photography to document a constructed artifice of identity. Each photograph is carefully composed with backdrops painted by Figueroa for his theatrical and/or portrait work. In front of these backdrops, an "Indian" model is made to recline, or the artist himself poses as stalking hunter, gypsy minstrel, meditative monk, or pensive artist. In another experiment, Figueroa skillfully manipulates and composes his negative so as to render the narrative flow of a sentiment gained and lost (fig. 10).

This photographic fascination with the malleability and staging of social identities reflects a broadening of Figueroa's bohemian or *walaychu* aesthetic to encompass the New Indianists's philosophy of constructed cultural identities. Like Figueroa's various bohemian selves, the New Indianists's cultural identity, or "ethnicity," was not a natural or historical identity waiting to be empirically discovered and described, as in Valcárcel's *indigenismo*. Rather, identities were to be constructed according to the consciously elaborated criteria of a political and artistic avant-garde. Photography fit into this philosophy of identity or self as a means to imagine new identities, although not as a medium to represent or to express them.

Throughout his life, Figueroa reserved specific media for different representational tasks: photography for self-portraiture, theater, and type; painting for Indians, allegories, and landscapes (fig. 11).[34] In the New Indianist conception of art, painters like Figueroa were to be praised for the "realism" with which they translated the emotion or beauty inherent to nature onto the canvas and not for the ways in which they actively rethought or imagined new forms or perspectives on the "truth" of nature. Photography, on the other hand, was unhampered by its ties to either nature or art. It could thus be used to document a shifting and formally constructed notion of identity more akin to contemporary forms of European modernist bohemianism than to the romantic notions of sentiment, nature, and art with which the Cusqueños had inscribed and restricted the artist's relation to paint.

This affinity between photography and the bohemian self was limited,

Deborah Poole

however, by the Cusqueños's doctrinal understandings of the telluric qualities of art in its relation to the land. Uriel García, along with the other Cusqueño critics, attributed both the sentiment and aesthetic success of Figueroa's paintings to his immersion in the rural Andean landscape of Paucartambo (where his in-laws owned land).[35] They argued that Figueroa's special bohemian sensibilities made him a fertile medium for translating onto canvas the spontaneous organic powers that nature had invested in the Paucartambo landscape and that constituted the essence of Andean cultural identity. This aestheticizing or sensitizing effect of the Andean landscape was restricted, however, to the medium of painting and could not pass through the modernizing mechanical medium of the camera. As a result, landscape photography—the *first* pictorialist form of photography to emerge in Europe and the United States—was never seriously developed in Cusco. Although Cusqueño photographers such as Martín Chambi, Alberto Ochoa, and Pablo Verdamendi shot extensive photography of archaeological sites, these photographs were meant to document the Inca historical past celebrated by *indigenista* writers such as Valcárcel.[36] The task of expressing the telluric essence of the landscape itself was meanwhile reserved for the vanguard of *indigenista* artists, who could translate this sentiment into the painterly art of color, emotion, and personal— as opposed to mechanical—sensibility.

Other Cusco artists followed Figueroa's example in the extent to which they experimented in both photography and painting. With the exception of Martín Chambi, however, the *indigenista* photographers of Figueroa's generation always turned back to painting as the preferred medium for expressing what they called *el sentimiento andino*. Because, for the *indigenistas*, beauty was inherent neither to the Indian nor to the landscape per se, it could not be captured by what Europeans considered to be the "magic" of photographic technology. Rather, the reality of the Andean world had to be transformed and reworked, carefully framed and skillfully tinted, before it could serve as an instrument of *indigenista* philosophy and aesthetics. As one *indigenista* critic expressed it, "The [*indigenista*] painters interpret the Indian landscape and carry pure Indianity to the objectivity of plastic arts."[37] Figueroa's importance in framing this aesthetic for both photography and painting is captured in the words of the *indigenista* writer José Gabriel Cosio, whose obituary for Figueroa lauded him as being "among the first to employ the *indigenista* thematic in a purely aesthetic sense with neither ethnological nor social preoccupations."[38]

7. "Tipo indigena."
(Below) 8. Figueroa Aznar
and friends in Cusco.
Both courtesy of Figueroa
Aznar Archive, Cusco,
Peru. Photo by Juan
Manuel Figueroa Aznar,
used by permission of
Luís Figueroa.

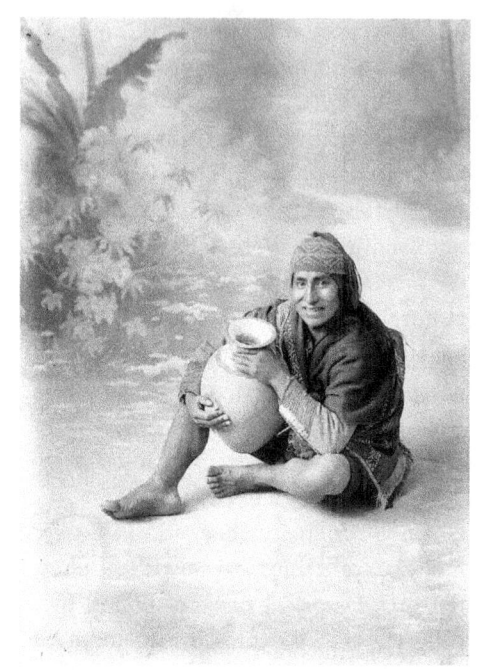

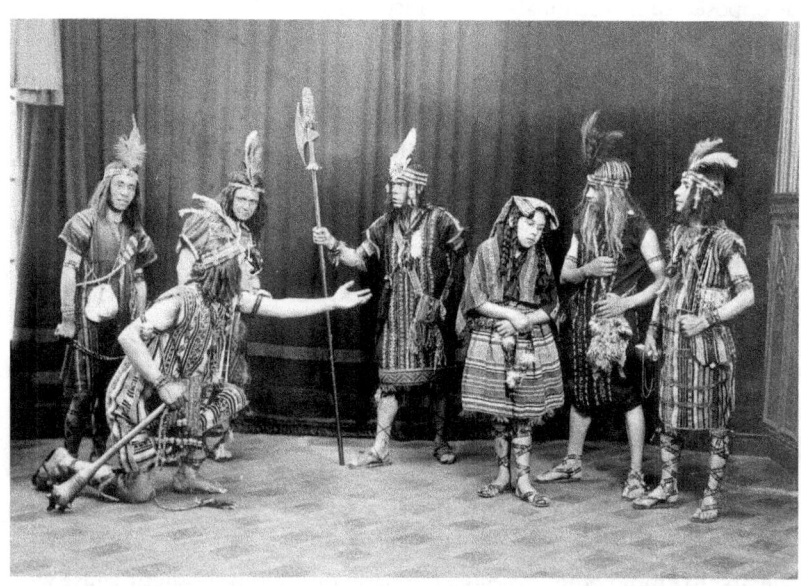

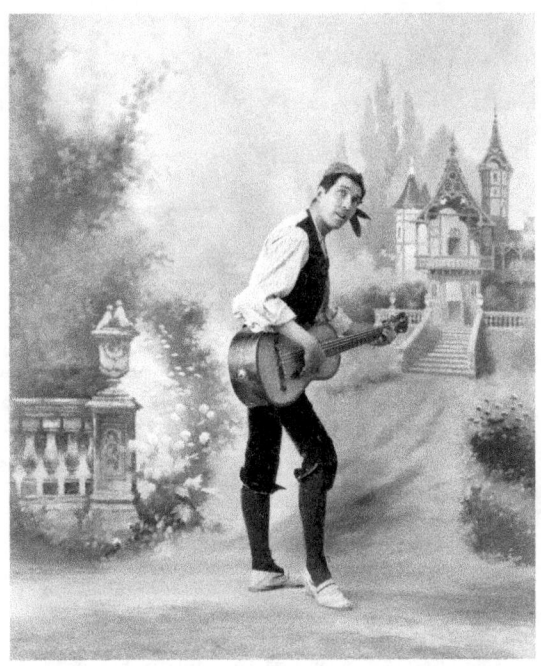

9. Self-portrait. *(Below)* 10. Self-portrait. Both courtesy of Figueroa Aznar Archive, Cusco, Peru. Photo by Juan Manuel Figueroa Aznar, used by permission of Luís Figueroa.

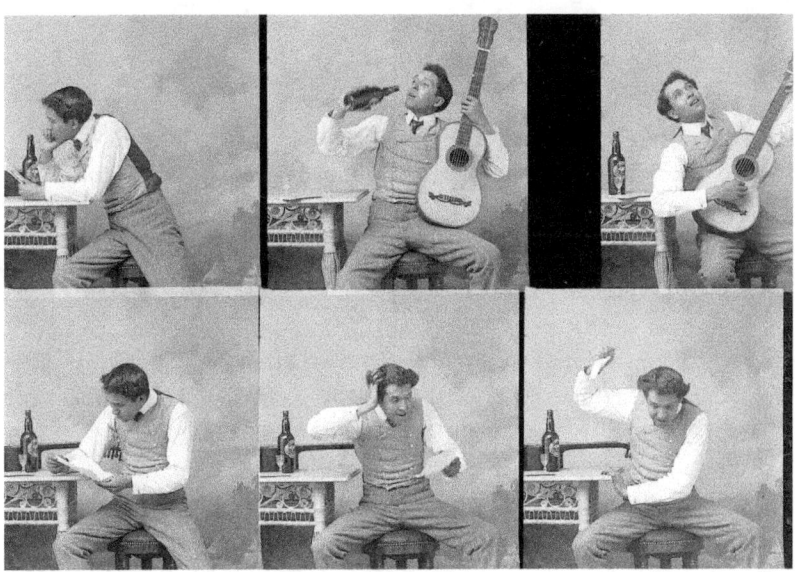

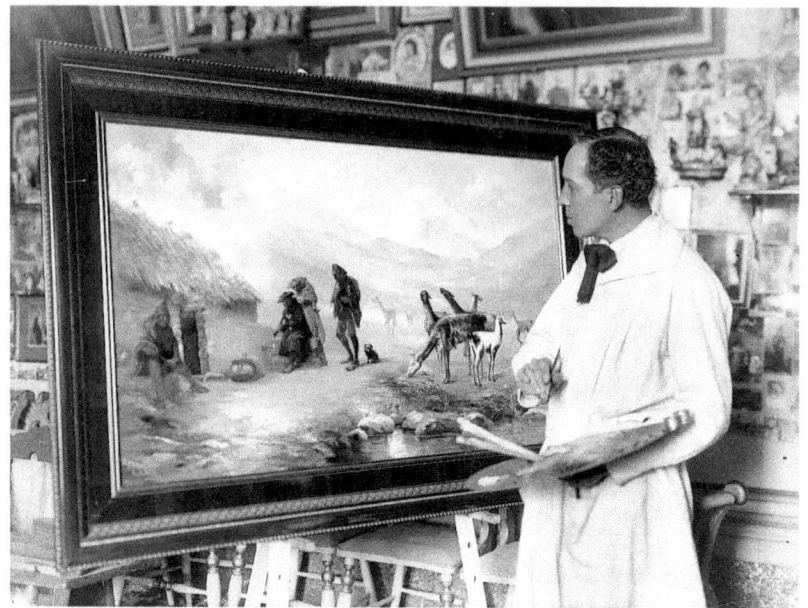

11. Self-portrait with painting *Amore y cellos andinos,* 1923. Courtesy of Figueroa Aznar Archive, Cusco, Peru. Photo by Juan Manuel Figueroa Aznar, used by permission of Luís Figueroa.

Conclusions

> Four hundred years of European science has compressed the
> expansion of the original spirit of our people. For this reason, the
> new ideas which are circulating in contemporary thinking must
> serve us only as short-term loans or reference points for the
> affirmation of our own values. —José Uriel García

By way of conclusion, I would like to return briefly to my original questions about the universality of the socially constructed divide between photography and art, and about Figueroa's specific, culturally and socially situated understanding of his artistic modernity. As I hope to have made clear in discussing the origins and formation of the *indigenista* movement in which he participated, intellectuals on the "periphery" consciously borrowed and made use of the philosophical and aesthetic philosophies through which, as they well knew, Europe had constructed its hegemonic discourse of art and the artist. They did not naively learn the "neutral"

Deborah Poole

technology of photography and then use it to record subjects appropriate to their own "indigenous" agenda. Even in far-off "preindustrial" Cusco the media of photography and painting were not neutral or transparent technologies acting simply to reflect social ideas and personal inspirations. Rather, as social and aesthetic technologies of representation, painting and photography in early-twentieth-century Cusco formed part of the complex discursive strategies of Western art. As the Cusco *indigenistas* themselves knew, they were representational technologies posited on post-Enlightenment forms of Western cultural production in which the aesthetic representation, classification, and idealization of social types, natural landscapes, and human forms had come to form an integral part of the humanistic philosophies and scientific knowledge through which the distribution of power in society is regulated and controlled.

Because of its close association with colonial expansion and the globalization of bourgeois culture in the late nineteenth and early twentieth centuries, photography is a particularly fascinating medium through which to study the dialogue through which intellectuals on the periphery contested this "controlling gaze." The Cusco New Indianists sought to counter this controlling gaze and positivist inventory of their history and geography by constructing an "imagined community" based on the philosophical and aesthetic values of intuition and sentiment informing their notion of *la emoción andina*.[39] Integral to this endeavor was the elaboration of a local tradition of the *walaychu*, or Andean-bohemian, as a person who replaces the bonds of social tradition and scientific history (or *pasadismo*) with an aggressive philosophy and aesthetic of nostalgia, sentiment, and music grounded in his close ties to the land. Out of this tradition came a certain repertoire of ideas regarding both the bohemian and painting as forms of spontaneous sentimental expression enabled by the telluric forces of Cusco's mountainous landscape.

At the same time, however, the emergence of a pictorial and literary imagery specific to the Cusco *indigenistas* was only enabled by other contemporary developments in European art and in the Latin American vanguardist movement. In Europe, first romanticism, with its peasants and bohemians, and then modernism, with its "colonial others," emerged as part of a broader discursive structure concerned with the elaboration and reproduction of social and racial difference as "a conscious strategy of exclusion" (Huyssen 1986, vi). This "strategy of exclusion" made it possible for European artists and writers to engage both industrial culture and the "colonial other" by transforming that encounter into an aesthetic act of bourgeois cultural production. For the Cusco artist, as well, it was the exclusionary discourse surrounding both the bohemian aesthetic and its successor, vanguard modernism—and not their pictorial or representational ideologies, which the *indigenistas* clearly rejected—that enabled the Indian to surface as the subject of early-twentieth-century Peruvian cultural discourse. This discursive explosion, through which "the Indian" entered the national artistic—and, somewhat later, political—imagination, was related to debates in Cusco concerning the desirability of modernizing the traditional (low-technology, unsalaried) forms and relations of production, and to the increasingly visible political organization and violence of the Indians themselves. It was this economic and social backdrop of rapid social change initiated from below that provided the institutional incitement for Peruvian intellectuals to speak, finally, about the previously forbidden subject of the Indian.

This discursive shift, however, was also to have specific implications for the development of photographic culture in Cusco. Once the hegemonic conceptual divide between photography (technology) and art had been surmounted, and *the foto-óleo* gone out of style, the directions in which Figueroa, and other Cusco artists, would take photography were determined by a new, regionally focused discourse on art. As Leguía's "Patria Nueva" (1919–1930) championed modernization and North American capital, Cusco politicians and philosophers elaborated an oppositional, regionalist doctrine of sentiment and antimodernity. In accordance with this new doctrine, *indigenista* critics celebrated the individual creativity and "sentimental realism" of painting for its ties to nature. They focused on both nature and the Indian as subjects whose essence or "sentiment" could not be captured by the technological realism (or "transparency") of photographic representation. What was needed for the *indigenista* cultural agenda was a directed rechanneling of sentiment and spirit to form the newly imagined community of "Cusqueñismo," and not the unmediated realism of either photography or the impoverished Indian that photography revealed. Photographic technology and photographic realism were therefore restricted to the private domain of photographic "studies" for both theater and painting and, in the case of Figueroa, for a remarkable series of self-portraits documenting the *indigenista* concern with constructing the vanguard or bohemian identities that would someday shape the New Indian culture of Cusco.

Notes

Research for this article was carried out in Cusco and Lima between 1986 and 1988 with the support of a J. Paul Getty Postdoctoral Fellowship in the History of Art and a Rackham Fellowship from the University of Michigan Society of Fellows. The work would not have been possible without the help and encouragement of Juan Manuel Figueroa's son, Luis Figueroa Yabar, and widow, Ubaldina Yabar de Figueroa. The glass plate negatives from which the photographs were reproduced are the property of the Figueroa family. The modern prints reproduced here are by Fran Antmann, with whom I share credit for the research in Peruvian photography archives. Adelma Benavente assisted with interviews and related research in Cusco. Unless otherwise noted, all translations from Spanish-language sources are mine.

1   In the years since this essay originally appeared a number of new publications on Andean anthropology, including that of Figueroa, have appeared. Although it has not been possible to incorporate into this essay all of the new findings and insights contained in these publications, several bear directly on my analysis here of Cusco modernism. For a comprehensive picture of Figueroa's place in the broader history of photography in Cusco and elsewhere in Peru, see Benavente 2002. For a somewhat different perspective on the importance of landscape in Peruvian photography, see Majluf 2002. Finally, for a different reading of Figueroa's work as an artifact of modernization, see Castro 1998.

2   From 1879 to 1883, Peru was at war with Chile. During much of this time, Lima was either occupied by, or under attack from, Chilean troops.

3   For a history and description of early-twentieth-century Peruvian society, see Flores-Galindo and Burga 1987.

4   Regarding the class origins of European pictorialist photography, see Hassner 1987 and Mélon 1987. Medellin, where the pictorialist-influenced photographers Melitón Rodriguez and Benjamin de la Calle lived and worked, was also home to a relatively progressive industrial and commercial bourgeoisie who distinguished themselves culturally, socially, and racially from the rest of Colombia. Medellin's literary and artistic community also had close contacts with both the United States and Europe (see Melo 1988).

5   The *carte de visite* format remained popular in Latin America for much longer than it did in either Europe or the United States. Even after the introduction of larger-format portraiture, the European élan of the *carte de visite* determined that its somewhat standardized poses, styles, and props would continue to be the norm for studio portraits of all social classes.

6   Fernando Castro, "Photographers of a Young Republic: Being French in Courret's Lima," *Lima Times*, 14 December 1990, 6–7.

7   Teófilo Castillo, *El Comercio* (Lima), 1919; reprinted as "Los triunfos artisticos de Figueroa Aznar en Lima" in *El Comercio* (Cusco), 8 May 1919.

8   Like Baudelaire, Castillo charged as well that art was necessarily private, visionary, and manual, and that while "photography can serve as a document to reconstruct a lost semblance . . . in no way can it [serve] to transform the semblance into a basic element of serious composition"; Teófilo Castillo, "Los triunfos artisticos de Figueroa Aznar en Lima," *El Comercio* (Cusco), 8 May 1919. Similar debates regarding the *foto-óleo* took place in Colombia (where *foto-óleos* were largely out of fashion by 1900) in the 1890s (see Serrano 1983, 213, 218–19).

9   Photography appeared in Lima only a few years after Daguerre's announcement in 1839 (see McElroy 1985).

10 Castillo's articles attacking the *foto-óleos* correspond to a period of dramatic change in Lima. The year 1918 was marked by a series of violent strikes by workers and artisans, and 1919 brought economic crisis for the traditional agricultural export economy of Lima's oligarchy. In July 1919, Augusto Leguía took office promising to build a modern, antioligarchical state called the "Patria Nueva" (Flores-Galindo and Burga 1987, 125–42).

11 *El Comercio* (Lima), 1901.

12 Obituary, 1951 (typescript). A contemporary of Figueroa, Julio G. Gutiérrez was an *indigenista* writer and painter and founder of the Peruvian Communist Party in Cusco.

13 "Un artista nacional," *La Bolsa* (Arequipa), 12 March 1903.

14 "Progresos fotográficos," *La Bolsa*, 13 January 1904.

15 This photography studio was founded in the 1890s by a congregation of English evangelical missionaries, who left the studio and all its equipment to the González family as payment for back rent. J. G. González retained the name Fotografía Inglesa for his business, which was inherited by his sons and grandsons (interview with Washington González, Cusco, July 1986).

16 "Arte nacional: Plumadas," *La Unión* (Cusco), 10 May 1905.

17 He was, for example, associate director of Cusco's Academia de Arte. He was also close to the circle of scholars who made up the Centro Científico del Cusco, an organization devoted to promoting progress through recuperation of Cusco's jungle resources. Figueroa would later serve as subprefect for one of these lowland provinces.

18 "Impresiones de arte," *El Sol* (Cusco), August 1907 (published anonymously; authorship attributed to José Angel Escalante in *El Sol*, 31 January 1908). Escalante was later director of the Cusco *indigenista* newspapers *El Ferrocarríl* and *La Sierra*.

19 See, for example, *El Sol*, 28 September 1907; *El Porvenir* (Cusco), 23 December 1907; *El Ferrocarríl*, 30 January 1908; and *El Sol*, 30 January 1908.

20 Figueroa's contributions included several copies of colonial religious paint-

ings, a "study of a head . . . in impressionist style," several beach landscapes, and two romantic compositions, one of "an unhappy woman sick with romanticism" and the other of "a voluptuous half nude woman . . . with a magnetic gaze" (*El Sol*, 28 September 1907).

21 "Notas de arte," *El Ferrocarríl*, 30 January 1908.

22 Similar discrepancies emerge between the European romantic tradition and its contemporary imitators in oligarchic Lima in the 1840s. Whereas European bohemians became associated with a public secular sphere of cultural discussion, Lima artists relied on the personal patronage of wealthy sponsors such as Don Miguel del Carpio. As one Peruvian critic has described the period: "Peruvian romanticism germinates . . . not in a *café*, nor on the street corner, but rather in an elegant mansion, perfumed and enriched by an atmosphere of patronage [*mecenazgo*] and protection" (Grande 1967, 19).

23 "La exposición de arte," *El Comercio* (Cusco), 4 October 1922.

24 "Teatro," *La Unión*, October 1907; theater poster dated Cusco, 30 May 1907, in the collection of Ubaldina Yabar de Figueroa, Lima. In Dicenta's play, written in 1893, Luciano is an artist "guided by revery, poetry, and the world of the muses" who battles a world of materialism and shallow bourgeois women. Although based on a thickly romantic conception of the suffering artistic soul, Dicenta's play touches as well on the modernist idea of the artist as alienated social being, pertinent to the incipient Spanish theatrical vanguard to which Dicenta belonged (see Ferrer 1978).

Local reviews praised Figueroa's performances for his miming talents, sentimentality, "natural Spirit and correct declamation" ("La funcion teatral," *El Sol*, 4 November 1907; "Teatro," *El Comercio* (Cusco), 9 November 1907; "Espectáculos: El concierto del 19," *El Ferrocarríl*, 21 March 1908; "El beneficio del centro espinar," *El Sol*, 20 May 1908; and "La muerte civil," *El Ferrocarríl*, 25 May 1908). Figueroa also painted the backdrops for the theater productions in which he performed. The conditions for theater in Cusco were, however, primitive at best, as judged by the fact that most reviewers accorded as much space to the chill winds and even rain that penetrated the theater hall as they did to the performance itself.

25 Obituary, *La Prensa* (Lima), 20 February 1951.

26 "Ante unos cuadros de J. M. Figueroa Aznar," *El Comercio* (Lima), April 1951. In a 1937 interview, for example, Figueroa describes himself as an "enemy of publicity" who had just arrived at his Arequipa exhibit from mines in "the furthest corner of the earth . . . removed from all contact with the civilized world" ("Una exposición de mas de 40 cuadros . . . ," *Noticias* (Arequipa), 20 January 1937.

27 "Azares," *El Sol*, 2 July 1908.

28 Prior to the 1920s, Indians appear in the work of only one Peruvian painter, Franciso Laso. In 1868, Laso photographed himself dressed in Indian clothes

as a model for these paintings. Although the similarities between Laso's and Figueroa's self-portrait work are suggestive, it is highly doubtful that Figueroa would have known about Laso's photographs, which were never publicly exhibited. Laso's photographs are reproduced in McElroy 1985 (plates 41 and 42).

More precedents exist for *indigenista* literature. These include the Cusquena writer Clorinda Matto de Turner, whose novel *Aves sin nido* (1889) marks a realist tradition leading up to twentieth-century *indigenismo*, as well José Arnaldo Marquez, Mariano Melgar, and Manuel Gonzalez Prada. José Santos Chocano marks the entry of the Indian into modernist poetry. The *indigenistas* of the 1920s and 1930s differed from these predecessors in that they were the first to claim to speak for contemporary Indians and the first to set forth a literary and artistic aesthetic based on a notion of authentic Indian culture (see Delgado 1980 and Polar 1980). Regarding *indigenista* jurisprudence, see Poole 1990.

29 In 1910, the American Alberto Giesecke was appointed rector of the University of Cusco. The new curriculum he imposed emphasized European philosophers such as Spengler, Ortega y Gasset, Leo Froebenius, Taine, and Georg Simmel. These writers provided the philosophical apparatus with which the Cusco *indigenistas* would authorize their arguments about Andean cultural identity (Herrera 1981, 123–26, and 1980, 187). At the other end of the "golden age," 1930 marks the end of President Augusto Leguía's dictatorship (see Herrera 1980; Deustua and Rénique 1984; and Valcárcel 1981).

30 By the 1920s, Cusco's land-owning elite was divided both ideologically and geographically between a modernizing export sector concentrated in the maize-producing Urubamba Valley to the northeast of the city of Cusco, and the traditional *gamonales* (agrarian lords) situated, for the most part, in the livestock-producing provinces to the south.

31 Yepez Miranda 1940, 30. Like other "New Indians," Yepez perceived modernity to be beneficial insofar as its rhythms "awaken" the *serranos* from their culturally dormant state, their introversion, and their latent *pasadismo*. It was dangerous insofar as it threatened to transform the very landscape responsible for the distinctively Andean emotions and sensibilities that were to be the foundations of a New Indian culture.

32 Cusco's New Indianist painting is best described as *costumbrista* in both style and composition. Influences came from Spanish localism and the *indigenista* painting of northern Argentina.

33 In one such denouncement, cubism—which the author describes as a "joke [*una tomadura de pelo*]" and "a craziness [*chifladura*] of a few"—is derided for portraying "what appears rather than what is" (Fernando Mollinedo, "Notas del dia: Palique," *El Sol*, 6 May 1911.

34 Early in the first decade of the twentieth century a shift occurs in Figueroa's work from *foto-óleos, plein aire* paintings, nudes, and copies of religious themes

to paintings focused almost exclusively on themes pertaining to Indian and Inca subjects. This shift is first reflected in the catalog for the 1916 exhibit sponsored by the Academia de Pintura of the Centro Nacional de Arte e Historia, a Cusco academy founded in 1914 by Figueroa and other prominent Cusco artists and intellectuals (*El Sol*, 3 October 1914). Figueroa's title in the Academia was "permanent director." At the Centro's 1916 exhibit, Figueroa won a gold medal for his oil painting *Inti Raymi* and a *diploma de close* for his *fotografía iluminada* ("El concurso de la nomina de arte," *El Comercio* [Cusco], 1 January 1916).

35 Uriel Garcia, *El Sol*, 2 July 1908. José Gabriel Cosio similarly describes Paucartambo's influence on Figueroa's work as a product of "dream and tragedy, because in the solemnity of its snow-capped mountains and the plasticity of its forests is where the tragedy of emotion resides" (José Pacheco Andia, *El Pueblo* [Arequipa], 17 February 1957). Another critic traces Figueroa's fame as a landscape artist to "that exuberant Paucartambo region, next to the jungle's domain but also, on the other hand, encased in the ruggedness of the Andes" ("La exposicion de Arte," *El Comercio* [Cusco], 4 October 1922). Because of its proximity to the jungle, Paucartambo was considered to have a peculiarly powerful telluric power. Figueroa lived much of his later life in Paucartambo and served as subprefect of the province from 1913 to 1914.

36 Even in the case of such archaeological landscapes, the New Indianists—who considered the camera an instrument of modernity that was therefore anathema to the telluric sentiments of Cusco—claimed that it was the landscape itself and not the camera that "captured" the scene. Thus, for example, in a recent film about Martín Chambi, Atilio Sivirichi describes a process whereby an (archaeological) landscape "casts a spell" (*hechizo*) on Chambi's film (Sivirichi, interviewed in the film *Martín Chambi and the Heirs of the Incas*, dir. Andy Harris and Paul Yule, 1986).

37 Sivirichi 1937, 21.

38 José Gabriel Cosio, "Obituario," *El Comercio* (Cusco), 1951.

39 Like Anderson's (1983) concept of "imagined community" as the basis for emergent nationalist projects, the *indigenista* effort to construct a common identity was based on sentiment and attachment to place (and history). The *indigenista* project differed from the nationalist projects described by Anderson, however, in both the scope and intent of their regionalist agendas.

Christopher Pinney

Notes from the Surface of the Image

PHOTOGRAPHY, POSTCOLONIALISM, AND

VERNACULAR MODERNISM

How do local visual traditions mediate modernity in ways that are independent from and critical of European modernity? Houston Baker, writing in *Modernism and the Harlem Renaissance* (1986) asks the question of how one can seriously understand, say, W. E. B. Du Bois or Langston Hughes in a manner that doesn't characterize them (and reduce them) to being either "like" (or "not like") T. S. Eliot or Ezra Pound. Baker's struggle is to break free from the model of a sovereign "Western" consciousness and reason of the sort that Dipesh Chakrabarty (2000) seeks to "provincialize" through the recovery of parallel practices. Part of Houston Baker's solution lies in his stress on the "deformation of mastery" (1986, 49) intrinsic to the Harlem Renaissance, an idea developed by Homi Bhabha in a rather different direction under the conjunction of the performative/deformative (1994, 241).

A similar idea is explored here: that is, the manner in which local photographic traditions creatively deform the geometrical spatializations of colonial worlds. Postcolonial photographic practices give rise to a "vernacular modernism"; images that project a materiality of the surface, or what Olu Oguibe (1996) calls "the substance of the image." In these practices the surface becomes a site of the refusal of the depth that characterized colonial representational regimes. "Surface" and "depth" refer here not simply to sedimentary layers, but rather to more profound positionalities that fuse the ethical/political with the chronotopic. What might be termed "colonial" schemata positioned people and objects deep within chronotopic certainties as they sought stable identities in places from which they could not escape. "Postcolonial" practice negates this, however, by siting its referents in a more mobile location on the surface. This performative/deformative transformation also reflects the opposition that Michel de Certeau made between the panoptic "lust to be a viewpoint" and the "opaque mobility [and] appropriation of the topographical system" by the ground-dwelling pedestrian (1984, 93, 97). Colonial depth practices implied, and strove to be guaranteed by, a photographic surface that was invisible. The surface was a window onto a field of spatial and temporal correlations that encoded a colonial "rationality." The opacity of the surface becomes a refusal of this rationality and an assertion of cultural singularity. There are resonances also with Michael Taussig's (1993, 19–32) attempt to refigure Walter Benjamin's "Work of Art" essay as serviceable for the late twentieth century. Taussig is concerned with the tactile and haptic dimension of what Benjamin termed the urge "to *get hold*" of objects [photographs] at close distance (1968, 217; emphasis added): the vernacular modernism described in this essay also reveals a desire to get hold of objects through photography, and this has a particular saliency in postcolonial contexts.

Photography and Depth

Taking our stand upon the island, we will make a leisurely
survey of the lake.... Let the reader endeavour to imagine this lovely
panorama spread around him—every object in which is faithfully
mirrored in the peaceful lake, whose surface on the first day that I
visited it was smooth as glass itself—and he will then be able to form
some idea of the kind of scenery which delights every visitor to
this celebrated valley. (Bourne 1866–67, 4)

Beckoned inside, through a hardboard partition and stepping
gingerly over trailing electric light cables, we follow Suresh into his
studio. [He] then pulls back the red curtain revealing the *piéce de résistance*
in this chamber of dreams. The great expanse of Dal Lake in Kashmir is
laid open, shimmering beneath cascading pine-encrusted mountains,

illuminated by efflorescent skies, and all offset by a foreground
luxuriating in multicoloured meadow flowers.

(Pinney 1997b, 14–15)

In a scene from the popular Hindi film *Beta*, a love-stricken Anil Kapoor rubs a photograph of Madhuri Dixit, the still-unrequiting object of his affections. Kapoor's hand passes over the surface of the image, detecting some secret libidinal undulation, some hardly visible texture of desire that triggers in the subject of the photo an ecstatic murmur. Looking becomes touching, and the referent of the photograph mutates from the imprisoning depths of the image to its sensual surface. Bombay cinema here plays out an erotics of looking and being, something close to the erotics described by Susan Sontag—a sensual immediacy.

I return to the "surfacism" that characterizes much popular small-town Indian photographic practice when later I explore its continuities with popular West African practices, notably the ways in which the use of backdrops, the creation of photographic mise-en-scène, and the postexposure manipulation of the image demonstrate a concern with the surface—or what Olu Oguibe calls "substance" of the image—rather than its narrativized indexical depths.

My later argument about popular "postcolonial" surfacist practices depends, however, on its opposition to an earlier practice that it repudiates and surpasses. This earlier practice privileges the time/space of photographic exposure and links these creational moments to the photographers' and photographic subjects' movements through time and space. The relationship between early photography and European travel is not accidental: the "normative" photograph encoded a practice of photography, which encoded a practice of travel. The ideology of indexicality authorized an autoptic practice of "being there." A flick through any basic history of photography reveals the powerful preoccupation with the changing location of the photographers and their equipment in real time/space conjunctions: early photographic technicians in their balloons, John McCosh in Burma, Roger Fenton in Russia and the Crimea, Francis Frith in Egypt, Felice Beato in Japan, Samuel Bourne in India (see Hershkowitz 1980), and Timothy O'Sullivan and W. H. Jackson in the American West.

There is a "newness" in photographic practice that authorizes this engagement with spaces of alterity but also a resonance with more enduring epistemologies. The parallelism between the technology of photography and techniques of travel has been explored by David Tomas (1982; 1988) who has noted the way in which the transformation of the negative into a positive encapsulates a journey between different states. But this technological narrative was layered on a much earlier European tradition of conceptualizing knowledge spatially. The frontispiece to Anton Wilhelm Schwart's 1693 *Der Adeliche Hofmeister* showing "the Grand Tour as part of the educational system of the Baroque" visualizes this spatialization in which different disciplines of knowledge—including "Universal History, Exotic Languages, Geography and Politics"—are depicted as steps along an ambitious "peregrination." Justin Stagl (1990, 325) has situated such images in the context of the rise of a systematic theory of travel in sixteenth- and seventeenth-century Europe.

In the rise of travel photography as practiced by those such as Roger Fenton, Samuel Bourne et al., whose sought-after work has now come to define a canonical nineteenth-century photographic practice, we can trace the alliance of photography's technological possibilities with a chronotopic expectation that emerges out of this long history of the theorization of travel and the rise of autopticism, of "seeing with one's own eye."

Samuel Bourne's 1866 "Narrative of a Photographic Trip to Kashmir (Cashmere) and Adjacent Districts" will serve for the purposes of this argument as the paradigmatic text of this normative practice. Bourne begins by suggesting that "if I am right in supposing that the readers of THE BRITISH JOURNAL OF PHOTOGRAPHY take an interest in narratives of photographic travel in foreign lands, I could scarcely hope to interest them more strongly perhaps than by presenting them with some notes of a trip with the camera to the far-famed Valley of Kashmir" (Bourne 1866, 471).

The weight and number of Bourne's photographic accoutrements necessitates the formation of a full-scale expedition with forty-two "coolies" plus his own retinue of servants, and the evidence of the insulating and world-conquering mentality that such militarylike expeditional formations engender is readily apparent in Bourne's narrative, which—as has often been remarked—is peppered with a dislike of the dialogical spaces of face-to-face encounters ("listening to nothing the whole time but barbarous Hindostani") juxtaposed with epiphanal moments of ascendancy ("The whole rich valley of Kangra which is about forty miles long by fifteen broad, was spread beneath, bounded on the opposite side by a superb mountain chain"). The expeditional mode and its hostility to dialogical encounter has been illuminatingly discussed by Gerd Spittler (1996), who contrasts it with the productive vulnerability of the individual traveler.

Ascendancy appeals to Bourne because it facilitates an encompassing view ("Here and there I could see far down into obscure and apparently inaccessible glens"). The systematicity of imperial penetration was also important to Bourne ("There is now scarcely a nook or corner, a glen, a valley, or mountain, much less a country, on the face of the globe which the penetrating eye of the camera has not searched" [cited in Ryan 1997, 47]) and his photographic images are offered as exemplary instances of these formerly inaccessible zones, now made visible. The successful outcome of travel is evaluated in these moments of height and distance, whereas closeness marks a failure ("I perceived that I should not be able to get a general view of the whole on account of the closeness of the wall which surrounded it" [475]). All these conflictual emotions and experiences are resolved in the epiphanal moment of his ascent above the Vale of Kashmir:

> The top was formed into a straight ridge or wall of snow about eight feet in width, on which I sat down to rest and survey the scene which opened around me. . . . The prospect was not only the most extensive but the most varied I have ever witnessed.
>
> Here I caught my first glimpse of the "Vale of Kashmir," which stretched away to the north like a level plain, with here and there a bright patch shining through the haze, like silver, the reflections from sheets of water. . . . To the right other pyramids of snow rose on the view in glorious and boundless succession, stretching, I presume, to the territory of Ladakh. Looking south (the way I had come) a succession of valleys and ridges followed each other for many a league, range beyond range, till they were lost in the higher summits and gigantic snows of Pangi, which in their turn mingle with the gloomy blackness of hovering clouds.
>
> What a scene was the whole to look upon! (584)

Bourne's sentiments here echo Gustave Flaubert's different responses to the varied spaces of Cairo during his 1850 trip with the photographer Maxine Du Camp: "What can I say about it all? What can I write you? As yet I am scarcely over the initial bedazzlement. . . . Each detail reaches out to grip you; it pinches you; and the more you concentrate on it the less you grasp the whole. Then gradually all this becomes harmonious and the pieces fall into place of themselves, in accordance with the laws of perspective. But the first days, by God, it is such a bewildering chaos of colours" (Flaubert, cited in Mitchell 1988, 21).

As Timothy Mitchell (who cites Flaubert in his great work *Colonising Egypt*) suggests, Flaubert contrasts a threatening experience of closeness (in which vision collapses into touch: "it pinches you") with the security of distance and height, which permits the detached observation of a totality ("in accordance with the laws of perspective"). Much later, Marcel Griaule —who had a well-known penchant for aerial photography—commented: "Perhaps it is a quirk acquired in military aircraft, but I always resent having to explore unknown terrain on foot. Seen from high in the air, a district holds few secrets" (Griaule, cited in Clifford 1988, 68). The theme of the superior colonial knowledge afforded by aircraft could be the theme of a short book, where a key text would be H. M. de Vries's *The Importance of Java as Seen from the Air* (c.1928), which included a recommendation by the chairman of the local Batavian aviation association: "Now we, the children of the age, are without ado floating thro' the air in our aeroplane or balloon, propelled by modern machinery whilst, enabled thereto by the perfection of camera-lenses, we are in a position to fix on the sensitive plate what, from the dizzy height, has drawn our attention, and afterwards, with the help of the graphic art, to demonstrate, how the world underneath presents itself to the eye spying from the clouds" (n.p.)

One of the photographs, *A Road Lined with Poplars*, that resulted from Bourne's excursion to Kashmir perfectly diagrams the diagonal sweep of a receding line of trees bisecting the picture plane into geometric fragments. Although for Rosalind Krauss, following Peter Galassi (1981, 93), Bourne's image "empties perspective of its spatial significance and reinvests it with a two dimensional order every bit as powerfully as does a contemporary Monet" (Krauss 1985, 135), this flattening and graphicization of Bourne's image is the function surely of its poor reproduction in the sources available to Krauss (presumably just Galassi) and her detachment of it from Bourne's narrative which inserts its pictorial line of flight in the penetrative camera/imperialist penetration of north India.

Bourne's narrative and images map a space in which the world is, in Heidegger's sense, a picture. In his fundamental and perplexing essay "The Age of the World Picture" (1977), Heidegger explored the manner in which a European modernity had produced a profound cleavage between man and the world. The world became a field of spatio-temporal certainty, a domain given over to measuring and executing what Merleau-Ponty later termed a "homogeneous isotropic spatiality." To Heidegger's characterization of this trope we might also add the crucial element of narrative: the world as picture also entailed interrogative pathways, forays in which lives became measured in terms of their "exploits" and the exploitation of the world as picture became the mark of lives successfully lived.

Contemporary African and Indian postcolonial photography is concerned with a realm of denarrativized, deperspectivalized surface effects that operate in a zone of tactility quite different from the detached viewpoint advocated by early European practitioners such as Bourne. However, I'm not suggesting that this refusal of narrative, perspective, and detachment is peculiar to photography. On the contrary, as I will show through a number of diverse examples this is a refusal made in other media as well. Indeed, it is also a refusal, apparent in "moments of unease" within dominant painterly schemata such as the northern "art of describing" discussed by Svetlana Alpers and the "madness of vision" apparent in the baroque.

Such an argument has been made by Martin Jay (1988) in his consideration of the multiple scopic regimes that have constituted modernity. Jay argues that the prevailing history of the dominance of a single scopic regime—which he calls "Cartesian perspectivalism"—is too simple. The term Cartesian perspectivalism conflates Cartesian subjective rationality with Albertian conceptualizations of single-point perspective. Central to this notion is a disembodied vision, what Norman Bryson terms "vision decarnalised" (Bryson 1983, 95) and which I have elsewhere examined (following Susan Buck-Morss) as an "anaesthetics" as opposed to a "corpothetics."[1] Within Cartesian perspectivalism, Bryson suggests, "the body is reduced to . . . its optical anatomy, the minimal diagram of monocular perspective. In the Founding Perception, the gaze of the painter arrests the flux of phenomena, contemplates the visual field from a vantage-point outside the mobility of duration, in an eternal moment of disclosed presence" (94). Jay outlines a number of related consequences stemming from the rise of this new visual order. The gap between the viewer and what was represented in the image widened, and there was a general "deeroticisation" of the visual order (Jay 1988, 8) as the world depicted in images was increasingly "situated in a mathematically regular spatio-temporal order filled with natural objects that could only be observed from without" (9).

Heidegger's "The Age of the World Picture" essay was produced in 1935 —one year before Benjamin's "Work of Art" essay—and there are certain intriguing parallels between the two arguments. Both essays develop extraordinarily broad and ambitious evolutionary narratives. In Benjamin's optimistic history, a decay of an earlier situated aura is pressaged by new technologies of picturing. In Heidegger's pessimistic history a positively valorized premodern dwelling is ruptured by Cartesian perspectivalism in which the world comes to be seen as picture—a zone of representation established as something exterior to existence. Picturing becomes inseparable from modernity: "The fact that the world becomes a picture at all is what distinguishes the modern age" (1977, 130).

Whereas for Parmenides "man is the one who is looked upon by that which is" in the modern age, "that which is ... come[s] into being ... through the fact that man first looks upon it" (1977, 131, 130). Looking upon the world and constructing the world as picture entails man placing himself against and before nature as something separate: the world is "placed in the realm of man's knowing and of his having disposal" (130).[2]

Jay opposes the assumption made by commentators as diverse as Richard Rorty and William Ivins Jr. that Cartesian perspectivalism has been the sole dominant regime since the Renaissance. He draws attention to other very different paradigms that at times dethroned the supposedly hegemonic Cartesian perspectival regime. Thus the "art of describing," which flourished in the Low Countries during the seventeenth century, rejected the narrative and perspective of earlier southern European Renaissance painting in favor of denarrativized visual texture. Instead of a fixed viewing position it demanded a mobile, roving eye, scanning the dispersed details in the images that frequently include words in addition to objects in its visual space (1988, 12). Among the contrasts Alpers draws between this art of describing and earlier perspectival imagery are "light reflected off objects versus objects modelled by light and shadow; the surface of objects, their colours and textures dealt with rather that their placement in a legible space" (1988, 12–13).

The second moment of unease described by Jay held the possibility of a more radical refusal of perspectivalism. The baroque (a term probably derived from the Portuguese word for a misshapen pearl) is advanced by Jay as "a permanent, if often repressed, visual possibility throughout the modern era" (1988, 16). Drawing on Christine Buci-Glucksmann's work, Jay stresses the baroque's rejection of "the monocular geometricalisation of the Cartesian tradition, with its illusion of homogenous three-dimensional space seen with a God's-eye view from afar." The baroque is fixated with opacity, with the recursivity of surface and depth and "reveals the conventional rather than the natural quality of 'normal' specularity by showing its dependence on the materiality of the medium of reflection" (17). Elsewhere (Pinney 1999) I have discussed popular Indian visual culture in terms of the baroque as invoked by Alejo Carpentier, who in a 1975 lecture outlined a theory of the baroque's relation to magical realism that has a peculiar applicability to the images I shall shortly consider.

Although the baroque was, for Carpentier, a "constant of the human spirit" (1995, 93), it needs also to be understood as a reaction to a spatial rationality. The baroque "is characterised by a horror of the vacuum, the naked surface, the harmony of linear geometry" (93); it "flees from geometrical arrangements" (94). Carpentier sees Bernini's Saint Peter's cathedral in Rome as an exemplar of the baroque; it is like a caged sun, "a sun that expands and explores the columns that circumscribe it, that pretend to demarcate its boundaries and literally disappear before its sumptuousness" (93). To Carpentier's stress on the creole and hybrid nature of magical realism we can add Luis Leal's observation that magical realism is an "attitude towards reality" (1995, 121) and not just as a literary genre,[3] as well as Amaryll Chanady's claim that magical realism "acquires a particular significance in the context of Latin America's status as a colonised society" and his observation that magical realism is a response to the "'rule, norm and tyranny' of the age of reason" (1995, 135).

This preoccupation with theoretical perspectives that have evolved out of the consideration of painting and literature may seem perplexing given that my concern is with photography. What I have tried to demonstrate, however, is that the "baroque"—the appeal to a haptic surface—is commonly invoked across different media. What all these surfacist strategies have in common is their emergence in specific postcolonial contexts as expressions of identities that in complex ways repudiate the projects of which Cartesian perspectivalist images are a part.

However, the distance is very slight between these abstract ideas and the practices of popular Indian and African photography to which I will very briefly turn. Judith Mara Gutman writes of one of Samuel Bourne's south Indian photographs (*View into Ootacummund*, 1867) in terms that closely mirror Dawn Ades's description of Claude's Italian landscapes: "A low level light is introduced into the foreground, then allowed to move in and out of trees, creating graceful lyrical turns among the leaves. The light builds to great majestic heights, with dramatic breaks of shadow, before fading out into the distance. Bourne wove a story into his image, guiding his viewers from the slower-paced rambling foreground through the building intensity of the middle ground, then quietly leading his viewers out into the distant future" (1982, 17). This image, which is so carefully constructed to permit the viewer's eye to travel through its internal space, can be con-

Christopher Pinney

trasted with another photograph discussed by Gutman, *Women at Sipi Fair* (c.1905). This image, by an unknown Indian photographer, is subject to a very different spatial regime: "With no 'invitation' into the picture, my eyes did not know how or where to enter. . . . There were no leads, as you find in Western imagery, to other parts of the image" (Gutman 1982, 6).

The Realist Backdrop

Writing about American Civil War photography, Alan Trachtenberg has noted what he calls "historicism-by-photography," the notion—in the wake of the consecration of photography by war—that "historical knowledge declares its true value by its photographability" (1985, 1). Perhaps the clearest statement of this transformation in the nature of historical events lies in Paul Valéry's conclusion, a hundred years after photography's introduction, that "the mere notion of photography, when we introduce it into our meditation on the genesis of historical knowledge and its true value, suggests the simple question: *Could such and such a fact, as it is narrated, have been photographed?*" (Valéry, cited in Trachtenberg 1989, xiii–xiv).

Valéry's observation expresses a standard view of photography as indexical—as a chemical trace of the light bounced off objects passed before the lens—and as having an element of randomness that always eludes the photographer's desire to frame and construct the image. It is the incompleteness of the photographic filter that sets it apart from other media, such as painting and drawing. Implicit in this view is a desire for imprisonment within the time space of the everyday world, captured by the camera.

Photography can be used to position bodies and faces within history, and it can also be used as a means of escape. What Eduardo Cadava (1997, xxix) terms "photographic self-archiving" positions bodies within specific chronotopes—it matters to some people when you went to France that the trace of the Eiffel Tower in the distance is the one in the center of Paris and not a simulacrum: as Bourdieu says, it "consecrates the unique encounter" (1990, 36). The central Indian chronotope I now want briefly to describe doesn't privilege these factors because its ludic photographic idiom is not concerned with fixing bodies in particular times and places; rather it is concerned with the body as a surface that is completely mutable and mobile, capable of being situated in any time and space.

Whereas in some photographic traditions, backdrops are valued as a record of the subject's position in a particular actual space (usually, as

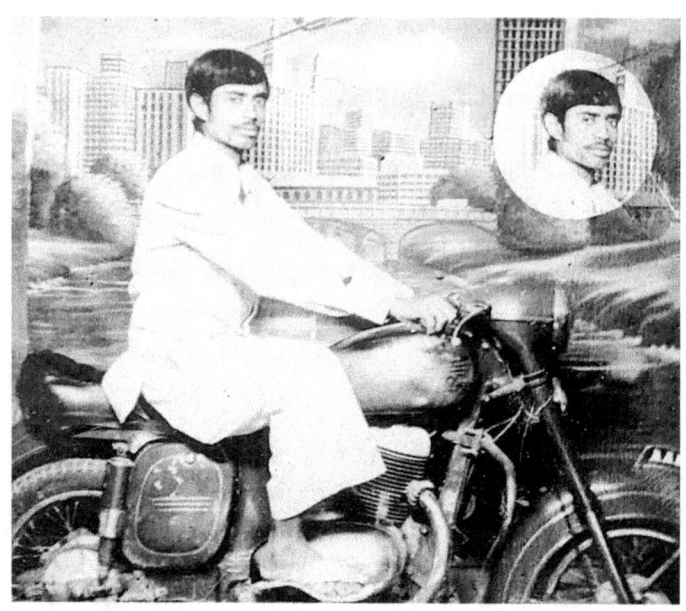

1. Guman Singh astride a traveling studio's motorbike, c. 1983.

Bourdieu notes, in encounters with places of high symbolic yield), very few people in Nagda (a town of 79,000 people in central India, about half-way between Delhi and Bombay) request to be photographed in the actual space of Nagda. This generally only happens in the process of photograph-ing wedding processions as they make their way through the town's streets, or in the gardens of the local Birla *mandir*, an elaborate pseudoarchaic temple whose grounds have become a popular picnic spot for the town's wealthier inhabitants. The photographs taken here (largely by professional photographers who stalk the gardens) spurn the topographical specificity of the location in favor of formulaic backdrops (of the sort to be seen in Hindi films) of flowers and fountains.

When Nagdarites seek a photograph of themselves they nearly always commission a photographer (for there are very few privately owned cam-eras) to photograph them *inside* a photographic studio. The "real" space of Nagda is continually rejected in favor of that within the photographer's premises (fig. 1). A backdrop will be chosen—perhaps the Taj Mahal, or a Dal Lake (Kashmir) scene, or a cityscape (seen from a motorbike). The same spatial/temporal dislocation can be achieved through "cutting"—the careful juxtaposition of cropped paper negatives and composite printing

Christopher Pinney

that allows brides and grooms in wedding albums to travel the length and breadth of India, one moment standing beside the Tower of Victory in Chittaurgarh and the next by the India Gateway in Delhi.

The "Subaltern" Backdrop

Writing in *Afterimage*, the anthropologist Arjun Appadurai has suggested that the widespread use of props and backdrops in popular postcolonial photography expresses a resistance to the documentary claims of photography and a foregrounding of critiques of modernity. Appadurai goes so far as to label the backdrop "subaltern," where "the backdrop resists, subverts or parodies the realist claims of photography in various ways. . . . In these postcolonial settings, photographic backdrops become less the site for debates about colonial subjectivity and more the place for . . . 'experiments with modernity.' That is, outside the taxonomising and coercive techniques of colonial observers and the colonial state, backdrops tend to become part of a more complicated dialogue between the posed photograph and the practices of everyday life" (1997, 5).

In Nagda, backgrounds are used not simply as a substitute in the absence of their referents, but as a space of exploration. This exploration is often geographic; within Nagda studios one can travel from Goa to Mandu to Agra and Kashmir merely by standing in front of different walls. But Nagda studios also function as chambers of dreams where personal explorations of an infinite range of alteregos is possible.

Double and triple portraits place a person beyond the space and identity that certain forms of Western portraiture enforce. These, along with the trick techniques of montage that are so common in Nagda portraiture, testify to the lack of any desire to "capture" sitters within bounded spatial and temporal frames. The replication of bodies and faces brought about by doubling and tripling fractures not only the spatial and temporal correlates that are implied by the perspectival window created by photography but also suggests a different conceptualization of the subjects who are made to appear within this window. It is as if there is a homology between the spatial and temporal infractions of this representational window and the fracture of these local subjects.

But it is not only backdrops that suggest this African/Indian parallelism. There is also an explicitly articulated recognition by photographers that their task is to produce not an imprisoning trace of their sitters but to act as impressarios, bringing forth an ideal and aspirational vision of the bodies that sitters wish themselves to be.

"Coming Out Better . . ."

No one in Nagda—apart, that is, from the police and other agents of the state—sees any value in photography's potential to fix quotidian reality. It is rarely there to record or to memorialize the events and conjunctions of the past. It is prized, rather, for its ability to make people and places "come out better than they really are."[4] This is a phrase used by customers of Nagda's Sagar Studio, which is famous for its double color exposures. The proprietor, Vijay Vyas, observes that Nagdarites rarely desire "realistic" (*vastavik*) photographs: "They always say I want to look good. . . . Everyone says I am like this but I want to come out better than this in my photo [*is se bhi zyada acchha mera photo ana chahie*]. So we try."

"Coming out better" in a Nagda photograph is achieved through two routes: through the adoption of gestures and through the deployment of costume and props. Frequently the one implies the other. Vijay Vyas refers to any photo involving a gesture with the English phrase "action shooting": "action shooting or an action photo means you've got your hand in a certain way, holding it up to show your watch, one leg is higher than another, these are action photos." This refers to a set of techniques agreed on between the sitter and the photographer that allow a particular pose to emerge and that may jointly involve a gesture or look by the subject and the adoption of an appropriate camera angle by the photographer. Thus there are "poet" and "filmi" (i.e., film star) poses that both require low camera angles, and the creation of these involves a sort of theatrical direction by the photographer (fig. 2).

Vijay, like several other Nagda studio owners, also has a collection of costumes available for the use of his clients, although they are the cause of considerable tribulations. The costumes include an all-in-one dress that can be arranged to give different regional, caste, and class flavors. I asked Vijay why his clients are so keen to wear different clothes when they are in front of the camera: "For *shauq* [pleasure, to satisfy a desire]. They don't want to wear their everyday clothes. They don't want *vastavik* [realistic] photos. . . . They brush and braid their hair, put on [talcum] powder, put on cream, put on lipstick, they change their dress, they wear good clothes,

Christopher Pinney

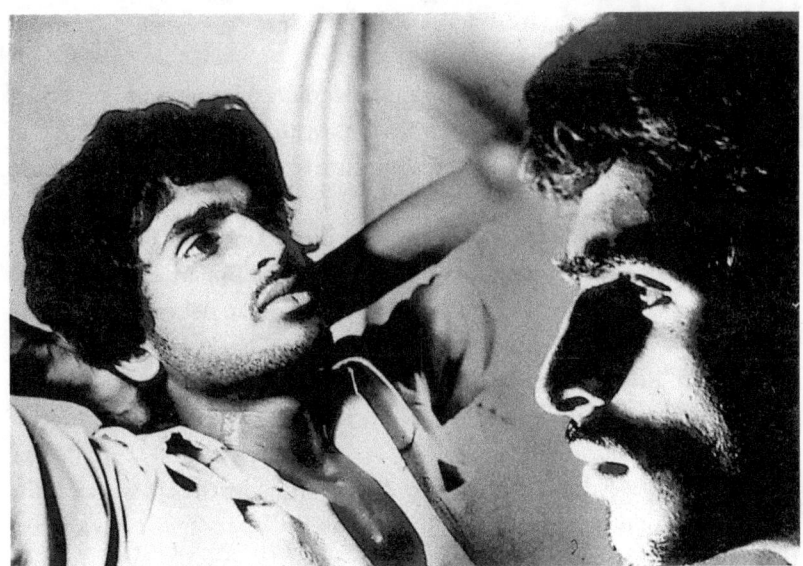

2. Composite print by Suhag Studios, Nagda, c. 1980.

put on a tie, wear a coat, they make sure their trousers are OK, then they say 'take an action photo,' 'take my photo with this type of dress, Rajasthani dress, with a *matka* [earthenware pot]' and so on."

Whereas Nagda popular photography does not seem to share much with the solemnizing function of French photography described by Pierre Bourdieu (1990, 24), there are insights to be gained from some West African practices. Kobena Mercer describes the approach of the photographer Seydou Keïta, active in Bamako, Mali, from the mid-1940s, as follows "With various props, accessories and backdrops, the photographer stylises the pictorial space, and through lighting, depth of field, and framing, the camera work heightens the mise-en-scène of the subject, whose poses, gestures and expression thus reveal a 'self' not as he or she actually is, but 'just a little more than what we really are'" (1995 n.p.). The comment at the end is by Seydou Keïta himself, and uncannily mirrors the observation by Vijay Vyas.

Coming from an immersion in popular Indian photographic practices, one is immediately struck by similarities with documented studies of popular African photography: there appears to be a similar disinterest in realist chronotopes, a similar refusal of Cartesian perspectivalism, even as it exists in its attenuated contemporary Euro-American popular incarnations. Some of the apparent continuities can be in part explained by a continuity of personnel: the studios studied by Heike Behrend (1998a; and paper in this volume) in Mombasa are largely Indian run, and the powerful influence of Bombay cinema throughout West Africa (Larkin 1997) and the impact of Indian-produced iconography in Mami Wata devotion suggest possible lineages of influence.

The work of Seydou Keïta (whose championing by the art world as the key African photographer could be the subject of another essay) is particularly resonant with popular Indian portraiture. Seydou Keïta's clients had, however, a much more restricted choice of backdrops. As Seydou reported to the *Guardian* on 19 April 1997, "Between 1949 and 1952, I used my fringed bedspread as my first backdrop. Then I changed the background every two or three years." In another source, he adds that this introduced an element of indeterminacy: "Sometimes the background went well with their clothes, especially for the women, but it was all haphazard" (Keïta, cited in Bigham 1999, 58).

These sporadically changed backdrops contribute significantly to the Seydou look—and to their refusal of the realist chronotope. Any location outside of the imaginary space of the studio is continually exceeded by the texture of Seydou's various bedspreads entering into harmonious and dissonant conversation with the clothes and accessories worn by his sitters (fig. 3). This conjunction produces a Malian "art of describing," a photographic surfacism that engages with texture, where everything springs out of the photograph toward the viewer, rather than a field of spatio-temporal certainty receding within the image.[5] This is what we might label "vernacular modernism": a refusal of external verification prompted not by Greenbergian angst but by a desire to consolidate the intimate space between viewer and image.

The most popular of Seydou's images date from the 1950s, perhaps because their subjects radiate the optimism of the winds of change of an imagined future (fig. 4), rather than the weariness of Mbembesque postcolonial "banality" (Mbembe 1992). The material discussed by Stephen

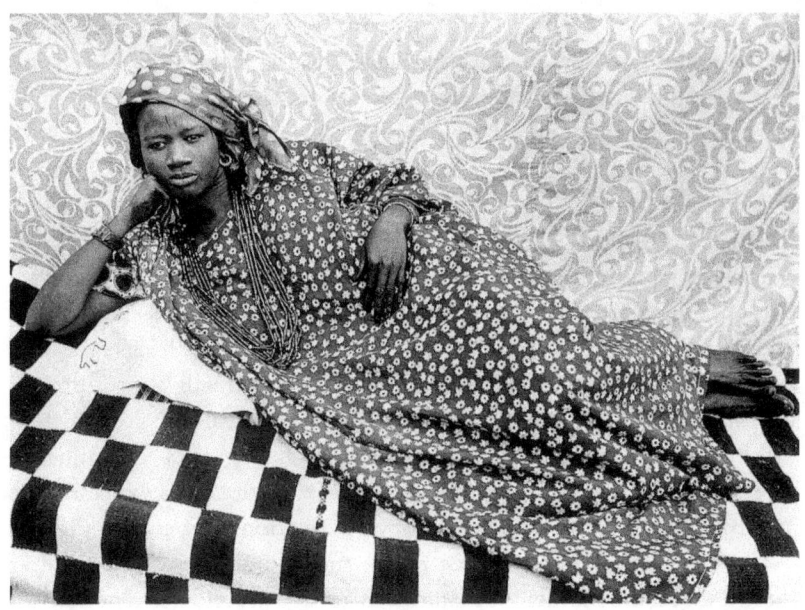

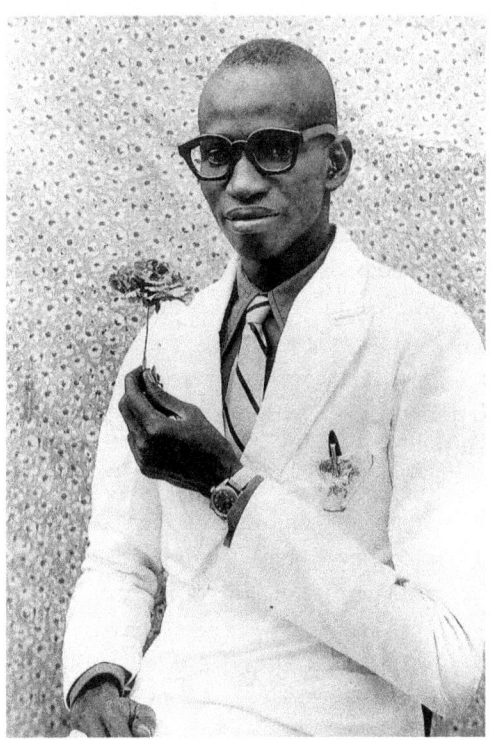

(*Above*) 3. Untitled, 1956–57.
(*Left*) 4. Untitled, 1958.
Both copyright Seydou
Keïta. Courtesy of Sean
Kelly Gallery, New York.

Sprague in his wonderful article (1978; reprinted in this volume) on Yoruba photography dates largely from the 1970s, and the resonances with popular Indian practice are even more marked: here is a world of surfaces and materiality that reach out to their embodied viewers.

As in Nagda there is a distrust of images that do not reciprocate their viewer's gaze: profiles and "unclear" images that do not fully reveal a face frustrate the real purpose of photography for Yoruba. Sprague describes a number of highly conventionalized poses and genres including the "formal photographic portrait" performed by older Yoruba. The subjects appear in their best traditional dress "squarely facing the camera" with legs well apart and hands on the knees or lap and "the eyes look directly at and through the camera" (1978, 54). Significantly, Sprague notes that although the technical constraints of early photographic processes and the enduring influence of early British portrait photography are often adduced to explain these Yoruba practices, there is in fact no obvious relationship between the two.

The concern with the surface of the image and its production after the photographic moment is manifest in Yoruba practices in a number of ways, all of which have Indian parallels. Photographic cutouts are commonly made by pasting photographic images (and in some cases images from magazines) onto thin sheets of wood, to which a supporting base is added.[6] Double and more complex composite printing, which fractures what Gombrich once called the "eye-witness principle"[7] is commonly used, particularly in the representation of deceased siblings in the *ibeji* twin cult. Some studios, such as Sir Special of Ila-Orangun, mounted photographic images within mirrored frames, carefully scratching away the tain so that the outline of the photographed body could be seen from the other side (Sprague 1978, 59), a common technique in the display of religious chromolithographs in central India. Yoruba studios also produce complex ensembles that juxtapose photographic images with textual inscriptions (Sprague reproduces one with the slogan "To be a man is a problem"), creations that would look familiar to Nagda producers.[8]

Both popular Indian and Yoruba surfacism is underwritten at every point by the desire for clarity and visibility, and in both locales the eyes of the subject become crucial markers of the image's ability to reciprocate the look of the viewer: the eyes become the fulcrum of the relationship between the picture and the world outside it. Sprague notes that one of the key conventions governing Yoruba photography is that "both of the subject's eyes must be always visible in a portrait. This convention . . . relates to

Christopher Pinney

the concept of *ifarahon*—of visibility of and clarity of form, line and identity" (1978, 56). This resonates very deeply with Nagda practices and with the more encompassing notion of *darshan*, of seeing and being seen, which also informs the Nagdarites's quest for frontality and visibility inscribed in a surface that looks out, thus reciprocating the gaze of the viewer.

But beyond this there is in much popular African and Indian photography a strikingly similar preoccupation with the materiality of the image and with the ways in which the surface of the photographic image becomes a site for the self-fashioning of postcolonial identities. What is striking about the practices discussed above is their discontinuity with the historical tradition out of which they emerge and their continuity with other contemporary postcolonial practices. Indian, African, Haitian (Houlberg 1992), and Chinese[9] popular practices are linked by a common concern, not with the space of the photograph as a window on a reality marked by internalized lines of flight, but with the photograph as a surface, a ground, on which presences that look out toward the viewer can be built. As Olu Oguibe elegantly describes this transformation, "the image in question is not the figure before the lens but that which emerges after the photographic moment" (1996, 246). If the photographic moment is dedicated to capturing the world as picture, what emerges afterward is the materiality of the image: what Oguibe calls its "substance" and what I discuss in terms of surface. A shallow picture space, collage and montage techniques, overpainting, and complex sculptural mediations transpose the focus of photographic images from the space between the image's window and its referents to the space between the images' surface and their beholders. It is this "visual decolonisation" (Appadurai 1997, 6) that I have tried to conjure in these notes from the surface of the image.

Notes

I am grateful to Michael Godby for his invitation to Cape Town in 1999, where I presented the first version of this essay.

1 Pinney 2001. By anaesthetics, following Buck-Morss, is meant the realm of anti-Kantian decorporealized aesthetics. The neologism "corpothetics" is intended to evoke the domain of sensuous and corporeal aesthetics.

2 For an extended application of these ideas to the European practice of travel, see Pinney 1994.

3 Leal argues that the magical realist "doesn't create imaginary worlds in which we can hide from everyday reality: In magical realism the writer confronts reality and tries to untangle it, to discover what is mysterious in things, in life, in human acts" (1995, 121).

4 The following three paragraphs are condensed from Pinney 1997a, 178–80; the quoted material is from interviews with the author, translated from Hindi.

5 Bigham (1999, 57) summarizes some of these pictorial characteristics as compositional centrality and stability, with centrally fixed figures often shown frontally, fully, and within a shallow picture space.

6 I have not encountered this in Nagda, but one photographer/artist, Bishumber Dutt of Mussoorie in north India (whose work is described in David and Judith MacDougall's film *Photo Wallahs*), makes his living from the production of such lifesize photographic cutouts (see MacDougall 1992).

7 That is, that an image depicts what one person could actually see.

8 For technical reasons, it was not possible to reproduce this image in the reprint of Sprague's essay in this volume.

9 In light of Sprague one could reread Sontag's account of popular Chinese photography to reveal its corpothetic and surfacist nature: "None is a candid photograph, not even of the kind that the most unsophisticated camera user in this society finds normal—a baby crawling on a floor, someone in midgesture . . . generally what people do with the camera is assemble for it, then line up in a row or two. There is no interest in catching movement" (1979, 173).

Heike Behrend

Imagined Journeys

THE LIKONI FERRY PHOTOGRAPHERS

OF MOMBASA, KENYA

There exists a longstanding association between travel and vision. However, in Europe before 1600, the aristocratic traveler went abroad mainly for "discourse"—to involve the reflective and disciplined exercise of the ear and the tongue, rather than for picturesque views (Adler 1989, 9). In the seventeenth and eighteenth centuries, in travel sermons and manuals, the eye slowly gained superiority over the ear. At this time, tourists carried Claude glasses, brownish convex mirrors named for the painter Claude Lorrain, which reflected condensed images of landscapes. With the help of the glass, they transformed the landscape they were traveling through into images often following the picturesque conventions of landscape painting. The Claude glass can be seen as a predecessor of the camera. As a technical instrument it privileged as well as mediated the gaze and sight and structured travel experience. Thus, touristic perception created its own imagined spaces (Wagner 1991, 330; Hennig 1997, 53).

Three months after the camera had been invented and presented to the Academy of Science in Paris in 1839, the first daguerreotypists reached Cairo in Africa and started "daguerreotyping like lions" (H. Vernet, cited in Howe 1994). A few years later, when Thomas Cook began organizing mass tourism in 1845, photographs offered indisputable evidence that the trip had been made. By taking pictures of pyramids and temples, tourists appropriated the things photographed and put themselves into a knowledgeable and powerful relation to the world. Photographs helped them to take possession of space in which they might have felt insecure (Sontag 1979, 4, 9). However, when the distance between tourists and Egyptian life grew, photographic representation came to provide a simulacrum of the experiences they had helped to avoid. Staged commercial photographs recapitulated exotic street scenes (Howe 1994, 41). Thus, since the invention of photography, a highly complex and symbiotic relationship has grown up between it and the activity of travel; photographic representations became inseparable from actual journey, the camera mediating the experience of travel. Western travelers used photographs, on the one hand, to produce "faithful pictorial records" by employing the camera as an instrument of evidence, thereby reinforcing the "culture of realism" (Green-Lewis 1996, 31), while photographic practices, on the other hand, paradoxically also subverted this realism. The commercial photographic studios that were built up at the turn of the twentieth century in various African towns produced a space of wish fulfillment and illusions that transcended "the culture of realism" while at the same time confirming it.

In the following I would like to present a group of young photographers in Mombasa, Kenya, who have made their studios the sites of a visual recycling of images produced by modern mass media. By localizing as well as domesticating the global flow of images, they have created a new space of wish fulfillment and imagination that allows their customers to participate in a world from which in actuality they are excluded.

The Likoni Ferry Photographers

In the course of my research on popular photography in Africa, I became acquainted with a group of young photographers who called themselves the Likoni ferry photographers.[1] At the beginning of the 1990s, they settled in Likoni, a quarter of Mombasa, on a steep bluff directly on the shore, opposite Old Town.

Already in the 1930s, Mombasa, an old Swahili town, became a place of particular attraction for white settlers. The sea that surrounds the island, as well as the island's creeks, provided immense pleasure for the devotees of deep-sea angling, sailing, and—later—water skiing. Numerous sports clubs were established and created an atmosphere of "sea level and sanity" (Jewell 1976, xiii). During this time, white settler tourism singled out and demarcated certain privileged spaces—the beach, the sea, and certain buildings in Old Town—from which Africans were excluded. Space was regionalized into different zones occupied by different classes of people. Pictures of these privileged places started circulating, reinforming and re-inforcing certain images.

In the 1960s, the forces of new technology and globalization processes allowed Western mass tourism to invade the coast. During the 1980s, Kenya's tourism industry was the country's number-one foreign exchange earner and one of the largest employers. Western mass tourism turned certain sites and landscapes into commodities and invested them with new meanings. Landscape, in its double role as commodity and potent cultural symbol, came to be presented and re-presented in "packaged tours": an object to be purchased, consumed, and even brought home in the form of souvenirs, such as postcards and photographs (Mitchell 1994a, 15).

This tourist boom attracted a large number of migrant workers, who came to the coast to work in tourist hotels, at the harbor, in game parks, or as photographers. Although the tourist trade has decreased strongly in recent years, migrant workers still travel to the coast to look for various opportunities. Most of the Likoni photographers came to Mombasa as migrant workers from Central Province or western Kenya. Strangers in Mombasa themselves, they recruited their customers from the pool of migrant labor and African tourists, people from up-country, whom the local city people contemptuously referred to as *washamba*—that is, peasants or field workers. On weekends and holidays many of these migrant laborers turned into tourists. Often they were visited by family members from up-country, and together with their relatives they went to see the Indian Ocean as well as the sites of Mombasa Old Town, and, as proof that they had been there, to have themselves photographed. As a photographer, Mr. Maina Hutchinson, explained to me, the "clic-clic culture" of Western tourists had reached Africa. Like Western tourists, who were "crazy" about taking pictures of every site they visited, Kenyans now also wanted to record everything in photographs, and today photography is an integral part of local African tourism. The Likoni ferry photographers profited from this trend, and they contributed substantially to molding and simultaneously transforming the conventions of this tourism.

Figure 1 shows three young migrant workers who returned to their homes up-country after the Likoni violence in August and September 1997.[2] They wanted to be photographed together with the camera, which is placed in the center in the position of greatest importance. Moreover,

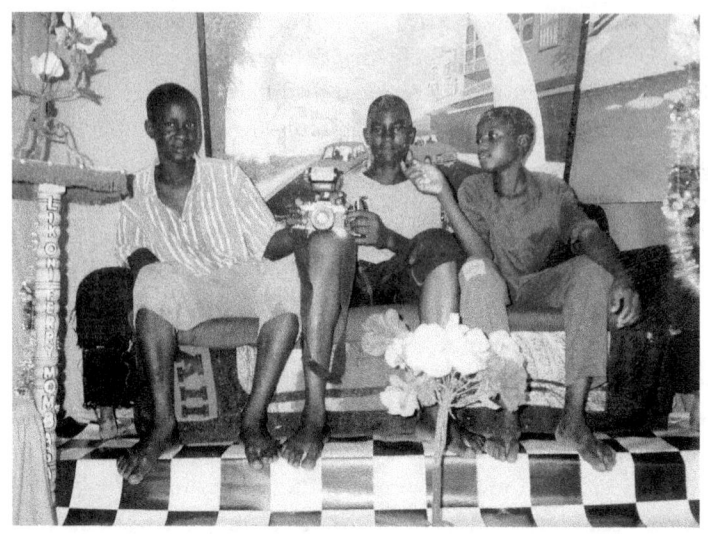

1. Photograph taken by Sheba Onyanga, Jay's Studio.

2. Mr. Sammy
Njuguma,
Sammy Big 7
Studio, 1996.

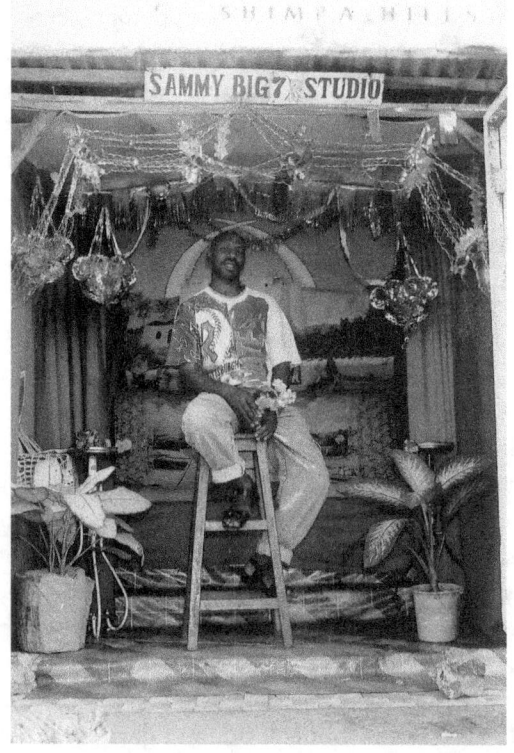

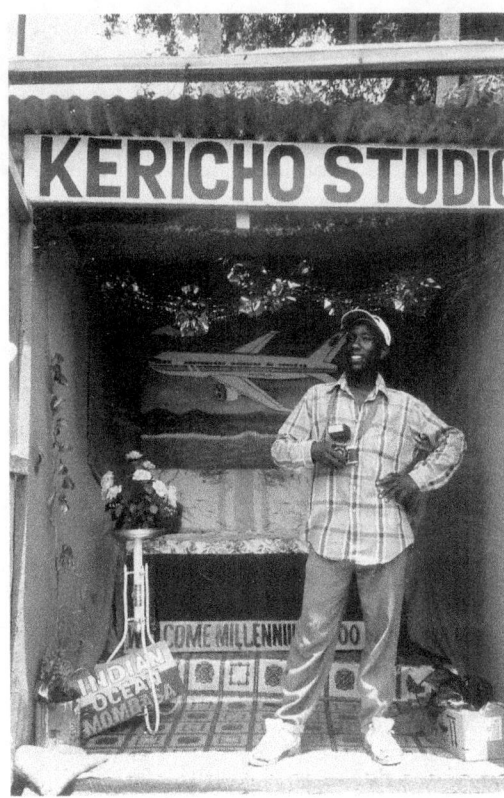

3. Mr. John Chege,
Kericho Photo Studio,
2000.

the boy on the right points at the camera, further underlining its significance. In the backdrop are the so-called Tusks on Moi Avenue, one of the tourist attractions of Mombasa. Thus, in this picture the relationship between tourism and photography is depicted in the photo itself.

Most of the Likoni photographers began as street photographers and then slowly, with little equipment, built up their studios (although without electricity and running water).[3] They called themselves *jua kali*, which is Swahili for "hot or sharp sun" and designates people who work in the "informal sector." Thus, in their small, mobile studios, they occupy an intermediate position between the established studios and the street photographers (figs. 2 and 3).

All told, about thirty photographers worked in Likoni, ten of which had their own studios and the rest, among them six young women, worked as roving photographers down by the dock or sometimes as touts for the studios. At the beginning, women worked only in subordinate positions, but when I returned to Likoni in April 2000 three women had managed to establish their own studios.

These young men and women were autodidacts or, as they themselves proudly put it, self-made men and women. They came from the ranks of those largely excluded from social and economic opportunities, and there was a strong feeling of marginalization and insecurity among them. It is not by chance, I suppose, that with a few exceptions they all belonged to various independent fundamentalist Christian churches, which demand of their members a radical rupture with their (sinful) past while at the same time promising them salvation and economic success in this world.

In my conversations with these photographers they emphasized the rivalry among themselves. They explained that they produced the differing decorations in their studios in opposition to each other—although this didn't prevent them from imitating or adopting a competitor's attractive decor. Their goal was to attract customers, and, for business reasons, each tried to outdo the others. They didn't see their decor as art but as an aspect of commerce or business. An installation was good and beautiful if it brought customers; their own creativity followed the logic of capitalistic competition and the law of accelerated innovation. Accordingly, they changed the backdrops and equipment of their studios frequently. They saw themselves as modern because, as one photographer explained, they always knew how to offer the newest things.

These photographers worked more or less illegally as squatters because the land occupied by their studios belonged to the city or to the ferry company. I believe that this illegal status contributed substantially to the particular aesthetic of the studios. The state rigidly prevents other street photographers, who work on public squares, from creatively altering these sites; as one street photographer put it, these sites must remain "natural." But the Likoni ferry photographers were not subject to this degree of state restrictions and sanctions. Their existence was repeatedly threatened and they had to fear being driven away, but their studios enjoyed "artistic freedom." Within the postcolonial Kenyan state, the photographers were able to occupy a space that eluded the state authorities. Indeed, the Likoni ferry photographers and their productions were a unique local development that made use of a great variety of global elements. As Daniel Miller (1995) describes, here we have an innovation, a discontinuity produced, so to speak, a posteriori out of the local consumption of global elements.

Heike Behrend

Remote Places

In their studios, the Likoni photographers created environments that made
use of the immense reservoir of images available in Mombasa. In their
decor they produced assemblages that singled out as well as juxtaposed
pictures of various places all over the world. Exotic tapestries made in
Turkey (reaching Kenya via Dubai) showing sublime Alpine landscapes or
playful horses in splashing water, wild tigers, roaring stags, Jesus as shep-
herd, the Last Supper, or the Kaaba of Mecca, as well as paintings picturing
airplanes, highways, and luxury steamliners, were brought together with
a homely sofa suggesting a modern middle-class salon or sitting room.
As I have shown elsewhere in more detail (Behrend 2000), by juxtaposing
and mixing the images of various places the Likoni photographers, as migrant workers, detached themselves from the logic of a fixed place, thereby
dissolving the separation between "here" and "there" by being global. In
their studios, they realized the vision of "the world-in-the-home" and "the
home-in-the-world" (Bhabha 1994, 141).

In their studios, the photographers offered their customers the chance to
enter a space from which in actuality they are excluded. Customers could
transform themselves into airplane passengers, part of the modern jet set,
and thus connected to a wider global world (figs. 4 and 5). In the photos,
the photographed persons are placed in an airport as a privileged place, a
"non-site," in the sense that it is a place of arriving and departing, a place
of passage not of staying (figs. 6 and 7). Through the photographs, the depicted persons participate in the increasing acceleration and mobility of
modern life, shifting boundaries and thus producing a cosmopolitan visu-
alized discourse of potentially being everywhere. In this context it is not
by chance that Mr. Jay Ngao, the owner of Jay's Studio, recently changed
the name of his studio to Global Studio. Mr. Jay Ngao explained to me that
most of the customers from up-country did not know ships; for them the
sea and ships formed part of a foreign exotic landscape that attracted them,
and that this is why, among the Likoni studio owners, painted backdrops
with luxury liners proliferated (figs. 8 and 9).

In the Francis Studio, ironically, the *Titanic* became a very successful
backdrop to celebrate the millennium. As I was told, it was, above all, the
recently produced film with the same title that made the ship an icon of a
(catastrophic) modernity (fig. 10).

In Mr. Jay Ngao's Studio in 1996 and in the Omalla Studio in 1998 there
were backdrops that showed two sites of Nairobi: the Kenyatta Conference

4. Simon Expert
Studio, 1996.

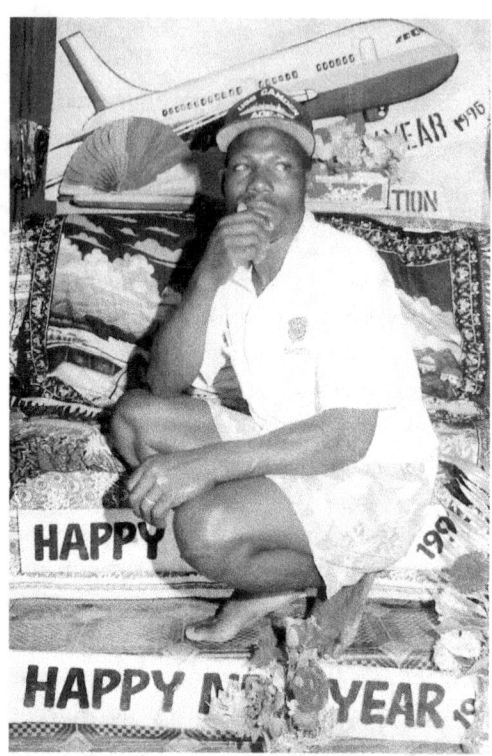

5. Jay's Studio,
now called Global
Studio, 1999.

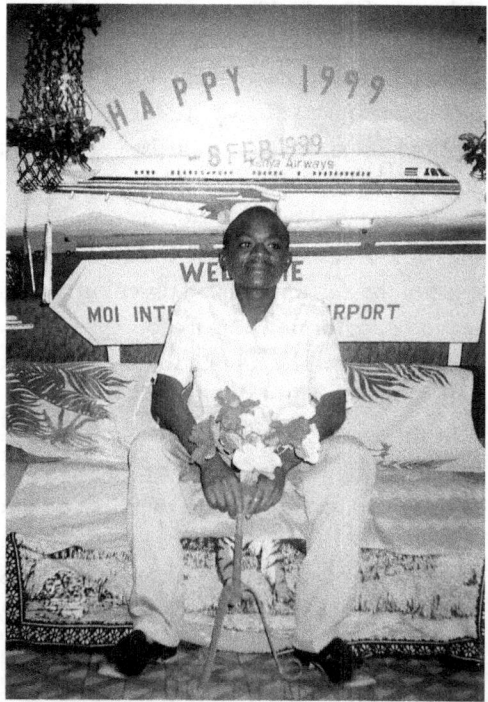

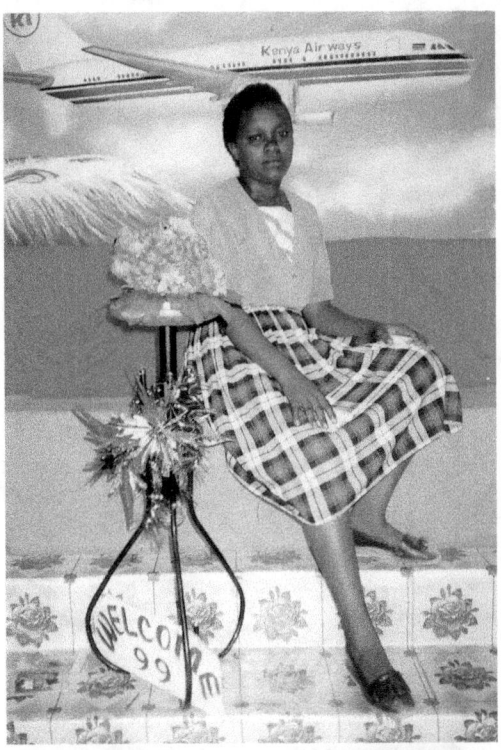

6. Omalla Studio,
1999.

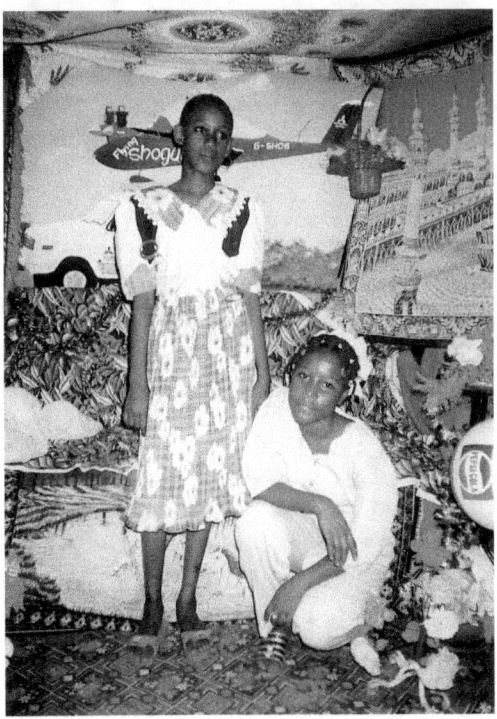

7. Omalla Studio,
1998.

8. Sheba Onyanga
Studio, 2000.

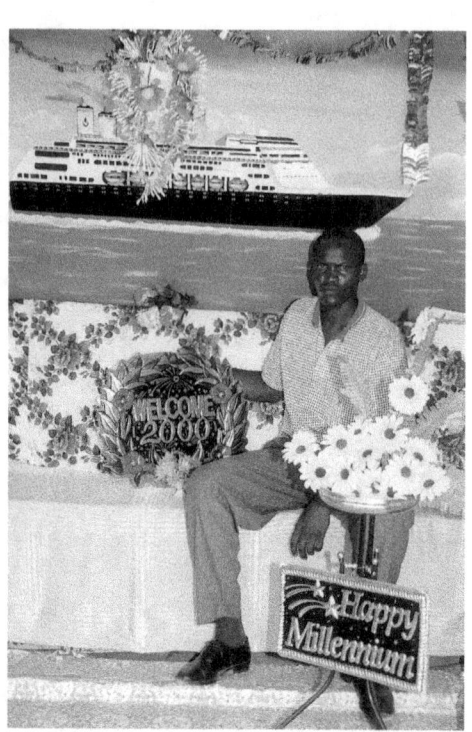

9. Omalla Studio,
1999.

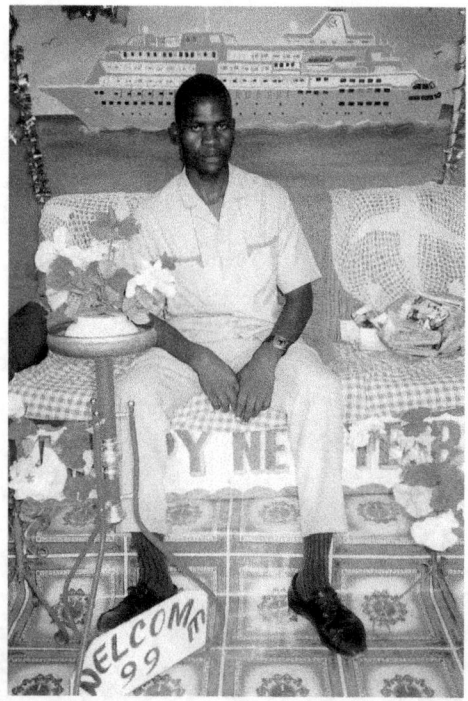

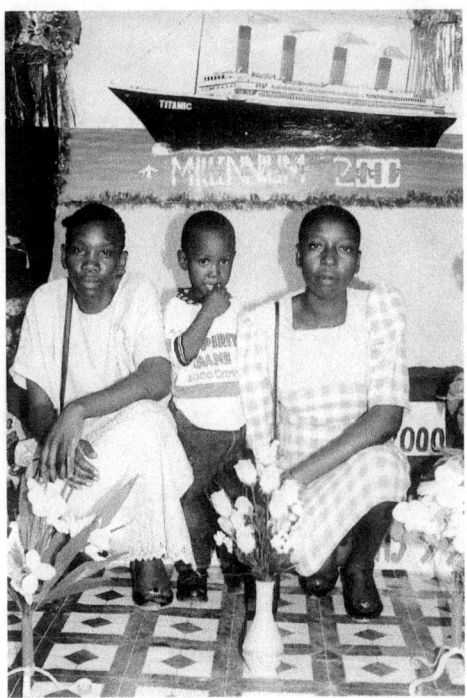

10. Francis Studio,
2000.

Center and the Nyayo Monument, both main tourist attractions representing the power of the postcolonial Kenyan nation state (figs. 11 and 12).

When I asked Mr. Jay Ngao whether migrant workers originating in the
Central Province, from Nairobi, came to be photographed at his studio because they were homesick and wanted to remember their native place, he
answered in the negative. Instead, he said, people from the coast who never
had been to the capital would come to his studio to take a picture that
allowed them to be in Nairobi. Thus, the Likoni photographers not only
used the exotic, more or less foreign, places and landscapes of Kenya as
well as other parts of the world to produce a specific cosmopolitan imaginary space, but they also used it as a space of exploration. Within their
studios, they and their customers would travel to various places all over the
world (compare Pinney 1997a, 175). While the photographers as well as their
customers could not afford to travel to Nairobi by airplane or to board a
luxury liner, in the studios they did. Here, modern means of transport and
exotic places were at their disposal, and the studios with their imaginative
geographies became a surrogate for travel.

11. Mutokaa Studio, 1995.

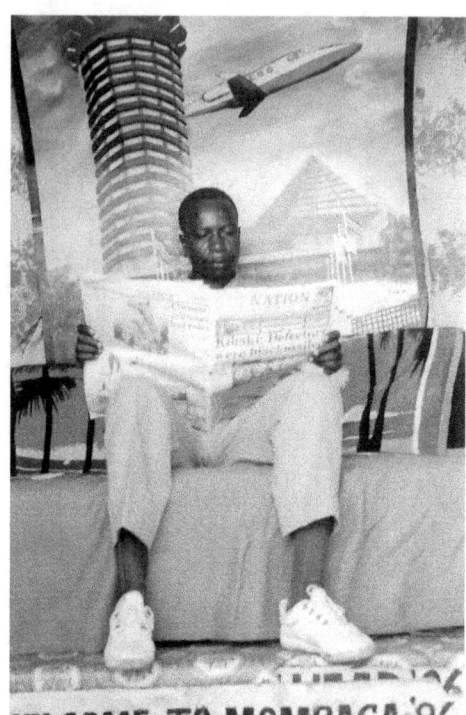

12. Omalla Studio, 1998.

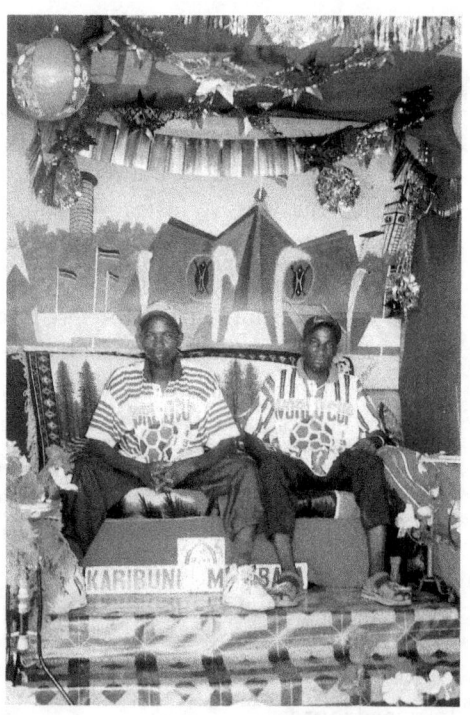

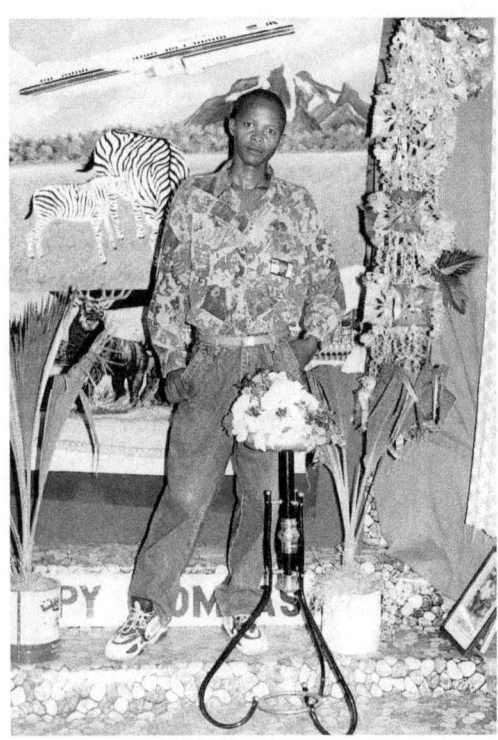

13. Simon Expert
Studio, 1998.

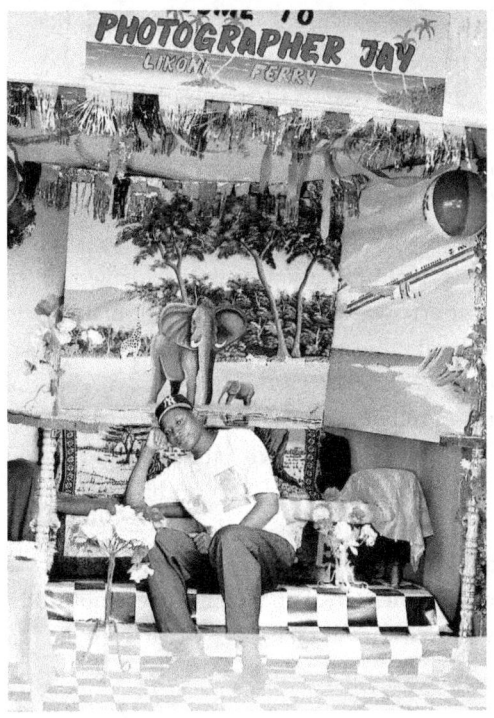

14. Jay's Studio, 1998.

Wildlife

In March 1998, when I again visited Likoni, the photographers had developed some new backdrops, this time referring to another touristic space: wildlife (figs. 13 and 14).

In their painted backdrops, they reproduced touristic pictures of an exotic, idyllic, naturalized African wilderness that originally had been produced as a counterimage to industrial capitalism, and had thus become the imaginary repository of value forms lost in the process of modernization (Bunn 1996, 38). The photographers also appropriated certain aspects of the "hunting tradition," and its cheaper variant of the nonhunting tours to the game parks, via existing touristic conventions. However, they "modernized" the images of a primordial wilderness by juxtaposing modern technology, such as an airplane, in the sky. Thus, in Likoni, the hegemonic space that belonged for some time more or less exclusively to Western tourists was appropriated and transformed into the vision of an African modernity.

Touristic Sites of Mombasa

In addition to sites in Nairobi and other parts of the world, the Likoni photographers in their studios also referred to certain places of their exile, of Mombasa—all of which were related to tourism (fig. 15).

The backdrops in figure 15 show Fort Jesus, a fortress built in 1593 by the Portuguese, and thus one of the oldest buildings on the coast. As its past history has shown, the island of Mombasa was at the mercy of whoever had command of Fort Jesus (Gray 1957, 49). Consequently, when the British protectorate was proclaimed, the fort was converted into a prison. In 1958 the building was declared a historical monument and transformed into a museum. Although originally constructed by Portuguese colonialists, the fort finally became a site of cultural value and a symbol of the Kenyan postcolonial nation—a symbol that was and still is reproduced in every school book.[4] Having been transformed into a national museum, Fort Jesus became one of the most important "attractions." With the fort's sound and light show three nights a week, it forms part of a "Mombasa by Night" package designed especially for Western tourists.

Another site the Likoni photographers depicted in their backdrops was the "Tusks" which, in addition to other triumphal arches, were put up in 1956 for Princess Margaret's visit to Mombasa. The idea came from the ten

Heike Behrend

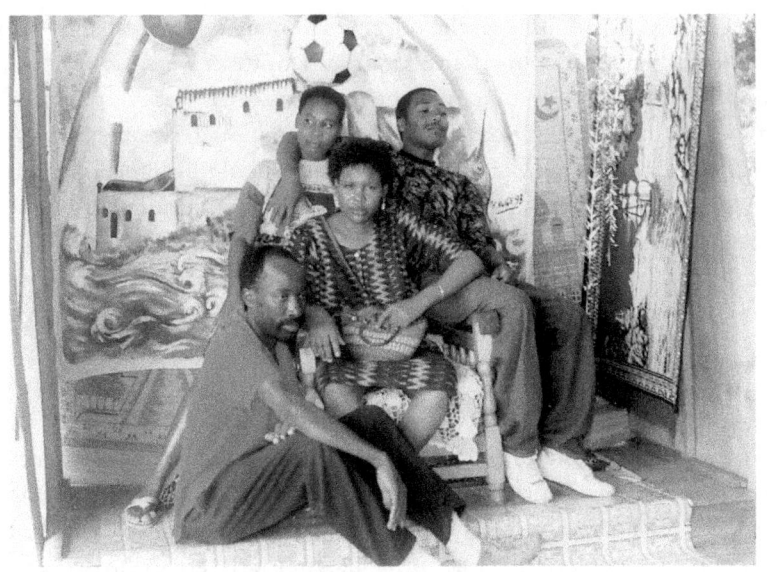

15. Simon Expert Studio, 1995.

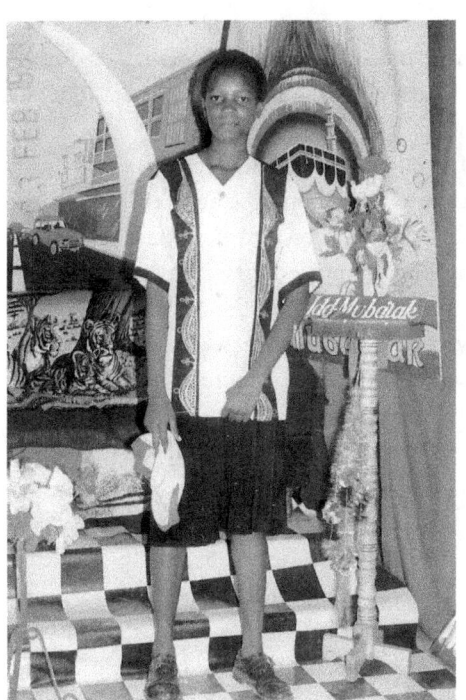

16. Jay's Studio, 1998.

cent coin, which had tusks on the obverse side, and was suggested by the treasurer of the town council. Two large pairs of tusks were constructed out of canvas on wooden frames by the municipal engineer's department and erected on Kilindini Road (now Moi Avenue). Such was the impression they made that the council decided they should become a permanent feature of the town. They were reconstructed in aluminum and put in their present position.[5] Today, some people without housing use them as shelters during the night. The tusks became a landmark of Mombasa and a favorite tourist site, and their picture widely circulates on postcards (fig. 16).

In addition, the Likoni photographers produced picturesque images of the sea, the beach, and palm trees, spaces that originally were occupied by and reserved for Western tourists. These images also followed the genre conventions of seaside paintings for tourists, above all postcards showing idyllic, untouched beaches, palm trees, and the blue sea. Thus, the Likoni photographers took over the basic principles of tourist art: the masking of specific cultural and political referents in an effort to broaden the popular appeal of a place and thereby create a larger audience (Jules-Rosette 1995, 43). They offered stereotyped, depoliticized souvenir images of an exotic landscape, sometimes even cleansed of African as well as Western tourists or inhabitants. Landscape here is thus a form of imaginary resolution or ideological naturalization, because the problematic issues of labor and land tenure are veiled (Bunn 1993, 50).

In their decor, however, the Likoni photographers reproduced not only the places of interest for Western tourists but also the Western tourist's gaze—the gaze from outside that took possession of African places and landscapes. Their visual agendas were strongly defined by the hegemonic tourist conventions. However, in appropriating in their photographs sites and landscapes that formerly were reserved for Western tourists, they reversed the processes of dispossession and exclusion. In addition, by positioning themselves as subjects in these touristic landscapes, they not only subverted the hegemonic conventions but also related to themselves as subjects of aesthetic experience (Battaglia 1995, 87). Furthermore, although Western tourist conventions single out sites and places as unique or as cultural markers of specific spaces, the Likoni photographers in their studios not only juxtaposed but piled up images of various places into a bricolage of a global world that is thereby decentered. In their "wild" assemblages, they dehierarchized the cultural values attached to various places, thus subverting the hegemonic Western discourse. I think it possible to

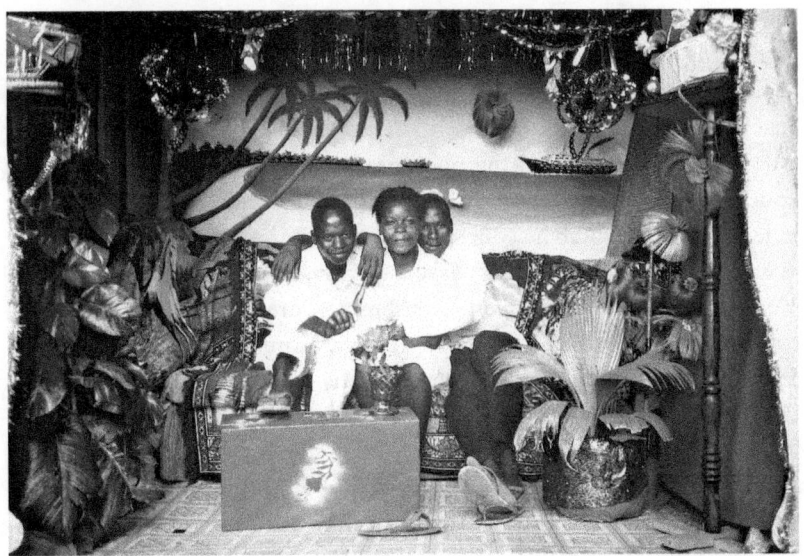

17. Sammy Big Seven Studio, 1996.

view their assemblages as a critical comment on representation because the representation in their montages is never complete in itself; instead, its effect lies in juxtaposing a heightened sense of reality with one of fantasy, thereby encouraging spectators and customers to speculate on representation itself (Marcus 1995, 47).

Truth and Fiction

When I asked the Likoni photographers why so many of their customers preferred to be photographed before painted backdrops showing, for example, the sea, instead of having pictures taken in front of the actual Indian Ocean, they explained that many of their customers preferred the painted backdrops "because they were more beautiful." They gave the example of the ferry connecting Likoni with the island or Old Town of Mombasa that in reality was old, rusty, and dirty, whereas as a backdrop it looked nice and clean (fig. 17).

In their images, the Likoni photographers did not so much attempt to produce an outside "reality" but rather they used the decor of their studios to improve the world and to transform and upgrade their own position in

Imagined Journeys

it. For them, the painted backdrops were "real"; they were not part of attempts to deceive or lie, although they did tell me that some customers would cheat and send photos to their relatives at home claiming that they had been at the airport or used a luxury liner. When I talked to the painter Mr. Masada, from whom the photographers ordered their backdrops, I found out that he extensively used photographs from journals, books, or calendars, from which he copied his pictures. Mr. Masada explained to me that as a painter he needed to have a camera. Thus, painting and photography were not so much seen as different genres or techniques of truth production, but rather formed phases in a more general process of producing images: in this process photographs were changed into paintings and paintings again into photographs, all of them deserving the status of representing "reality."

To return to the beginning of this essay: in their studios, the Likoni photographers produced a space of wish fulfillment, illusions, and imaginations that transcended "the culture of realism" while at the same time confirming it. By taking photographs of painted backdrops that had previously been photographs, they took part in the production of a new regime of fiction that molds the West as well as Africa: in this regime, it is not so much the world outside that is real; instead, the images have now gained reality (Flusser 1997, 349).

Notes

1   I am grateful to the German Research Foundation, which generously funded my research.
2   In Mombasa in August 1997 (before the elections in December), armed gangs attacked various groups of people, mainly migrant workers. In a letter dated 1 September 1997, Sammy Njugunda of the Sammy Big Seven Studio wrote to us that all the studios of the Likoni photographers had been destroyed and burned, and they had to run for their lives. Fortunately, however, in 1998, they returned to Likoni.
3   During my ethnographic work on popular Kenyan studio photography (Behrend 1998a, 1998b, 2000; Behrend and Wendl 1998) in 1996, 1998, and April 2000, I realized that I had to expand my field of research and include so-called street photographers. In the 1980s, when manual black-and-white photography was gradually replaced by quasi-industrial color photography, numerous studios had to close down, but at the same time this decline gave a chance to many young men and a few young women, who started to work as street

Heike Behrend

photographers; that is, without the greater investment a studio would require (Behrend and Wendl 1997; Werner and Nimes 1998). Street photographers usually congregate in small groups at more or less touristy sites and photograph primarily African tourists, who have the photos taken as proof that they were "there." But these photographers also often have access to a substantial network and take pictures of people in the neighborhood—for example, women who want to be photographed with a new coiffure, a new dress, or a new lover; or they are invited to festivities in the homes of customers, where they capture a wedding or birthday on film. Needless to say, intense competition emerged between street photographers and studios. Many owners of studios to whom I talked complained that they lost customers to street photographers, who sell their services much more cheaply than the studios.

4 Compare the history of Elmina Castle in Ghana discussed in Bruner 1996.

5 I am grateful to Judy Aldrick, who kindly gave me this information.

Stephen F. Sprague

Yoruba Photography

HOW THE YORUBA SEE THEMSELVES

Photographers and photographic studios are prevalent throughout many areas of Africa today, and particularly in West Africa many indigenous societies make use of this medium. The Yoruba, though not unique, are certainly exceptional in the extent to which they have integrated photography into many contemporary and traditional aspects of their culture. Some Yoruba photographs reflect traditional cultural values, and some are even utilized in certain traditional rituals (fig. 1). These more conventionalized forms of photography seem to exist in the smaller, more isolated Yoruba towns and villages. In the large cities such as Ibadan and Lagos, where contemporary Western photography is more influential, the work exhibits a greater sophistication and a wider range of styles and techniques.

Photography is no newcomer to Africa. Three months after Daguerre publicly announced his daguerreotype process in 1839, the French romantic painter Horace Vernet wrote from Alexandria, Egypt, "We keep daguerreotyping like lions, and from Cairo hope to send home an interesting batch" (Bensusan 1966, 7). In colonial South and East Africa, the first studios were opened in the 1840s (11), and photography immediately became a part of colonial life. In West Africa it is likely that photography was introduced more slowly and coincided with the later nineteenth-century expansion of permanent European colonies and political rule. It was past 1900, for instance, before the interior of Nigeria was completely under British rule,

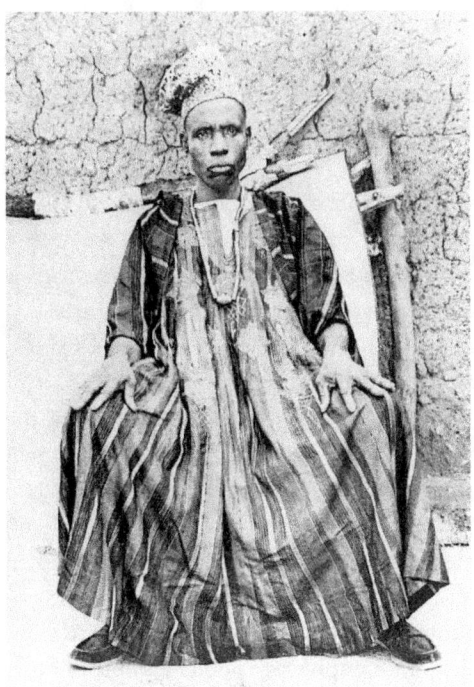

1. This chief and *Babalawo* (Ifa diviner) requested that I make a portrait of him. He had his family set up the mats and background, and he proceeded to pose in the traditional manner.

and 1895 before some of the first photographs of the River Niger were made (82).

Considering the long history of photography in colonial Africa, it seems reasonable to assume that many indigenous societies would have had ample opportunity to become familiar with the medium and to make it as much a part of their own cultures as seemed appropriate. Indigenous photographers have indeed been working in West Africa at least since the 1930s and probably very much earlier, as their actual existence would likely predate by a considerable number of years their recognition and documentation in the literature. A picture by a Gold Coast photographer appeared in a pre–World War II British book on commercial photography with the condescending comment that "crude though the result it had virtues which showed that the mind of the photographer was at work" (Charles 1938, 17). A possibly much earlier example is the large framed photograph hanging over the doorway to a traditional *abiku*[1] shrine in the Yoruba town of Ila-Orangun. It depicts the mother of the old priestess who is presently head of the society, and it could date from as early as pre–World War I.

The Yoruba may have been substituting photographs in place of traditional sculpture since the 1930s and probably much earlier, provided the substance of this ethnocentric quote is correct: "The *Oba* was constrained to relax his patronage of the artists' works: very much like other African chiefs he thought he could hand on his image to posterity more beautifully by means of an enlarged photograph than by a wooden statue" (Westermann 1939, 102).

Most of the material for this article was collected in the Igbomina Yoruba town of Ila-Orangun during summer 1975. Some comparative material was collected in the Ijebu-Remo area and in the large cities of Lagos, Ibadan, and Kano. Ila-Orangun is a typical Yoruba community of about 30,000 inhabitants, which did not have either electricity or running water at the time of this investigation. In spite of the lack of modern facilities, the town supported ten flourishing photographic studios. I investigated the negative files of each studio and requested ten to fifteen postcard-size prints (3″ × 5″) from each (fig. 2). These were selected on the basis of criteria established, in part, from a stylistic and subject matter analysis of three hundred sample postcards kept by Sir Special photo studio for prospective clients to view. Briefly, these criteria were: (1) the photograph was a good example of a distinct subset of Yoruba photographs as previously defined by the analysis of Sir Special's postcards; (2) the photograph was unique in some way or did not fit into any previously defined category; (3) the photograph seemed to contain anthropological information useful to Marilyn Houlberg, who was also in Ila-Orangun continuing her research on Yoruba sacred children; and (4) the photograph particularly pleased my own aesthetic tastes.

All ten photographers were interviewed, and they willingly discussed their profession and demonstrated their personal camera and darkroom techniques.[2] In addition, members of the community contributed information about the subject matter and function of photographs they owned. Finally, I myself took pictures of the photographers, their studios and darkrooms, and the use and display of Yoruba photographs within the context of the community. Yoruba photography in Ila-Orangun was studied, then, from the points of view of the producer and the consumer, and by looking at the photographs themselves. Although this investigation was primarily restricted to Ila-Orangun, observations in other areas of Yorubaland strongly suggest that the use of photography in Ila-Orangun is typical of many Yoruba communities and probably has much in common with other areas of West Africa.

The photographers of Ila-Orangun claim that practically any subject may

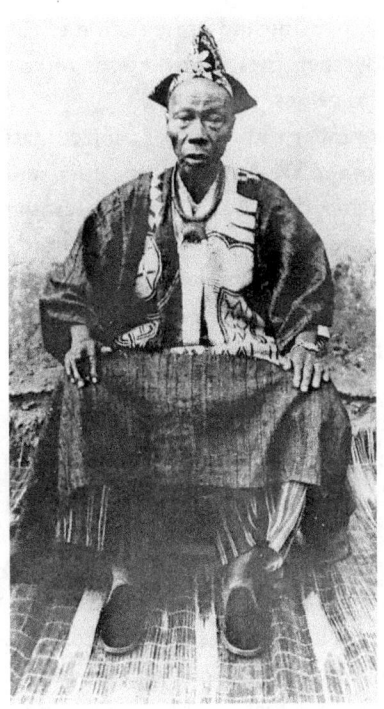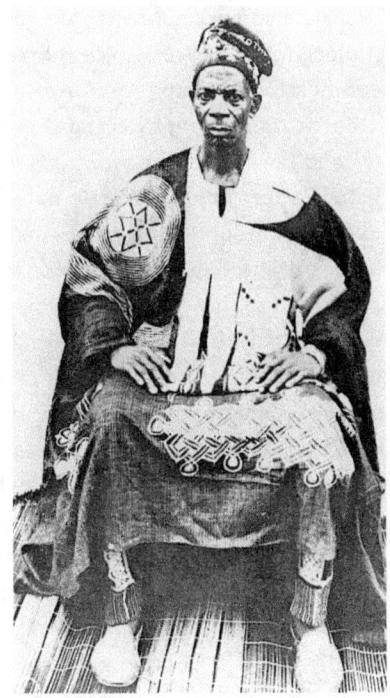

2. Two traditional formal portraits, postcard-size contact prints made for me by the photographers of Ila-Orangun from glass plate negatives selected from their studio files. The clients would have commissioned prints in a variety of sizes and frames.

be photographed except for those ritual objects, masquerades, and ceremonies that some segments of the public are traditionally prohibited from viewing. Also, they say that a good photographer will take a picture of whatever the client requests. However, a study of the kinds of photographs most commonly produced indicates that the actual practice of the profession is generally much more restricted than is claimed.

Yoruba photography in Ila-Orangun and elsewhere is, almost exclusively, posed portraiture of individuals or groups of people, which are often commissioned in order to commemorate an event of some importance to those depicted. Though an important ritual object or prized possession, such as a traditional sculpture or a new car, might occasionally be photographed, general subjects such as landscapes, architecture, or ordinary objects and events are seldom taken by local photographers.[3] In short, the Yoruba have developed unstated but clearly discernible conventions regarding the appropriate subject matter; those governing posing and presentation of the subject matter have also developed. Together, these conventions offer a codification of a range of Yoruba cultural values.[4]

Yoruba photography certainly shares similar categories of subject matter and formalistic conventions with other West African societies and with Western cultures, particularly British culture. But cultural patterning exists, not in subtle differences in these conventions but more importantly in the unique, culturally derived symbolic meanings and specific functions attributed to these seemingly similar forms. It is beyond the scope of this essay to analyze all the diverse external and indigenous factors that might have contributed to the development of Yoruba photography. Instead, I simply seek here to establish Yoruba photography as a genuine expression of the culture by discussing several specific examples with respect to how their subject matter, formal and stylistic conventions, symbolic meanings, and function within Yoruba society are in part a reflection of Yoruba cultural values and perceptions of the world.

Older Yoruba in traditional dress often sit in a particular stylized manner at traditional ceremonies and events. This pose has become codified usually through photography and now seems to be the accepted way for traditional Yoruba to present themselves in a formal photographic portrait. What I call the "traditional formal portrait" is highly conventionalized both in the manner in which the subject poses and the manner in which the photograph is composed (see figs. 1 and 2). The subject always wears his best traditional dress and sits squarely facing the camera. Both hands are placed on the lap or on the knees, and the legs are well apart to spread the garments and display the fabrics. The face has a dignified but distant expression as the eyes look directly at and through the camera. Symbols of the subject's position in Yoruba society are worn, held, or placed conspicuously nearby (fig. 3). The photographer enhances the sense of dignified stateliness by a camera viewpoint either level with the subject's waist or looking slightly upward, as if from the position of one paying homage. The entire body is always included within the frame, and a neutral vertical background immediately behind serves to isolate the subject in a shallow three-dimensional space. The figure gives a feeling of sculptural massiveness and solidarity, and the whole pose is one of symmetry and balance.[5]

It might be argued that the traditional formal portrait is in part a synthesis of certain traditional Yoruba cultural values, the inherent attributes of nineteenth-century photography and nineteenth-century British attitudes

Stephen Sprague

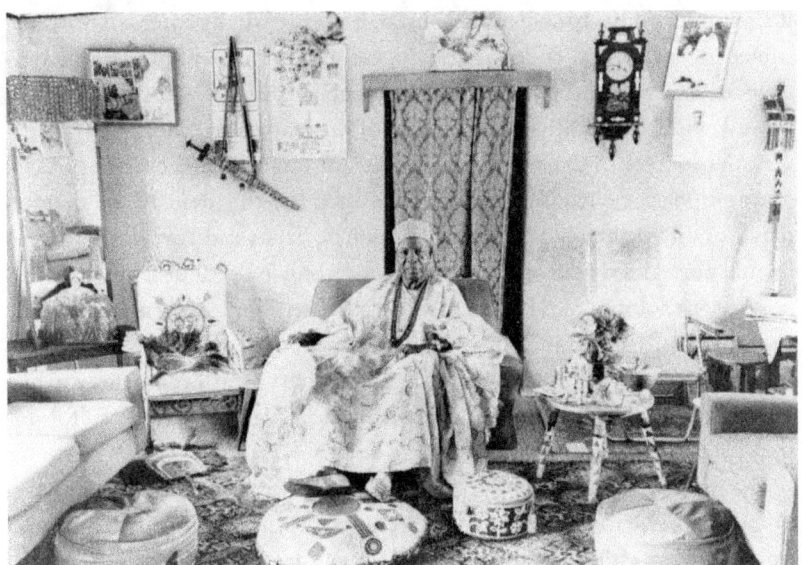

3. The Orangun of Ila-Orangun in his private sitting room in the palace. The horsetail flywhisk, necklace, beaded crown, and the other beaded objects surrounding him are all symbols of his position. The traditional formal pose and many of the same symbols are repeated in the freestanding cutout photographs on display.

toward the medium. Its formality might be partly explained as a convention that developed out of the practical difficulties of making portraits when photography was first introduced. The early technology (the large-view cameras, slow lenses, and insensitive emulsions) made taking a photograph a laborious process and forced the sitter to assume a rigid pose that could be held for the duration of a long exposure. Consequently, in the hands of an inexperienced operator many portraits turned out unnaturally serious and stiffly formal.

However, the particular style of posing represented by the Yoruba traditional formal portrait is almost never seen in nineteenth- and twentieth-century British portrait photography.[6] In the latter, the subject does not squarely confront the camera but usually turns asymmetrically to one side and looks out of the frame and away from the lens. The whole body is seldom shown; most British portraits range from three-quarter length to extreme close-ups that include only the head. Also, studio props are often cropped by the frame rather than being entirely included in the picture.

If a painted studio background is used, it often visually interacts with the subject. These visual codes are, of course, common to photographic portraits in many societies, and they often appear in many Yoruba examples as well, with the significant exception of the traditional formal portrait.

Both nineteenth-century British and traditional Yoruba cultures placed great emphasis on tradition, proper conduct, and the identity and maintenance of one's social position. Early British portraits and Yoruba traditional formal portraits visually codify these commonly held values: the dignified pose, proper clothes, and often the display of symbolic objects identify the subject's profession and social station. British portraits, however, also emphasize the Western values of individuality and even eccentricity, while the traditional formal portrait emphasizes how well the subject fulfills his traditional role in Yoruba society.

The traditional formal portrait, of all the forms of Yoruba photography, most clearly embodies in its composition not only certain traditional Yoruba cultural values, but also their aesthetic values as outlined by R. F. Thompson in his discussion of Yoruba sculpture (1971, 374–81). The concept of *jijora*—mimesis at the midpoint—implies the work should exist somewhere between complete abstraction and individual likeness. It should resemble the individual and at the same time embody all the ideal Yoruba characteristics without overemphasizing any one. The extreme stylization of pose and facial expression of the traditional formal portrait is an attempt to achieve this state by circumventing to a degree the inherent specificity of the photographic portrait. *Odo*, depiction midway between infancy and old age, at the prime of life, is seen in the strength of the pose and in the facial expression, both of which seem to imply the subject's maturity and wisdom. *Ifarahon*, "visibility," implies clarity and definition of form and line, and a subsequent clarity of identity. This is emphasized in the photograph by the isolation of the subject against the neutral background, in the sculptural dimensions and symmetry of the figure, and in the inclusion of objects symbolizing the subject's position in Yoruba society.

A comparison of much Yoruba sculpture with the traditional formal portrait reveals two obvious similarities in form: in both, the head invariably faces forward with respect to the body, and when the sculpture is viewed from directly in front (the point of view at which the traditional formal portrait is taken) both characteristically appear bilaterally symmetrical. Another relationship between photography and the sculptural tradition can be seen in the practice of mounting a photo of a person on a thin sheet of wood, then cutting out the subject and adding a flat base to make a freestanding, three-dimensional portrait. Any style of photographic portrait may be treated in this way. A studio in Ibadan features an entire display case of freestanding portraits ranging from a very Westernized close-up of the head to the traditional formal portrait. Yesufu Ejigboye from the Ijebu-Remo area, in addition to carving traditional sculpture and silver airplanes (Houlberg 1976a), has cut out and mounted full-color magazine portraits of two lovely ladies. These are displayed in his parlor surrounded by photographs and other fascinating items (fig. 4). The Orangun of Ila-Orangun has at least three cutout portraits of himself in the traditional formal pose displayed in his sitting room (fig. 5). When I requested permission to take his picture, he posed in the sitting room in an identical manner. He wore a traditional gown and included similar symbols of his office: the horsetail flywhisk, beaded crown, and large beads around the neck (see fig. 3).

The traditional formal portrait, then, seems to have been functioning as an integral part of Yoruba culture for a significant length of time. It is meant to memorialize the subject not so much as a unique individual, as in much British portraiture, but rather in terms of how well he has embodied traditional Yoruba ideals and fulfilled his given position in society. When the subject dies, this portrait might be carried in his funeral procession to particularize the ancestral Egungun (Schiltz 1978, 51). It is the portrait that might be hung in his crypt or laminated to his tombstone, and published in memoriam each year in the Lagos *Daily Times*.

The memorial pages of the *Daily Times* are a manifestation in contemporary Nigerian Culture of traditional respect for, and veneration of, ancestors. Every day the *Daily Times* has several pages of memorials to the deceased, many of whom have been dead ten or twenty years or longer. Each memorial almost always includes a photograph and a brief tribute and description of the person's accomplishments and social position.[7] A limited survey of a few recent editions of the Lagos *Daily Times* indicates that those Yoruba whose accomplishments could be identified with the traditional culture were often pictured in traditional dress in the traditional formal pose, while Yoruba whose accomplishments could be identified with contemporary Nigerian culture were often pictured in modern dress in a variety of more casual, Europeanized poses. An extended survey should show a definite correlation, which might change over time, between dress and pose in the memorial photograph and the subjects' wealth, social position, and education.[8]

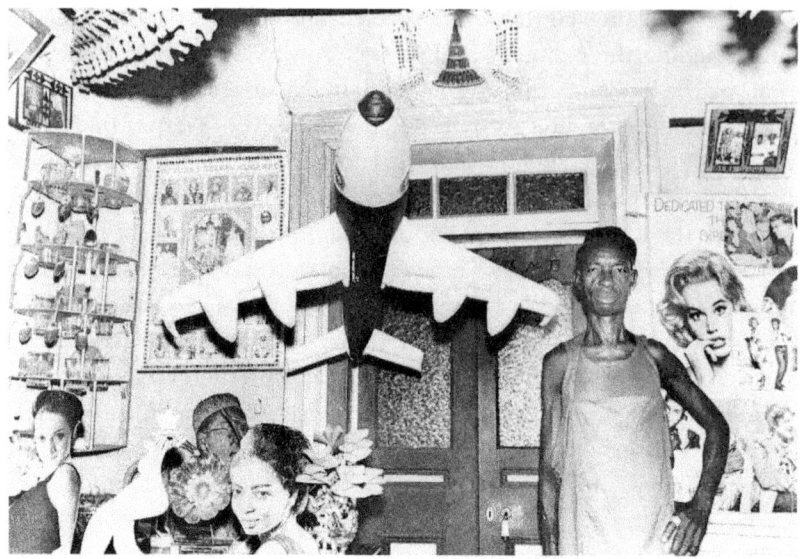

4. Carver Yesufu Ejigboye from the Ijebu-Remo area. The two lovely ladies on either side of the egret have been cut out from magazines and mounted on thin board as freestanding sculpture figures.

5. One of the freestanding cutout portraits.

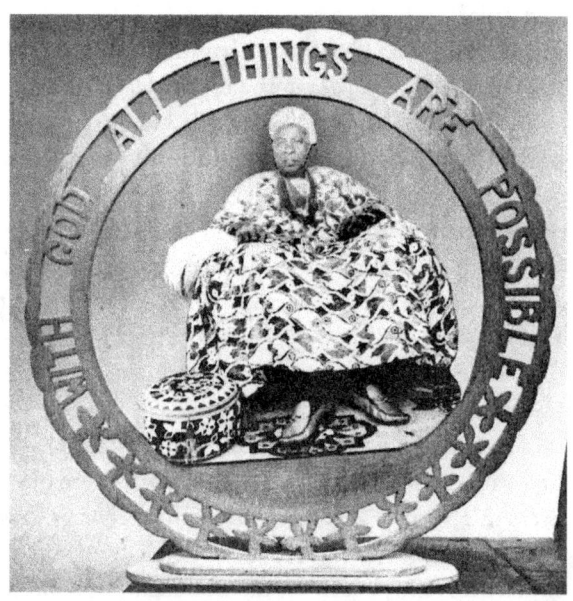

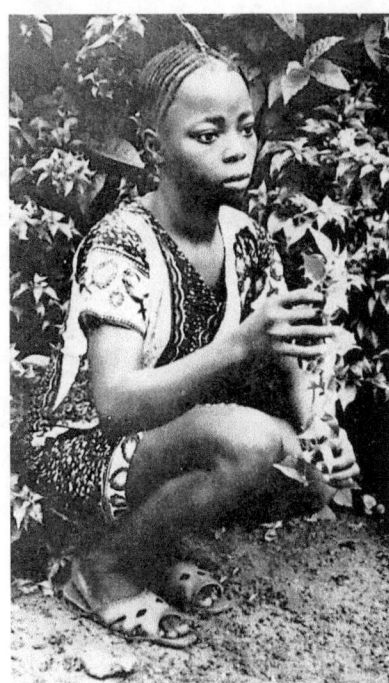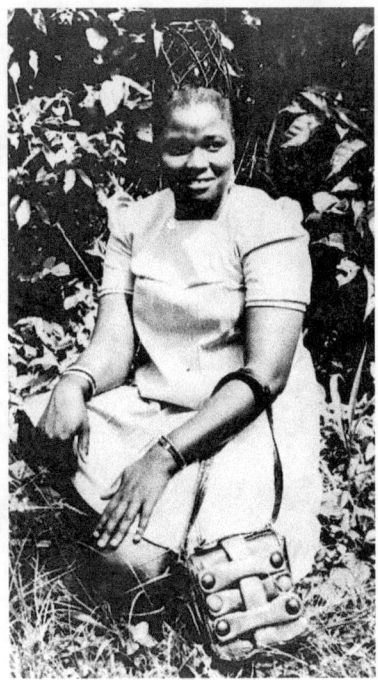

6. The squatting pose. Postcard-size prints collected from photographs in Ila-Orangun.

There are many other styles of formal, informal, and even humorous portraiture; and many reflect more directly Western conventions in their manner of posing than does the traditional formal portrait. However, as a particular pose is adapted into Yoruba culture, its meanings may also be modified. What I call the squatting pose is one such example (fig. 6). This pose seems restricted to young Yoruba ladies dressed in modern styles, and may be in part a fusion of the deferent behavior traditionally required of young women toward their social superiors with the rather innocent, physical allure shown in American "cheesecake" pin-up photographs circa 1950. A painted studio backdrop from Ila-Orangun featuring such a pin-up girl squatting on top of a modern skyscraper (fig. 7) is but one indication of this Western influence. This pose might be seen to express the ambiguous position of Yoruba women in a changing society: the impression is that of a young lady who, while maintaining her proper place in traditional society, has turned her fascinated eyes to the modern world.

Many conventions that reflect Yoruba cultural values are independent

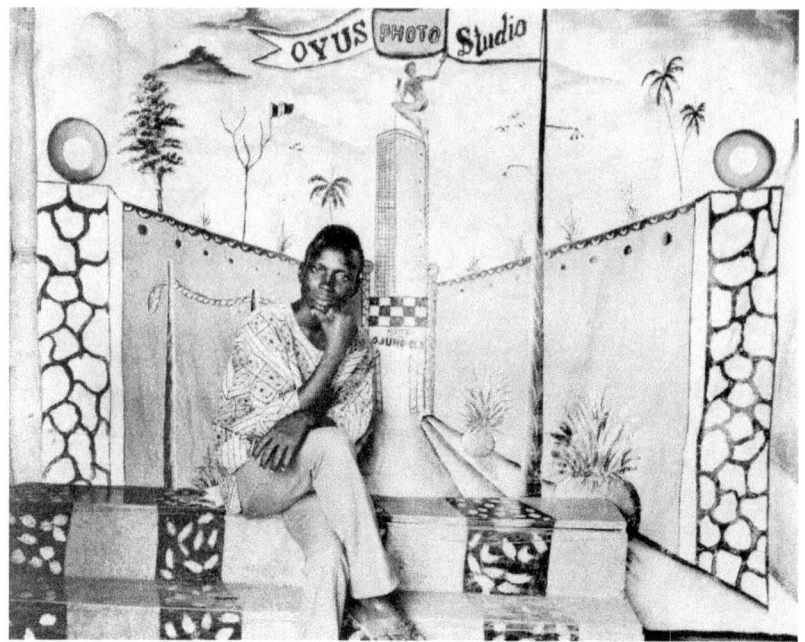

7. The backdrop of Oyus Photo Studio is particularly interesting with its varieties of foliage and architecture, inconsistent perspective, and mixture of contemporary and traditional motifs.

of any particular subject matter or style of posing. One such convention is that both of the subject's eyes must always be visible in a portrait. This convention again relates to the concept of *ifarahon*—of visibility and clarity of form, line, and identity. Both older, traditional Yorubas and those younger and more Westernized expect this convention to be upheld. In one case, an American photographer made a series of photographs of a contemporary *juju* musician and offered him a profile view as being the best. The musician, however, rejected the photograph, saying that it was "not clear." In another case, Houlberg asked an Ijebu-Remo priestess to evaluate and rank in order of preference eight photographs of herself previously taken by Houlberg. The priestess ranked lowest the one portrait that showed her in profile.[9]

Many photographs are made to commemorate a particular ceremony or event, and another convention is the prominent inclusion in the photograph of the proper symbolic objects to adequately identify this event. In a group photograph the social hierarchy must also be made clear by the

Stephen Sprague

positions of individuals within the frame. The most important person is seated (often in the traditional formal pose) in the center of the first row, with the next most important seated to his left. Persons of least status stand farthest toward the back and edges of the frame. Children are exceptions, being allowed to squat or sit anywhere in the foreground. The poet George Awooner-Williams expresses this status ordering in the second stanza of his poem "Song of Sorrow" "I am on the world's extreme/corner./I am not sitting in the row/with the eminent./But those who are lucky/sit in the middle and forget/I am on the world's extreme/corner/I can only go beyond and/forget" (1967).

These few examples establish Yoruba photography as a genuine expression of the culture by showing how some cultural values have been given visual form in certain kinds of photographs. Many Yoruba would not consciously know, or be able to articulate, how their photographs reflect commonly held values and myths—and many members of our own culture would find it equally difficult to explain the symbolic meanings of their family photographs. Instead, photographically unsophisticated members of both cultures assume that the photographic image is simply a visual record, which serves as a device to bring to mind at some future time the people and events depicted. The actual structure and symbolic meaning of the photographic image are not consciously considered; it serves only to trigger the viewer's memory of the subject. Even the traditional formal portrait, though meant to invoke a specific, culturally determined image, still functions basically as a memory device.

The Yoruba photograph itself, as an object, also serves specific functions in the community. Photographs are prominently displayed in the parlor or sitting room of homes, and at the front of many shops and offices. Family members, relatives, friends, and important gatherings are the dominant subjects. The largest and most elaborate photographs are of senior family members and distinguished ancestors. Local and national leaders and other famous people are often included in either original photographs or in magazine and poster reproductions. By displaying these photographs, the owner publicly acknowledges his respect for, and his involvement with, the subjects. There is often an additional implication of status. A person of relatively little wealth will own a few photographs, and they will be mounted and displayed in a simple fashion. Those of greater wealth and social standing will have more and larger photographs on display, and many of them may be elaborately hand colored and framed, and occasionally made into a freestanding cutout.

Educated Yorubas and wealthy families who have been exposed to Western culture often own photograph albums that can date back a number
of generations. These albums contain mostly postcard-size photographs
and other memorabilia arranged in a rough chronological order, forming
a culturally conditioned visual history of the family or individual. Again,
there is the implication of status; it is considered progressive and modern to own photo albums, and the mere fact that a visual record has been
kept validates one's importance. Wealth is also implied. Since the concept
of the amateur family snapshot is not prevalent among the Yoruba, only
the relatively well-off could afford over the years to hire a photographer
for practically every occasion of any importance.

There are fascinating exceptions to the general function of the photograph as literal record, memory device, and an object symbolizing respect
and status. The photograph is sometimes believed to possess additional
power and spiritual meanings and can be used in traditional rituals. A few
instances appear to be simply individual beliefs, while others are widely accepted practices. The most fascinating and widespread example is the inte-
gration of photography into the traditional beliefs and rituals surrounding
twins. Because twins are sacred children with connections to the spirit
world, it is especially important to show them proper respect. Photographs
are often made of twins and other children to hang in the parlor with the
photographs of other family members. Then, if a child dies, there is a portrait by which to remember him or her. The procedure becomes more
complex when one twin dies before their photograph is taken. If the twins
were of the same sex, the surviving twin is photographed alone, and the
photographer prints this single negative twice, so that the twins appear to
be sitting side by side in the final photograph (fig. 8). If the twins were of
opposite sexes, the surviving twin is photographed once in male clothing
and once in female clothing. Sometimes these two exposures are made on
separate negatives, which must then be printed together; and sometimes
they are made on opposite halves of a single 3″ × 5″ glass plate negative,
which can be printed without any darkroom manipulation (fig. 9). In either
case the photographer attempts to conceal the line blending the two separate exposures in order to maintain the illusion of twins sitting together
in a single photograph.

Though twins are quite common, not only among the Yoruba but
throughout Africa, the incidence of triplets is much lower, and a photographer would seldom be confronted with the problem of representing triplets. In one unusual case the two brothers died, and the surviving girl was

Stephen Sprague

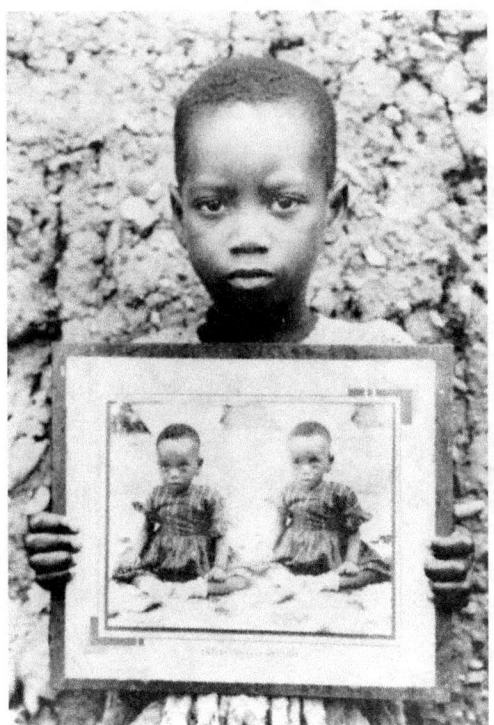

8. This little girl, Taiwo, holds a multiple-printed hand-colored photograph representing herself and her dead twin sister sitting together. It is actually the same image of Taiwo printed twice. The photograph is used by her mother in place of the traditional *ibeji* (twin sculpture).

photographed once as herself in girl's clothes and once in matching boy's clothes. The two exposures were made on the same 3″ × 5″ glass plate. The photographer then printed the "boy" image twice, once on either side of the girl, to give the proper illusion of triplets (fig. 10).

The traditional procedure when a twin dies is for the parents to commission the carving of a twin figure, or *ibeji*, which then participates in the twin ceremonies along with the living twin. In some areas, it is now accepted practice for the photograph to be substituted for the *ibeji*. This picture is then kept on the twin shrine and participates in the traditional ceremonies. The multiple-printed photograph of the little girl, Taiwo (see fig. 8), is used by her mother in this way.[10]

The exact function of these twin photographs seems to depend in part on the religious convictions of the parents. Houlberg (1973) states that the Christian and Muslim prohibition against the use of Yoruba traditional sculpture has been a major influence in the simplification of *ibeji* forms used by Christian and Muslim Yoruba, and in the substitution of other objects, such as plastic dolls, for *ibeji* in the traditional twin rituals. She sug-

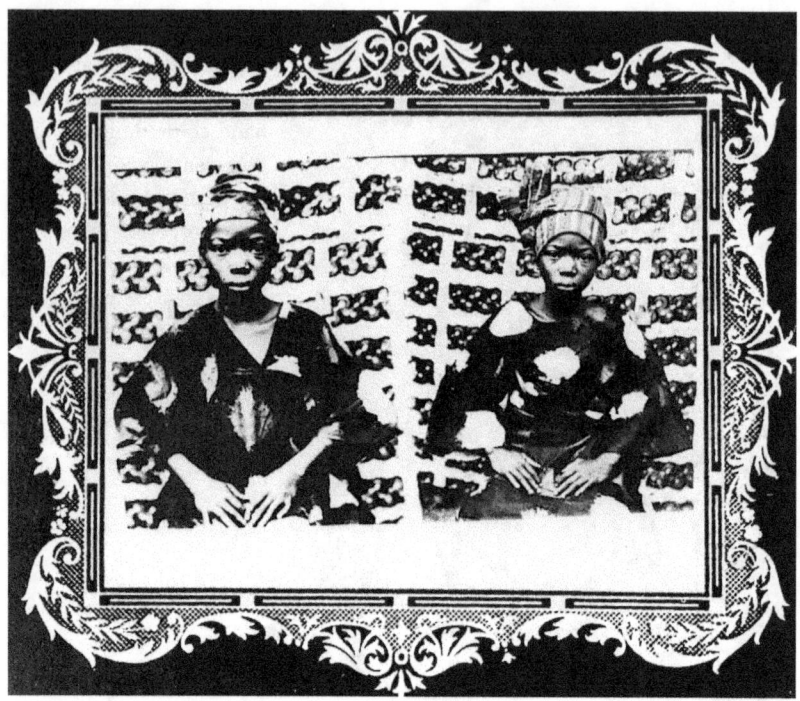

9. In this photo the surviving girl twin was photographed once as herself in her own clothes, and once as her dead twin brother in matching boy's clothes. The photographer, Simple Photo, made a "full plate" enlargement for me in the same way that he would for a client. He mounted the finished enlargement in the usual manner on a 10″ by 12″ cardboard mount with a printed border.

gests in a more recent article (1976a) that this prohibition has been a major influence in the substitution of photographs for *ibeji*. Through the use or possession of a twin photograph, Christian and Muslim Yoruba seek to distinguish themselves from believers in the traditional religion. The cycle of substitution can, on occasion, come full circle when both twins die before their pictures have been taken. Then, if the traditional *ibeji* are carved, these are sometimes photographed and the photo of the carvings is hung in the parlor in place of the usual twin photograph.

The photographers themselves and the craft of Yoruba photography deserve some discussion. Photography enjoys a respected position within the community, similar to hairdressing, barbering, or tailoring. It is considered a good modern profession for young people to enter, and though the vast majority of photographers are men, there are no restrictions against

Stephen Sprague

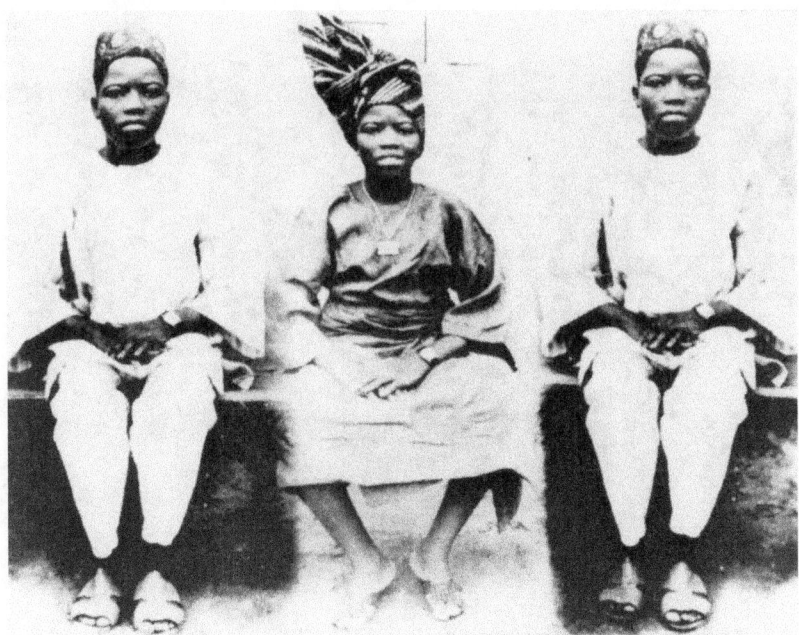

10. A rare representation of triplets. The two boys died, and the surviving girl was photographed first as herself, then in matching boy's clothes to represent her brothers. The male image was printed twice, once on either side of the girl's image to show the triplets sitting together. By Simple Photo.

women. In Ila-Orangun the ten photographers included eight young men, one young woman, and one older, retired photographer who served as head of the photographers' union. Though it tends to be a young person's profession and is seldom handed down from father to son, there are often family connections between photographers in the smaller towns. In Ila-Orangun four of the ten photographers belonged to the same family compound, and the younger three had all been apprenticed to their senior brother.

To become a photographer a young person must first complete primary six (sixth grade). He then must apprentice to a master photographer for a period of one to three years. If he has learned well, he is given his freedom in a special ceremony at the end of his apprenticeship. He can then open a studio and eventually attract his own apprentices. Photographers are highly organized. There is a union in each town to which every photographer automatically belongs, and which meets at least once a month. These

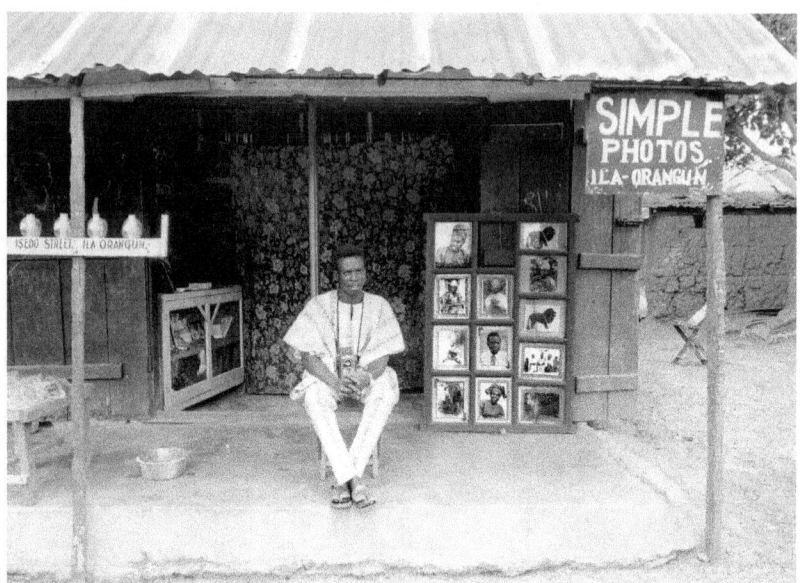

11. The photographer "Simple" sits in front of his studio holding his twin-lens reflex camera. It is the custom for a photographer to be known by his studio title rather than by his given name. Simple's studio is typical of those in Ila-Orangun.

local unions form regional unions, which meet about every six months. The unions regulate such things as the price structure of the various types of photographs and services, the details of apprenticeship, and the professional conduct of its members.

The typical photography studio, such as those in Ila-Orangun, is usually small but efficiently laid out. Double doors swing open to reveal to the passerby samples of the photographer's work (fig. 11). A backdrop hangs a few feet inside the studio, with a bench for the sitter placed immediately in front of it (see fig. 7). These backdrops are painted by sign painters in various shades of black, white, and gray. They often show a fascinating but naive use of Western perspective, and usually mix traditional and contemporary motifs. Behind the backdrop is a tiny darkroom, often without either electricity or running water. Along one wall is a narrow table on which are set the processing solutions in enameled bowls from the market. A kerosene lantern with a red cloth surrounding the globe serves as a safelight. An old postcard-size view camera is installed with its back to a window for use as a solar enlarger; a mirror, located outside the window, is

Stephen Sprague

tilted to reflect the sunlight through the system. An enlargement is made by placing a negative in the back of the camera and projecting its image onto a sheet of photographic paper clipped to a vertical easel. Except for minor variations, this makes up the photographer's entire facilities.

The traditional view camera that takes postcard-size glass plates has been increasingly relegated to the darkroom as an enlarger. Since about 1960 there has become available a wide variety of more flexible, twin-lens reflex cameras that take twelve two-inch square negatives on inexpensive 120 roll film. The success and status of a photographer are often indicated by the camera and other equipment he owns. A beginning photographer will own a cheap plastic Russian Lubitel or Chinese Sea Gull; the majority own Japanese Yashicas, and a few photographers in the large cities own expensive German Rollicords or Rolliflexes.

From the two-inch square negative of these cameras, the photographers offer standardized photograph sizes based on the old British view camera negative formats. These are passport ($2'' \times 2''$), postcard ($3'' \times 5''$), half plate ($3'' \times 4''$), and full plate ($6'' \times 8''$). The larger sizes of $11'' \times 14''$ or $16'' \times 20''$ and occasionally $20'' \times 30''$ conform to the sizes of photographic paper available.

Many photographers offer additional services, including multiple-printing and hand coloring, and mounting techniques ranging from simple cardboard mounts to elaborate frames and freestanding cutouts. Some photographers have a specialty; for example, Sir Special Photo of Ila-Orangun is known for his skill in mounting a portrait behind a mirror. He says the technique came to him in a dream. He scratches away the mirror coating in the shape of the subject and then places the photograph behind the mirror, allowing only the subject to show through.

If the customer does not like what the studio has to offer, other frames are available in the market and from the sign painters. Sign painters make very popular frames by painting a design and a proverb in English or Yoruba on the back of a sheet of glass while leaving room for one or more postcard-size photographs to show through.

This brief introduction to Yoruba photography suggests some broader implications and questions.[11] One of the first questions that might be asked is why certain groups in West Africa, like the Yoruba, have integrated photography into their cultures, while other groups, such as the Hausa, appear to make little use of the medium.[12] It is suggested that societies with a strong tradition of figurative art, such as the Yoruba, have aesthetic values and a need for representation that could be satisfied and understood in a photograph. For example, the Yoruba were initially introduced to the medium of photography by the British, whose photographic portraits appeared to display values important to the Yoruba. This made the usefulness of the photography immediately apparent. On the other hand, societies such as the Hausa, which have a more abstract aesthetic tradition involving decorative pattern and design, would have less use for, or even understanding of, the photographic image. Also, any society that has a long history of dominant Muslim influence, again the Hausa, would be less likely to make use of the medium because of the strong Muslim prohibition against graven images, which specifically includes photographs. Another important consideration is that a society with an economic system that could accommodate the commissioning and production of photographs would be more likely to make use of the medium. The Yoruba have a long history of urbanization with a developed tradition of individual enterprise in the production of goods and the marketing of specialized skills.

The large number of photographs available from individual Yorubas and from photographers' negative files form a vast visual data bank that is unique because it has been generated entirely by members of a non-Western culture. This material might be utilized in a number of ways. The most obvious would be simply to study the subject matter of photographs available in a particular community in order to discover the existence of people, ceremonies, events, and even objects and masquerades that otherwise might not be known. Copies of these photographs could be used to elicit more information from other members of the community.

More important, as this essay has shown, these photographs are "coded in Yoruba" and can also give us much information about how the Yoruba see themselves—about their cultural values and their view of the world. But understanding all the implications of this wealth of visual information will not be easy. A coherent methodology does not exist for extracting cultural and historical data from even our own heritage of family snapshots and anonymous photographs, and the formulation of a methodology for interpreting the photographic heritage of a non-Western society has never been attempted as far as I am aware. One hopes that continued investigation will eventually lead not only to a better knowledge of the Yoruba view of themselves, but also to a better cross-cultural understanding of how we communicate through mediated visual images of the world, and to the formulation of a methodology to deal with these images.

Notes

1 *Abiku* means, literally, "we are born to die." Children who are discovered to be *abiku* must be paid special ritual attention in order to keep them in this world; otherwise they will surely die and return to their spirit world. See Mobolade 1973 for more information.

2 I would like to thank the photographers in Ila-Orangun, and especially Sir Special Photo, for their cooperation in providing information and in allowing me access to their negative files.

3 Newspaper photographers in the cities have adapted a more candid journalistic approach, but their range of subject matter is much the same—predominantly people at ceremonial or other newsworthy events. News photographs typical of Western papers, such as accidents, disasters, or action pictures of sports, seldom appear.

4 I am particularly indebted to the thinking and research of Sol Worth, who in his book *Through Navajo Eyes* (Worth and Adair 1972) has demonstrated that members of a culture or subculture who learn to use a new medium of communication (in this case, film) will produce work that is structured in part by their own cultural values and by their culture's perception of the world.

5 This describes the ideal form; sometimes the figure will be cut by the edge of the frame, and occasionally the subject will be smiling. Although minor variations are common, the traditional formal portrait always maintains its distinct identity.

6 Many types of nineteenth- and early twentieth-century British photographic portraits were looked at in detail. This included the work of artistic photographers such as Julia Margaret Cameron (Gernsheim 1975), commercial studio photographs (Hillier 1976), and colonial British photographs of India (Worswick and Embree 1976).

7 The concept of the memorial pages may have been adapted from the obituaries in the London *Daily Times*. But the emphasis on the photograph, the brief tribute in different type faces, and the deemphasis on text mark this as a distinct form.

8 Betty Wass (1975) has shown that Yoruba dress, as depicted in six hundred photographs dating from 1900 to 1974, does relate to the event photographed and to the social position and education of the subject, and that the percentage of indigenous dress increases from 1900 to 1974 as a function of increased national consciousness and pride.

9 The full results of this research were presented by Houlberg in her "Image and Inquiry: Photography and Film in the Study of Yoruba Art and Religion" (1976b). The profile portrait rejected by the priestess was selected for publication in the *1973 World Book Yearbook* (95).

10 I would like to credit Marilyn Houlberg who, through her research on Yoruba sacred children during a field trip to Nigeria in 1971, first heard of the existence of this particular twin photograph and its use in traditional twin ritual (Houlberg 1973). It was my fascination with this unsubstantiated fact that compelled me to undertake this investigation of Yoruba photography, which was conducted in part with Houlberg's assistance during summer 1975. Houlberg (1976a, 18) has published a similar photograph of Taiwo in connection with her discussion of new forms of *ibeji* and of twin photos replacing *ibeji*.

11 Additional photographs taken by me and by the Yoruba photographers of Ila-Orangun, along with a brief statement of methodology, have been published as a photographic essay titled "How I See the Yoruba See Themselves" (Sprague 1978). These photographs present visually the main point of this present paper, as well as show more of the photographers themselves, their studios, and the display of photographs within the context of the community.

12 A week of searching throughout Kano, a predominantly Hausa area, revealed very few photographic studios or photographs on display. When questioned about this, Hausa traders repeatedly said that I must go to the Yoruba area of Kano because all of the photographers were either Yoruba or Ibo.

Works Cited

Adams, Bluford. 1997. *E Pluribus Barnum: The Greatest Showman and the Making of U.S. Popular Culture.* Minneapolis: University of Minnesota Press.

Adler, J. 1989. "Origins of Sightseeing." *Annals of Tourism Research* 19: 7–29.

Aird, Michael. 1993. *Portraits of Our Elders.* Brisbane: Queensland Museum.

———. 1996. *I Know a Few Words.* Southport, Qld.: Keeaira Publications.

Alloula, Malek. 1987. *The Colonial Harem.* Minneapolis: University of Minnesota Press.

Anderson, Benedict. 1983 [1991]. *Imagined Communities: Reflections on the Origin and Spread of Nationalism.* London: Verso.

Anderson, Patricia. 1991. *The Printed Image and the Transformation of Popular Culture.* Oxford: Oxford University Press.

Annear, Judy, ed. 1997. *Portraits of Oceania.* Sydney: Art Gallery of New South Wales.

Appadurai, Arjun. 1997. "The Colonial Backdrop." *Afterimage* 24 (5) (March/April): 4–7.

Arango, Juan Luis Mejía. 1988. "La fotografía." In *Historia de antioquia,* ed. Jorge Orlando Melo. Medellín, Colombia.

Attenborough, David. 1963. *Quest under Capricorn.* London: Lutterworth.

Awooner-Williams, George. 1967. "Songs of Sorrow." In *West African Verse: An Anthology,* annotated by Donatus Ibe Nwoga. London: Longmans.

Baker, Houston, A. 1986. *Modernism and the Harlem Renaissance.* Chicago: University of Chicago Press.

Bakhtin, M. M. 1981. *The Dialogic Imagination.* Austin: University of Texas Press.

Barnhart, Michael A. 1987. *Japan Prepares for Total War: The Search for Economic Security.* Ithaca: Cornell University Press.

Barthes, Roland. 1977. *Image, Music, Text.* Trans. Stephen Heath. London: Fontana Paperbacks.

————. 1984. *Camera Lucida: Reflections on Photography.* Trans. Richard Howard. London: Fontana Paperbacks.

Barton, Francis R. 1908. "Children's Games in British New Guinea." *Journal of the Royal Anthropological Institute* 38: 259–79.

————. 1910. "The Annual Trading Expedition to the Papuan Gulf." In *The Melanesians of British New Guinea,* by Charles G. Seligman. Cambridge: Cambridge University Press.

————. 1918. "Tattooing in South Eastern New Guinea." *Journal of the Royal Anthropological Institute* 48: 22–79.

Batchen, Geoff. 1997. *Burning with Desire: The Conception of Photography.* Cambridge: MIT Press.

Battaglia, Debbora, ed. 1995. *Rhetorics of Self-Making.* Berkeley: University of California Press.

Baudelaire, Charles. [1859] 1980. "The Modern Public and Photography." In *Classic Essays on Photography,* ed. Alan Trachtenberg. New Haven: Leete's Island Books.

Behrend, Heike. 1998a. "Love à la Hollywood and Bombay: Kenyan Postcolonial Studio Photography." *Paideuma* 44: 139–53.

————. 1998b. "Populäre Fotografie und die Konstruktion einer afrikanischen Moderne. In *"Snap Me One": Studiofotografen in Afrika,* ed. Tobias Wendl and Heike Behrend. Munich: Prestel.

————. 2000. "'Feeling global': The Likoni Ferry Photographers in Mombasa, Kenya." *African Arts* 33 (3): 70–77.

Behrend, Heike, and Tobias Wendl. 1997. "Social Aspects of African Photography." In *Encyclopedia of Subsaharan Africa,* ed. John Middleton. New York: Simon and Schuster.

————. 1998. "Introduction." In *"Snap Me One": Studiofotografen in Afrika,* ed. Tobias Wendl and Heike Behrend. Munich: Prestel.

Benavente, Adelma. 2002. "Cronología de la fotografía peruana." In *La recuperación de la memoria, Perú 1842–1942.* Lima.

Benjamin, Roger. 1997. "Post-Colonial Taste: Non-Western Markets for Orientalist Art." In *Orientalism: From Delacroix to Klee.* Sydney: Art Gallery of New South Wales.

Benjamin, Walter. 1968. "The Work of Art in the Age of Mechanical Reproduction." In *Illuminations,* ed. Hannah Arendt. Trans. Harry Zohn. New York: Schocken Books.

————. 1985. "A Small History of Photography." In *One Way Street and Other Writings,* trans. E. Jephcott and K. Shorter. London: Verso.

Bensusan, A. D. 1966. *Silver Images: The History of Photography in Africa.* Capetown: Howard Timmons.

Berger, John, and Jean Mohr. 1982. *Another Way of Telling.* Cambridge: Granta.

Bhabha, Homi K. 1983. "The Other Question: The Stereotype and Colonial Discourse." *Screen* 24: 6.

———. 1994. *The Location of Culture.* London: Routledge.

Bigham, Elizabeth. 1999. "Issues of Authorship in the Portrait Photographs of Seydou Keita." *African Arts* 32 (1): 56–67.

Bourdieu, Pierre. 1990. *Photography: A Middle-Brow Art.* Cambridge: Polity.

Bourne, Samuel. 1866–67. "Narrative of a Photographic Trip to Kashmir (Cashmere) and Adjacent Districts." *British Journal of Photography* (9 parts; 5 October 1866 to 8 February 1867).

Bretschneider, E. 1898. *History of European Botanical Discoveries in China.* London: Sampson Low, Marston and Co.

Brown, Marilyn R. 1985. *Gypsies and Other Bohemians: The Myth of the Artist in Nineteenth-Century France.* Ann Arbor: University of Michigan Press.

Brumbaugh, Lee P. 1996. "Shadow Catchers or Shadow Snatchers? Ethical Issues for Photographers of Contemporary Native Americans." *American Indian Culture and Research Journal* 20 (3): 33–49.

Bruner, Edward. 1996. "Tourism in Ghana." *American Anthropologist* 98 (2): 290–304.

Bryson, Ian. 2002. *Bringing to Light: A History of Ethnographic Filmmaking at the Australian Institute of Aboriginal and Torres Strait Islander Studies Film Unit.* Canberra: Aboriginal Studies Press.

Bryson, Norman. 1983. *Vision and Painting: The Logic of the Gaze.* New Haven: Yale University Press.

Buck-Morss, Susan. 1991. *The Dialectics of Seeing: Walter Benjamin and the Arcades Project.* Cambridge: MIT Press.

Bunn, D. 1993. "Relocations: Landscape Theory, South African Landscape Practice, and the Transmission of Political Value." *Pretexts* 4 (2): 44–67.

———. 1996. "Comparative Barbarism, Game Reserves, Sugar Plantations, and the Modernization of South African Landscape." In *Text, Theory, Space: Land, Literature, and History in South Africa and Australia,* ed. Kate Darian-Smith, Liz Gunner, and Sarah Nuttall. London: Routledge.

Cadava, Eduardo. 1997. *Words of Light: Theses on the Photography of History.* Princeton: Princeton University Press.

Cantrill, A., and C. Cantrill. 1982. "The Baldwin Spencer Film Material: Conflict of Interests." *Cantrills Filmnotes* 37, 38: 42–43, 56.

Carpentier, Alejo. 1995. "The Baroque and the Marvellous Real." In *Magical Realism: Theory, History, Community,* ed. Lois Parkinson Zamora and Wendy B. Faris. Durham: Duke University Press.

———. 1998. *Image and Memory: Photography from Latin America, 1866-1994.* Austin: University of Texas Press.

Catnach, J. 1832 [1985]. *Catalogue of Songs and Song Books, Sheets, Half Sheets, etc. etc.* Facsimile reprint by Steve Roud and Paul Smith. London: January Press.

Chakrabarty, Dipesh. 2000. *Provincializing Europe: Postcolonial Thought and Historical Difference*. Princeton: Princeton University Press.

Chanady, Amaryll. 1995. "The Territorialization of the Imaginary in Latin America: Self-Affirmation and Resistance to Metropolitan Paradigms." In *Magical Realism: Theory, History, Community*, ed. Lois Parkinson Zamora and Wendy B. Faris. Durham: Duke University Press.

Charles, David. 1938. *The Camera in Commerce*. London: Pitman Greenwood.

Chiappelli, Fredi, ed. 1976. *First Images of America: The Impact of the New World on the Old*. Vol. 2. Berkeley: University of California Press.

Clark, John. 2000. "Indices of Modernity: Changes in Popular Reprographic Representation." In *Being Modern in Japan: Culture and Society from the 1910s to the 1930s*, ed. Elise K. Tipton and John Clark. Sydney: Australian Humanities Research Foundation and Fine Arts Press.

Clifford, James. 1988. "Tell Me about Your Trip: Michel Leiris." In *The Predicament of Culture: Twentieth-Century Ethnography, Literature and Art*. Cambridge: Harvard University Press.

Cook, Thomas, and Son. 1920. *Peking, North China, South Manchuria, and Korea*. 4th ed. London: Thomas Cook and Son.

Corby, Raymond. 1993. "Ethnographic Showcases, 1870–1930." *Cultural Anthropology* 8 (3): 338–69.

Cowling, Margaret. 1989. *The Artist as Anthropologist: The Representation of Type and Character in Victorian Art*. Cambridge: Cambridge University Press.

Cunningham, R. A. 1884. *History of R. A. Cunningham's Australian Aborigines*. London: Elliot.

Curran, James. 1982. "Communications, Power, and Social Order." In *Culture, Society, and Media*, ed. M. Gurevitch, Tony Bennett, J. Curran, and Jane Woollacott. London: Routledge.

Curtis, Edward S. 1907. *The North American Indian*. Vol. 1 (and supplemental portfolio). Cambridge: Cambridge University Press.

Davies, Alan, and Peter Stanbury. 1985. *The Mechanical Eye in Australia: Photographers, 1841–1900*. Melbourne: Oxford University Press.

Dean and Munday. 1837. *The Shipwreck of Mrs Frazer [sic] and the Loss of the Stirling Castle on a Coral Reef in the Pacific Ocean*. London: Dean and Munday.

de Certeau, Michel. 1984. *The Practice of Everyday Life*. Trans. Steven Rendall. Berkeley: University of California Press.

Delgado, Washington. 1980. *Historia de la literature republicans*. Lima.

de Lorenzo, Catherine. 1993. "Ethnophotography: Photographic Images of Aboriginal Australians". Ph.D. thesis, University of Sydney.

Deustua, José, and José Luis Renique. 1984. *Intelectuales, indigenismo, y decentralismo en el Peru, 1897–1932*. Cusco.

de Vries, H. M., ed. c.1928. *The Importance of Java as Seen from the Air*. Batavia: H. M. de Vries.

Dickens, Charles, ed., 1853. "The Noble Savage." *Household Words* 7 (168) (11 June): 337–39.

Dixon, Robert M. W. 1983. "Wargamay" (1: 1–144); "Nyawaygi" (3: 430–35). In *Handbook of Australian Languages*, ed. Robert M. W. Dixon and Barry J. Blake. Amsterdam: Bejamins B.V.

Dussart, Françoise. 2000. *The Politics of Ritual in an Aboriginal Settlement*. Washington, D.C.: Smithsonian Institution Press.

Duus, Peter, Ramon H. Myers, and Mark R. Peattie, eds. 1989. *The Japanese Informal Empire in China, 1895–1937*. Princeton: Princeton University Press.

Eléspuru, Juan M. Ugarte. 1968. "Notas sobre la pintura peruana entre 1890 y 1930." In *Historia de la Republica del Perú*, vol. 16, ed. Jorge Basadre. Lima.

Elliott, Mark C. 2000. "The Limits of Tartary: Manchuria in Imperial and National Geographies." *Journal of Asian Studies* 59 (3): 603–46.

Ellis, Catherine. 1970. "The Role of the Ethnomusicologist in the Study of Andagarinja Women's Ceremonies." *Miscellanea Musicologica* 5: 76–208.

Endō Ryūji [Endo Riuji] and Charles E. Resser. 1937. "The Sinian and Cambrian Formations and Fossils of Southern Manchukuo." *Manchurian Science Museum Bulletin* 1.

Etherton, Colonel P. T., and Hessell H. Tiltman. 1934. *Manchuria: The Cockpit of Asia*. 2nd ed. London: Jarrolds.

Faris, James. 1996. *Navajo and Photography: A Critical History of the Representations of an American People*. Albuquerque: University of New Mexico Press.

Faure, Bernard. 1998. "The Buddhist Icon and the Modern Gaze." *Critical Inquiry* 24: 768–813.

Ferrer, Jaime Mas. 1978. *Vida, teatro, y mito de Joaquin Dicenta*. Alicante, Spain.

Finch-Hatton, Harold. 1885. *Advance Australia! An Account of Eight Years Work, Wandering, and Amusement in Queensland, New South Wales, and Victoria*. London: H. Allen and Co.

Flint, Richard W. 1977. "The Evolution of the Circus in Nineteenth Century America." In *American Popular Entertainment*, ed. Myron Matlaw. Westport, Conn.: Greenwood Press.

———. 1983. "The Circus Is the World's Largest, Grandest, Best Amusement Institution." *Quarterly Journal, Library of Congress* 40 (3): 202–33.

Flores-Galindo, Alberto. 1978. *Arequipa y el sur andino*. Lima.

Flores-Galindo, Alberto, and Manuel Burga. 1987. *Apogeo y crisis de la república aristocrática*. 4th ed. Lima.

Flusser, V. 1997. *Für eine Philosophie der Fotografie*. Göttingen.

Fogel, Joshua A. 1996. *The Literature of Travel in the Japanese Rediscovery of China, 1862–1945*. Stanford: Stanford University Press.

Foucault, Michel. 1979. *Discipline and Punish: The Birth of the Prison*. Trans. Alan Sheridan. New York: Pantheon.

Works Cited

Fox, Celina. 1988. *Graphic Journalism in England during the 1830s and 1840s*. New York: Garland Publishing.

Friedberg, Anne. 1993. *Window Shopping: Cinema and the Postmodern*. Berkeley: University of California Press.

Galassi, Peter. 1981. *Before Photography: Painting and the Invention of Photography*. New York: Museum of Modern Art.

Gell, Alfred. 1993. *Wrapping in Images: Tattooing in Polynesia*. Oxford: Clarendon Press.

Gernsheim, Helmut. 1975. *Julia Margaret Cameron*. Millerton, N.Y.: Aperture.

Gilman, Sanders L. 1991. *Inscribing the Other*. Lincoln: University of Nebraska Press.

Ginzburg, Carlo. 1989. "From Aby Warburg to E. H. Gombrich: A Problem of Method." In *Clues, Myths, and the Historical Method*. Baltimore: Johns Hopkins University Press.

Gould, Richard A. 1969. *Yiwara: Foragers of the Australian Desert*. London: Collins.

Grana, César. 1964. *Bohemian versus Bourgeois: French Society and the French Man of Letters in the Nineteenth Century*. New York: Basic Books.

Grana, César, and Marigay Grana. 1990. *On Bohemia: The Codes of the Self-Exile*. New Brunswick: Rutgers University Press.

Grande, Maurilio Arriola. 1967. *Jose Arnaldo Marquez y Martin Fierro*. Lima.

Gray, J. 1957. *The British in Mombasa*. London: Macmillan; New York: St. Martin's Press.

Grayden, William. 1957. *Adam and Atoms*. Perth: F. Daniels.

Green-Lewis, Jennifer. 1996. *Framing the Victorians: Photography and the Culture of Realism*. Ithaca: Cornell University Press.

Groger-Wurm, Helen M. 1973. *Australian Aboriginal Bark Paintings and Their Mythological Interpretation*. Canberra: Australian Institute of Aboriginal Studies.

Guise, R. E. 1899. "On the Tribes Inhabiting the Mouth of the Wanigela River, New Guinea." *Journal of the Royal Anthropological Institute* 29: 205–19.

Gutman, Judith Mara. 1982. *Through Indian Eyes: Nineteenth and Early-Twentierh-Century Photography from India*. New York: Oxford University Press / International Center for Photography.

Hardt, Michael, and Antonio Negri. 2000. *Empire*. Cambridge: Harvard University Press.

Hassner, Rune. 1987. "Amateur Photography." In *A History of Photography*, ed. Jean-Claude Lemagny and André Rouillé. Cambridge: Cambridge University Press.

Healy, Chris. 1997. *From the Ruins of Colonialism: History as Social Memory*. Cambridge: Cambridge University Press.

Heidegger, Martin. 1977. "The Age of the World Picture" (1935). In *The Question Concerning Technology, and Other Essays*. Trans. William Lovitt. New York: Harper.

Helms, Richard. 1896. "Anthropology." *Transactions of the Royal Society of South Australia* 16 (3): 237–386.

Henderson, L. 1988. "Access and Consent in Public Photography." In *Image Ethics: The Moral Rights of Subjects in Photographs, Film, and Television,* ed. Larry Gross, John Katz, and Jay Ruby. New York: Oxford University Press.

Hennig, C. 1997. *Reiselust: Touristen, Tourismus, und Urlaubskultur.* Frankfurt: Insel Verlag.

Herrera, Tamayo. 1980. *Historia del indigenismo cusqueño.* Lima.

———. 1981. *Historia social del Cusco republicans.* Lima.

Hershkowitz, Robert. 1980. *The British Photographer Abroad: The First Thirty Years.* London: Robert Hershkowitz.

Higonnet, Anne. 1998. *Pictures of Innocence: The History and Crisis of Ideal Childhood.* London: Thames and Hudson.

Hillier, Bevis. 1976. *Victorian Studio Photographs.* Boston: David Godine.

Honour, Hugh. 1989. "From the American Revolution to World War I." In *The Image of the Black in Western Art.* Vol. 4. Cambridge: Harvard University Press.

Houlberg, Marilyn. 1973. "Ibeji Images of the Yoruba." *African Arts* 7 (1): 20–27.

———. 1976a. "Collecting the Anthropology of African Art." *African Arts* 9 (3): 15–19.

———. 1976b. "Image and Inquiry: Photography and Film in the Study of Yoruba Art and Religion." Paper presented at the panel "Methods in Visual Anthropology—Recent Research in Yoruba Art and Religion." Nineteenth annual meeting of the African Studies Association, Boston.

———. 1992. "Haitian Studio Photography: A Hidden World of Images." *Aperture* 126: 58–65.

Houzé, E., and Jacques, V. 1884. "Communications de MM. Houzé et Jacques sur les Australiens du Musée du Nord: Séance du 28 Mai, 1884." *Bulletin de la Société d'Anthropologie de Bruxelles* 3–4: 53–153.

Howe, K. S. 1994. *Excursions along the Nile: The Photographic Discovery of Ancient Egypt.* Santa Barbara: Santa Barbara Museum of Art.

Hulme, Peter. 1986. *Colonial Encounters: Europe and the Native Carribean, 1492–1797.* New York: Routledge.

Huyssen, Andreas. 1986. *After the Great Divide: Modernism, Mass Culture, Postmodernism.* Bloomington: Indiana University Press.

Iizawa, Kōtarō. 1989. *Toshi no shisen: Nihon no shashin, 1920–1930 nendai.* Osaka: Sōgensha.

———. 1995. "The Shock of the Real: Early Photography in Japan." In *Photography and Beyond in Japan: Space, Time and Memory,* ed. Robert Stearns. Tokyo: Hara Museum of Contemporary Art; New York: Harry N. Abrams.

Itō, Takeo, 1988. *Life along the South Manchurian Railway: The Memoirs of Itō Takeo.* Trans. Joshua A. Fogel. Armonk, N.Y.: M. E. Sharpe.

Ivins, William M. 1953. *Prints and Visual Communication.* Cambridge: MIT Press.

Jackson, Mason. 1885. *The Pictorial Press, Its Origins and Progress*. London: Hurst and Blackett.

Japan Times and Mail. 1937. *The Truth Behind the Sino-Japanese Crisis: Japan Acts to Keep Eastern Civilization Safe for the World*. Tokyo: Japan Times and Mail.

Jay, Martin. 1988. "Scopic Regimes of Modernity." In *Vision and Visuality*, ed. Hal Foster. Seattle: Bay Press.

———. 1993. *Downcast Eyes: The Denigration of Vision in Twentieth-Century French Thought*. Berkeley: University of California Press.

Jewell, J. 1976. *Mombasa, the Friendly Town*. Nairobi: East African Publishing House.

Johns, Adrian. 1993. "The Ideal of Scientific Collaboration: The 'Man of Science' and the Diffusion of Knowledge." Unpublished ms.

Jones, Dorothy. 1961. *The Cardwellshire Story*. Brisbane: Jacaranda.

Jones, Francis C. 1949. *Manchuria since 1931*. London: Royal Institute of International Affairs.

Jules-Rosette, Bennetta. 1995. "Simulations of Postmodernity: Images of Technology in African Tourist and Popular Art." In *Visualizing Theory*, ed. Lucien Taylor. New York: Routledge.

Kaberry, Phyllis. 1939. *Aboriginal Woman: Sacred and Profane*. London: Routledge.

Kaneko, Ryūichi. 1996. "A Brief History of Photography in Japan." In *Japanese Photography: Form In / Out. Part 1: From Its Introduction to 1945*. Tokyo: Metropolitan Museum of Photography.

Kelly, Rob Roy. 1969. *American Woodtype 1828–1900*. New York: Van Norstrand Reinhold.

Kerry, Charles. 1899. "Note." *Journal of the Royal Society of New South Wales* 33: xxvii–xxviii.

Kidd, Rosalind. 1997. *The Way We Civilise: Aboriginal Affairs — The Untold Story*. St. Lucia: Queensland University Press.

Killingray D., and A. Roberts. 1988. "An Outline History of Photography in Africa." In *Photographs as Sources for African History*, ed. A. Roberts. London: School of Oriental and African Studies.

Kimber, Dick. 1992. "T. G. H. Strehlow." In *Northern Territory Dictionary of Biography*, vol. 2, ed. D. Carment and B. James. Darwin: NTU Press.

Kinney, Henry W. 1928. *Modern Manchuria and the South Manchuria Railway Company*. Dairen and Tokyo: Japan Advertiser Press.

Krauss, Rosalind E. 1985. "Photography's Discursive Space." In *The Originality of the Avant-Garde and Other Modernist Myths*. Cambridge: MIT Press.

Larkin, Brian. 1997. "Indian Films and Nigerian Lovers: Media and the Creation of Parallel Modernities." *Africa* 67 (3): 406–40.

Lauer, Mirko. 1976. *Introducción a la pintura peruana del Sigio XX*. Lima.

Lavater, J. C. 1775-78. *Essays on Physiognomy, for the Promotion of Knowledge and the Love of Mankind*. 3 vols. Trans. Thomas Holcroft. London: G. G. J. and J. Robinson.

Leal, Luis. 1995. "Magical Realism in Spanish American Literature." In *Magical Realism: Theory, History, Community*, ed. Lois Parkinson Zamora and Wendy B. Faris. Durham: Duke University Press.

Lett, Lewis. 1949. *Sir Hubert Murray of Papua*. London: Collins.

Lindsay, David. 1893. *Journal of the Elder Scientific Exploring Expedition, 1891-2, under the Command of D. Lindsay*. Adelaide: Government Printer.

Lippard, Lucy, ed. 1992. *Partial Recall: Photographs of Native North Americans*. New York: New Press.

Lutkehaus, Nancy C., and Paul B. Roscoe. 1995. *Gender Rituals: Female Initiation in Melanesia*. London: Routledge.

MacCannell, Dean. 1976. *The Tourist: A New Theory of the Leisure Class*. London: Macmillan.

MacDougall, David. 1992. "Photo Wallahs: An Encounter with Photography." *Visual Anthropology Review* (fall): 96–100.

Mackie, Vera. 2000. "Modern Selves and Modern Spaces: An overview." In *Being Modern in Japan: Culture and Society from the 1910s to the 1930s*, ed. Elise K. Tipton and John Clark. Sydney: Australian Humanities Research Foundation and Fine Arts Press.

Majluf, Natalia. 2002. "La fotografía pictórica." In *La recuperacíon de la memoria, Perú 1842–1942*. Lima.

Marcus, George E. 1995. "The Modernist Sensibility in Recent Ethnographic Writing and the Cinematic Metaphor of Montage." In *Fields of Vision*, ed. Leslie Devereux and Roger Hillman. Berkeley: University of California Press.

Maschio, Thomas. 1995. "Mythic Images and Objects of Myth in Rauto Female Puberty Ritual." In *Gender Rituals: Female Initiation in Melanesia*, ed. Nancy Lutkehaus and P. Roscoe. London: Routledge.

Mavor, Carol. 1995. *Pleasures Taken: Performances of Sexuality and Loss in Victorian Photographs*. Durham: Duke University Press.

Mbembe, Achille. 1992. "The Banality of Power and the Aesthetics of Vulgarity in the Postcolony." *Public Culture* 4(2).

McBryde, Isabel. 1985. "Thomas Dick's Photographic Vision." In *Seeing the First Australians*, ed. Ian Donaldson and Tamsin Donaldson. Sydney: Allen and Unwin.

McCandless, Barbara. 1992. *Equal Before the Lens: Jno. Trlica's Photographs of Granger, Texas*. College Station: Texas A&M University Press.

McCarthy, Frederick D. 1957. *Australia's Aborigines: Their Life and Culture*. Melbourne: Colorgravure.

McCorquodale, John. 1987. *Aborigines and the Law: A Digest*. Canberra: Aboriginal Studies Press.

McElroy, Keith. 1985. *Early Peruvian Photography: A Critical Case Study*. Ann Arbor: University of Michigan Press.

McKenzie, E. E. 1975. "Growing Up with Aborigines." *The Queensland Naturalists: Journal of the Queensland Naturalists Club* 21 (3–4).

McNiven, Ian J., Lynette Russell, and Kay Schaffer, eds. 1998. *Constructions of Colonialism: Perspectives on Eliza Fraser's Shipwreck*. London: Cassell / Leicester University Press.

Meggs, Philip B. 1998. *A History of Graphic Design*. 3rd ed. New York: Wiley.

Melo, Jorge Orlando. 1988. *Historia de antioqua*. Medellín, Colombia.

Mélon, Marc. 1987. "Beyond Reality: Art Photography." In *A History of Photography*, ed. Jean-Claude Lemagny and André Rouillé. Cambridge: Cambridge University Press.

Mercer, Kobena. 1995. "Home from Home: Portraits from Places In Between." In *Self Evident*. Birmingham: Ikon Gallery.

Michaels, Eric. 1994. "For a Cultural Future: Francis Jupurrurla Makes TV at Yuendumu." In *Bad Aboriginal Art: Tradition, Media, and Technological Horizons*. Minneapolis: University of Minnesota Press.

Miller, Daniel. 1995. "Introduction: Anthropology, Modernity and Consumption." In *Worlds Apart: Modernity Through the Prism of the Local*, ed. Daniel Miller. London: Routledge.

Mitchell, Timothy. 1988. *Colonising Egypt*. Cambridge: Cambridge University Press.

Mitchell, W. J. T. 1994a. "Imperial landscape." In *Landscape and Power*, ed. W. J. T. Mitchell. Chicago: University of Chicago Press.

———. 1994b. *Picture Theory*. Chicago: University of Chicago Press.

Mitter, Rana. 2000. *The Manchurian Myth*. Berkeley: University of California Press.

Mobolade, Timothy. 1973. "The Concept of Abiku." *African Arts* 7 (1): 62–67.

Moreland, William J. 1991. "American Indians and the Right to Privacy: A Psycholegal Investigation of the Unauthorized Publication of Portraits of American Indians." *American Indian Law Review* 15 (2): 237–77.

Morphy, Howard, and Robert Layton. 1981. "Choosing among Alternatives: Cultural Transformations and Social Change in Aboriginal Australia and the French Jura." *Mankind* 13 (1): 56–73.

Mountford, Charles P. 1976. *Nomads of the Australian Desert*. Adelaide: Rigby.

Mudimbe, V. Y. 1994. *The Idea of Africa*. Bloomington: Indiana University Press.

Mulvaney, John, Howard Morphy, and Alison Petch, eds. 1997. *"My Dear Spencer": The Letters of F. J. Gillen to Baldwin Spencer*. Melbourne: Hyland House.

Myers, Ramon H. 1973. "Taiwan as an Imperial Colony of Japan: 1895–1945." *Journal of the Institute of Chinese Studies* 6: 425–51.

———. 1989. "Japanese Imperialism in Manchuria: The South Manchuria Railway Company, 1906–1933." In *The Japanese Informal Empire in China, 1895–1937*, ed. Peter Duus, Ramon H. Myers, and Mark R. Peattie. Princeton: Princeton University Press.

Nathan, Carl F. 1967. *Plague Prevention and Politics in Manchuria, 1910–1931.* Cambridge: East Asian Research Center, Harvard University.

Nochlin, Linda. 1983. "The Imaginary Orient." *Art in America* (May): 121–31.

Noda, Mitsuzō. 1971. *Chūgoku tōhoku (Manshū) no shokubutsushi.* Tokyo: Kazema Shobō.

O'Connell, Sheila. 1999. *The Popular Print in England.* London: British Museum Press.

Oguibe, Olu. 1996. "Photography and the Substance of the Image." In *In/sight: African Photographers, 1940 to the Present.* New York: Guggenheim Museum.

Ohmann, Richard. 1996. *Selling Culture: Magazines, Markets, and Class at the Turn of the Century.* London: Verso.

Ono, Philbert. 1998. "Chronological History of Japanese Photography; Part 1: 1646–1945." Online at philbert@photojpn.org.

Parkinson, Bob. n.d. [c.1896]. "The Circus and the Press." *Bandwagon* news cutting. Chicago: Chicago Historical Society.

Peattie, Mark R. 1983. "Japanese Colonialism: Discarding the Stereotypes." In *Japan Examined: Perspectives on Modern Japanese History,* ed. H. Wray and H. Conroy. Honolulu: University of Hawaii Press.

Peirce, Charles Saunders. 1958. *Selected Writings (Values in a Universe of Chance).* New York: Dover.

Pinney, Christopher. 1992. "The Parallel Histories of Anthropology and Photography." In *Anthropology and Photography: 1860–1920,* ed. E. Edwards. New Haven: Yale University Press.

———. 1994. "Future Travel." In *Visualizing Theory,* ed. Lucien Taylor. New York: Routledge.

———. 1997a. *Camera Indica: The Social Life of Indian Photographs.* London: Reaktion Books; Chicago: University of Chicago Press.

———. 1997b. "The Nation (Un)pictured? Chromolithography and 'Popular' Politics in India, 1978–1995." *Critical Inquiry* 23 (4): 834–67.

———. 1999. "Indian Magical Realism: Notes on Popular Visual Culture." In *Subaltern Studies X.,* ed. Gautam Bhadra, Gyan Prakash, and Susie Tharu. Delhi: Oxford University Press.

———. 2001. "Piercing the Skin of the Idol." In *Beyond Aesthetics: Art and the Technologies of Enchantment,* ed. Christopher Pinney and Nicholas Thomas. Oxford: Berg.

Poignant, Axel. 1957. *Piccaninny Walkabout: A Story of Two Aboriginal Children.* Sydney: Angus and Robertson.

Poignant, Roslyn. 1996. *Encounter at Nagalarramba.* Canberra: National Library of Australia.

———. 1997. "Looking for Tambo." *The Olive Pink Society Bulletin* 9 (1–2): 27–37.

Polar, Antonio Cornejo. 1980. *Literatura y sociedad en el Perú: La novela indigenista.* Lima.

Poole, Deborah. 1990. "Ciencia, peligrosidad, y represion en la criminologia peruana." In *Bandoleros, abigeos, y montoneros: Criminalidad y violencia en el Peru, siglos XVIII-XX*, ed. C. Walker and C. Aguirre. Lima.

————. 1997. *Vision, Race, and Modernity: A Visual Economy of the Andean Image World.* Princeton: Princeton University Press.

Powers, Willow R. 1996. "Images across Boundaries. History, Use, and Ethics of Photographs of American Indians." *American Indian Culture and Research Journal* 20 (3): 129–36.

Reed, David. 1997. *The Popular Magazine in Britain and the United States, 1880–1960.* London: British Library.

Reeves, John. 1998. *Building on Land Rights for the Next Generation: Report of the Review of the Aboriginal Land Rights (Northern Territory) Act 1976.* Canberra: Australian Government Publishing Service.

Reiss, Benjamin. 2001. *The Showman and the Slave: Race, Death, and Memory in Barnum's America.* Cambridge: Harvard University Press.

Report of the First Scientific Expedition to Manchoukuo: Under the Leadership of Shigeyasu Tokunaga, June-October 1933. 25 vols. 1934–40. Tokyo: Office of the Scientific Expedition to Manchoukuo, Faculty of Science and Engineering, Waseda University.

Rhodes, Jon. 1998. *Whichaway? Photographs from Kiwirrkura, 1974–1996.* Thora, N.S.W.: Jon Rhodes.

Riffenburgh, Beau. 1994. *The Myth of the Explorer: The Press, Sensationalism, and Geographical Discovery.* Oxford: Oxford University Press.

Riis, Jacob A. 1997 [1890]. *How the Other Half Lives.* New York: Penguin Books.

Russell, Henry Stuart. 1888. *The Genesis of Queensland.* London: Vintage Books.

Ryan, James. 1997. *Picturing Empire: Photography and the Visualization of the British Empire.* London: Reaktion.

Said, Edward W. 1978. *Orientalism.* London: Routledge and Kegan Paul.

Sandall, Roger. 1976. "A Curious Case of Censorship." *Encounter* 47 (1): 42–44.

Schadow, Gottfried. 1835. *National-Physiognomieen; Text, vol. 1; Illustrations, vol. 2.* Berlin.

Schaffer, Kay. 1993. *In the Wake of First Contact.* Cambridge: Cambridge University Press.

Schiltz, Marc. 1978. "Engungun Masquerades in Iganna." *African Arts* 11 (3): 48–55.

Schneider William H. 1982. *An Empire for the Masses: The French Popular Image of Africa, 1870–1900.* Westport, Conn.: Greenwood Press.

Sekula, Allan. 1983. "Photography between Labor and Capital." In *Mining Photographs and Other Pictures: A Selection from the Negative Archives of Shedden Studio, Glace Bay, Cape Breton, 1948-1968*, ed. H. D. Buchloh and Robert Wilkie. Halifax: Press of the Nova Scotia College of Art and Design.

————. 1984. "Dismantling Modernism, Reinventing Documentary." In *Photog-*

raphy against the Grain. Halifax: Press of the Nova Scotia College of Art and Design.

Seligman, Charles G. 1910. *The Melanesians of British New Guinea*. Cambridge: Cambridge University Press.

Serrano, Eduardo. 1983. *Historia de la fotografía en Colombia*. Bogotá.

Simpson, Colin. 1951. *Adam in Ochre: Inside Aboriginal Australia*. Sydney: Angus and Robertson.

Sivirichi, Atilio. 1937. "El contenido espiritual del movimiento indigenista." *Revista Universitaria del Cuzco* 72: 21–22.

Smith, Bernard. 1960. *European Vision and the South Pacific, 1768–1850*. Oxford: Oxford University Press.

———. 1992. *Imaging the Pacific in the Wake of the Cook Voyages*. Melbourne: Melbourne University Press.

Smith, Heide. 1990. *Tiwi: The Life and Art of Australia's Tiwi People*. Sydney: Angus and Robertson.

Smith, Lindsay. 1998. *The Politics of Focus: Women, Children, and Nineteenth-Century Photography*. Manchester: Manchester University Press.

Smith, W. Ramsay. 1924. *In Southern Seas: Wanderings of a Naturalist*. London: John Murray.

Sontag, Susan. 1979. *On Photography*. New York: Farrar, Straus & Giroux; Harmondsworth, Eng.: Penguin.

Spittler, Gerd. 1996. "Explorers in Transit: Travels to Timbuktu and Agades in the Nineteenth Century." *History and Anthropology* 9 (2–3).

Sprague, Stephen. F. 1978. "Yoruba Photography: How the Yoruba See Themselves." *African Arts* 12: 52–59.

———. 1978. "How I See the Yoruba See Themselves." *Studies in the Anthropology of Visual Communication* 5 (1).

Stagl, Justin. 1990. "The Methodising of Travel in the Sixteenth Century: A Tale of Three Cities." *History and Anthropology* 4 (2): 303–39.

Stewart, Susan. 1991. *Crimes of Writing: Problems in the Containment of Representation*. London: Oxford University Press.

———. 1993. *On Longing: Narratives of the Miniature, the Gigantic, the Souvenir, the Collection*. Durham: Duke University Press.

Stirling, A. W. 1884. *The Never-Never Land: Rides in North Queensland*. London.

Strathern, Marilyn. 1988. *The Gender of the Gift: Problems with Women and Problems with Society in Melanesia*. Berkeley: University of California Press.

———. 1997. "Prefigured Features: A View from the New Guinea Highlands." In *Australian Journal of Anthropology* 8 (1): 89–103.

Sugita, Nozomu. 1990. *Mantetsu chūō shikenjo*. Tokyo: Kōdansha.

Swain, Tony. 1993. *A Place for Strangers: Towards a History of Australian Aboriginal Being*. Melbourne: Cambridge University Press.

Tagg, John. 1988. *Burden of Representation: Essays on Photographies and Histories*. London: Macmillan.

Tanaka, Stefan. 1993. *Japan's Orient: Rendering Pasts into History*. Berkeley: University of California Press.

Taussig, Michael. 1986. *Shamanism, Colonialism, and the Wild Man*. Chicago: University of Chicago Press.

———. 1993. *Mimesis and Alterity: A Particular History of the Senses*. New York: Routledge.

Taylor, Penny, ed. 1988. *After Two Hundred Years: Photographic Essays on Aboriginal and Islander Australia*. Canberra: Aboriginal Studies Press.

Thomas, Nicholas. 1994. *Colonialism's Culture: Anthropology, Travel and Government*. Oxford: Polity.

———. 1995. *Oceanic Art*. London: Thames and Hudson.

———. 1997. "Marked Men." *Art Asia Pacific* 13: 66–73.

Thompson, Robert Farris. 1971. "Aesthetics in Traditional Africa." In *Art and Aesthetics in Primitive Societies*, ed. Carol F. Jopling. New York: E. P. Dutton.

Thomson, Donald. 1972. *Kinship and Behaviour in North Queensland: A Preliminary Account of Kinship and Social Organisation on Cape York Peninsula*. Canberra: Australian Institute of Aboriginal Studies.

———. 1983. *Children of the Wilderness*. Melbourne: Currey O'Neil.

Tindale, Norman. 1974. *Aboriginal Tribes of Australia: Their Terrain, Environmental Controls, Distribution, Limits, and Proper Names*. Canberra: Australian National University Press.

Tokunaga, Shigeyasu. 1934. "Natural Science Research of the First Scientific Expedition to Manchoukuo." In *Report of the First Scientific Expedition to Manchoukuo: Under the Leadership of Shigeyasu Tokunaga, June-October 1933*. Vol. 1. Tokyo: Office of the Scientific Expedition to Manchoukuo, Faculty of Science and Engineering, Waseda University.

———. 1940. "Epilogue." In *Report of the First Scientific Expedition to Manchoukuo: Under the Leadership of Shigeyasu Tokunaga, June-October 1933, Epilogue, General Index, and Obituary*. Tokyo: Office of the Scientific Expedition to Manchoukuo, Faculty of Science and Engineering, Waseda University.

Tomas, David. 1982. "The Ritual of Photography." *Semiotica* 40 (1–2): 1–25.

———. 1988. "Towards an Anthropology of Sight: Ritual Performance and the Photographic Process." *Semiotica* 68 (3–4): 245–70.

Topinard, Paul. 1885. "Presentation de trois Australiens vivants: Séance du 19 Novembre 1885." *Bulletin de la Société d'Anthropologie de Paris*, 3: 683–99.

Trachtenberg, Alan. 1985. "Albums of War: On Reading Civil War Photographs." *Representations* 9.

———. 1989. *Reading American Photographs: Images as History. Mathew Brady to Walker Evans*. New York: Hill and Wang.

Tsinhnahjinnie, Hulleah J. 1993. "Proving Nothing." *Crosswinds* 5 (9): 13.

Tweedie, Penny. 1998. *Spirit of Arnhem Land: Aboriginal Australians*. Sydney: New Holland.

Valcárcel, Luís. 1981. *Memorias*. Lima.

Vale, V., and Andrea Juno. 1991. *Modern Primitives. Tattoo, Piercing, Scarification: An Investigation of Contemporary Adornment and Ritual*. San Francisco: RE/Search.

Vogan, J. 1890. *The Black Police. A Story of Modern Australia*. London: Hutchinson.

Wagner, M. 1991. "Ansichten ohne Ende—oder das Ende der Ansicht? Wahrnehmungsumbrüche im Reisebild um 1830." In *Reisekultur: Vonder Pilgerfahrt zum modernen Tourismus*, ed. H. Bausinger et al. Munich: C. H. Beck.

Wallace, Phyl, and Noel Wallace. 1968. *Children of the Desert*. Melbourne: Thomas Nelson.

Warner, William L. 1937. *A Black Civilization: A Social Study of an Australian Tribe*. New York: Harper.

Wass, Betty M. 1975. "Communicative Aspects of the Dress of Yoruba: A Case Study of Five Generations of a Lagos Family." Paper presented at the panel "The Social Significance and Aesthetics of African Dress." Eighteenth annual meeting of the African Studies Association, San Francisco.

The Way We Civilise. 1880. Brisbane: G. & J. Black.

Wei Chao. 1980. "Foreign Railroad Interests in Manchuria: An Irritant in Chinese-Japanese Relations (1903–1937)." Ph.D. diss., St. John's University.

Weiner, James F. 1997. "Televisualist Anthropology: Representation, Aesthetics, Politics." *Current Anthropology* 38 (2): 197–236.

Westermann, Diedrich. 1939. *The African Today and Tomorrow*. London: Oxford University Press; International Institute of African Languages and Culture.

Williams, Raymond. 1983. "The Romantic Artist." In *Culture and Society: 1780–1950*. New York: Columbia University Press.

Willis, Anne-Marie. 1988. *Picturing Australia: A History of Photography*. North Ryde, N.S.W.: Angus and Robertson.

Wilson, Sandra. 1995. "The 'New Paradise': Japanese Emigration to Manchuria in the 1930s and 1940s." *International History Review* 17 (2): 221–40.

Worswick, Clark, and Ainslie T. Embree. 1976. *The Last Empire: Photography in British India, 1855–1911*. Millerton, N.Y.: Aperture.

Worth, Sol, and John Adair. 1972. *Through Navajo Eyes: An Exploration in Film Communication and Anthropology*. Bloomington: Indiana University Press.

Wright, Christopher. 1997. "An Unsuitable Man: The Photographs of Francis R. Barton." *Pacific Arts* (15–16): 42–60.

Yepez Miranda, Alfredo. 1940. "El process cultural del Perú: La unidad geografica y cultural de la costa." *Revista Universitaria* 78: 27–37.

Young, John. 1966. *The Research Activities of the South Manchurian Railway Company, 1907–1945: A History and Bibliography*. New York: East Asian Institute, Columbia University.

Young, Louise. 1998. *Japan's Total Empire: Manchuria and the Culture of Wartime Imperialism*. Berkeley: University of California Press.

Young, Robert. 1990. *White Mythologies: Writing History and the West*. London: Routledge and Kegan Paul.

Zeki, Semir. 1999. *An Exploration of Art and the Brain*. Oxford: Oxford University Press.

Contributors

MICHAEL AIRD runs his own publishing company, Keeaira Press, in Queensland, Australia, specializing in books on photography and Aboriginal history. His most recent publication is *Brisbane Blacks* (2001). Prior to his work as a publisher he was a Curator in the Queensland Museum in Brisbane. He organized an exhibition of studio portraiture of indigenous Australians, published as *Portraits of Our Elders* (1993).

HEIKE BEHREND is Professor in the Institute for African Studies, University of Cologne, and author of *Alice und Die Geister: Krieg im Norden Ugandas* (1993; English translation *Alice Lakwena and the Holy Spirits*, 2000). In 1998 she published *Snap Me One: Studiofotografen in Afrika* (with Tobias Wendl).

JO-ANNE DRIESSENS works as an Indigenous Resource Officer in Indigenous Library Services at the State Library of Queensland in Brisbane.

JAMES FARIS, currently of Santa Fe, New Mexico, is Professor Emeritus of Anthropology at the University of Connecticut. He is the author of *Navajo and Photography* (1997) and has written widely on art, politics, and representation.

MORRIS LOW is Senior Lecturer in Asian Studies at the University of Queensland. He is coauthor of *Science, Technology, and Society in Contemporary Japan* (1999), editor of *Science, Technology, and R&D in Japan* (3 vols. 2001) and coeditor of *Asian Masculinities: The Meaning and Practice of Manhood in China and Japan* (2003).

NICOLAS PETERSON is Reader in Anthropology in the School of Archaeology and Anthropology, Australian National University. He has a longstanding interest in ethnographic film and photography. He recently coedited the volume *Citizenship and Indigenous Australians* (with W. Sanders; 1998).

CHRISTOPHER PINNEY is Reader in Anthropology and Visual Culture at University College in London, and was Visiting Fellow at the Centre for Cross-Cultural

Research, Australian National University, in 1997–98, and Visiting Professor in the History of Culture program at the University of Chicago in spring 1999. He is the author of a study of popular Indian photography, *Camera Indica: The social life of Indian photographs* (1997).

ROSLYN POIGNANT, an independent scholar and curator of a number of photographic exhibitions over the past twenty years, is based in London. Recently she curated "Captive Lives: Looking for Tambo and His Companions," a National Library of Australia touring exhibition (1997–2001). Her book *Encounter at Nagalar-ramba* (1996) is about a photographic encounter with an Aboriginal community in Arnhem Land in 1952 and the "return" of the photographs to the community forty years later.

DEBORAH POOLE is Professor of Anthropology at Johns Hopkins University. She is author of *Race and Modernity: A Visual Economy of the Andean Image World* (1997).

STEPHEN SPRAGUE received an M.F.A. from the School of the Art Institute of Chicago in 1970. At the time of writing the essay in this volume he was Assistant Professor of Photography and Film at Purdue University. Sadly, he has since died, but many of his photographs are housed in the Sprague Archive at the Center for Creative Photography at the University of Arizona.

HULLEAH J. TSINHNAHJINNIE was born into the Bear and Racoon Clans of the Seminole and Muskogee Nations, and born for the Tsinajinnie Clan of the Diné Nation. Exhibited nationally and internationally, Tsinhnahjinnie claims photography as her primary language. Creating fluent images of Native thought, her emphasis is art for indigenous communities.

CHRISTOPHER WRIGHT is Lecturer at Goldsmith's College, London. He co-curated "The Impossible Science of Being: Dialogues between Anthropology and Photography" at the Photographer's Gallery, London (1995–96), as well as archival photographic exhibitions in Sikkim and the Solomon Islands.

Index

Index

Library of Congress Cataloging-in-Publication Data

Photography's other histories / edited by Christopher Pinney and Nicolas Peterson.
p. cm. — (Objects/histories) Includes bibiographical references and index.
ISBN 0-8223-3126-8 (cloth : alk.paper) ISBN 0-8223-3113-6 (pbk. : alk.paper)
1. Photography—History. 2. Photography—Social aspects—History. I. Pinney,
Christopher. II. Peterson, Nicolas. III. Series.
TR145.P495 2003
770—dc21   2002151232

www.ingramcontent.com/pod-product-compliance
Lightning Source LLC
Chambersburg PA
CBHW072131170526
45158CB00004BA/1332